BEYOND CONTINU

Beyond Continuity

Institutional Change in Advanced Political Economies

Edited by

WOLFGANG STREECK

and

KATHLEEN THELEN

OXFORD
UNIVERSITY PRESS

OXFORD
UNIVERSITY PRESS

Great Clarendon Street, Oxford OX2 6DP

Oxford University Press is a department of the University of Oxford.
It furthers the University's objective of excellence in research, scholarship,
and education by publishing worldwide in

Oxford New York

Auckland Cape Town Dar es Salaam Hong Kong Karachi
Kuala Lumpur Madrid Melbourne Mexico City Nairobi
New Delhi Shanghai Taipei Toronto
With offices in
Argentina Austria Brazil Chile Czech Republic France Greece
Guatemala Hungary Italy Japan South Korea Poland Portugal
Singapore Switzerland Thailand Turkey Ukraine Vietnam

ISBN 978-0-19-928046-9

Printed in the United Kingdom by
Lightning Source UK Ltd., Milton Keynes

K.T. to A.M.T.

Preface

This volume grew out of a conference we convened in Cologne in December 2002. The project was motivated by a sense of the limitations of existing approaches to institutions, which emphasize continuity over change and which—to the extent that they deal with change—tend to fall back on a strong punctuated equilibrium model that distinguishes sharply between periods of institutional innovation and institutional 'stasis'. Our feeling was that the kind of abrupt, discontinuous change captured in the traditional model does not come close to exhausting the ways in which institutions change, and misses entirely some of the most important ways in which institutions can evolve gradually over time. To move the debate forward, we invited contributions that investigate in a theoretically self-conscious way specific empirical cases of institutional change in the political economic or social institutions of advanced industrial societies. We asked that contributions aim at producing general insights into the character and mechanisms of institutional change—insights grounded in the careful empirical research of contemporary developments within and across individual countries. Taken together, the chapters assembled here provide a powerful corrective to existing theoretical frameworks by showing (as one reviewer has put it) how transformative changes can happen one step at a time. Beyond critique, however, they also provide the basis for a broader typology that goes beyond the traditional literature, drawing attention to common modes of change that typically go unrecognized and enriching the conceptual and theoretical tools we can bring to bear in understanding such change.

We would like to thank the participants in the Cologne workshop, including and especially Peter Hall, Ellen Immergut, and Philip Manow, who provided important insights and commentary. Since that meeting, we have also received valuable input from Suzanne Berger and three anonymous reviewers for Oxford University Press. We thank David Musson and Oxford University Press for facilitating the timely publication of this book. Kathleen Thelen gratefully acknowledges the support of the Max Planck Gesellschaft and of the Institute for Policy Research at Northwestern University.

Cologne and Evanston, June 2004
Wolfgang Streeck and Kathleen Thelen

Contents

List of Contributors   xi

List of Figures   xv

List of Tables   xvi

Abbreviations   xvii

1 Introduction: Institutional Change in Advanced
   Political Economies   1
   Wolfgang Streeck and Kathleen Thelen

2 Policy Drift: The Hidden Politics of US Welfare State
   Retrenchment   40
   Jacob S. Hacker

3 Changing Dominant Practice: Making use of Institutional
   Diversity in Hungary and the United Kingdom   83
   Colin Crouch and Maarten Keune

4 Redeploying the State: Liberalization and Social
   Policy in France   103
   Jonah D. Levy

5 Ambiguous Agreement, Cumulative Change: French
   Social Policy in the 1990s   127
   Bruno Palier

6 Routine Adjustment and Bounded Innovation: The
   Changing Political Economy of Japan   145
   Steven K. Vogel

7 Change from Within: German and Italian Finance in the 1990s   169
   Richard Deeg

8 Institutional Resettlement: The Case of Early Retirement
   in Germany   203
   Christine Trampusch

9 Contested Boundaries: Ambiguity and Creativity in the
  Evolution of German Codetermination   229

  Gregory Jackson

10 Adaptation, Recombination, and Reinforcement: The
   Story of Antitrust and Competition Law in
   Germany and Europe   255

   Sigrid Quack and Marie-Laure Djelic

Index   282

List of Contributors

Colin Crouch is currently head of the Department of Social and Political Sciences and Professor of Sociology at the European University Institute, Florence. He is also the External Scientific Member of the Max Planck Institute for the Study of Societies in Cologne. He previously taught sociology at the London School of Economics (LSE), and was fellow and tutor in politics at Trinity College, Oxford, and Professor of Sociology at the University of Oxford. He is currently the President of the Society for the Advancement of Socio-Economics (SASE) and has published within the fields of comparative European sociology and industrial relations, on economic sociology, and on contemporary issues in British and European politics. His most recent books include: *Political Economy of Modern Capitalism: Mapping Convergence and Diversity* (with Wolfgang Streeck 1997); *Are Skills the Answer?* (with David Finegold and Mari Sako 1999); *Social Change in Western Europe* (1999); *Local Production Systems in Europe: Rise or Demise* (with others 2001); *Postdemocrazia* (2003); and *Changing Governance of Local Economies: Response of European Local Production Systems* (with others 2004).

Richard Deeg (Ph.D., MIT) is Associate Professor of Political Science at Temple University. During 1995 he was a Postdoctoral Fellow at the Max Planck Institute for the Study of Societies in Cologne, Germany, where he was also a visiting scholar in 2001. His publications include *Finance Capitalism Unveiled: Banks and the German Political Economy* (1999). He has also published numerous articles on the German and European political economy, as well as on German federalism, in journals including *Comparative Political Studies, West European Politics, Governance, Small Business Economics,* and *Publius.*

Marie-Laure Djelic (Ph.D., Harvard) is Professor at ESSEC Business School, Paris, where she teaches Organization Theory, Business History, and Comparative Capitalism. In 2002–3 she held the Kerstin Hesselgren Professorship at Uppsala University, and in 2000 she was Visiting Professor in the Sociology Department at Stanford University. She is the author of *Exporting the American Model* (1998) which obtained the 2000 Max Weber Award for the Best Book in Organizational Sociology from the American Sociological Association. Together with Sigrid Quack she has edited *Globalization and Institutions* (2003). Currently she is working on a new edited volume, *Transnational Regulation in the Making* (together with Kerstin Sahlin-Andersson; forthcoming in 2005).

Jacob S. Hacker (Ph.D., Yale) is Peter Strauss Family Assistant Professor of Political Science at Yale University. He was previously a Junior Fellow of the Harvard Society of Fellows and a Guest Scholar and Research Fellow at the Brookings Institution. His articles have appeared in the *American Political Science Review,* the *British Journal of Political Science, Politics and Society, Studies in American Political*

Development; the *Journal of Health Politics, Policy and Law*, and the *Journal of Policy History*. He is also the author of two books: *The Divided Welfare State: The Battle over Public and Private Social Benefits in the United States* (2002), and *The Road to Nowhere: The Genesis of President Clinton's Plan for Health Security* (1997), which received the 1997 Louis Brownlow Book Award of the National Academy of Public Administration. He is currently chairing a working group of the American Political Science Association's Task Force on Inequality and Democracy.

Gregory Jackson (Ph.D., Columbia) joined Kings College, London, as Senior Lecturer in Management in September 2004. He was previously a Fellow at the Research Institute of Economy, Trade and Industry in Tokyo (2002–4) and researcher at the Max Planck Institute for the Study of Societies in Cologne, Germany (1996–2002). He has written widely on historical and comparative aspects of corporate governance, particularly in Germany and Japan, including 'The Cross-National Diversity of Corporate Governance' (with Ruth Aguilera) in *Academy of Management Review*, July 2003. He is editor of *Corporate Governance in Japan: Institutional Change and Organizational Diversity* (with Masahiko Aoki and Hideaki Miyajima 2004).

Maarten Keune is Research Associate at the European University Institute in Florence. He has published on institutional change, labor markets, and local development in central and eastern Europe. He is editor of *Local Development, Institutions and Conflicts in Post-Socialist Hungary* (with József Nemes Nagy 2001) and *Regional Development and Employment Promotion: Lessons from Central and Eastern Europe* (1998).

Jonah D. Levy (Ph.D., MIT) is Associate Professor of Political Science at the University of California, Berkeley. He works on economic and social policy among the affluent democracies, particularly France. Levy's publications include: *Tocqueville's Revenge: State, Society, and Economy in Contemporary France* (1999); 'Vice into Virtue? Progressive Politics and Welfare Reform in Continental Europe', *Politics and Society* (1999); and 'Activation through Thick and Thin: Progressive Approaches to Labor Market Reform', in Martin Levin and Martin Shapiro (eds.), *Transatlantic Policy-Making: Policy Drift and Innovation in the Age of Austerity*, Georgetown University Press, forthcoming 2004. Levy is currently completing an edited volume, *The State after Statism: New State Activities in the Age of Globalization and Liberalization*.

Bruno Palier is CNRS researcher in the Centre d'études de la vie politique française (CEVIPOF) in Paris. He works on welfare state reforms, from both a French and a comparative perspective. Palier is a member of the Management Committee of Cost A15, 'Reforming the Welfare Systems in Europe'. He is author of *'Facing pension crisis in France'*. In: Noel Whiteside and Gordon Clarke (eds.), *Pension Security in the 21st Century: Redrawing the Public-Private Divide* (2003), *Gouverner la Sécurité sociale* (2002), and ' "Defrosting" the French Welfare State',

West European Politics (2000). He has coedited *Globalization and European Welfare States: Challenges and Changes* (with Rob S. Sykes and P. Prior 2001).

Sigrid Quack (Ph.D., Free University of Berlin) is a Research Fellow at the Social Science Research Center (WZB) in Berlin, Germany. She lectured at the Department of Sociology of the Free University of Berlin from 1990 to 1992. Her books include *Dynamik der Teilzeitarbeit* (1993), *National Capitalisms, Global Competition and Economic Performance* (2000), which she edited together with Glenn Morgan and Richard Whitley, and *Globalization and Institutions: Redefining the Rules of the Economic Game* (2003), edited with Marie–Laure Djelic. Ms. Quack has been a member of the Board of the European Group of Organization Studies (EGOS) since 2002.

Wolfgang Streeck (Ph.D., Frankfurt am Main) is Director at the Max Planck Institute for the Study of Societies in Cologne, Germany. From 1988 to 1995 he was Professor of Sociology and Industrial Relations at the University of Wisconsin, Madison. He is author of *Social Institutions and Economic Performance* (1992) and editor of *Germany: Beyond the Stable State* (with Herbert Kitschelt 2003); *The End of Diversity: Prospects for German and Japanese Capitalism* (with Kozo Yamamura 2003); *The Origins of Nonliberal Capitalism: Germany and Japan* (with Kozo Yamamura 2001); and *Political Economy of Modern Capitalism: Mapping Convergence and Diversity* (with Colin Crouch 1997). He was the president of the Society for the Advancement of Socio-economics in 1998/9.

Kathleen Thelen (Ph.D., Berkeley) is Professor of Political Science at Northwestern University. She is author of *Union of Parts: Labor Politics in Postwar Germany* (1991) and *How Institutions Evolve: The Political Economy of Skills in Germany, Britain, the United States and Japan* (2004), and coeditor of *Structuring Politics: Historical Institutionalism in Comparative Analysis* (1992). Her work on labor politics and on historical institutionalism has appeared in, among others, *World Politics, Comparative Political Studies, The Annual Review of Political Science, Politics and Society,* and *Comparative Politics.*

Christine Trampusch (Ph.D., Göttingen) is Researcher at the Max Planck Institute for the Study of Societies in Cologne, Germany. From 1997 to 2000 she was a Ph.D. student at the Graduate Program 'Die Zukunft des Europäischen Sozialmodells' at the Center for Studies of Europe and North America, University of Göttingen. Her doctoral thesis on 'Labor Market Policy, Trade Unions and Employers' Associations: A Comparison of the Formation and Transformation of Public Employment Services in Germany, Great Britain and the Netherlands between 1909 and 1999' (in German) was published in 2001. She has also published articles and papers on German and Dutch labor market and social policy.

Steven K. Vogel (Ph.D., Berkeley) is Associate Professor of Political Science at the University of California, Berkeley. He specializes in the political economy of advanced industrialized nations, especially Japan. He has recently completed an edited volume entitled *US–Japan Relations in a Changing World* (2002). His book, *Freer Markets, More Rules: Regulatory Reform in Advanced Industrial Countries* (1996) won the 1998 Masayoshi Ohira Memorial Prize. He is currently working on a book project on how the Japanese model of capitalism is adapting in the face of new pressures since the 1990s. He has written extensively on Japanese politics, industrial policy, trade, and defense policy. He is a regular columnist for *Newsweek—Japan*. He has worked as a reporter for the *Japan Times* in Tokyo and as a freelance journalist in France. He has taught at the University of California, Irvine and Harvard University.

List of Figures

1.1 Types of institutional change: processes and results 9
1.2 Institutions as regimes 13
2.1 Four modes of policy change 48
2.2 Inequality and instability of American family income, 1972–98 53
2.3 Income redistribution via taxes and transfers
   in selected nations, 1981–2000 55
2.4 Share of Americans covered by private health insurance
   and Medicare/Medicaid, 1940–98 60
2.5 Pension contributions and benefits, as a less share of
   compensation, 1948–2001 64
2.6 IRA and 401(k) plan assets, as a percentage of GDP, 1985–98 66
2.7 Actual and projected retirement income streams, 1992, 2025
   (in thousands of 1992 dollars) 67
2.8 Occupational pension and old-age insurance benefits,
   as a share of combined benefits, 1950–2001 69
4.1 Total French tax revenues as a percentage of GDP, 1981–99 104
4.2 Number of French workers in public labor market programs 109
4.3 The 1998 Public social expenditures as a percentage
   of GDP, select OECD nations 110
8.1 Early retirement in Germany: inflow of male employees
   between 1960 and 1989 208
8.2 Early retirement in East Germany: inflow of male
   employees between 1993 and 2002 211
8.3 Contribution rates to pension, health, and unemployment
   insurance between 1949 and 2002 213
8.4 Early retirement in West Germany: inflow of male
   employees between 1993 and 2002 215
9.1 A subjective game model of institutionalization 233

List of Tables

1.1 Institutional change: five types of gradual transformation   31

6.1 What would it take to turn Japan into a liberal market
economy? Selected examples from labor and finance   146

6.2 If Japan is not turning into a liberal market economy,
then how is it changing? Selected examples from
labor and finance   148

7.1 Market share of loans to firms and manufacturing
industry by bank group (% of total)   178

8.1 Proportion of unemployed social plan recipients to all
social plan beneficiaries by age and industry, 1974–84   211

8.2 Development of part-time retirement: claims for
reimbursement to the Federal Labor Office
between 1996 and 2002   219

9.1 Codetermination as an institution: a schematic overview   237

Abbreviations

ADEPA	Agency for the Development of Applied Production Technology
ANVAR	National Agency for the Valorization of Research
APA	Aide Personnalisée à l' Autonomie
AsU	Arbeitsgemeinschaft Selbständiger Unternehmer
BDA	Bundesvereinigung der Deutschen Arbeitgeberverbände
BDI	Bundesverband der Deutschen Industrie
BGH	Bundesgerichtshof
BKA	Bundeskartellamt
CDU	Christian Democratic Union
CEE	Central and East European
CEVIPOF	Centre d'études de la vie politique française
CME	Coordinated Market Economy
CMU	Couverture Maladie Universelle
CSG	Contribution Sociale Généralisée
CSU	Christian Social Union
DG	Directorate General
DIHT	Deutscher Industrie –und Handelstag
DRIRE	Regional Directions of Industry, Research, and the Environment
ECJ	European Court of Justice
ECSC	European Coal and Steel Community
EEC	European Economic Community
EITC	Earned income tax credit
EMS	European Monetary System
EMU	European Monetary Union
ERISA	Employee Retirement Income Security Act
EU	European Union
FDI	Foreign direct investment
FDP	Federal Demonstration Partnership
FDP	Freie Demokratische Partei
FTC	Federal Trade Council
GWB	Gesetz gegen Wettbewersbeschränkungen
IRA	Individual Retirement Account
IRC	Industrial Revitalization Corporation
KapAEG	Kapitalaufnahmeerleichterungsgesetz
LDP	Liberal Democratic Party
LIS	Luxembourg Income Study
LFSS	Loi de Financement de la Securité Sociale
LME	Liberal Market Economy
LSE	London School of Economics
LTCB	Long-Term Credit Bank

MEDEF	Movement of French Enterprises
METI	Ministry of Economy, Trade and Industry
MITI	Ministry of International Trade and Industry
NGISC	North German Iron and Steel Control
NIE	New Institutional Economics
NPL	Non-Performing Loan
PEJ	Programme Emploi Jeunes
PSD	Prestation spécifique de dépendance
PSID	Panel Study of Income Dynamics
R&D	Research and development
RMI	Revenue minimum d'insertion
RPR	Rally for the Republic
SASE	Society for the Advancement of Socio-Economics
SEA	Single European Act
SEC	Securities and Exchange Commission
SME	Small- and medium-size enterprise
SSA	Social Security Administration
TEU	Treaty on the European Union
WTO	World Trade Organization

1

Introduction: Institutional Change in Advanced Political Economies

Wolfgang Streeck and Kathleen Thelen

The chapters in this volume were written as a collective contribution to the current debate in political science and sociology on institutional change. Instead of abstract theoretical reasoning, they offer in-depth empirical case studies. The underlying assumption, amply supported by recent literature, is that there is *a wide but not infinite variety* of modes of institutional change that can meaningfully be distinguished and analytically compared. It is also assumed that an empirically grounded typology of institutional change that does justice to the complexity and versatility of the subject can offer important insights on mechanisms of social and political stability and evolution generally.

Empirically the chapters of this book deal with current changes in selected political-economic institutions of rich, mostly Western democracies. To us the most prominent theoretical frameworks employed in the analysis of the welfare state and of contemporary political economy generally seem singularly ill-equipped to capture significant developments underway in many if not all of them. While we join with a large literature that rejects the notion that previously diverse political economies are all converging on a single model of capitalism, we notice that many arguments in support of the idea of distinctive and stable national models lack the analytic tools necessary to capture the changes that are indisputably going on in these countries. One consequence is a tendency in the literature to understate the extent of change, or alternatively to code all observed changes as minor adaptive adjustments to altered circumstances in the service of continuous reproduction of existing systems.

The conservative bias in much of this literature—the widespread propensity to explain what might seem to be new as just another version of the old—is at least partly a consequence of the impoverished state of theorizing on issues of institutional change. In the absence of analytic tools to characterize and explain modes of gradual change, much of the institutionalist literature relies—explicitly or implicitly—on a strong punctuated equilibrium model that draws an overly sharp distinction between long periods of institutional stasis periodically interrupted by some sort of exogenous shock that opens things up, allowing for more or less radical reorganization. As the problems of the literature on the political economies of advanced capitalism are symptomatic of broader theoretical deficits in the institutionalist literature as a whole, we submit that a close analysis of the

We are grateful to the participants in this project for the ideas and insights they contributed, and to Suzanne Berger and Peter A. Hall, for their comments on this chapter.

processes through which they are currently changing can provide a particularly fertile terrain within which to explore frequently overlooked mechanisms and modes of change more generally.

The opening section of this chapter will address three general issues. It begins with a summary account of the *historical setting* of the cases of institutional change analyzed in subsequent chapters. In particular, it describes the secular process of *liberalization* that constitutes the common denominator of many of the changes presently occurring in advanced political economies. Second, it characterizes and places in context the *type* of institutional change associated with current processes of liberalization, change that is at the same time *incremental* and *transformative*. And third, a definition of the concept of institution is provided that is to allow for an adequate conceptualization, not only of institutional statics, but also of institutional change. In the second part, we review the lessons that the case studies in the volume hold for the theorization of institutional change. First we ask how we may distinguish 'real' change from 'superficial', merely adaptive change, and how to detect change in the absence of disruptive events leading to institutional breakdown. Then we explore the contribution of our cases to an empirical inventory and analytical typology of modes of *gradual transformative change* of modern political-economic institutions. The Introduction ends with a concluding summary that returns to the substantive theme of the volume, the current liberalization of advanced political economies.

Institutional change in advanced political economies

Institutional change as liberalization

In the 1980s and 1990s, the political economies of the second postwar settlement began to undergo major changes. What exactly these changes were—or rather, are—is far from being unanimously agreed upon. At a very general level, however, most observers describe a secular expansion of market relations inside and across the borders of national political-economic systems, significantly beyond the limits that the organized capitalism of the postwar 'mixed economy' had set for them. With due caution, it would therefore seem justified to characterize the prevailing trend in the advanced economies during the last two decades of the twentieth century and beyond as a broad process of *liberalization*.

Clearly, differences between countries are of importance, and we would be making a severe mistake if we were to belittle them. But commonalities also count and must be taken no less seriously. Major differences between them notwithstanding, the postwar political economies of the countries that after 1945 under American leadership came to form the 'Free World' of democratic capitalism shared a number of features that set them apart from the capitalism of the interwar period and of the Great Depression. After the Second World War, governments accepted political responsibility for full employment, to be discharged by means of a Keynesian economic policy that, if necessary, placed the interests of workers above that of capitalist 'rentiers'. Trade unions were conceded constitutional or quasi-constitutional rights to free collective bargaining; large parts of industrial capacity were nationalized or in other ways controlled by the state, sometimes together with organized business and trade unions, in various ways exempting industries from market pressure and providing safe employment at good pay; economic growth was to a significant extent spent on an expanding welfare state that insured rising standards of mass consumption against the vagaries of the market while partly 'de-commodifying' the supply of labor; and sophisticated international arrangements enabled national governments democratically to respond to popular demands for social protection without upsetting an international free trade regime that made for ever increasing productivity and growing demand for mass-produced consumer goods.

Why the 'Golden Age' of postwar capitalism came to an end is the subject of an extensive debate that we cannot and need not summarize in this essay. First fissures began to show in the 1970s, in the aftermath of a worldwide wave of worker militancy that, among other things, reflected a new level of material and social aspirations after twenty years of peace, prosperity, and democracy. For a few years after, a new generation of workers and citizens used the institutions of democratic capitalism without being restrained by the cultural inhibitions and the historical traumas that had helped make economic democracy compatible with capitalist markets and hierarchies. Then the tide began to turn. In most Western countries heightened distributional conflict, reinforced by the welfare losses imparted on the rich industrialized world by the two oil crises, caused rising inflation and, subsequently, unemployment. In some places earlier than in others, but ultimately throughout the countries of the second postwar settlement, governments gradually reneged on their promise to provide for full employment and began to return to the market growing segments of national economies that had become too politicized to be governable by democratic politics.

Again, time and pathways of liberalization differed greatly between countries. There is also no doubt that a number of factors were at work that had little if anything to do with the explosion of popular economic and political demands after the demise of the disciplining memories of war and depression. The new microelectronic technology comes to mind that revolutionized work, skill requirements, employment structures, products, and product markets. In addition there also was internationalization and globalization, in part unquestionably accelerated and indeed called upon by governments striving to defend themselves against ever more demanding constituents, but in part clearly not. Rising competition in world markets both forced and legitimated sometimes deep revisions of welfare state policies, and the same can be said of fundamental demographic changes especially in Europe that originated in the 1970s and seemed to hang together in complex ways with increased consumer prosperity and citizen equality. In the 1990s at the latest, tightening political and economic limits on public budgets, in part constructed by international agreement between national executives that were about to lose their room for fiscal maneuver, combined with intensified international and domestic competition to discredit collective solutions to economic and social problems, providing strong ideological support for privatization, deregulation, self-reliance, and a general opening-up of social and economic arrangements to the logic of 'free' competitive markets—not just in the traditionally 'liberal' but also in the so-called 'coordinated' market economies.

Liberalization, then, may be described both as an inevitable economic adjustment in organized political economies to growing internal and external market pressures, and as a political strategy of either governments overwhelmed by unsatisfiable political demands or of business extricating itself through internationalization from the profit squeeze imposed on it by labor at the height of its postwar power in the early 1970s. As already emphasized, the liberalization of the institutions of organized capitalism—their 'disorganization', as it was called by Offe (1985) and Lash and Urry (1987)—took different forms and proceeded at different speeds in different countries, due in part to the effects of different institutional endowments interacting with what may in shorthand be described as identical exogenous and, in part, endogenous challenges. Indeed as pointed out prominently by the economic historian, Karl Polanyi, liberalization always comes with, and is enveloped in, all sorts of countermeasures taken by 'society'—or by specific societies in line with their respective traditions—against the destructive effects of free, 'self-regulating' markets. This, however, must clearly not be read with the unquenchable optimism of much of functionalist reasoning, which seems to accept as a general premise that liberalization can never be destructive because ultimately it will always be balanced by newly invented institutions and methods of social regulation. Rather it puts us on alert that in studying liberalization as a direction of institutional change, we should expect also to observe changes in institutions intended to reembed the very same market relations that liberalization sets free from traditional social constraints.

Transformation without disruption

Institutional change that we observe in the political economies of today's advanced capitalist societies is associated with a significant renegotiation of the politically regulated social market economy of the postwar period. Important qualifications notwithstanding, the current transformation of modern capitalism is making it more market-driven and market-accommodating as it releases ever more economic transactions from public–political control and turns them over to private contracts. One particularly intriguing aspect of this broad and multi-faceted development is that it unfolds by and large incrementally, without dramatic disruptions like the wars and revolutions that were characteristic of the first half of the twentieth century. In fact, an essential and defining characteristic of the ongoing worldwide liberalization of advanced political economies is that it evolves in the form of gradual change that takes place within, and is conditioned and constrained by, the very same postwar institutions that it is reforming or even dissolving.

Clearly it is hard to determine with any degree of accuracy whether the difference between the capitalist political economies of today and of the early 1950s is greater or smaller than that between capitalism in the middle and at the beginning of the nineteenth century. Perhaps the convulsive transformations associated with the First and Second World Wars did in fact unsettle the societies of western Europe and, to a lesser extent, North America more deeply than the gradual changes that began to chisel away at the postwar mixed economy in the 1980s and 1990s. But to us this cannot mean that the changes we are observing today throughout the advanced capitalist world are only of minor significance, or are merely modifications on the surface of a fundamentally stable and self-reproductive social order. For a few years when one could still speak of a 'crisis'—usually in the expectation of a return to a stable state similar to what the world was like when its transformation began—this might have seemed plausible. But ongoing change and its accumulating results increasingly suggest that the current process of liberalization involves a major recasting of the system of democratic capitalism as we know it, issuing in a social order dissociated from fundamental assumptions of social integration and political-economic conflict resolution that underlay the construction of the postwar settlement after 1945.

In our view, central properties of the developments currently underway in the advanced political economies are not being adequately theorized, nor even fully recognized, in the most influential theoretical frameworks guiding research on political economy and the welfare state. For different reasons, contemporary scholarship both on 'varieties of capitalism' and on the welfare state seem to be producing analyses that understate the magnitude and significance of current changes. Hall and Soskice's highly influential work on varieties of capitalism is one example (Hall and Soskice 2001). The framework they propose is premised on a broad distinction between 'coordinated' and 'liberal' market economies based on the extent to which employers can coordinate among themselves to achieve joint gains. Differences between the two types of economies are expressed in different clusters of institutions—including particular kinds of financial arrangements, collective bargaining institutions, vocational training institutions, and welfare state institutions—that together support distinctive types of employer strategies in the market. Against popular convergence theories that see all systems bending toward the Anglo Saxon model, Hall and Soskice's argument predicts continuing cross-national divergence. Specifically, and most directly at odds with convergence theories, Hall and Soskice argue that employers in coordinated market economies who have invested in and organized their strategies around indigenous institutions will not abandon these arrangements in the face of new market pressures. While providing a compelling account of observed institutional resiliency, the theory is much less suited to understanding contemporary changes. Emphasizing divergent employer preferences rooted in preexisting institutional configurations, the theory, in fact, seems to regard almost all feedback within a system as positive and operating to maintain traditional structures (Thelen and van Wijnbergen 2003; Kume and Thelen 2004).

Similarly in the welfare state literature, the most influential theoretical frameworks stress continuity over change. Pierson's agenda-setting work on welfare state retrenchment paints a picture that emphasizes the obstacles and political risks of change. Contrary to previous accounts, Pierson argues that the politics involved in dismantling the welfare state are not simply the mirror image of the politics of constructing and expanding it. For instance, even if organized labor and Left political parties had been crucial to the construction of the welfare state, their declining political power does not necessarily imperil its continuity. The reason, Pierson argues, is that large-scale public welfare programs are subject to important feedback effects, as they create new constituencies and beneficiaries that develop vested interests in their maintenance. Following Pierson, conventional wisdom in the welfare state literature today largely focuses on the difficulties of retrenchment. As Hacker points out (Chapter 2, p. 40), the dominant view is that while the welfare state is perhaps under greater strain than before 'social policy frameworks remain secure, anchored by their enduring popularity, powerful constituencies, and centrality within the post-war order'.

The prevailing emphasis on institutional stability even in the face of indisputable and important change points to a general problem in contemporary institutional analysis, which has always emphasized structural constraints and continuity. In the past, this involved a highly static conception of institutions as 'frozen' residues, or 'crystallizations', of previous political conflict. Presently a growing body of work has begun to conceive of institutional reproduction as a dynamic political process. Recent work on path dependence in particular has emphasized mechanisms of increasing returns and positive feedback that sustain and reinforce institutions through time. Still, however, increasing returns and positive feedback are more helpful in understanding institutional resiliency than institutional change (the following paragraphs draw on Thelen 2004, pp. 27–30).

In fact, when it comes to the latter, the notion of path dependence seems to encourage scholars to think of change in one of two ways, *either* as very minor and more or less continuous (the more frequent type) *or* as very major but then abrupt and discontinuous (the much rarer type). This has yielded a strangely bifurcated literature that links path dependence as a concept to two completely different and in some ways diametrically opposed conceptions of change. Some scholars invoke the term to support the broad assertion that legacies of the past always weigh on choices and changes in the present (e.g. Sewell 1996). Especially studies of transitions to democracy and market economy in contemporary eastern Europe, for example, employ path dependence in this way, as in: 'Path-dependency suggests that the institutional legacies of the past limit the range of current possibilities and/or options in institutional innovation' (Nielson, Jessop, and Hausner 1995: 6). Invoked in this way, the concept is to stress the *limited degrees of freedom* that exist for innovation, even in moments of extreme upheaval. In many such cases, the characterization of change as 'path dependent' is meant as a refutation of and an alternative to voluntarist ('rational design') accounts that view institution-building as a matter of constructing efficient incentive structures on a more or less 'clean slate' (e.g. Stark 1995).

Others, however, and often those who insist on a more precise definition of path dependence, tend toward a very different view of change, one that is closer to a strong version of a punctuated equilibrium model that draws a sharp distinction between the dynamics of institutional innovation on the one hand and of institutional reproduction on the other (Krasner 1988). Mahoney, for instance, criticizes loose definitions of path dependence and argues that 'path-dependence characterizes specifically those historical sequences in which contingent events set in motion institutional patterns or event chains that have deterministic properties' (Mahoney 2000: 507). By emphasizing the very different logic of contingent institutional choice and deterministic institutional reproduction, this definition implies and encourages a strong distinction between 'critical juncture' moments in which institutions are originally formed, and long periods of stasis characterized by institutional continuity. Any number of examples could be given here but the idea is generally captured in what Pempel calls 'long continuities' periodically interrupted by 'radical shifts' (Pempel 1998: 1). In his words: 'Path-dependent equilibrium is periodically ruptured by radical change, making for sudden bends in the path of history' (Pempel 1998: 3).

Claims about relative contingency at historic choice points and relative determinism in trajectories once chosen are pervasive in the social science literature and they are by no means exclusively associated with scholars invoking the concept of path dependence.[1] In sociology, Ann Swidler has drawn a distinction between 'settled' and 'unsettled' times, in which the latter are seen as 'periods of social transformation' or 'historical junctures where new cultural complexes make possible new or reorganized strategies of action' (Swidler 1986: 278, 283, respectively). Ira Katznelson adopts this formulation and links it to the age-old debate on the balance between agency and structure, arguing that structure figures heavily in the 'settled' while agency reigns in 'unsettled' times. He writes of 'multiple possibilities inside unsettled moments of uncommon choice', such moments being defined as periods in which the 'constraints on agency are broken or relaxed and opportunities expand so that purposive action may be especially consequential' (Katznelson 2003: 277, 283). This kind of perspective is reflected, among others, in Jowitt's work on eastern Europe, which sees post-Leninist societies as 'genesis environments' characterized by a new openness in which 'leaders will matter more than institutions, and charisma more than political economy' (quoted in Stark 1995: 68).

Rational-choice scholarship, too, has mostly gravitated to a model of discontinuous institutional change (Weingast 2002: 692), though from a different starting point. This is because some of the core premises underlying rational-choice theorizing—above all, the view of institutions as self-enforcing equilibria in which behavior is generated endogenously—suggest a sharp line between the logics and the analysis of institutional reproduction and change. Here again, there is a tendency to see change mostly in terms of dynamics unleashed by some exogenous shift or shock, ignoring the possibility of endogenously generated institutional change that is more than just adaptive (but see Greif and Laitin 2003: 2).[2]

Moreover, similar to perspectives such as Katznelson's that stress agency and openness in 'critical junctures', the *direction* of change (i.e. the reason why a particular institutional equilibrium prevails over other possible ones) seems to be a function of factors exogenous to the institutions.[3] As Pierson points out, this perspective has little to say 'about what is likely to happen if a particular institutional equilibrium does give way', and in fact the implication often is that 'any new equilibrium may be as likely as any other' (Pierson 2004: 143–4). In other words, where the problem of change is posed in terms of breakdown and replacement, there is often no sense of a 'path' at all.

The analyses offered in this volume suggest that there are severe limits to models of change that draw a sharp line between institutional stability and institutional change and that see all major changes as exogenously generated. Sometimes institutional change *is* abrupt and sharp (e.g. see Beissinger 2002). However, it is not at all clear that this exhausts the possibilities, nor even that it captures the most important ways in which institutions evolve over time. Certainly, the cases examined in this volume do not conform to a strong punctuated equilibrium model. On the contrary, they suggest that we must avoid being caught in a conceptual schema that provides only for either incremental change supporting institutional continuity through reproductive adaptation, or disruptive change causing institutional breakdown and innovation and thereby resulting in discontinuity. In short, we argue that equating incremental with adaptive and reproductive *minor* change, and *major* change with, mostly exogenous, disruption of continuity, makes excessively high demands on 'real' change to be recognized as such and tends to reduce most or all observable changes to adjustment for the purpose of stability.

The biases inherent in existing conceptual frameworks are particularly limiting in a time, like ours, when incremental processes of change appear to cause gradual institutional transformations that add up to major historical discontinuities. As various authors have suggested, far-reaching change can be accomplished through the accumulation of small, often seemingly insignificant adjustments (e.g. Pierson 2004 and others on 'tipping points'). To be able to take due account of this, we suggest that we distinguish between *processes* of change, which may be incremental or abrupt, and *results* of change, which may amount to either continuity or discontinuity (Figure 1.1). From the perspective of a punctuated equilibrium model, 'real' change that results in discontinuity takes place through abrupt institutional breakdown and replacement (the cell on the lower right of Figure 1.1). Authors writing in this tradition do recognize that there is also incremental change; but they tend to conceive of this as fundamentally reactive and adaptive and serving to protect institutional continuity (upper left cell). In reality, however, there often is considerable continuity through and in spite of historical break points, as well as dramatic institutional reconfiguration beneath the surface of apparent stability or adaptive self-reproduction, as a result of an accumulation over longer periods of time of subtle incremental changes (see also Thelen 2004). The former, which we tentatively refer to as 'survival and return' (lower left cell), is of less

		Result of change	
		Continuity	Discontinuity
Process of change	Incremental	Reproduction by adaptation	Gradual transformation
	Abrupt	Survival and return	Breakdown and replacement

Figure 1.1 Types of institutional change: processes and results

interest to us in the present context than the latter, which we call *gradual transformation* and which stands for institutional discontinuity caused by incremental, 'creeping' change (upper right cell).

It is to the exploration of this type of change that the present volume is devoted—and, we believe, should be if we want to be able to conceptualize properly current developments in the political economy of modern capitalism. Rather than big changes in response to big shocks, we will be looking for *incremental change with transformative results*.[4] To move beyond the punctuated equilibrium models that are employed, almost by default, by most political scientists, sociologists, and economists working on institutional change, we have invited contributions organized around a theoretically self-conscious investigation of empirical cases of institutional change in advanced industrial societies that do not fit received conceptualizations. As our volume demonstrates, such cases are not just frequent but they are also found in core areas of contemporary political economies. Authors were asked to work toward general insights in the character and the mechanisms of the sort of change they observed within and across individual countries. Contributions were to draw on ongoing or completed empirical work and highlight the significance of its findings for an improved theoretical understanding of institutional change, in particular of the relationship between continuity and discontinuity, and between incremental and fundamental change.

Institutions as regimes

Definitions of institutions abound. As none of them has yet become firmly institutionalized in the social and political sciences, a brief conceptual exercise cannot be avoided.[5] Very generally, institutions may be defined *as building-blocks of social order:* they represent socially sanctioned, that is, collectively enforced expectations with respect to the behavior of specific categories of actors or to the performance of certain activities. Typically they involve *mutually related rights and obligations* for actors, distinguishing between appropriate and inappropriate, 'right' and 'wrong', 'possible' and 'impossible' actions and thereby organizing behavior into predictable and reliable patterns.

In this volume we focus on institutions that govern behavior in the political economies of advanced capitalism. As we believe in historically grounded concepts and theories, this relieves us of the need to define institutions so generally that all possible forms of normative regulation of social action are covered. For example, anthropologists might conceive of mores and customs, like shaking hands with everyone present in a certain order when one enters a meeting room, as institutions, provided there are strong enough sanctions against deviating from them. Indeed in more conservative social settings in Germany, like a business meeting, not shaking hands is very likely to reflect negatively on someone, and those present will in one way or other make the deviant feel that they disapprove of what is disrespectful and impolite behavior to them.

Mores and customs are no trivial matter. The sanctions that are applied to enforce them may be extremely painful—in the case above, they may mean that business is lost to the competition, or that an overdue promotion is refused. But what is important for us in the example is that the sanctions that are available to the group to enforce the norm are strictly *informal* in nature, as indeed is the 'institution' of the handshake that such sanctions are supposed to protect. Informal institutions exist by no means only in premodern societies; in fact informal norms enforced by community disapproval are universally present in social life. *They are, however, not the subject of our study.* This is because to the extent that modern economies are *political* economies—that is, governed by politics—they are mainly controlled by norms and sanctions that are *formalized*.[6]

Modern, formal, legal–political institutions differ in a variety of ways from informal, 'anthropological' ones, not least in how they change: the former by decision and the latter by cultural evolution. Still, they also have important properties in common. Foremost among these is their *obligatory character*. Actors may and frequently will voluntarily comply with the demands of an institutionalized social norm, either because they believe in its value or because they find compliance with its expedient. This, however, is not what *defines* an institution. Defining of an institution is, rather, that actors are *expected* to conform to it, regardless of what they would want to do on their own. Moreover, such expectations are held, not just by actors directly affected by the expected behavior, but by 'society' as a whole. Someone who does not know how to greet people properly in a meeting room and in what order will incur the disapproval of *all* well-socialized middle- or upper-class Germans, whether or not they themselves have been refused the opportunity to shake hands with him or her. And in a country with an institutionalized right to collective bargaining, an employer who turns his shop into a 'union-free environment' will not just be reproached by the unions he has locked out, but also by the courts that will remind him of the obligations the law of the land imposes on an employer of labor as a matter of legal duty.

In sum, the institutions in which we are interested here are formalized rules that may be enforced by calling upon a third party. Following Stinchcombe (1968), it is this possibility of third party enforcement that indicates whether a rule has legitimacy. As long as the breach of a rule or the violation of an expectation, informal or formal, leads to no more than a strategic response by the actors directly affected, we are dealing, *not* with an institution, but with a more or less voluntarily agreed social convention.[7] With an institution we are dealing only if and to the extent that third parties predictably and reliably come to the support of actors whose institutionalized, and therefore *legitimate*, normative expectations have been disappointed. This they do not necessarily because they identify with the interests of such actors, although they may. Rather, they intervene as an expression of moral disapproval (in traditional societies, or on behalf of informal institutions), or because they are specifically charged by an organized modern society with ensuring the reliability of certain expectations of actors with respect to the behavior of others.

By emphasizing the obligatory character of institutions, and in particular of the formal institutions of modern political economies with which we are concerned, we exclude from our discussion empirical phenomena and dissociate ourselves from conceptual constructions that would make our subject too broad to be meaningful. Our definition shares with the more economistic treatments associated with 'rational choice' theory an emphasis on strategic behavior within institutional constraints, rejecting the shared cognitive templates that some sociologists associate with institutions (e.g. Meyer and Rowan 1991). But against the rational-choice view of institutions as coordinating mechanisms, we draw attention to relations of authority, obligation, and enforcement as opposed to voluntarism.[8] In this way we distinguish institutions from private pacts or conventions that lack third party or societal support and with it, in our definition, legitimacy. Pacts or conventions, in other words, become institutions only when their stability ceases to depend exclusively on the self-interested behavior of those directly involved and rather becomes, in a strict sense, a matter of 'public interest'.[9]

Defining institutions in this way, we believe we gain at least three advantages. First, our emphasis on enforcement as a social process by which institutions are translated in behavior distinguishes our approach from the voluntaristic variety of 'rational choice' where institutions are seen in functional terms, as facilitating coordination for actors to achieve joint gains—which does not allow for the possibility of a gap between the institution as designed and the behavior under it. Similarly, at the other end of the spectrum, it sets us off against a view of institutions as shared scripts where also, by definition, there is no gap between institution and behavior, and therefore no conflict over competing interpretations that could be explored as a source of change.[10] Put otherwise, the way we include obligation and enforcement into our concept of institution, we can explicitly provide for a significant amount of 'play' in the rules actors are expected to follow, and thus for the possibility that institutional change may be generated *as a result of the normal, everyday implementation and enactment of an institution*. We will return to this theme shortly when we introduce the concept of an institutional 'regime'.

Second, especially when political scientists write about institutions, the question sometimes arises whether *policies*, like, for example, early retirement or the provision of state support to small- and medium-sized firms, should be included or not—and to what extent theories of institutional change may at the same time be theories of policy change. To us this depends on the character of the policy in question. If a government agrees or refuses to support the American occupation of Iraq by sending troops, this certainly is a policy but we would not consider it as an institution. There are policies, however, which stipulate rules that assign normatively backed rights and responsibilities to actors and provide for their 'public', that is, third party enforcement. Thus early retirement policies create expectations among workers and employers with respect to when people become entitled to draw a pension from the state, and to the extent that stipulated conditions are met, they can consider their expectations to be legitimate and indeed go to the courts to have them vindicated. Policies, that is to say, are institutions in our sense to the extent that they constitute rules for actors other than for the policymakers themselves—rules that can and need to be implemented and that are legitimate in that they will if necessary be enforced by agents acting on behalf of the society as a whole.

Third, in colloquial language the word institution is sometimes used for a specific category of actors, usually corporate actors or organizations, rather than for legitimate rules of behavior. The Federal Reserve Bank, for example, certainly falls in this category, and so does a state as a whole. Even private organizations are sometimes considered institutions, for example, trade unions in Scandinavian countries or the Deutsche Bank in the German postwar economy. To us this does not pose a big conceptual problem. We suggest that organizations come to be regarded as institutions to the extent that their existence and operation become in a specific way publicly guaranteed and privileged, by becoming backed up by societal norms and the enforcement capacities related to them. A central bank is considered an institution because its existence is an outflow of the strongly sanctioned state monopoly on issuing legal tender. It stands for the collectively enforced expectation that other actors will stay away from printing money and instead will accept for payment the money issued by the central bank. Also, as long as trade unions are mere organizations, they can be suppressed and may even be outlawed by a hostile government. In some societies, however, where their existence and their activities have become protected by collective values and politically enacted norms, they constitute a socially sanctioned constraint for economic actors. Similarly, a bank is just a bank as long as it is not performing semipublic functions in a country's industrial policy; if it is, however, the opportunities and constraints its decisions create for others can be disregarded only at the price of disapproval, not just by the bank, but also by other agents that represent the community as a whole.

Summing up so far, to us the closest general concept for the kind of institution in whose dynamics of change we are interested is that of a social *regime*. By regime we mean a set of rules stipulating expected behavior and 'ruling out' behavior deemed to be undesirable. A regime is legitimate in the sense and to the extent that the expectations it represents are enforced by the society in which it is embedded. Regimes involve rule makers and rule takers, the former setting and modifying, often in conflict and competition, the rules with which the latter are expected to comply. In the limiting case, rule makers and rule takers are identical; in any case, relations and interactions between the two are crucial for the content and the evolution of the regime as such. An institution conceived as a regime resembles what Weber calls a *Herrschaftsverband*, translated by Guenther Roth as a 'ruling organization' (Weber 1978 [1956] 53).[11] Conceiving of institutions as regimes not only makes them eminently accessible to empirical research as it translates institutional relations into relations between identifiable social actors. Even more importantly, as the analyses in this volume confirm, it is only if we can distinguish analytically between the rules and their implementation or 'enactment'—and, by extension, if we can identify the gaps between the two that are due to or open up opportunities for strategic action on the part of actors—that we can capture important features of incremental endogenous change.

In Figure 1.2 we have summarized the main properties of *institutions as regimes*. Embedded in a societal context of supportive third parties that makes for institutional legitimacy, we locate our ideal–typical distinction between rule

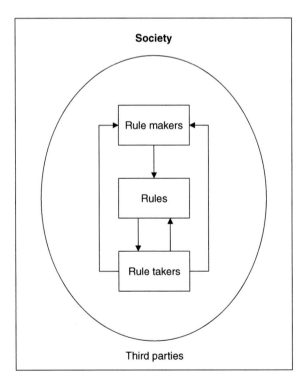

Figure 1.2 Institutions as regimes

makers (or institutional designers) and rule takers. Note that we provide for a direct feedback from the latter to the former, which we expect to be of relevance certainly in democratic societies. In order not to make our Figure too confusing, we have decided not to indicate the relations between both rule makers and rule takers with the surrounding society and the values the latter enforces on them. Just as the surrounding society affects both parties through the constraints and opportunities it creates for socially backed rule making and rule enforcement, it is itself affected by the social and political influence exercised by agents lobbying for their interpretation of social rules and norms. We will address this in more detail further below.

Defining institutions as regimes has the advantage for us that it directs attention to important sources of institutional change. They all have to do with the fact that the *enactment of a social rule is never perfect* and that there always is a gap between the *ideal pattern* of a rule and the *real pattern* of life under it. In the following we will address four facets of this complex relationship for purposes of illustration:

1. As we have learned from sociologists such as Reinhard Bendix (1974 [1956]), the meaning of a rule is never self-evident and always subject to and in need of interpretation. This is relevant especially in the relationship that is indicated in Figure 1.2 by the downward arrow from rules to rule takers. Life in a social, that is, normatively ordered community requires ongoing efforts to develop and maintain a shared understanding of what exactly the rule says that one has to apply to a given situation. As ideal patterns are necessarily less complex than real patterns, honest disagreement over how a norm is to be applied may always arise. Rather than simply a matter of logical deduction, applying a general rule to a specific situation is a creative act that must take into account, not just the rule itself, but also the unique circumstances to which it is to be applied. This holds for highly formalized norms, like written law, no less than for informal ones. Lawyers know the complexities of subsuming the empirical properties of an individual case under a general rule. Recourse to what is called in some legal systems 'the will of the legislator' is for good reason just one way among others to discover what a rule really demands in a concrete context. This is because no rule maker can be assumed to have been aware of the full variety of situations to which his law might in the future have to be applied. In fact he might find it difficult to remember with hindsight the complex variety of motives that may have driven his decision. Sociologists have pointed out that typically, clarification of the operative meaning of formal law presupposes a shared culturally based tacit understanding between the actors involved that may, however, either not really exist or change over time, in which case the rule *in effect* changes with it. Indeed often what a rule 'really means' can be established only by the rulings of a legitimate authority charged with adjudicating between different interpretations. Such rulings, too, can and are likely to change with time and circumstances, which may be entirely functional as they may provide a regime with the sort of ground flexibility that it may require for its reproduction.

2. A related issue is the cognitive limits of rule makers, which become relevant in the downward relationship in our Figure between rule makers and rules. Even the honest application in good will of a rule to empirical conditions may cause unanticipated results that may differ from what was intended when the rule was written, which in turn may cause its corrective rewriting. On the other hand, that rules cannot be unambiguously and definitively stated facilitates their creative application in uncertain circumstances, keeping them valid in spite of the inevitably imperfect information of their designers on the circumstances of their implementation. In fact regimes capable of survival in a complex environment are likely to have built-in feedbacks that inform rule makers how their rules are working out in practice. (In Figure 1.2, these are indicated by the upward arrows from rule takers to rule makers.) Supported by intelligence of this sort rule makers may then revise the rules, setting in motion another sequence of practical exploration of their real meaning, observation of their real consequences, and further revision in the light of the latter.

3. Questioning the true meaning of institutionalized rules happens of course not only in good will. Rule takers do not just implement the rules made for them, but also try to revise them in the process of implementation, making use of their inherent openness and under-definition (see the upward arrow in Figure 1.2 from rule takers to rules). One advantage of defining institutions as *Herrschaftsverbände* within which rule makers and rule takers interact is that this avoids an 'over-socialized' (Wrong 1961) conception of human actors as is often implied by purely normative, or cultural, concepts of institution. While sometimes rule takers are socialized to follow a rule for its own sake, sometimes they clearly are not, and this seems to apply particularly in modern societies and economies. To the extent that rules impose uncomfortable and costly obligations, less than perfectly social-ized rational actors may look for ways to circumvent them. Finding loopholes in a law is a specialty of lawyers, especially tax lawyers. Their continuous probing of the boundary between the legal and the illegal is part of the interpretative strug-gle that begins as soon as a rule is laid down: it is one mechanism by which the meaning of a rule is both clarified and modified ('worked out') in practice. Favorable discoveries made by adventurous interpretative entrepreneurs may spread fast among the subjects of a regime, forcing rule makers to revise the law in order to restore it. Sometimes the only way this can happen is by more special rules being added to cover unforeseen cases. As this makes the regime more complex, it may further extend the opportunities for inventive opportunists to evade or subvert it to their advantage.

4. Finally, there are limits to the extent to which socially authorized agencies of social control can prevent and correct unintentional or subversive deviation from social rules. A case in point is the phenomenon of illegal employment, or more generally of the underground economy. Some labor market regimes are more likely than others to give rise to anomic behavior of this sort. In fact, under-ground employment seems to be most frequent in highly regulated economies. Mass deviant behavior in breach of a social or legal regime can often be ended

only by changing the regime and making the behavior legal. Sometimes, however, rule makers are willing to live with a great deal of anomie since the stability of a norm may, as famously pointed out by Durkheim, require that it be broken. For example, illegal employment may furnish a modicum of flexibility to an economy that would otherwise be too rigidly regulated to perform well (what Berger and Piore (1980) have some time ago described as economic 'dualism').

What all this amounts to is that those who control social institutions, whoever they may be in a concrete case, are likely to have less than perfect control over the way in which their creations work in reality. What an institution *is* is defined by continuous interaction between rule makers and rule takers during which ever new interpretations of the rule will be discovered, invented, suggested, rejected, or for the time being, adopted. The real meaning of an institution, that is to say, is inevitably and because of the very nature of social order subject to evolution driven, if by nothing else, by its necessarily imperfect enactment on the ground, in directions that are often unpredictable. Indeed the more sophisticated the makers of a regime are, the more they recognize that a good part of institutional and political life consists of unanticipated consequences of their 'institutional design' decisions, requiring that these are continuously adjusted and revised if they are to be made to stick.

We conclude this section by noting that, conceived as systems of social interaction under formalized normative control, institutions cease to appear as a rigid hardware of social life mechanistically relegating actors and action to narrowly circumscribed residual spaces for spontaneous voluntarism and rational calculation. Instead a grounded, 'realistic' concept of social institutions, as adopted in this volume, emphasizes their being continuously created and recreated by a great number of actors with divergent interests, varying normative commitments, different powers, and limited cognition. This process no single actor fully controls; its outcomes are far from being standardized across different sites of enactment; and its results are contingent, often unpredictable, and may be fully understood only with hindsight.[12]

Dynamics of institutional change: lessons from the present volume

What counts as change? Or, when is a change a 'real' change?

As suggested above, the most influential frameworks for the study of the political economy of advanced countries exhibit a distinct if inadvertent conservative bias, in that the sophisticated analytic tools they provide for understanding stability are not matched by equally sophisticated tools for understanding change. As a consequence, whether such frameworks are premised on an equilibrium model (as in the varieties of capitalism literature) or not (as in much of the welfare state literature), current scholarship is prone to ignore or downplay observed changes, or to code all that appears to be new as a variation of the old.

The chapters in this volume demonstrate how much is missed when contemporary trends are analyzed from the perspective of these theoretical frameworks.

Jacob Hacker's chapter on the US welfare state documents a trend toward the privatization of risk across a number of policy areas. The traditional literature on the welfare state rightly suggests that most large-scale social welfare policies have proven very resistant to overt cutback efforts. However, as Hacker argues, 'the conventional story about retrenchment appears only half right', for as he shows, risk coverage in the United States has narrowed significantly as policymakers have failed to adapt welfare programs to cover new risks that have emerged outside the scope of existing policies. As Hacker puts it, in a context in which social risks are changing and where the gap between them and the 'reach' of social programs is growing, 'conservatives have not had to enact major policy reforms to move toward many of their favored ends' (pp. 46–7). Analyses that focus exclusively on the lock-in effects characteristic of large entitlement programs miss the story of a major de facto shrinkage of welfare state coverage in the United States over the past two decades.

The chapters by Jonah Levy and Steven Vogel, on the French and Japanese political economies, respectively, make a similar point. Anyone looking for evidence of the continued viability of the traditional French and Japanese political-economic 'models' will find a lot of it. France has traditionally been considered the classic example of a state-led political economy and as Levy points out, the French state still looms extremely large in the lives of its citizens. In fact, by many conventional measures, like spending and taxation, the state is bigger than ever, and certainly no less economically active. However, as Levy argues, if we focus on these continuities, we miss an enormous and highly consequential transformation: the abandonment of the traditional *dirigiste* strategy of directing capital while excluding labor, in favor of a strategy of aggressively promoting market liberalization while cushioning its social effects. Levy's account shows how existing state capacities, far from being dismantled, were 'redeployed' in a major way during the post *dirigiste* period.

Vogel's chapter on Japan describes a similar phenomenon. Despite the strains of prolonged economic crisis, traditional Japanese political-economic institutions have exhibited remarkable staying power. Much remains of the institutions that support and sustain Japan's version of a 'coordinated' market economy—like long-term employment in the area of labor relations, or corporate and financial networks. Vogel documents these continuities but notes that stability should not obscure change, particularly in the way in which old institutions and policies are being used in the service of new ends. Among other things, the corporate ties that are often seen as defining a distinctively 'coordinated' as opposed to a 'liberal' model of capitalism are being tapped as mechanisms through which to accomplish corporate downsizing and a move toward more liberalized labor markets. Liberalization in Japan, that is to say, has unfolded above all by traditional institutions being deployed in novel and, indeed over the long run, transformative ways.

One thing the three cases have in common is that they illustrate, as suggested by our definition of institutions as regimes, that formal institutions do not fully determine the uses to which they may be put. This is one important reason why major change in institutional practice may be observed together with strong continuity in institutional structures. Gregory Jackson's analysis of German code-termination is a case in point, documenting as it does profound changes in the way codetermination has functioned over successive historical periods in the absence of major institutional discontinuity. At its inception, codetermination was partly intended as an independent, workplace-based counterweight to Germany's rather radical national labor movement at the time. By the 1950s, however, works councils had been fully though not formally incorporated into the strategies of, now moderate, trade unions. Now, not only did codetermination not detract from the strength of the unions, but it magnified their voice by providing them with a stable, legally anchored foothold in workplaces across the entire economy. Clearly this is change of a quite fundamental sort although it has taken place within an institutional form that has remained recognizably similar, or was reconstructed in recognizably similar forms, over a long period of time.

How can transformative change result from incremental change, in the absence of exogenous shocks? Institutional structures, our chapters suggest, may be stickier than what they do and what is done through them. If the latter changes significantly, however gradually, analytical frameworks that take the absence of disruption as sufficient evidence of institutional continuity miss the point, given that *the practical enactment of an institution is as much part of its reality as its formal structure.* In this vein, Hacker rightly suggests including in institutional analysis the actual *consequences* of institutionalized behavior, while Jackson emphasizes the possibility of changing *meanings* and *functions* being attached to an otherwise stable institution. Similarly, Vogel and Levy point to the different purposes that may be pursued by means of a given institutional arrangement, and Deeg locates the beginning of a new 'path' where a new 'logic of action' is established. The latter he defines as a *general orientation* of actors that, one might add, operates like a 'meta-rule' governing the interpretation of a given structure of institutional constraints and opportunities—whose meaning, as we have argued, is never self-evident and therefore needs to be continuously constituted in practice.

Fundamental change, then, ensues when a multitude of actors switch from one logic of action to another. This may happen in a variety of ways, and it certainly can happen gradually and continuously. For example, given that logics and institutional structures are not one-to-one related, enterprising actors often have enough 'play' to test new behaviors inside old institutions, perhaps in response to new and as yet incompletely understood external conditions, and encourage other actors to behave correspondingly. We will return to the concept of logic of action below.

How institutions change

Contemporary theories of institutional development mostly locate significant change in convulsive historic ruptures or openings. This is not what the essays in this volume do. Rather than abrupt and discontinuous, they find transformative change often to result from an accumulation of gradual and incremental change (see also Djelic and Quack 2003: 309–10). Moreover, rather than emanating on the outside, change is often endogenous and in some cases is produced by the very behavior an institution itself generates. Reminded of this by their empirical material, the analyses in this volume provide an angle on institutional change that is different from dominant punctuated equilibrium models. In particular, they document from different perspectives how significant change can emanate from inherent ambiguities and 'gaps' that exist by design or emerge over time between formal institutions and their actual implementation or enforcement (see also Pierson 2004: ch. 4). As several of our chapters show, these gaps may become key sites of political contestation over the form, functions, and salience of specific institutions whose outcome may be an important engine of institutional change (see also Thelen 2004).

'Agency' and 'structure', in other words, do not just matter sequentially—unlike in Katznelson (2003) where institutions mostly constrain and where change has to wait for those rare moments when agency defeats structure. Political institutions are not only periodically contested; they are the object of ongoing skirmishing as actors try to achieve advantage by interpreting or redirecting institutions in pursuit of their goals, or by subverting or circumventing rules that clash with their interests. Instead of separating institutional development into periods in which agency matters more than structure or the other way around, the aim must be to understand, as Deeg puts it, the way actors cultivate change from within the context of existing opportunities and constraints—working around elements they cannot change while attempting to harness and utilize others in novel ways.

Overall the chapters of this book suggest to us five broad modes of gradual but nevertheless transformative change that we will call *displacement, layering, drift, conversion,* and *exhaustion.* We discuss each of these modes briefly, drawing on the contributions to this volume[13] but also on a broader literature. After this we will close with a consideration of the lessons the essays assembled here can tell us, substantively, about current processes of liberalization in advanced industrial democracies.

Displacement   From the perspective of whole systems (or what some sociologists call 'organizational fields') change can occur through a process of displacement. In the 'new' institutionalism in sociology, displacement happens as new models emerge and diffuse which call into question existing, previously taken-for-granted organizational forms and practices (Fligstein 1990, 1997; DiMaggio and Powell 1991; Dobbin 1994; Clemens 1997; Schneiberg n.d). In the political science literature, the emphasis is typically more on political than on cognitive or normative factors, with change emanating mostly from shifts in the societal balance of power (see, among others, Collier and Collier 1991; Skowronek 1995; Huber and Stephens 2001).

For our present purposes, the important point (associated above all with the works of Karen Orren and Stephen Skowronek) is that the institutional frameworks that exist in any particular society are never completely coherent. While some institutional arrangements may impose a dominant logic of action, these typically coexist with other arrangements, created at different points in time and under different historical circumstances, that embody conflicting and even contradictory logics (Orren and Skowronek 1994, 2004). Beyond this, and equally important, even within dominant frameworks there will normally remain possibilities of action that institutions neither prescribe nor eliminate. Where either of these is the case, institutional configurations are vulnerable to change through displacement as traditional arrangements are discredited or pushed to the side in favor of new institutions and associated behavioral logics. Such change often occurs through the rediscovery or activation—and, always, the cultivation—of alternative institutional forms. As growing numbers of actors defect to a new system, previously deviant, aberrant, anachronistic, or 'foreign' practices gain salience at the expense of traditional institutional forms and behaviors.[14]

Where the institutions and behaviors enacted by *displacement through defection* come from can vary widely. For example, an older literature in political science drew attention to the 'reactivation' or 'rediscovery' of what Barrington Moore once called 'suppressed historical alternatives' (Moore 1979: 376). Thus Michael Piore and Charles Sabel (1984) attributed the success of the German political economy in the 1980s in large part to the survival of institutional and organizational forms (among others a vibrant and flexible small business sector and a skill system that preserved and promoted the acquisition of traditional 'craft' skills) that had been declared anachronistic and irrelevant in the heyday of Fordist mass production. As the terms of competition shifted in the 1980s, these institutions could be tapped and activated to become the basis for alternative competitive strategies premised on what one of us has elsewhere called 'diversified quality production' (Streeck 1991).

In this volume, a similar logic of change is at work in the chapter by Colin Crouch and Maarten Keune. In the two cases they analyzed, change occurred as actors 'worked creatively with institutional materials that were at hand ... [by virtue of their historic] legacies, but submerged by more dominant or more recent practices' (pp. 84–5). In the case of the rejuvenation of the Hungarian region of Győr, this involved tapping into and cultivating the Western-oriented, market countenancing practices that had developed alongside and under the dominant state-socialist economy. When the time came for the transition to capitalism, the ruling local elite needed merely to '[bring] to the fore the previously secondary development path of the region' (Crouch and Keune, p. 99). Similarly in their analysis of Britain's transition to neoliberalism in the early 1980s, Crouch and Keune show how displacement was facilitated by the related facts that the foundations of Keynesianism had been precarious to begin with, and that they had coexisted with alternative institutions and practices firmly anchored in the country's financial sector. The point in both cases is that in critical moments or periods latent subsidiary ways of action can be rediscovered, and by switching over actors then promote them to dominance or move them from the periphery of the institutional system to its center.

Underlying Crouch and Keune's analysis is an image of social structure in which different institutions inside one and the same society may embody conflicting, mutually contradictory 'logics'—with one institution requiring or licensing behavior that is *in principle* incompatible with the behavior required or licensed by another institution. Human actors seem to be quite capable to operate simultaneously in different institutional contexts governed by different 'logics', moving back and forth between them, or playing them off against one another. Also, human societies appear to have enough slack, and their causal texture usually seems to be loose enough (or cause takes enough time to turn into effect) to be tolerant of considerable friction between differently constructed institutions or action spaces. All societies, in other words, are in some way hybrids, some more and some less.[15]

Change through displacement can occur endogenously through the rediscovery or activation of previously suppressed or suspended possibilities. But it can also occur through what Castaldi and Dosi call 'invasion', in either a literal or metaphoric sense (Castaldi and Dosi n.d.: 24). Literally, invasion refers to the supplanting of indigenous institutions and practices with foreign ones, presumably those of the victor or occupying power—although we know from historical work that this is never complete and more typically produces hybrids of one variety or another (Herrigel 2000, also Quack and Djelic, this volume). In a broader literature (e.g. the sociological literature on diffusion) and for our purposes, the more relevant version of invasion is the metaphorical one, which involves the importation and then cultivation by local actors of 'foreign' institutions and practices.

Chapter 7 by Deeg provides an example of change of this variety. His analysis of contemporary trends in the German financial sector documents the coexistence of two different and, in many ways, competing logics of action. One is based on 'traditional' German institutions including strong long-term links between banks and firms and relying heavily on mutual obligation and trust, and involving what Deeg calls a logic of 'voice'. The other, closer to Anglo-Saxon countries and indeed copied from them, is associated with more distant relations both among firms and between firms and banks that operate according to a logic of 'exit'. In Deeg's case, unlike in Crouch and Keune's, the 'new' institutional forms have not (yet?) come to dominate the old. Rather, both coexist, but with the availability of the former calling into question the primacy and taken-for-grantedness of the latter.[16]

Crucial to Deeg's analysis is the idea that change requires active cultivation by enterprising actors (in Crouch and Keune's chapter, by economic elites in Győr and by financial interests in Britain; in Deeg's chapter, by Germany's large commercial banks). Such actors either see their interests at odds with prevailing institutions and practices, or they test new behaviors inside old institutions, perhaps in a tentative response to emerging new external conditions. Change is most likely to be effective if actors are willing to pay a price for their 'incongruent' behavior (this is the core of what Deeg means by the 'cultivation' of a new 'path'). This is because promoting new institutions typically requires the exercise of power or the expenditure of resources, for example, to underwrite new forms of coordination.[17]

At some point, to put it in terms of the model we introduced earlier, innovating actors may also be able to get rule makers to make changes to the formal institutions, or rule takers to demand such changes. In the process, deviant behavior becomes less deviant, and indeed traditional behavior may increasingly run into formal and informal sanctions.

Other variations on the displacement theme appear in Chapter 10 by Sigrid Quack and Marie-Laure Djelic. Quack and Djelic show how ordo-liberalism—a school of economic thought that had been entirely marginal in Germany before 1945—came to shape German competition law under the pressure of the American occupation government seeking to transplant its antitrust legislation to Germany. Here endogenous displacement and what we have referred to as displacement by invasion come together, illustrating a point that also Deeg makes: that exogenous change is often advanced by endogenous forces pushing in the same direction but needing to be activated by outside support. A similar configuration of forces was at work later in the unfolding complex interaction between developments in European and German competition law when in what the authors refer to as the 'public turn' of European competition law, an almost forgotten section of the European Treaty became 'activated' by proponents of a type of liberalization that no one had envisaged when the law was originally written.[18] In cases such as these, elements or possibilities of an institution that have fallen dormant and were for all practical purposes forgotten, may turn into crucial resources for actors interested in making fundamental change appear as an incremental, 'natural' evolution of an existing social order.

In all of the instances of displacement discussed above,[19] change occurred, not through explicit revision or amendment of existing arrangements, but rather through shifts in the relative salience of different institutional arrangements within a 'field' or 'system'. This type of change, as Chapter 7 by Deeg and Chapter 10 by Quack and Djelic emphasize, requires active cultivation by agents whose interests are better served by new arrangements. Deeg's analysis in particular hints, incidentally, at an important, often overlooked relationship between endogenous and exogenous change: for external shocks to bring about fundamental transformation, it helps if endogenous change has prepared the ground. Endogenous evolution of a social system may generate potentials that, when activated by interested parties in response to changing external conditions, can provide the foundation for a new logic of action (on this see also Schneiberg n.d.).

Layering   Institutional change can also occur through a process that one of us has elsewhere, following Eric Schickler, called layering (Schickler 2001; Thelen 2002). Paul Pierson has convincingly argued that not just economic institutions but also political ones may be subject to increasing returns and lock-in effects. In his work on social security, he has demonstrated how each new client added to a pay-as-you-go pension system creates additional vested interests in the maintenance of that system. The older the system, therefore, the more costly it becomes both politically and fiscally to dismantle it (Pierson 1994; Myles and Pierson 2001).

Many other kinds of institutional arrangements are subject to this sort of effect. However, as Schickler points out, this does not preclude change altogether provided reformers learn to work around those elements of an institution that have become unchangeable. Layering is the term he uses to characterize the nature of such reform. In his empirical work Schickler shows how, in the case of the US Congress, successive rounds of institutional reform produced a highly 'disjointed' pattern and a much higher degree of institutional incoherence than prevailing functionalist accounts of congressional institutions would predict.

For our purposes what is most interesting about change through layering is that it can set in motion path-altering dynamics through a mechanism of what we might think of as *differential growth*. The classic example from the welfare state literature is the layering of a voluntary private pension system onto an existing public system. While the established public system may well be unassailable, faster growth of the new private system can effect profound change, among other things by draining off political support for the public system. In Chapter 2 this mechanism of change is analyzed by Jacob Hacker, who shows how opponents of the public pension system in the United States consciously orchestrated the expansion of individual, privatized retirement accounts. Importantly, the original innovations—the introduction of 401(k) and IRA accounts—appeared to be minor measures and went virtually unnoticed at their time of enactment. Their subsequent explosive growth, however, amounted to the rise of an alternative pension system premised on a voluntaristic logic wholly different from that of the public system alongside which the new arrangements had been created.

Bo Rothstein has written of analogous reform efforts in the Swedish context in which customized private alternatives, for example, in schools or day care centers, are offered alongside the uniform public system (Rothstein 1998). As he points out, fundamental change can be—gradually—effected, not through a frontal attack on traditional institutions, but through differential growth of private and public sector institutions siphoning off the support of key constituencies for the latter, in particular the middle class which occupies the politically pivotal position. In cases like this, new dynamics are set in motion by political actors working on the margins by introducing amendments that can initially be 'sold' as refinements of or correctives to existing institutions. Since the new layers created in this way do not as such and directly undermine existing institutions, they typically do not provoke countermobilization by defenders of the status quo. To the extent, however, that they operate on a different logic and grow more quickly than the traditional system, over time they may fundamentally alter the overall trajectory of development as the old institutions stagnate or lose their grip and the new ones assume an ever more prominent role in governing individual behavior.

The chapter by Bruno Palier (Chapter 5) provides an additional example of layering as a mode of institutional change. Palier describes the gradual transformation of French social policy over the past two decades. The backdrop to Palier's analysis is the liberalization of French economic policy, which for political reasons had to be embedded initially in an expanding conservative welfare state. (This historical period and broader context is analyzed in the chapter by Levy.) Palier examines the subsequent liberalization of the welfare state, which may have been an inevitable next step forced by the high costs to the state of full compensation and status maintenance for the losers of economic change. Welfare state liberalization, as Palier shows, departs from the logic of the traditional corporatist welfare state, and in particular entails increasing reliance on means-tested, minimum-level protection paid out of public funds. Importantly, it also involves 'activation' instead of decommodification or status maintenance outside employment. In Palier's account, liberalization policies were designed to avoid generating too much resistance, proceeding incrementally and without much rupture or fanfare, and avoiding a direct assault on existing institutions and policies. In fact, Palier notes that reformers introduced change mainly at the margins and 'as if their purpose were only to fix or complement the system' (p. 131). New programs were introduced alongside the immovable and politically firmly established old ones, adding to the 'enduring realm of social insurance' based on contributions and on a traditional social-conservative logic a wholly new and thoroughly liberal welfare regime of targeted minimum benefits financed by taxes. Palier shows how, despite their incremental nature, and despite the fact that they were introduced as minor additions and repairs to make the existing system more stable, the reforms set in motion dynamics that produced a deep transformation of the French welfare state.[20]

Layering involves active sponsorship of amendments, additions, or revisions to an existing set of institutions. The actual mechanism for change is differential growth; the introduction of new elements setting in motion dynamics through which they, over time, actively crowd out or supplant by default the old system as the domain of the latter progressively shrinks relative to that of the former. Unlike Schickler, who mostly emphasizes the institutional incongruence that layering can produce, for us it is an important question to what extent the fringe and the core can peacefully coexist, or whether the fringe can attract enough defectors from the core eventually to displace it.

Drift There is nothing automatic about institutional stability—despite the language of stasis and stickiness often invoked in relation to institutions. Institutions do not survive by standing still, nor is their stable reproduction always simply a matter of positive feedback or increasing returns (Thelen 2004: ch. 1). Quite to the contrary institutions require active maintenance; to remain what they are they need to be reset and refocused, or sometimes more fundamentally recalibrated and renegotiated, in response to changes in the political and economic environment in which they are embedded. Without such 'tending', as Hacker's analysis of health care policy in the United States illustrates, they can be subject to erosion or atrophy through *drift*. As with layering, change through drift, while potentially fundamental, may be masked by stability on the surface. Indeed Hacker begins by noting that, as other analysts have shown, social programs in the United States have indeed 'resisted major retrenchment'. However, Hacker also observes that the American welfare system has failed to be adapted to cover a set of risks that have newly emerged or increased in salience. The result is a significant shrinkage in the social protections enjoyed by American citizens as a matter of right. Hacker's analysis suggests that in addition to the formal attributes of institutions, we must take account of their implementation, and especially of the gaps that may emerge between the two as a consequence of shifting contextual conditions. Analyses that focus only on the continuity of existing rules miss the potential slippage between these and the real world to which they are supposed to apply.

A disjuncture between social programs and changing profiles of social risk can result from 'natural' trends. For example, slow changes in family structures may alter the composition of risk and therefore also de facto welfare state coverage. In cases like this, drift occurs without explicit political maneuvering: the world surrounding an institution evolves in ways that alter its scope, meaning, and function. Drift can also be caused by gaps in rules allowing actors to abdicate previous responsibilities. In Hacker's analysis, changes in the incentives faced by employers (as important private sector welfare providers in the United States) caused many of them to scale back their efforts. Again, the result was declining welfare state coverage even without major retrenchment and indeed in the absence of any public debate or decision at all.

Hacker also emphasizes, however, that drift does not just happen. Like change by layering, change by drift can also be promoted by political cultivation. The difference between the two is exemplified by the different types of change at work in the two policy areas that Hacker analyzes. In the case of pensions where change took place through layering, active political sponsorship put new programs in place that could then be upgraded to attract more clients. In the case of health, by contrast, where the mode of change was drift, change was above all the result of *nondecisions* as conservative policymakers deliberately declined to close emerging gaps in coverage. In health policy just as in pensions, a stable core remained due to opponents of the welfare state refraining, for good political reasons, from attacking popular old programs directly. But change took place nevertheless—in the case of health by way of a kind of passive aggressive behavior refusing to end the 'slippage' caused by exogenous developments that made existing institutions slowly lose their grip. Failure actively to maintain an institution, that is to say, may amount to actively allowing it to decay.

Parallels exist between Hacker's analysis of drift in US health care policy today and Skocpol's analysis of civil war benefits, which provides us with another, especially dramatic, example of change through drift (Skocpol 1992). Civil war pensions, Skocpol argues, could have become the core of a general public pension system had its supporters been able to forge the broader alliances needed to secure its political foundation. That they did not succeed in this was, by Skocpol's account, in large measure due to opponents of expansion being able to invoke a connection between civil war pensions on the one hand and the patronage politics and corruption of the Progressive Era on the other, 'as a reason for opposing or delaying any move toward more general old-age pensions' (Skocpol 1992: 59). Failure to extend benefits to new groups made the atrophy and ultimate demise of the original system a foregone conclusion: the program literally died out as civil war veterans and their spouses themselves passed away.

Conversion   A fourth mode of change documented in the Chapters below is what Thelen (2002, 2004) has elsewhere called conversion. Different from layering and drift, here institutions are not so much amended or allowed to decay as they are *redirected to new goals, functions, or purposes*. Such redirection may come about as a result of new environmental challenges, to which policymakers respond by deploying existing institutional resources to new ends. Or it can come about through changes in power relations, such that actors who were not involved in the original design of an institution and whose participation in it may not have been reckoned with, take it over and turn it to new ends. Here, too, there are elements of stability and even lock-in. However, whereas conventional increasing returns arguments point to a dynamic in which actors adapt their strategies to existing institutions, conversion works the other way around: existing institutions are adapted to serve new goals or fit the interests of new actors.[21]

The redirection of institutional resources that we associate with conversion may occur through political contestation over what functions and purposes an existing institution should serve. Political contestation driving change through conversion is made possible by the gaps that exist by design or emerge over time between institutionalized rules and their local enactment. Four sources of such gaps are of particular relevance in the present context (see also the discussion in Pierson 2004: ch. 4). The first is the cognitive limits of institutions' builders and associated problem of *unintended consequences*. As Elster (2003) and others have pointed out, designers of institutions are not all seeing; they make mistakes and in any event they can 'never do just one thing' (Pierson 2004: 115). For Elster the point is to challenge the presumption, pervasive in the rational-choice literature, that institutions can be thought of as rational solutions to specific social problems. Elster's analysis, of successive waves of constitution writing in France, ends on the note that behavior in general and institutional design in particular are almost by definition irrational—the implication of which could be that they are not amenable to systematic analysis. Our conclusion here is somewhat less sweeping as we limit ourselves to noting that unintended consequences of institutional design may offer opportunities for political contestation that theoretical treatments that assume an identity between design and effect by definition cannot account for.

Second, institution-building, to the extent that it occurs through political negotiation, typically involves *compromise*. As Schickler has argued, new institutions often constitute 'common carriers' for coalitions of actors who support them for highly diverse reasons (Schickler 1999; Pierson 2004). The resulting *ambiguities* in the rules that define institutionalized behavior provide space for political contestation over how rules should be interpreted and applied. In the present volume, an example of this is given by Palier (Chapter 5). Welfare state reform in France, his chapter shows, was premised on highly ambiguous agreements, with all parties accepting the need for reform in general while consensus on any particular reform was based on widely different understandings of what the reform was to mean. Similar ambiguities seem to have made possible economic liberalization in France which, according to Levy, was embedded in the same rhetoric that was in the past used to legitimate state planning.

Similarly, as shown in the chapter by Jackson (Chapter 9), the institutions and rules governing German codetermination were always characterized by deep ambiguities as rule makers had in part to leave open their meaning lest they lose support from necessary allies. As a result, both the uncertainty that is inherent in all rules that need to be applied to varying conditions and the discretion rule takers must inevitably exercise in following a rule are amplified considerably. Jackson's analysis in fact describes the continuous reinterpretation of the institution of codetermination over a long period of time under widely varying market and political conditions. It shows how very different ambitions and purposes came to be connected to the same institution, causing a considerable amount of change over time on the background of much formal continuity. Sometimes this was the result of changing power relations among the actors involved, altering the way the institution was practiced. In other periods the environment of the regime changed, confronting rule takers with new contingencies that made them apply the rules differently or forced rule makers to reinterpret them.

Third, and again echoing points made earlier in this chapter, actors are strategic and even those not involved in the design of an institution will do everything in their power to interpret its rules in their own interest (or *circumvent* or *subvert* rules that clash with their interests). Elizabeth Clemens' work, among others, has drawn attention to processes through which familiar organizational forms were redeployed by 'marginal' actors who had been blocked out of the system—in ways that subverted and undermined received behaviors and logics of action (Clemens 1997). An example of the strategic use of institutions not of their own making can be found in the present volume in Quack and Djelic's discussion of multilevel governance systems like the European Union (EU). Lower-order institutions regulated from above in a multilevel institutional structure are not once and for all determined by the latter: like rule takers in general, those in control of national institutions inevitably have some leeway to adjust the supranational rules that apply to them, and they can also try to change such rules by putting pressure on rule makers or rule enforcers. Moreover, those governed by a national institution which is in turn governed by a supranational one often have wide-ranging strategic capacities as they can try to use political resources mobilized at one level to influence decisions at the other. This, at least, is what the study of interest group behavior in the EU increasingly shows, and it also becomes apparent in the complex stratagems of national and international policymakers and judges in the field of European and national competition law, as described by Quack and Djelic in this volume.

Fourth and as most forcefully argued by Pierson, *time matters* (Pierson 2004). Many institutions—and certainly some of those in which we are most likely to have an interest—have been around long enough to have outlived, not just their designers and the social coalition on which they were founded, but also the external conditions of the time of their foundation. Changes in the nature of the challenges actors face or in the balance of power allow for institutions created to serve certain interests to be redirected to very different and even diametrically opposed goals and ends. Time, in other words, and the changes it brings in actors and problems, opens gaps that entail possibilities for institutional conversion. An example explored elsewhere by one of us (Thelen 2004: chs 2 and 5) are the institutional arrangements comprising Germany's celebrated system for vocational training. The 'founding' legislation around which this system came to be constructed was passed in 1897 by an authoritarian government and was above all directed against the country's social democratic labor movement. A hundred years later, some of the central institutional pillars are still recognizable, even though the system has been turned completely on its head in political-distributional terms, serving now as a key source of strength for organized labor and a pillar of social partnership between labor and business. The process of conversion through which this occurred was not one of dramatic and sudden renegotiation in moments of historic rupture—of which Germany of course experienced several over the twentieth century. Rather, conversion was the result of ongoing political contestation and periodic incremental adjustment through which inherited institutions were adapted and fitted to changes in their social, economic, and political environment.

Chapter 4 on France by Jonah Levy provides another example of this mode of change. Levy characterizes the transformation he documents as an instance of 'redeployment', consisting of the formidable interventionist powers of the French state being diverted away from industrial to social policy, and in the process also from market correcting to market conforming ends. The failure of the old statist model precipitated the transition. However, rather than dismantling previous institutional capacities (and in the absence of societal actors to whom social policy could be handed—itself a consequence of statism as Levy's work has instructed us) political elites redirected them to new ends. For our purposes, the important message of Levy's analysis is not so much that state activism continues in France—although it does and this is in itself an outcome of considerable interest. Rather it is that the French state has managed to move gradually in a decidedly liberal direction, with policymakers taking full advantage of the considerable institutional capacities at their disposal to make change appear less fundamental than it was, or to make fundamental change proceed gradually enough so that it was not recognized as such.

Finally, the chapter by Steven Vogel shows that even in a political economy as tightly coupled as the Japanese, change that goes beyond routine adjustment is possible. Vogel emphasizes the contribution to change of external shocks, in a system in which typically deviation from established rules immediately causes costly side effects or painful social sanctions or both. (Somewhat more room for deviant behavior seems to exist for foreigners who are less integrated in existing institutions—suggesting a parallel to the chapter by Crouch and Keune, Chapter 3.)

Even Japanese institutions, Vogel emphasizes, do not only impede change but also condition it, facilitating certain kinds of innovation precisely as they proscribe others. Vogel's analysis describes a process of gradual liberalization that advances by way of growing variation between firms and sectors, as well as through redeployment of key institutional supports for the traditional Japanese system to new, more liberal, ends (see the redefinition of lifetime employment into lifetime career support). In this case again, considerable continuities on the surface mask important underlying changes resulting from the way in which traditional rules and institutions are reinterpreted and converted to new goals.

Exhaustion We call our fifth mode of change institutional exhaustion. We include it although, unlike the four others, the processes we have in mind here strictly speaking lead to institutional breakdown rather than change—although the collapse is gradual rather than abrupt. As argued most famously by Marx, social arrangements may set in motion dynamics that sow the seeds of their own destruction. Different from institutional drift, in which institutions may retain their formal integrity even as they increasingly lose their grip on social reality, institutional exhaustion is a process in which behaviors invoked or allowed under existing rules operate to undermine these.

Recent work by Avner Greif and David Laitin provides an example (Greif and Laitin 2003). Greif and Laitin begin, as we do, with a critique of theories of institutions in which change by definition must be generated exogenously. By examining the divergent fate of governing institutions in Venice and Genoa in the early modern period, they try to specify the conditions under which such arrangements either become self-reinforcing or self-undermining over time.[22] In both cases, political institutions were created that provided a foundation for cooperation among rival clans, generating returns for all. Institutional arrangements in Venice operated in ways that weakened the clan structure, however, whereas in Genoa they 'contained inter-clan rivalry, but did not eliminate it' (Greif and Laitin 2003: 18). In both cases cooperative arrangements led to economic prosperity. But in the Genoese case this heightened competition among rival elites, not least by raising the stakes. In this way the institution gave rise to dynamics that made it more and more vulnerable and, indeed, self-undermining over time.

In the present volume, Christine Trampusch's analysis of the exhaustion of early retirement policies in Germany points out that these had originally been conceived in a period of full employment, to deal in a targeted way with the decline of specific industries. The regime 'worked' as long as it applied only to a limited number of cases and had not yet given rise to a general expectation that workers would be entitled to retire early. However, as the context shifted to high levels of long-term unemployment, and especially with German unification, early retirement as an institution became overextended as it was used to facilitate restructuring and soften the impact of redundancies on a massive scale. Since early retirement was financed by the social insurance system, its extension set in motion a perverse dynamic, driving increases in nonwage labor costs that in turn contributed to unemployment, which then for its part lowered the revenue and raised the expenditure of the social insurance system. Over time, early retirement thus came to consume the very resources that would have been necessary for its continuation, at which point the institution began to yield declining rather than increasing returns.

Yet another facet of time-related exhaustion concerns the *age* of an institution, which may be much underrated as a subject of research. 'Young' institutions require elaboration of their meaning in practice, by a sequence of decisions on the part of rule makers as well as rule takers. The 'path' along which an institution is 'worked out' in this sense is shaped by exogenous circumstances as well as a myriad of strategic choices, deciding together which of the many possible meanings of a young institution are practically explored and which are foreclosed or left behind by the wayside. Institutions may, however, also age. For example, viz. Trampusch, they may meet 'limits to growth' where their further expansion destroys or uses up resources that they require for their continued operation. Or they may become ever more complex in a process by which, like in the decline of a Kuhnian 'paradigm', more and more exceptions and special provisions have to be added to a given set of institutionalized rules, thereby depriving it of its legitimacy or practicability or both.

In Table 1.1, we have summarized the main properties of the five types of gradual but nevertheless transformative institutional change that we have identified.

Liberalization as gradual transformation

The dominant trend in advanced political economies, we have stated early in this chapter, is liberalization: the steady expansion of market relations in areas that under the postwar settlement of democratic capitalism were reserved to collective political decisionmaking. Although liberalization amounts to a quite fundamental transformation, it proceeds gradually and continuously, apart from occasional but short-lived episodes of turmoil like in Britain under Thatcher when the Keynesian model of economic policy was replaced with a rediscovered neoliberal model.

Whatever its economic and political deserts—on which one can have different views—it cannot be doubted that the advance of liberalism in the countries of democratic capitalism is greatly supported by the fact that it mainly moves forward only slowly, through what we have called displacement, layering, drift, conversion, and the exhaustion of existing institutions and policies. This raises the question—which we can no more than raise here—whether liberalization under modern capitalism is in whatever way *a privileged direction of 'normal' institutional change* in the absence of historic ruptures. Notably, as Levy reports, the instruments of postwar state interventionism in France were available to promote liberalization in a way that a liberal state could hardly be used for nonliberal, corporatist, or even socialist purposes. Levy's account confirms that liberalization, as already Polanyi knew, tends to come together with a 'countermovement' that

Table 1.1 Institutional change: five types of gradual transformation

	Displacement	Layering	Drift	Conversion	Exhaustion
Definition	Slowly rising salience of subordinate relative to dominant institutions	New elements attached to existing institutions gradually change their status and structure	Neglect of institutional maintenance in spite of external change resulting in slippage in institutional practice on the ground	Redeployment of old institutions to new purposes; new purposes attached to old structures	Gradual breakdown (withering away) of institutions over time
Mechanism	Defection	Differential growth	Deliberate neglect	Redirection, reinterpretation	Depletion
Elaboration	Institutional incoherence opening space for deviant behavior	Faster growth of new institutions created on the edges of old ones	Change in institutional outcomes effected by (strategically) neglecting adaptation to changing circumstances	Gaps between rules and enactment due to:	Self-consumption: the normal working of an institution undermines its external preconditions
	Active cultivation of a new 'logic' of action inside an existing institutional setting	New fringe eats into old core	Enactment of institution changed, not by reform of rules, but by rules remaining unchanged in the face of evolving external conditions	(1) Lack of foresight: limits to (unintended consequences of) institutional design	Decreasing returns: generalization changes cost–benefit relations
	Rediscovery and activation of dormant or latent institutional resources	New institutional layer siphons off support for old layer		(2) Intended ambiguity of institutional rules: institutions are compromises	Overextension: limits to growth
	'Invasion' and assimilation of foreign practices	Presumed 'fix' destabilizing existing institutions		(3) Subversion: rules reinterpreted from below	
		Compromise between old and new slowly turning into defeat of the old		(4) Time: changing contextual conditions and coalitions open up space for redeployment	

're-embeds' emerging and expanding market relations. But the redeployment of French state capacities after 1983 to social policy was mainly designed to 'anaesthetize' society and 'demobilize' potential resistance. Indeed it did the job quite successfully, only to become afterward the subject of more reform, as described by Palier. Not only was that reform again presented in ambiguous ideological terms so as to be acceptable to actors with widely divergent world-views, but it was also introduced as a series of minor additions and repairs to fix the existing system to make it more stable, rather than to replace it.

Liberalization, our chapters show, can take many forms: not only can it be advanced by the state, like in France, but state functions can also, like in Germany, be delegated to civil society. The resettlement of German early retirement in the collective bargaining system amounts to a move back from the sphere of social rights, in Marshall's sense, to that of industrial rights. This may well be regarded as quite far-reaching change, in spite of the fact that it progressed more slowly and went less far than French social security reform. It also represents change towards liberalization: instead of 'de-commodifying' state legislation, it is now by collective contract negotiated under market constraints that early retirement is made possi-ble and paid for. Collective contracts are concluded in the economic rather than in the political arena; moreover, they are by definition less universal than social rights based on legislation since they apply only to the core and no longer to the periphery. Internalizing the costs of early retirement in workers' pay helps in the consolidation of public budgets. But it also, again, brings in private insurance companies and employers with their company-based pension plans who can be relied upon further to promote liberalization out of their own interests.

Codetermination, too, is undergoing a process of liberalization, according to Jackson, in that its practice is increasingly becoming enmeshed in and circumscribed by market relations. Just as changing capital markets manifest themselves in growing pressure by nonstrategic shareholders, changing product markets intensify needs for corporate restructuring to defend and increase competitiveness. As workforce representatives cannot afford to overlook the changed external conditions, they become increasingly part of a joint comanage-ment of change for which the continued economic viability of the firm is the uppermost goal. While under German institutional conditions restructuring does not and cannot result in workplaces being turned into 'union-free environments', codetermination slowly mutates in practice toward the institutional base of a tight economic community of face between managers and core workforces.

How powerful and at the same time necessary the slow shift of functions between and within institutions is for the progress of liberalization is demon-strated by the Japanese case. In Japan there is no welfare state to relieve firms of the social obligations they have entered into in the past, nor is there a collective bargaining system to relieve the state of functions it can no longer perform. This seems to be a main reason why liberalization in Japan proceeds even more slowly than in Europe. As Vogel reports and as we have noted above, now small adjustments are being undertaken within firms themselves, with attempts to expand internal labor markets beyond company boundaries and, simultaneously, redefine on the margins traditional institutions such as long-term employment. In a world in which workers cannot distinguish between the social contract and their employment contract, liberalization has a higher threshold to cross and must take a different path than in Western social democracies.

Could it be that measures of liberalization are somehow particularly suited to being imposed gradually and without disruption? Is, in other words, the relationship we observe between gradual transformative change in institutions and liberalization more than historically contingent? Nonliberal reforms in a market economy seem to require 'political moments' in which strong governments create and enforce rules that individual actors have to follow, even if they would on their own prefer not to do so. Liberalization, by comparison, can often proceed without political mobilization, simply by encouraging or tolerating self-interested subversion of collective institutions from below, or by unleashing individual interests and the subversive intelligence of self-interested actors bent on maximizing their utilities. To this extent, liberalization within capitalism may face far fewer collective action problems than the organization of capitalism, and much more than the latter it may be achievable by default: by letting things happen that are happening anyway. All that may be needed for liberalization to progress in this case would be to give people a market alternative to an existing system based on collective solidarity, and then give free rein to the private insurance companies and their sales forces.

Put otherwise, if we follow Deeg (in this volume) and define a liberal regime as one in which exit is favored as a dominant logic of action over voice, individual actors may find it easier to start a movement toward liberalization than one toward constraining market relations by institutional obligations. This is because encouraging others to exit from a previously obligatory social relationship for self-regarding reasons may require no more than setting an example, while tightening normative controls would need collective rather than individual action followed, importantly, by collectively binding decisions. We conclude this chapter by speculating that it may not be by accident that it is predominantly through our five modes of gradual yet transformative change—displacement of dominant with dormant institutions, institutional layering and subsequent differential growth, tolerated drift of institutions away from social reality, slow conversion of existing institutions to new purposes, and exhaustion due to systemic incompatibility and erosion of resources—that the current liberalization of advanced political economies mainly proceeds.

Notes

1. Nor, conversely, do all path dependence theorists subscribe to a strong punctuated equilibrium model of change.
2. As Barry Weingast has argued: 'Rational choice theory provides a variety of mechanisms that afford predictions of discontinuous change'. However, questions of 'endogenous

emergence, choice and survival of institutions' he regards as 'frontier issues' (Weingast 2002: 692).

3. The difference is that, in the historical institutionalist version, 'new' arrangements are mostly assumed to be very different from the 'old' ones as a result. In the rational choice version the distance between the new and the old equilibrium could in fact be small; the change, in other words, need not be particularly 'big'.

4. Djelic and Quack (2003: 309) have also drawn attention to the phenomenon of 'incremental but consequential change' and, for metaphorical illustration of the mechanism behind such change, propose a 'stalactite model of change'. See their contribution to this volume.

5. For an excellent overview see Voss (2001).

6. We deliberately say 'mainly' as we do not generally preclude that informal sanctions may also be of importance. Typically, however, as Colin Crouch reminds us, these are today studied by lawyers as 'soft law', indicating that in modern societies even informal rules, like those governing certain production networks, may sometimes become legally enforceable.

7. We might also say: with a private contract. But this may be misleading since, as Durkheim has pointed out, 'in a contract not everything is contractual' (Durkheim 1984 [1893]: 158), meaning that *the contract as such* is a social institution precisely because individual contracts can be and are enforced by agencies of social control that are not parties to them.

8. A few rational choice scholars have criticized the voluntaristic conception of institutions characteristic of their school (see, for example, Knight 1992; Moe 2003). But even in revisionist versions the treatment of power is sometimes thin, coming in mainly by virtue of the fact that some actors need an institution more than others, or that the opportunity costs of revising existing institutions are different for different actors. More on this below.

9. As a result their stability increases. 'Self-interest is, in fact, the least constant thing in the world. Today it is useful for me to unite with you; tomorrow the same reason will make me your enemy. Thus such a cause can give rise only to transitory links and associations of a fleeting kind' (Durkheim 1984 [1893]: 152).

10. By noting that institutions are always interpreted, and thus can be interpreted differently, we also reintroduce room for agency and political conflict that is eliminated when institutions are conceived either in purely functional terms or as shared cognitive frames (taken-for-granted understandings).

11. A *policy* may give rise to a *Herrschaftsverband* to the extent that it creates a distinction between policymakers and policy takers. Socially backed *corporate actors* may be *Herrschaftsverbände* themselves, or may be included in them at their center.

12. Constraint, of course, remains constraint. In fact as we have pointed out above in criticizing rational voluntaristic concepts of institutions, enforceable obligation is for us among the most important defining characteristics of social institutions. Our point is simply that obligations may be ambiguous and are in any event generally subject to interpretation and contestation.

13. To be sure, without even attempting to exhaust the full range of possible interpretations of their empirical material. Each chapter stands on its own feet and our reading in this Introduction is not intended to be anything other than selective. Moreover, empirical cases are always more complex than typological constructs and may contain relationships that are illustrative of different types of change.

14. See also Kuran (1991) for an analogous model of change, which however draws attention to changes in the revealed preferences of growing numbers of actors and relies more heavily on a tipping point logic. Another example, based more on what one could call a 'cascading logic', is Beissinger's analysis of the development and success of nationalist movements across the states of the former Soviet Union in the late 1980s and very early 1990s (Beissinger 2002). In this case, the impact of events and processes in a densely, temporally and spatially, connected context produced what Beissinger calls a 'tidal' dynamic, such that nationalism in countries lacking the structural prerequisites of success ('improbable nationalisms', as Beissinger calls them) nonetheless succeeded as a result of linkages to other unfolding nationalisms and the ability of politicians to 'ride nationalism's tidal force'.

15. Although it appears that the closeness of interinstitutional coupling, and the degree to which a society insists on congruence between its institutions, is a variable; see the image Vogel projects of the Japanese political economy.

16. Nor, in fact, would we expect displacement ever to be complete, since the premise of these analyses is precisely that dominant forms never completely 'crowd out' alternatives.

17. Within the rational choice literature on institutions as coordinating devices, Terry Moe's work is most sensitive to the connections between power and coordination. As he puts it, 'it is cooperation that makes the exercise of power possible, and the prospect of exercising power that motivates the cooperation' (Moe 2003: 12).

18. The logic here is similar to Pierson's (1996) analysis of European social policy. In one instance (the case of EU policy on gender equality), he shows how provisions adopted by the EU member states in one period—largely symbolic and without much 'meaning'—were later picked up by emergent women's groups, who used these provisions to achieve gains at the EU level that had eluded them domestically.

19. See also the chapter by Trampusch, which analyzes the migration of a particular policy from one institutional context to another—as it were, to a reserve system ready to take over as the primary system became overloaded.

20. It is perhaps important to underscore the subtle but important difference between displacement and layering. A central feature in both Deeg's account of displacement and Palier's and Hacker's examples of layering is differential growth of parallel systems— an expanding fringe that potentially crowds out a shrinking core. The difference is that in Deeg's case proponents of change are cultivating a wholly new set of institutions on the fringes of an existing system, thus setting up a competition between two alternative logics. In Hacker's and Palier's cases, by contrast, innovators are attaching new elements to existing institutions, effecting change gradually within the traditional arrangements themselves.

21. Building new institutions from scratch may take longer than the rise of new goals or purposes, so it often makes sense to try to accomplish new goals with old institutions. This is nicely illustrated by Levy who in his chapter explains the conversion of French statism from industrial to social policy in part by the fact that institutions other than the state that could have carried the new social policies simply were not available— not least as a result of statism itself which by default, as it were, had to be converted instead of dismantled.

22. Where most rational-choice theories see change as emanating from a shift in an institution's parameters, Grief and Laitin pay attention to what they call 'quasi-parameters', which 'are assumed in the rules of the game but in reality are part of the broader

context within which an institution is embedded' (Greif and Laitin 2003: 3). In the language that they employ, the question is whether the behavioral effects that an institution generates either expand or narrow the range of situations (quasi-parameters) in which the institution is self-reinforcing.

References

Bates, Robert H. (1988). Contra Contractarianism: Some Reflections on the New Institutionalism. *Politics and Society* 16(2): 387–401.

Beissinger, Mark R. (2002). *Nationalist Mobilization and the Collapse of the Soviet State*. New York: Cambridge University Press.

Bendix, Reinhard (1974 [1956]). *Work and Authority in Industry: Ideologies of Management in the Course of Industrialization*. Berkeley, CA: University of California Press.

Berger, Suzanne and Michael Piore (1980). *Dualism and Discontinuity in Industrial Societies*. Cambridge: Cambridge University Press.

Castaldi, Carolina and Giovanni Dosi (n.d.). The Grip of History and the Scope for Novelty: Some Results and Open Questions on Path Dependence in Economic Processes. Unpublished manuscript.

Clemens, Elisabeth (1997). *The People's Lobby: Organizational Innovation and the Rise of Interest Group Politics in the United States*. Chicago: University of Chicago Press.

Collier, Ruth B. and David Collier (1991). *Shaping the Political Arena*. Princeton, NJ: Princeton University Press.

DiMaggio, P. and Walter W. Powell (1991). Introduction. In: W. W. Powell and P. DiMaggio (eds.), *The New Institutionalism in Organizational Analysis*. Chicago, IL: University of Chicago Press.

Djelic, Marie-Laure and Sigrid Quack (2003). Conclusion: Globalization as a Double Process of Institutional Change and Institution Building. In: M.-L. Djelic and S. Quack (eds.), *Globalization and Institutions*. Cheltenham, UK: Edward Elgar, pp. 302–33.

Dobbin, Frank (1994). *Forging Industrial Policy: The United States, Britain and France in the Railway Age*. New York: Cambridge University Press.

Durkheim, Emile (1984 [1893]). The Division of Labor in Society. Translated by W.D. Halls. New York: The Free Press.

Elster, Jon (2003). Authors and Actors. Paper presented at conference on Crafting and Operating Institutions. Yale University, April 11–13.

Fligstein, Neil (1990). *The Transformation of Corporate Control*. Cambridge, MA: Harvard University Press.

—— (1997). A Political Cultural Approach to Market Institutions. *American Sociological Review* 4: 656–73.

Greif, Avner and David Laitin (2003). How do Self-enforcing Institutions Endogenously Change? Unpublished manuscript, Stanford University.

Hall, Peter A. and David Soskice (2001). An Introduction to Varieties of Capitalism. In: Hall and Soskice (eds.), *Varieties of Capitalism: The Institutional Foundations of Comparative Advantage*. Oxford: Oxford University Press, pp. 1–68.

Herrigel, Gary (2000). American Occupation, Market Order, and Democracy: Reconfiguring the Steel Industry in Japan and Germany after the Second World War.

In: J. Zeitlin and G. Herrigel (eds.), *Americanization and its Limits: Reworking US Technology and Management in Post-War Europe and Japan*. New York: Oxford University Press.

HUBER, EVELYNE and JOHN D. STEPHENS (2001). *Development and Crisis of the Welfare States: Parties and Policies in Global Markets*. Chicago, IL: University of Chicago Press.

KATZNELSON, IRA (2003). Periodization and Preferences: Reflections on Purposive Action in Comparative Historical Social Science. In: J. Mahoney and D. Rueschemeyer (eds.), *Comparative Historical Analysis in the Social Sciences*. New York: Cambridge University Press.

KNIGHT, JACK (1992). *Institutions and Social Conflict*. New York: Cambridge University Press.

KRASNER, STEPHEN D. (1988). Sovereignty: An Institutional Perspective. *Comparative Political Studies* 21(1): 66–94.

KUME, IKUO and KATHLEEN THELEN (2004). Coordination as a Political Problem in Coordinated Market Economies. Forthcoming in *Governance*.

KURAN, TIMOR (1991). Now out of Never: The Element of Surprise in the East European Revolution of 1989. *World Politics* 44(1): 7–48.

LASH, SCOTT and JOHN URRY (1987). *The End of Organized Capitalism*. Cambridge, UK: Polity Press.

MAHONEY, JAMES (2000). Path Dependence in Historical Sociology. *Theory and Society* 29: 507–48.

MEYER, JOHN and BRIAN ROWAN (1991). Institutionalized Organizations: Formal Strategy as Myth and Ceremony. In: Walter Powell and Paul DiMaggio (eds.), *The New Institutionalism in Organizational Analysis*. Chicago, IL: University of Chicago Press.

MOE, TERRY (2003). Power and Political Institutions. Paper presented at conference on Crafting and Operating Institutions, April 11–13 at Yale University.

MOORE, BARRINGTON (1979). *Injustice: The Social Bases of Obedience and Revolt*. New York: Random House.

MYLES, JOHN and PAUL PIERSON (2001). The Comparative Political Economy of Pension Reform. In: P. Pierson (ed.), *The New Politics of the Welfare State*. Oxford: Oxford University Press.

NIELSON, KLAUS, BOB JESSOP, and JERZY HAUSNER (1995). Institutional Change in Post-socialism. In: J. Hausner, B. Jessop, and K. Nielsen (eds.), *Strategic Choice and Path-Dependency in Post-socialism: Institutional Dynamics in the Transformation Process*. Hants, UK: Edward Elgar.

NORTH, DOUGLASS (1990). *Institutions, Institutional Change and Economic Performance*. New York: Cambridge University Press.

OFFE, CLAUS (1985). *Disorganized Capitalism: Contemporary Transformations of Work and Politics*. Cambridge, MA: The MIT Press.

ORREN, KAREN and STEPHEN SKOWRONEK (1994). Beyond the Iconography of Order: Notes for a 'New' Institutionalism. In: L.C. Dodd and C. Jillson (eds.), *The Dynamics of American Politics*. Boulder, CO: Westview.

ORREN, KAREN and STEPHEN SKOWRONEK (2004). *The Search for American Political Development*. New York: Cambridge University Press.

PEMPEL, T. J. (1998). *Regime Shift: Comparative Dynamics of the Japanese Political Economy*. Ithaca, NY: Cornell University Press.

PIERSON, PAUL (1994). *Dismantling the Welfare State? Reagan, Thatcher, and the Politics of Retrenchment*. Cambridge: Cambridge University Press.

PIERSON, PAUL (1996). The Path to European Integration: A Historical Institutionalist Approach. *Comparative Political Studies* 29(2): 123–63.

—— (2004). *Politics in Time: History, Institutions, and Political Analysis*. Princeton, NJ: Princeton University Press.

PIORE, MICHAEL J. and CHARLES F. SABEL (1984). *The Second Industrial Divide*. New York: Basic Books.

ROTHSTEIN, BO (1998). *Just Institutions Matter: The Moral and Political Logic of the Universal Welfare State*. New York: Cambridge University Press.

SCHICKLER, ERIC (1999). Disjointed Pluralism and Congressional Development: An Overview. Paper read at the 95th Annual Meeting of the American Political Science Association, September 2–5, at Atlanta.

—— (2001). *Disjointed Pluralism: Institutional Innovation and the Development of the U.S. Congress*. Princeton, NJ: Princeton University Press.

SCHNEIBERG, MARC (n.d.). Combining New Institutionalisms: Market Failures, Models of Order, and Endogenous Institutional Change in American Property Insurance. Reed College Manuscript. Portland, OR.

SEWELL, WILLIAM H. (1996). Three Temporalities: Toward an Eventful Sociology. In: T. J. McDonald (ed.), *The Historic Turn in the Human Sciences*. Ann Arbor, MI: University of Michigan Press.

SKOCPOL, THEDA (1992). *Protecting Soldiers and Mothers: The Political Origins of Social Policy in the United States*. Cambridge, MA: Belknap.

SKOWRONEK, STEVEN (1995). Order and Change. *Polity* 28(1): 91–6.

STARK, DAVID (1995). Not by Design: The Myth of Designer Capitalism in Eastern Europe. In: J. Hausner, B. Jessop, and K. Nielsen (eds.), *Strategic Choice and Path-Dependency in Post-Socialism*. Hants, UK: Edward Elgar.

STINCHCOMBE, ARTHUR L. (1968). *Constructing Social Theories*. New York: Harcourt, Brace and World.

STREECK, WOLFGANG (1991). On the Institutional Conditions of Diversified Quality Production. In: E. Matzner and W. Streeck (eds.), *Beyond Keynesianism*. Aldershot, UK: Edward Elgar.

SWIDLER, ANN (1986). Culture in Action: Symbols and Strategies. *American Sociological Review* 51: 273–86.

THELEN, KATHLEEN (2002). How Institutions Evolve: Insights from Comparative-Historical Analysis. In: J. Mahoney and D. Rueschemeyer (eds.), *Comparative Historical Analysis in the Social Sciences*. New York: Cambridge University Press.

—— (2004). *How Institutions Evolve: The Political Economy of Skills in Germany, Britain, the United States and Japan*. New York: Cambridge University Press.

—— and CHRISTA VAN WIJNBERGEN (2003). The Paradox of Globalization: Labor Relations in Germany and Beyond. *Comparative Political Studies* 36(8): 859–80.

VOSS, T.R. (2001). Institutions. In: Neil J. Smelser and Paul B. Baltes (eds.), *International Encyclopedia of the Social and Behavioral Sciences*, vol. 7. Amsterdam: Elsevier, pp. 7561–6.

WEBER, MAX. (1978 [1956]). In: Guenther Roth and Claus Wittich (eds.), *Economy and Society*. Berkeley, CA: University of California Press.

WEINGAST, BARRY (2002). Rational-choice Institutionalism. In: I. Katznelson and H. Milner (eds.), *Political Science: The State of the Discipline*. New York: Norton.

—— and William J. Marshall (1988). The Industrial Organization of Congress; or, Why Legislatures, like Firms, are not Organized as Markets. *Journal of Political Economy* 96(1): 132–63.

Wrong, Dennis (1961). The Oversocialized Conception of Man in Modern Sociology. *American Sociological Review* 26(2): 183–93.

2

Policy Drift: The Hidden Politics of US Welfare State Retrenchment

Jacob S. Hacker

For over two decades, the social policies of advanced democracies have faced major strains.[1] Yet only recently have analysts devoted themselves in earnest to exploring the changes that these pressures have wrought. These inquiries have produced a large, growing, and increasingly sophisticated body of research, the overwhelming verdict of which is that remarkably few systems of social protection have experienced fundamental shifts (e.g. Pierson 1994, 1996, 2001; Esping-Andersen 1999; Bonoli, George, and Taylor-Gooby 2000; Huber and Stephens 2001; Korpi and Palme 2001). In this now-conventional wisdom, welfare states are under strain, cuts have occurred, but social policy frameworks remain secure, anchored by their enduring popularity, powerful constituencies, and centrality within the postwar order.

Yet, if there is now broad agreement on what has *not* happened to the welfare state—namely, across-the-board retrenchment—the new wave of interest in welfare state reform has not produced anything like common ground on the question of what *has*. Observers have offered a blizzard of terms to describe recent trends, but they have failed to reach even minimal consensus on how much and what kind of change has taken place, much less on how these shifts should be characterized and explained. The result is a situation in which most discussions in the field are still 'devoted to determining *what* is happening to systems of social provision, rather than the more typical challenge of explaining *why* . . . outcomes have occurred' (Pierson 2002: 1).

In these roiling and muddy waters, one important line of argument that has surfaced in recent years is that mature welfare states are characterized by a growing mismatch between traditional structures of social provision and the new sorts of social risks that citizens face. Gøsta Esping-Andersen (1999: 5), the dean of welfare state scholars, argues, for example, that 'the real "crisis" of contemporary welfare regimes lies in the disjuncture between the existing institutional configuration and exogenous change. Contemporary welfare states . . . have their origins in, and mirror, a society that no longer obtains'. Public social programs have weathered the storms of the past two decades, on this view. But major transformations in the employment sector and family relations have significantly altered the effects (and effectiveness) of long-standing policy strategies.

This observation, if true, raises critical questions: Is the increased mismatch between risks and social protections the result of exogenous change alone? Or are systems of social provision and the political processes that shape them implicated in the outcome? And why have some systems been so slow to adapt to the new realities they confront? This chapter develops a conceptual framework for studying these questions and offers a preliminary verdict for one 'crucial case' (Eckstein 1975), the United States. It shows that there has indeed been a growing mismatch between risk profiles and welfare state protections in the United States and that much of the disjuncture is rooted, as recent welfare state scholarship suggests, in the very institutional and political resilience that has protected the American welfare state against retrenchment.

Yet, contrary to the usual framing of this disjuncture as a result of exogenous shocks to stable systems, this chapter demonstrates that many of these mismatches should be seen as a direct outgrowth of political struggles over social policy—a manifestation of an important but often hidden 'second face' (Bachrach and Baratz 1962) of welfare state debate. No less important, the chapter shows that crucial forms of policy change have in fact taken place over the past three decades, despite general stability in formal policies. The key mechanism of change, however, is not large-scale legislative reforms, but a set of alternative, and often less visible, processes of adaptation—'conversion' (Thelen 2003), 'layering' (Schickler 2001), and, perhaps most important, 'drift' (Hacker 2004).[2] In focusing on active changes in policy rules, welfare state scholars have thus missed fundamental ways in which the welfare state is changing.

To see this, however, requires that we shift our focus—from the welfare state narrowly defined to the complex of public and private social benefits that characterize the mixed economy of welfare, from the income-redistributive effects of social policies to their risk-spreading functions, and from the highly visible interactions that are the usual stuff of welfare state scholarship to the more hidden processes that shape the ground-level alteration of social policies. Indeed, a key argument of this chapter is that a conception of the welfare state centered around risk protection, rather than exclusively or predominantly around income redistribution, provides a different and clearer picture of welfare state development. This shift in focus, in turn, demands more intensive (and more genuinely historical) analysis of the ground-level consequences of policies, as well as greater attention to the dynamics of agenda formation and path dependence that have helped keep new or worsening risks from being addressed. It also requires more detailed consideration of how *private* social benefits, such as employer-provided health and pension plans, have changed alongside public programs. As I will show, despite general stability in the rules and incentives that shape them, private benefits have changed dramatically in the United States in recent decades—in ways that have profoundly limited their ability to protect higher-risk and lower-income citizens against pressing social contingencies.

The choice of the American welfare state as the focus of these claims may appear unconventional. Comparative analysts who disagree on much nonetheless typically view the American welfare state as lying on a wholly different plane from other nations, or at the very least on the outer frontiers of the 'liberal' category of market-oriented welfare states (Esping-Andersen 1990). Yet the American case, with its multiple institutional 'veto points' (Immergut 1992; see also Tsebelis 1995), has also long been treated as the quintessential example of welfare state resilience in the face of attack–indeed, the principal validating case of the leading approach to retrenchment: the 'new politics of the welfare state' perspective associated with the work of Paul Pierson (1994). If, therefore, the surface stability of US social programs has in fact masked a major constriction in the bounds of shared risk, then a strong case can be made that the prevailing scholarly approach to retrenchment has overlooked core dimensions of welfare state reform. Moreover, certain unusual aspects of the US framework, in particular its heavy reliance on private benefits, are becoming more common in other nations (Adema and Einerhand 1998), making the American experience a potential guide to the long-term effects of these nascent but powerful trends.

Nonetheless, the American experience remains distinctive in key respects. In other rich democracies, policymakers have often responded to changing social risks with new interventions aimed at reconciling traditional policy goals with new realities. Ironically, the very political fragmentation that has helped protect US social programs against radical change has also allowed the gradual deterioration of their risk-protection functions, while encouraging opponents of the welfare state to pursue stealth reforms that have increasingly succeeded in shifting risk from collective intermediaries onto individuals and families, fundamentally recasting the US debate.

This chapter therefore carries two important messages about processes of institutional change. The first is that changes in an institution's functioning and effects can occur without fundamental shifts in formal institutional structures. Shifts in the context of an institution and in the goals that agents pursue through an institution can alter an institution's character and effect fundamentally, even without shifts in formal structure. I argue that changes of this kind lie at the heart of the transformed role of the American welfare state.

This leads to the second overarching message—that processes of institutional change are not hopelessly idiosyncratic or complex, but instead systematically conditioned by two specific, identifiable characteristics of institutions: (1) the extent to which they permit internal shifts in institutional operation and goals, and (2) the degree to which their political context facilitates authoritative external reform. When, for example, institutions are highly malleable yet substantial barriers block authoritative change, then advocates of reform are likely to pursue strategies of 'conversion' (Thelen 2003), refashioning existing institutions from within rather than from without. By contrast, when institutional structures are highly change-resistant but the political environment is conducive to action, reform is more likely to take the form of 'layering' (Schickler 2001), in which new institutions are established alongside older ones. And when neither internal structures nor political contexts favor reform, advocates may instead aim to foster 'drift', preventing the updating of institutions to changing circumstances.

In short, actors who wish to change a popular and embedded institution in a political setting that places steep hurdles in the path of large-scale authoritative reform may find it prudent *not* to attack that institution directly. Instead, they may block adaptation of an institution to its context, shift its ground-level operation, or establish new institutions on top of it. These are reform strategies that are little studied and even less well-understood. They are also strategies, I shall demonstrate, that critics of the welfare state—rebuffed in their direct assaults on public social programs—have increasingly attempted to pursue, at times with considerable success.

The analysis of retrenchment

The beginning of the recent wave of interest in retrenchment can be conveniently dated to Pierson's pathbreaking 1994 book on welfare state reform in Britain and the United States, *Dismantling the Welfare State?* Pierson was certainly not the first to examine the 'crisis' of the welfare state, nor was he even the first to argue that welfare states had successfully weathered the storm. But he was the first to assess systematically the progress of reform across a range of policy areas using a clear conceptual framework. Indeed, a chief reason for the influence of *Dismantling the Welfare State?* is that Pierson was unusually attuned to issues of definition. 'Retrenchment', Pierson notes in the opening of the book, 'is one of those cases in which identifying what is to be explained is almost as difficult as formulating persuasive explanations for it'. Spending cuts alone do not define the concept; analysts need also to consider structural reforms that move the welfare state toward a more 'residual' role, in which government does little to shift the distribution of income and services in a progressive direction. Retrenchment thus describes 'policy changes that either cut social expenditure, restructure welfare state programs to conform more closely to the residual welfare state model, or alter the political environment in ways that enhance the probability of such outcomes in the future' (Pierson 1994: 17). The last of these—changes in the welfare state's long-term context—Pierson labeled 'systemic retrenchment', to distinguish it from immediate changes in policies, which he termed 'programmatic retrenchment'.[3]

Having defined retrenchment, Pierson went on to evaluate the success of British and US conservatives in pursuing it. Based on studies of several key policy areas, as well as comparative data on social spending and public opinion, he concluded that efforts at retrenchment largely failed and 'the fundamental structure of social policy remains comparatively stable' (Pierson 1994: 182). Expanding the welfare state involved imposing relatively diffuse costs in return for relatively concentrated benefits. Cutting social programs, by contrast, entails imposing relatively concentrated costs in return for diffuse gains—a far more challenging project. More important, social programs remain popular, and the welfare state has created powerful constituencies, such as pensioners and nonprofit service providers, that are well positioned to fight efforts at retrenchment. In short, the prospects for retrenchment are—to use a phrase Pierson deploys in more recent writings—highly 'path dependent' (Pierson 2000). Past social policy choices, which create strong vested interests and expectations, are extremely difficult to undo even in the present era.

Pierson's argument is clear and logical, and it carries a straightforward prescription—namely, that analysts should look for efforts to introduce residualizing reforms into existing social programs. A significant body of writing has followed this prescription and, in doing so, made major advances in our understanding of the politics and progress of welfare state reform. Indeed, even predominantly quantitative work now routinely concedes that analysis of the politics of retrenchment requires careful probing of actual case histories to show that spending trends reflect affirmative political decisions (e.g. Huber and Stephens 2001).

Yet, for all its virtues, Pierson's approach also has real limits.[4] The first and most straightforward is the emphasis on active 'policy changes'. Although Pierson notes that one strategy for retrenchment is 'decrementalism', whereby benefits are simply allowed to erode, his emphasis is on decisions rather than 'nondecisions', on affirmative attempts to change policies rather than failure to act in the face of contrary pressures. Like the pluralists who made the case for widely distributed political influence during the famous community power debate, Pierson and others who have followed his lead have examined retrenchment principally by tracing observable decisions—in this case, decisions that change the contours of public social programs.[5] The influential critique made against pluralism thus carries weight here, too: By looking only at what reformers have done to public programs, retrenchment analyses tend to downplay the important ways in which these actors have shaped and restricted the agenda of debate—agenda-setting and blocking activities that may be crucial to the welfare state's long-term evolution.

A second limitation of Pierson's approach concerns the relationship between welfare states and their environment. Researchers have cautioned that we should take into account major economic shocks in assessing welfare state spending, because economic distress is likely to increase social expenditures while at the same time lowering economic growth. We surely would not want to say that a country in crisis, its citizens hanging precariously onto countercyclical supports, has a more generous welfare state simply because it is devoting more of its GDP to social benefits. Yet Pierson's approach does something quite similar. In emphasizing affirmative policy departures, it pushes analysts to assess changes in programs independently of any consideration of how those programs interact with the broader life circumstances of citizens, thus missing the potentially shifting ways in which policies intersect with their larger economic and social context.

This point can and should be applied to a variety of social policy areas. Welfare states have historically been directed not just at alleviating economic distress, but at providing security against a vast range of life risks: childbirth, unemployment, death of a spouse, retirement, disability, sickness. Yet the incidence of many of these risks has changed dramatically over the past three decades, leading to potentially significant transformations in the consequences of social policy interventions.

To be sure, we should not assume that the welfare state *should* naturally adjust to deal with changing risks, or that gaps between risks and benefits are always deliberate—as they clearly are, for example, in the case of active attempts to prevent policies from being updated to achieve their historical goals in response to demands to do so. And yet, we cannot ignore these gaps either. Welfare states, after all, constitute institutionalized aims as well as an arsenal of policy means for achieving them, and their development over time must be assessed in that dual light.

In fact, even within the relatively narrow conception of the welfare state that Pierson adopts, there are important policies he largely overlooks. Notable here are two overlapping policy realms central to the American social welfare framework: tax expenditures with social welfare aims and regulatory and tax policies governing privately provided social welfare benefits (Howard 1997; Hacker 2002). The United States has an extremely large employment-based private benefit system that is extensively buttressed and shaped by government policy (Hacker 2002). Controlling for tax burdens, for instance, private social benefits constituted more than a third of US social spending in 1995, compared with an average of less than a tenth in the other nations for which data exist. Furthermore, there has been a major shift in the distribution and character of private benefits in recent decades, with rates of coverage plummeting among lower-income workers and benefit plans providing increasingly insecure income guarantees. Leaving policies that govern private social benefits out of the analysis entirely, as nearly all retrenchment studies do, thus misses a critically important dimension of social policy change, particularly within the United States.

Hidden forms of retrenchment: drift, conversion, and layering

The decline of private social benefits in the United States represents a huge change in the scope of American risk protection. Yet it is a change that has occurred, for the most part, without the kinds of large-scale formal policy reforms that retrenchment scholars typically analyze. For this reason, it provides a revealing example of the less visible, but no less consequential, forms of institutional change that the standard lens on retrenchment tends to occlude.

These hidden types of change take three main forms, each of which is elaborated more fully in the introduction to this volume: *drift*, *conversion*, and *layering*. The first type, which I have termed *drift*, may also be the most important for understanding recent social policy developments. *Drift* describes a shift in the context of policies that significantly alters their effects. If, for example, unemployment insurance excludes service workers, a shift of employment from manufacturing into services effectively decreases the extent of protection, despite stability in overall policy. Or, to use the example at the heart of this chapter, if the constellation of social risks that citizens face fundamentally shifts, yet policies remain stable, then the universe of social protection effectively constricts—again, without formal policy revision.

Esping-Andersen (1999) and others who discuss the inability of existing welfare state policies to deal with changing social risks imply that it is largely an apolitical process, driven by exogenous social shifts over which politicians have little or no control. To the extent that arguments in this vein concern the *politics* of reform, their ambition is limited to explaining welfare state responses to the disjunction between risks and benefits *once* it has arisen. Yet the emergence of this mismatch should itself be seen as a process that is highly mediated by politics. In an environment of new or worsening social risks, opponents of expanded state responsibility do not have to enact major policy reforms to move policy toward their favored ends. Merely by delegitimizing and blocking compensatory interventions designed to ameliorate intensified risks, they can gradually transform the orientation of existing programs. To be sure, externally induced policy drift may sometimes be wholly inadvertent. But much of it is quite clearly mediated by politics—a result not of failures of foresight or perception, but of deliberate efforts by political actors to prevent the recalibration of social programs.

Drift is not, however, the only means by which policies may change without formal revision. In addition, what Kathleen Thelen (2003) calls *conversion* may also cause ground-level change. In the realm of social policy, conversion describes changes in implementation that occur without formal policy revision. It is, in short, change driven by the deployment of existing policy levers in new ways, rather than the revision of those policies through normal procedures of collective political decisionmaking.

Policies vary greatly in their susceptibility to conversion. Some policies, for example, have procedures and aims that are clearly specified, consistent, and widely understood; others do not. Some give central leaders strong tools for controlling front-line agents who shape ultimate results; others do not. At one extreme, then, are policies whose dictates are unambiguous and whose front-line agents have little discretion. On the other are policies whose rules are opaque and contested, and whose interpretation and implementation by front-line actors are highly variable. In the realm of social policy, public retirement programs provide perhaps the best example of the first ideal type; tax breaks for voluntarily provided workplace benefits of the second. More generally, the difficulty of converting a policy to new ends should be lower when it delegates administration or lacks clear overarching rules or aims, as in decentralized federal-state programs or subsidy arrangements that shape voluntary benefits.

A less studied but no less important force shaping the internal malleability of policies is the degree to which a policy gives rise to self-reinforcing 'policy feedbacks' (Skocpol 1992; Pierson 1993) that cement in place stable constituencies, operating procedures, and definitions of mission. Although research on policy feedback is still in its youth, existing scholarship demonstrates that social policies do differ markedly in the extent to which they give rise to politically efficacious support coalitions. Social Security, for example, promotes widespread mobilization among the American aged, who are well poised to fight cuts (Campbell 2003). Cash assistance for the poor, by contrast, gives rise to an extremely weak, fragmented, and politically demobilized constituency, which was unable to present an effective and united front against the 1996 welfare reform law. In general, policies are more durable if they create or encourage the creation of large-scale organizations with substantial set-up costs, directly or indirectly benefits sizable organized groups or constituencies, and embody long-lived commitments upon which beneficiaries and those around them premise crucial life and organizational decisions (Hacker 2002).

Awareness of the internal convertibility of policies is largely missing from work on welfare state reform. This is in part because welfare state scholars have restricted their analysis almost entirely to policies with explicit and elaborate rules governing eligibility and benefits—policies for which it makes sense to begin by looking at policy rules and attempts to change them. And yet, there are many key realms of social policy in which the link between policies and effects is much weaker. Regulatory and tax policies governing private benefits, for example, leave virtually unfettered discretion to employers, allowing companies to change what they do within government guidelines fundamentally. Many social policies divide authority between units of government or between government and private actors, such as providers, unions, and employers. Even programs run entirely by public organizations may allow significant 'street-level bureaucracy' (Lipsky 1980), making problematic the assumption that what a policy dictates is what is actually done. And such decentralized arrangements are, it appears, becoming more prevalent (Gidron, Kramer, and Salamon 1992; Rein and Wandensjö 1997; Clayton and Pontusson 1998; Gilbert 2002). If this is so, it may become increasingly difficult to judge policy effects simply by reading the statute books or examining disputes over policy rules. We will need to look at what really happens on the ground.

In contrast to internal policy change, the cost of eliminating or replacing a policy is principally determined by the barriers to authoritative policy change through normal decisionmaking procedures. These barriers, as institutionalists have long argued, are systematically shaped by decisionmakers' preference distributions as well as by generic features of political systems, particularly the degree to which procedural rules create a status-quo bias (Immergut 1992; Tsebelis 1995; Krehbiel 1998). According to Tsebelis's (1995) widely used 'veto players' framework, for example, policy stability increases when more actors or decisionmaking bodies must give assent for change to occur, when the ideological distance between them is greater, and when they are more internally cohesive. All this suggests that the American institutional and political context of the 1980s and 1990s—with its bicameral and presidential structure, frequent periods of divided government, and increasingly polarized and internally homogenous parties—was particularly inhospitable to large-scale legislative change.

In sum, a policy is more resilient to challenge when it is situated in a political structure and partisan context that strongly privileges the status quo (making reversal difficult) and when it has strong support (making reversal undesirable). Pragmatic advocates of change in such settings may find it more attractive to adapt existing policies to their ends than to wage a frontal assault. For this reason, *political settings that make authoritative change more difficult encourage reformers to seek change through drift or conversion.* In these contexts, not only is their ability to pass new legislation or replace existing policies limited, but they are also better able to block efforts to close gaps between a policy's original goals and its actual effects.

Figure 2.1 presents the argument thus far in a simple two-by-two matrix. As the bottom-right quadrant indicates, when a policy is easy to convert and easy to alter through authoritative decisionmaking, it is highly vulnerable to elimination or replacement. Quite obviously, however, this is not the normal state of affairs in welfare state politics. The most illuminating possibilities for the study of retrenchment, therefore, are the other three combinations. When the barriers to authoritative policy action are relatively low but policies are difficult to convert, the dominant pattern of change is likely to be *layering*—in which proponents of change work around institutions that have fostered powerful vested interests and long-term expectations 'by adding new institutions rather than dismantling the old' (Schickler 2001: 13). When the barriers to authoritative action are high but policies are relatively easy to change internally, by contrast, the dominant pattern is instead likely to be *conversion*, in which policies are adapted over time rather than replaced or eliminated. Finally, *drift* is most likely when the barriers to internal change are high (meaning it is hard to shift them to new ends) and the status-quo bias of the external political context is also high (meaning it is hard to eliminate or supplant existing institutions). If successful in undermining policies'

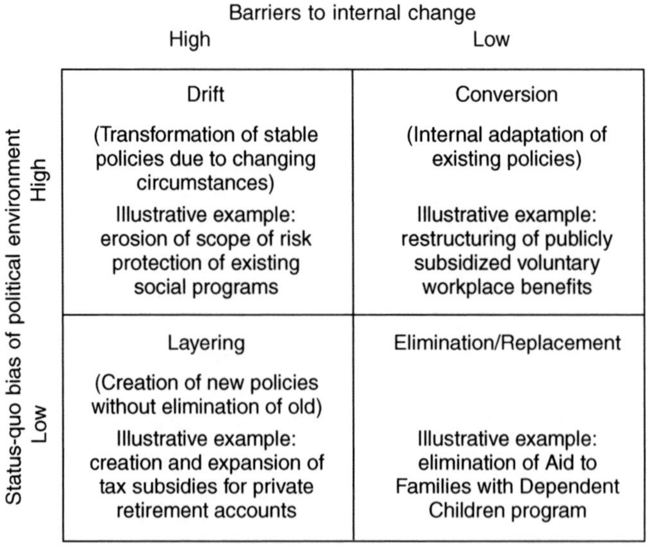

	Barriers to internal change	
	High	Low
High	Drift (Transformation of stable policies due to changing circumstances) Illustrative example: erosion of scope of risk protection of existing social programs	Conversion (Internal adaptation of existing policies) Illustrative example: restructuring of publicly subsidized voluntary workplace benefits
Low	Layering (Creation of new policies without elimination of old) Illustrative example: creation and expansion of tax subsidies for private retirement accounts	Elimination/Replacement Illustrative example: elimination of Aid to Families with Dependent Children program

Status-quo bias of political environment

Figure 2.1 Four modes of policy change

support coalitions or the ability of policies to achieve their goals, all these forms of change should also lower the barriers to *future* policy changes.

As we shall see, each of these forms of change were on vivid display in American welfare state debates during the 1980s and 1990s. *Drift* was the most pervasive dynamic, as critics of the welfare state grew increasingly adept at using the famously fragmented American political system to block legislative reforms that would close the growing gulf between social risks and social benefits. Yet this was not the only pattern. When critics gained sufficient leverage to enact authoritative reforms (yet not to dismantle existing policies outright), they also sought to layer new policies onto old. *Layering* in fact aptly describes conservatives' use of political openings in the early 1980s (due to Reagan's election) and late 1990s (due to the Republican capture of Congress) to create tax breaks encouraging individualized private benefits that compete with public programs. Throughout the period, moreover, opponents of existing programs also sought to convert existing policies to new ends by granting greater discretion to front-line policy actors, such as employers and states—actors that, opponents anticipated, would use their increased latitude to revamp policy operations along more conservative lines.

Because these changes largely occurred without formal legislative revision, examining them call for an analytic approach attuned to the internal reworking of otherwise stable policies and the shifting interaction of programs and their environment. This is, of course, a formidable challenge. We are a long way from having good data on what has happened to benefit rules, much less on how these rules are actually implemented or affect citizens. But the claim that drift, layering, and conversion are crucial does carry with it prescriptions that run counter to the methodological thrust of much previous work on retrenchment. Most straightforward, it suggests that we should be interested in the effects of programs as well as their formal structure. That is, we should look not merely at rules governing benefits or eligibility, but also at the effects that those rules have as they are actually carried out by front-line policy actors in the context of other sources of social protection and shifting constellations of social risk. In all these inquiries, however, one question should be central: Have welfare states continued to provide the inclusive risk protection that defined their structure and goals in the immediate decades after the Second World War?

New social risks, old social policies

Despite many observations about the 'new social risks' and welfare state rigidities in coping with them, the changing ability of social policies to deal with major life contingencies has not been intensively studied. This reflects a larger blind spot in the vast literature on the welfare state. Though everyone knows that welfare states serve vital insurance functions, most commentary assumes rather reflexively that income redistribution is, if not the defining goal of social programs, at least the strongest indicator of their performance.[6] Yet the reasons for making risk protection a key independent topic of concern are compelling. Not only are the largest social programs—pensions, health insurance, unemployment compensation, survivors' benefits—centrally about insuring against risks to income, but also many aspects of the welfare state that we do not typically think of as risk protection (such as child care and worker retraining) contain important insurance elements insofar that they cushion families against the income shock of major life events.[7]

Risk protection and income redistribution are related but distinct. Although social insurance does redistribute income, both in the short-term and over time, its principal goal is to 'moderate the risks of current income loss or inadequacy by providing secure cash or near-cash entitlements on the occurrence of defined risks' (Graetz and Mashaw 1999: 65). The animating aim of social insurance is to spread the risk of costly life contingencies that are recognized as a collective, rather than private, responsibility. The bounds of social insurance thus delimit the scope of shared risk—the degree to which potent threats to income are spread across citizens of varying circumstances ('risk-socialization') or left to individuals or families to cope with on their own ('risk-privatization').[8] To 'privatize' risk, in this parlance, is thus to fragment and undermine collective insurance pools that offer reduced-cost protection to higher-risk and lower-income citizens in favor of arrangements that leave individuals and families responsible for social risks largely on their own.

Intuitively, the boundaries of such collective risk pools can be changed in three ways. The first is explicit alterations of rules governing eligibility or benefits—the subject of most retrenchment analyses. The second and more subtle means is a transformation in the translation of these rules into outcomes. Do all those eligible receive the benefits specified in law, for example? Do policies permit discretion on the part of administrators or providers? The final source of change is a shift in the constellation of risks itself. Risks that insurance covers may become more severe, leading to an effective decline in protection, or new risks could arise that fall outside the universe of shared responsibility. Neither this type of change nor changing policy effectiveness is likely to be picked up by the conventional focus on active reform. Nor, it should be noted, are these forms of change likely to be captured fully by data on redistribution—which can tell us whether more or less is redistributed at any time, but not how well policies protect citizens *over* time.[9]

About one point there can be little question: The constellation of risks that citizens face has changed significantly in the past three decades due to linked changes in work and family (Esping-Andersen 1999; Skocpol 2000). In the employment sector, the shifts include rising levels of earnings inequality, growing instability of income, increased employment in services and in part-time and contingent work, and increased structural (rather than cyclical) unemployment. In the realm of family relations, the changes include rising rates of divorce and separation, and the increasing prevalence of lone-parent, female-headed families. Connecting the two domains is perhaps the most fundamental shift in the worlds of work and family—the dramatic movement of women into paid employment. Each of these changes has placed new strain on social protections constructed during an era in which the social risks that families faced flowed almost entirely out of the employment status of the male breadwinner. In the brave new world of work and family, even stable full-time employment of household heads is not a guarantee of security, and citizens are barraged with a host of risks emanating from families themselves.

Foremost among the economic changes is a major transformation in the employment opportunities and earnings of men that began in the 1970s. In a startling break with the past, 'the earnings of less skilled American men began dropping after 1973 and fell precipitously during the 1980s, when young male high school graduates and dropouts suffered exceptional losses relative to their college graduate peers' (Blackburn, Bloom, and Freeman 1990: 31). Moreover, average rates of unemployment among these workers nearly doubled between 1974 and 1988, and the nature of unemployment also changed, shifting from cyclical lay-offs during economic downturns toward permanent job losses. At the same time, employment in the (often low-wage) service sector and in part-time and contingent positions that offered relatively low pay and few or no benefits increased.

The most easily tracked manifestation of these trends is a marked increase in economic inequality. Between 1979 and 2000, for example, the post-tax and -transfer income of the top 1 percent of American households on the income scale increased by 201 percent in real terms, and that of the top fifth by more than 68 percent. By contrast, the post-tax and -transfer income of the bottom fifth of households rose by just 8.7 percent, while that of the second fifth and middle fifth rose by just 13.3 percent and 15.1 percent, respectively (Greenstein and Shapiro 2003). The growth in inequality of wealth during this period was even more dramatic (Wolff 2002).

This is, to many, *the* story of the post-1970s American experience: the reversal of long-standing expectations about rapidly rising standards of living among average workers. Yet simultaneously, and in many ways in concert, the 1970s ushered in equally profound changes in American families. Most striking by far was the continued entry of women into the paid workforce, a trend that by 2000 had made two-earner families, once an exotic species, the majority of married couples. Even women with children younger than six years grew more likely to work than not, their labor force participation increasing from 19 percent in 1960 to 59 percent in 1990 (Skocpol 2000: 124–5). But if two-earner families became more common, marriages did not become more durable. Rates of divorce and single parenthood (in most cases, single motherhood) increased dramatically.

These trends both fueled and were fueled by the economic shifts just described. Single parenthood is concentrated among less educated women, who have increasingly delayed marriage but not childbearing, in part because the men they are most likely to marry have faced poor economic prospects. More educated women, by contrast, are delaying childbearing but not marriage and having fewer children overall, which seems to reflect the economic costs to female professionals of having children (Ellwood and Jencks 2001). In addition, the increasing prevalence of two-earner families must be seen in part as a private response to the pressures that families face—a form of intra-family risk sharing that decreases vulnerability to the shocks to income caused by interruptions of earnings or the high cost of services that housewives once provided.

Whatever their cause, these changes in family structure are clearly a significant contributor to economic inequality and hardship. The rise of two-earner families exacerbated family income inequality because high-earning women tend to be married to high-earning men. On the other side of the coin, single-parent families are, unsurprisingly, much more likely to have low incomes than families in which two parents are present. And with dual paychecks now a prerequisite for middle-class life, divorce and separation have come to represent potent risks to the economic well-being of families with children. A partial glimpse of the effects that these transformations have wrought can be gleaned from statistics concerning the characteristics of people in poverty. Although poverty rates dipped in the strong economy of the mid- to late 1990s, they rose over the 1970s and 1980s (and are now rising again). But no less striking than the overall rise is the change in the characteristics of those affected: Poverty among the elderly fell sharply in the 1970s and has remained relatively low since, while a sizable and increasing portion of the poverty population is made up of parents with young children (for a comparative review, see Ritakallio 2001; Smeeding 2001).

A similar, but in many ways more nuanced, portrait is provided by evidence on the number and characteristics of Americans filing for bankruptcy. As is well known, personal bankruptcy has risen dramatically, with filings increasing fivefold between 1980 and 2002, to more than 1.5 million. Less well known is that the characteristics of filers have also changed dramatically. Elizabeth Warren (2003) reports, for example, that women have emerged as the largest single group of filers, their share of filings rising eightfold between 1981 and 2001. Revealingly, half of filers cite health problems, childbirth, a death in the family, or substantial medical bills as a prime reason for filing. By comparison, a 1970s study found just 11 percent of filers citing one or more of these reasons in 1964 (cited in Jacoby, Sullivan, and Warren 2001).

The rise in economic inequality and the changing composition of the poor and bankrupt are each strongly suggestive of the changing composition of social risks that citizens face. Yet perhaps the most powerful evidence of increased risks to family income is the growing *instability* of earnings over the past two decades. Robert Moffit and Peter Gottschalk (2002), for example, have documented a marked increase in the variability of male wages during the 1980s and 1990s—an increase driven more by instability in workers' wages than by instability of employment. Figure 2.2 presents the results of an investigation of family income instability conducted by myself and Nigar Nargis of the University of Dhaka using the Panel Study of Income Dynamics (PSID), a longitudinal study that traces a representative sample of US individuals and the family units in which they reside. In the figure, 'permanent variance' measures differences across families (controlling for family size), while 'transitory variance' measures differences over time in the income of any given family. The substantial rise in permanent variance confirms

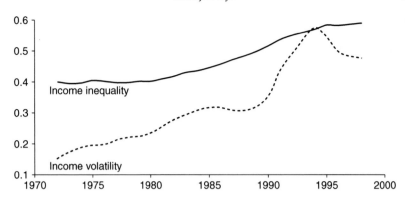

Figure 2.2 Inequality and instability of American family income, 1972–98

Notes: The sample consists of adult household members aged 25–61. Income is adjusted for household size by dividing it by the square root of family size. The contribution of each component of income to the variance of total family income is weighted by its relative share in total family income.

Source: Calculated from the Panel Study of Income Dynamics, Institute for Social Research, University of Michigan. Lines are five-year moving averages of permanent variance (inequality) and transitory variance (volatility) of log of family income, adjusted for household size.

the well-known finding that family income inequality increased over this period. More striking, however, is doubling of transitory variance between 1974 and 1998—and the fact that it exceeded five times its initial level at its peak in the mid-1990s.[10] This is a potent indication of the increased risks to income that American families confront.

These trends have exposed serious gaps in the American framework of social protection—which, while widely criticized, is also widely misunderstood (Marmor, Mashaw, and Harvey 1990). Comparative researchers, for example, commonly describe the American welfare regime as one in which 'benefits cater mainly to a clientele of low-income, usually working-class, state dependents' (Esping-Andersen 1990: 26). But although public social spending is much lower in the United States than other affluent democracies, it is debatable whether it is notably more targeted on the poor (see, for example, the evidence in Korpi and Palme 1998). Public cash assistance for the poor represents only a tiny fraction of US social welfare spending, and means-tested benefits as a whole make up less than a third of public social spending. This picture is considerably reinforced when we consider tax expenditures with social welfare purposes and private social welfare benefits, both of which primarily benefit upper-income Americans (Howard 1997; Hacker 2002).

The bulk of public and private social spending in the United States, as in other rich democracies, is devoted to major areas of social insurance—particularly health insurance and pensions. In part because the United States is the only nation in which contributory public health insurance is limited to the aged, public spending is highly concentrated on the elderly (Lynch 2000). By contrast, public and private support for working adults and families with children is comparatively anemic. The United States lacks the universal health insurance and family allowances common in other affluent nations, benefit levels under cash-assistance programs that aid families are low and falling, public and private support for child care is extremely modest, and employers have been reluctant to provide paid family leave even as they have cut back other benefits for spouses and children. Unlike Germany, Japan, and the Nordic countries, the United States also lacks universal long-term care for the elderly (Campbell and Morgan 2002).

In principle, US social policy could have adapted to changing social realities. As the pathbreaking feminist writings on the welfare state show (e.g. Orloff 1993; Stetson and Mazur 1995), some nations—most strikingly, the Scandinavian welfare states—have dramatically expanded public protections that help women enter the labor force and balance work and child rearing. Many of these same nations have also tackled the new realities of the labor market with active employment and training polices (Levy 1999). Putting aside some modest exceptions, however, the United States clearly did not follow this path. Increases in the Earned Income Tax Credit (EITC) for low-wage workers and their families, shifts of money from cash assistance to child care and job retraining, and new family leave legislation were all steps toward a response. But lower-wage workers continued to receive only meager public supports and the US tax and benefit structure continued to penalize two-earner families (CBO 1997). Family leave rules did not apply to small employers and, more important, did not provide any income support to leave-takers. Government assistance for child care remained scant, and unavailable even for families eligible for it (Levy and Michel 2002). Despite new forms of job insecurity, unemployment insurance dramatically contracted, particularly for lower-income and intermittently employed workers (GAO 2000), while the 1996 welfare reform legislation removed important elements of the safety net for the most disadvantaged. Perhaps most striking, however, was a massive decline in employment-based health and pension protections among lower-wage workers—which was only weakly offset by public coverage expansions.

Suzanne Mettler and Andrew Milstein (2003) provide concrete dollar figures for some of these changes. The inflation-adjusted value of the minimum wage, for example, dropped by more than a third between 1968 and 2002. The real value of unemployment benefits also fell significantly, as did benefits under the Food Stamps and Aid to Families with Dependent Children programs. As Mettler and Milstein note, moreover, unionization rates plummeted during this period, in part because of the Reagan administration's aggressive antiunion policies. Although, as Pierson (1994) argues, declining unionization does not necessarily imperil public programs that enjoy strong popular support, it is difficult to deny that it has weakened the leverage of those who wish to reorient social policy toward new risks, or that it has strengthened the political standing of employers, particularly in negotiations over private benefits.

A further glimpse into these trends is provided by the cross-national measures of redistribution provided by the Luxembourg Income Study (LIS). Figure 2.3 shows

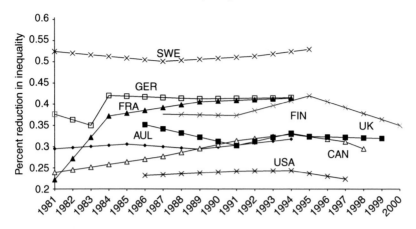

Figure 2.3 Income redistribution via taxes and transfers in selected nations, 1981–2000
Source: Unpublished LIS data, kindly supplied by David Jesuit, Vincent Mahler, and Timothy Smeeding.

the percentage reduction in income inequality produced by taxes and transfers in selected nations. The LIS statistics confirms that inequality before taxes and transfers rose sharply in the United States and a number of other nations during the 1980s. The United States, in fact, has the highest levels of inequality, both before taxes and transfers take effect and afterward. Compared with other nations, however, the United States appears to have done much less to offset the rise in inequality that many nations experienced during this period. Averaging across the twelve other nations for which data exist, for example, the reduction in inequality created by taxes and transfers increased 10 percent between the first and last observation. In the United States, by contrast, taxes and transfers reduced inequality slightly less by the end of the series (1997) than at the outset (1986). This contrast would probably be starker if LIS statistics went back to the 1970s.

It is important to emphasize that these were not uncontested issues. There were, most obviously, major attempts to scale back existing public social programs in the early 1980s and then after the ascendance of the GOP in Congress in 1994. Although these efforts had only limited success, they were not without effect—and a number yielded substantial restrictions of program scope and generosity (Weaver 2000; Shapiro and Greenstein 2001). Perhaps more important, these struggles unquestionably helped produce a major shift in the terms of social policy discourse, immortalized in President Clinton's 1995 declaration that the 'era of big government is over'. While in both periods conservatives quickly moved to protect themselves against charges that they were hostile to popular programs, the larger drift was clearly toward the conservative pole of the debate. Proposals for major structural reform of Medicare and Social Security gained grounds, liberals found themselves vying with conservatives over the depth of their commitment to making welfare recipients work, tax cuts that threatened future social spending passed into law, and calls for the creation of new social interventions all but vanished from public debate. This new climate has shaped the orientation and structure of the few new policy innovations that have been put in place, leading to an increased emphasis on tax expenditures and private provision. In more decentralized and discretionary programs, it has also shaped the character of front-line administration and even, some evidence suggests, the degree to which citizens take advantage of benefits for which they qualify (Levy and Michel 2002; Zedlewski 2002).

In addition, although few big new policy departures took place, a series of often-unnoticed incremental changes have produced, or seem likely to produce, significant longer-term effects. Most notable here are a deliberate expansion of tax-favored investment accounts for retirement—sold as an alternative to both older company pension plans and Social Security—the creation and expansion of opportunities for private health plans to contract with Medicare and Medicaid, and a significant loosening through both legislative changes and administrative processes (such as federal waivers) of federal restrictions on state and local social welfare activities. As Steven Teles (1996: 141) argues with regard to cash public assistance, waivers were deliberately used by the Republican-led executive branch in the late 1980s because the 'left was strong enough to veto certain policies in the legislative context that it has been unable to stop when pursued through the waiver process'—a textbook example of strategic adaptation to a political context preventing authoritative policy change. Moreover, all of these more subterranean changes, whether through drift or layering, have been aided by the inherent difficulty in a fragmented polity of closing gaps that have opened between original policy aims and ground-level policy effects.

Finally, overshadowing and dominating these other events were active campaigns to block the passage of policies that might extend social protections to new risks or that could limit the weakening of existing protections. The Family and Medical Leave Act, for example, was passed in 1993 only after it was whittled down for more than a decade—and vetoed not once but twice by President George H.W. Bush (Elving 1996). But this was a (marginally) successful example: Most proposals ended up in the political graveyard, stymied by budgetary constraints, actual or threatened filibusters and vetoes, and formidable conservative resistance. The signal case here, of course, is the failure to pass any proposal for significantly expanded health coverage in the early 1990s, despite declining levels of private coverage, President Clinton's strong support for the goal, and public enthusiasm for some action (Skocpol 1996; Jacobs and Shapiro 2000).

This is an impressionistic tally, to be sure. But, as we shall see, its general message is confirmed by a closer review of recent policy developments in the two largest areas of US social policy: health insurance and pensions. These policy areas are inviting as a target of in-depth inquiry for two reasons. First, they collectively comprise the majority of social spending in the United States (and, indeed, in all affluent democracies). Second, by virtue of their size and the unquestionable popularity of the policies that comprise them, these two domains are also widely seen as the most resilient components of the postwar social welfare order. As the next two sections detail, however, in both of these bedrock areas, relative stability in public social programs has masked major declines in the ability of social policies to provide inclusive risk protection. Social risks have shifted from collective intermediaries—government, employers—onto individuals and families. Efforts to address new (and newly intensified) risks have failed. New social policies sharply at odds with established ones have been created and expanded, breeding new tensions and conflicts. Although the paths of health and pension policy differ in crucial and revealing ways, their overarching trajectories appear the same: toward a significant privatization of risk.

The unraveling of American health insurance

By the 1970s, the basic structure of American health insurance was firmly in place. For most Americans—more than 80 percent by the mid-1970s—private health insurance provided the first line of protection against the risks of medical costs. Historically, employment-based health insurance was provided by large commercial and nonprofit insurers, which pooled risks across many workplaces (and, originally, even charged all subscribers essentially the same rate—a practice favorable to higher-risk groups).

Employment-based health protection was (and is) heavily subsidized through the tax code, which treats virtually all workplace health benefits as exempt from taxation as compensation. (The estimated revenue loss created by this tax expenditure is roughly $188 billion, an amount roughly half as large as employer contributions to health coverage for their workers, Sheils and Hogan 2004.) From 1965 onwards, the federal Medicare program provided public coverage for elderly—and, later, the disabled—and the joint federal-state Medicaid program covered poor people with ties to public assistance, although most Medicaid spending has gone to the disabled and indigent elderly, rather than families with children.

Since the 1970s, the private foundation of this system has undergone a radical contraction—in what amounts to a textbook case of conversion within the bounds of stable policies. From a peak of more than 80 percent of Americans, private insurance coverage (both employment-based and individually purchased) fell during the 1980s and early 1990s to less than 70 percent, before rebounding slightly in the strong economy of the late 1990s (Health Insurance Association of America 1996; Uninsured 2002). Employment-based protection was the biggest casualty: Between 1979 and 1998, the share of workers who received health insurance coverage from their own employers fell from 66 to 54 percent (Medoff and Calabrese 2000). At the same time, employers have grown less willing to cover workers' dependents and required that workers pay a larger share of the cost of coverage, which has discouraged some from taking coverage even when it is offered.

The result has been a marked rise in the proportion of Americans who are without health insurance (along with a lengthening of spells without insurance). For more than a decade, the number of Americans uninsured for the entire year has been rising by about 1 million a year and now hovers around 45 million, with some 75 million—one out of three nonelderly Americans—uninsured at some point during a two-year period (FamiliesUSA 2003). The vast majority of the uninsured are members of households with at least one head working.

The gravest effects have been felt by those most disadvantaged by the trends of the past three decades. The share of workers in the lowest 20 percent of the wage spectrum receiving health insurance from their employers fell from almost 42 percent to just over 26 percent between 1979 and 1998 (Medoff and Calabrese 2000), with workers lacking a high school degree experiencing a 35 percent drop in the probability of employment-based coverage. African Americans and Hispanics have been hit particularly hard: The share of the nonelderly with job-based coverage contracted by 18 percent among African Americans between 1977 and 1996, and by 28 percent among Hispanics—to 47.9 and 42.1 percent, respectively, versus 71 percent for whites (calculated from Gabel 1999). These trends reflect multiple factors, including declining unionization and changing employment patterns. But above all, they mirror the simple reality that medical costs have risen much faster than most workers' wages, outstripping the ability of workers (and their employers) to finance protection (Kronick and Gilmer 1999). With employers free to drop coverage, and workers under financial pressure to decline it even when it is offered, the risk of medical costs is being shifted from insurers and employers back onto workers and their families.

This view is reinforced when we consider one of the most fundamental transformations in American health insurance since the 1970s: the rise of 'self-insurance' among employers. As already discussed, corporate self-insurance—the paying of medical claims directly—was encouraged by the 1974 Employee Retirement Income Security Act (ERISA), the so-called preemption clause of which protects self-insured health plans from most state insurance regulations and lawsuits in state courts. But an additional crucial underlying motive for self-insurance has been the desire of larger employers to limit the cross-subsidization of the medical expenses of workers outside their own employment pool. Rather than purchase insurance from external companies that provide coverage to multiple firms (and, as noted, traditionally charged relatively similar rates to all subscribers), employers increasingly finance just their own workers' claims, thereby pooling risks within—and only within—their own labor force. Self-insurance has thus seriously worsened the situation of smaller employers, which have employment groups too small to self-insure safely, while encouraging private insurers to weed out subscribers with high expected costs. The chronically ill, near-elderly, and those with expensive conditions have all faced increasingly serious barriers to obtaining insurance as a result.

Meanwhile, employers (and in some cases unions, which jointly manage many self-insured plans) have joined with conservative politicians to beat back any attempt to revisit the provisions of ERISA that exempt self-insured health plans from regulation (Gottschalk 2000). The ERISA Industry Committee, an organization of large employers created in 1976, has been perhaps the most vociferous champion of the preemption clause, supporting 'legislation that preserves and strengthens ERISA preemption and reduces government interference with employers' efforts to provide cutting-edge, comprehensive health care benefits to their employees' (ERIC 2003). As a consequence, government regulation of private health plans has changed relatively little since the mid-1970s, despite a massive swing away from inclusive risk protection in the private sector.

Although Americans' prime source of health protection is eroding, public programs have largely failed to fill the gap and, in some key respects, have also eroded significantly. The Medicare program—a centerpiece of US social insurance—has essentially been caught in a holding pattern (Marmor 2000): Its popularity and the political strength of its beneficiaries, as well as the multiple veto points in the American political structure, have blocked radical retrenchment, but the program has grown increasingly inadequate as the health costs of the elderly have rapidly outstripped the program's constrained spending. In a striking demonstration of drift, beneficiaries pay more out of their own pockets for medical care today than they did at Medicare's passage (Moon 1993, 10–11). A benefit package that was roughly the norm in the mid-1960s is now far less generous than the private-sector standard. Employment-based coverage for retirees has also contracted, and the supplemental protection offered by private insurers has been in a tailspin, as insurers find that they cannot bear the large and concentrated financial risks Medicare does not cover. These risks are thus shifting by default to Medicare beneficiaries and their families.

Medicare has not been static, of course. But few of the changes made can be described as expansionary. Even the prescription drug benefit enacted in 2003 will cover only a very small share of seniors' expected drug expenses (while outlawing supplemental coverage that fills its huge gaps in protection). And other recent policy changes, including some contained within the 2003 prescription drug law itself, pose the possibility that the program's risk protection could deteriorate even further. The crucial example here is Medicare contracting with private health plans, an effort at policy layering that originated in demonstration projects first pursued by the Reagan administration. Conservatives have aggressively pursued the transformation of contracting into a full-fledged system of competing, risk-bearing private plans. To date, these efforts have been hampered by an essential contradiction: private plans have generally cost the program money, but the primary reform imperative is to contain spending. Yet for Medicare's critics, the creation of a more competitive system—in which the public component of Medicare competes with private plans, and in which the experience and premiums of beneficiaries vary greatly across these options—holds out the promise of fragmenting the Medicare risk pool and, with it, the unified constituency that has blocked direct benefit cuts in the past. Although studiously careful not to challenge Medicare directly, the strongest advocates of a competitive system clearly believe that the traditional program should, as Republican House Speaker Newt Gingrich infamously put in 1995, 'wither on the vine'. (Gingrich, in fact, was unusually candid about Medicare reformers' covert strategy, noting of Medicare that 'we don't get rid of it in Round One because we don't think it's politically smart', Clymer 1995.)

In contrast, coverage of the poor has unquestionably grown. This is clear in spending statistics, but the rapid growth of Medicaid spending is somewhat misleading, because it has only partially translated into coverage expansions. Still, coverage has indeed expanded: first with federally mandated extensions of Medicaid to additional categories of poor women and children in the 1980s, and, second, with the creation of the Children's Health Insurance (CHIP) program for uninsured kids in 1997. These were important expansions, all the more remarkable because they occurred in such a hostile climate. Before ending the story, however, two important points should be emphasized. First, as Figure 2.4 shows, the expansion of Medicaid has only partially offset the decline in private coverage. Second, the trend toward expanding coverage has at least temporarily run its course. After a period in which states controlled spending by enrolling beneficiaries in low-cost

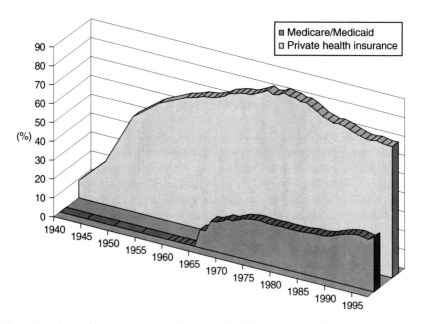

Figure 2.4 Share of Americans covered by private health insurance and Medicare/Medicaid, 1940–98

Note: Medicaid figures begin in 1968 and are not fully reliable until 1973.

Source: Compiled from Centers for Medicare & Medicaid Services, 'Medicare Enrollment: National Trends, 1966–2001'; US Census Bureau, table HI-7, 'Health Insurance Coverage Status and Type of Coverage by Age: 1987–2001'; Social Security Administration, *Annual Statistical Supplement, 2002* (Washington DC: SSA, 1998), p. 327; Health Insurance Association of America, *Source Book of Health Insurance Data* (Washington DC: HIAA, 1998), p. 39.

private plans, health care costs are rising rapidly again across-the-board. Even before the current economic downturn, enrollment in Medicaid had slowed dramatically. States are now actively using federal waivers to retool their programs in ways that are likely to increase the number of insured and to shift an increasing share of costs and risks onto covered populations. Finally, the 1996 welfare reform bill has created a massive exodus from the welfare rolls, and those who leave are moving into the low-wage employment sector, where private coverage is rare. Millions eligible for CHIP and Medicaid are not enrolled, and this is likely to become more true as the time limits on assistance in the welfare reform legislation kick in. While crucial in softening the blow of private-sector reversals, then, public coverage expansions appear more like band-aids on a festering wound than an inexorable expansion of public protection.

In strategic terms, critics of Medicaid have been greatly aided by the joint-federal-state structure of the program, which has facilitated cutbacks by fostering interstate competitive pressures in favor of budgetary stringency, while making cutbacks more difficult to identify and assign responsibility for. Since 2000, federal waivers have been aggressively used to encourage state-based program restructuring by the Bush administration, which also hopes to shift from the current guaranteed matching formula to so-called block grants, in which the states are provided a fixed amount of funds. Like Medicare reform, Medicaid block grants last became a major issue in the mid-1990s—when, as now, advocates of block grants espoused 'an ideological commitment to shrink the welfare state and return power to states from Washington' (Weaver 1996: 52).

No discussion of the recent evolution of US health insurance is complete without mention of the stunning defeat of the Clinton health plan—arguably the most dissected legislative failure in modern history. Rather than rehash this familiar saga, I wish simply to emphasize that it represents a paradigm example of politically mediated policy drift. The Clinton health plan and its major competitors reflected a recognition that the American policy of relying on voluntary employer provision of tax-subsidized health benefits was increasingly unworkable as a secure foundation for risk pooling. The opposition to the plan, centered among hardcore political conservatives, employers, insurers, and private medical interests, in turn reflected not simply the recognition that many of these groups would be immediately hurt by the plan, but also the awareness that its passage would create a new and valued entitlement for anxious middle-class and working-class voters whose long-term political allegiances were very much up for grabs. Thus conservative activist William Kristol warned that the Clinton plan would 'relegitimize middle-class dependence for "security" on government spending and regulation' and 'revive the reputation of . . . the Democrats . . . as the generous protector of middle-class interests' (quoted in Skocpol 1996: 145). On the other side, Clinton explicitly cast his crusade as an effort to undo the policy drift of the past two decades—drift that had created, in the words of the White House's Health Security report, 'growing insecurity'. 'From the 1940s through the 1970s', the report explained, 'the United States made steady progress toward broader health care coverage. . . . Beginning in the 1980s, however, the number of Americans lacking health insurance has increased steadily—while health care costs have increased at ever-rising rates' (Domestic Policy Council 1993: 2).

In the end, the Clinton health plan was brought down by much the same political dynamic that stymied conservatives' efforts to dismantle Medicare: the easily ignited fears of Americans that reform would compromise the health protections upon which they relied—in this case, employment-based insurance (Hacker 2002). But what is crucial to emphasize is that America's leaders fiercely debated whether the US social welfare framework would adapt to the changing job market and declines in private protection. The privatization of risk in American health care occurred without major policy reforms, but it was very much a matter of political struggle.

In sum, when one considers the broader framework of US risk protection, the direction of change is clearly toward a marked narrowing of the bounds of collective protection. To be sure, major public social programs have been preserved. The demise of conservative efforts to scale back Medicare and Medicaid in 1995, courtesy of the veto of a politically fortified President Clinton (Peterson 1998), is a powerful illustration of the hurdles thrown up by American political institutions and the enduring popularity of established programs. But resilience in the overall policy framework of American health insurance has not prevented a major shift in the distribution and intensity of the risks faced by citizens. The Medicare program has stagnated in the face of rapidly rising medical costs. The Medicaid program has expanded, but not nearly enough to offset the implosion of private coverage. There has been a massive decline in private health protection, which has increasingly ceased to be available or affordable for workers on the lower half of the pay scale and their dependents. Serious efforts to deal with this have been effectively blocked by a formidable constellation of ideologically committed opponents and vested interests. The outcome has been a significant privatization of risk.

Individualizing retirement security

The American approach to retirement security is also a public–private hybrid, blending public social insurance and employment-based benefits—and, increasingly, tax-favored savings accounts. But pension policy differs crucially from health policy in the respective roles of public and private benefits. Whereas Medicare and Medicaid emerged after the large-scale development of private health insurance, private retirement pensions were largely built on top of the public foundation of Social Security. This supplementary role was embodied most concretely in the practice of 'integration', in which employers that qualified for tax breaks for their private retirement plans were allowed to reduce pension benefits sharply for lower- and middle-income workers to reflect expected Social Security benefits. It was also embodied in the 1974 ERISA statute, which regulated private plans to ensure that they would be secure counterparts to the public foundation established by Social Security and even created a quasi-public insurance company to protect defined-benefit plans against insolvency. Put simply, while employers offered health insurance as workers' first line of defense, they offered retirement pensions to 'top off' expected Social Security benefits—a role sanctioned, regulated, and insured by the federal government. Thus, in its underlying structure— guaranteed, insured benefits based on earnings and years spent working—the private pension system looked very much like the public, though it was much more favorable to the highly paid than was Social Security.

The core role that Social Security continues to play in America's public–private system of social benefits has put opponents of the welfare state in a different strategic position in the pension realm than in the health insurance domain. In health policy, critics of the welfare state have mainly had to play a defensive role, preventing the expansion of public protections to cover those ill-served by the predominantly private insurance system. In pension policy, by contrast, conservatives have had to work much more actively to introduce new measures that undercut Social Security's primary role—in a context, moreover, in which employers' basic commitment to private retirement provision has seriously eroded. As a result, changes in the pension realm have more frequently taken the form of 'layering' than in the health insurance domain, as conservatives have assiduously championed the creation of new tax breaks for individualized retirement benefits and the alteration of rules governing private pensions to encourage a shift away from traditional fixed-benefit pension structures toward higher-risk investment accounts.

In this effort, critics of Social Security have benefited from two larger trends. First, since the economic slowdown of the 1970s, Social Security has been under serious financial pressure, both because slower wage growth has reduced the revenues of the payroll tax-financed program and because the number of workers who are paying into the system has decreased while the number of retirees collecting benefits has increased. This reversal of fortune has made Social Security the target of repeated calls for overhaul, facilitating the passage of two major packages of reform legislation, in 1977 and 1983. While preserving the program, these reforms have effectively ended its postwar expansion.

Second, employers have rapidly shifted away from the traditional 'defined-benefit' plans that were the subject of ERISA. Instead, they have adopted so-called defined-contribution plans that are not tied to Social Security and, unlike defined-benefit plans, place most of the risk of investment decisions onto workers. Although this momentous transformation is mostly a case of conversion, in that employers have restructured their plans within relatively stable federal rules, it is important to note that defined-contribution plans were enabled and greatly encouraged by new tax subsidies and regulatory requirements that were layered onto existing policies during periods of conservative ascendance in the late 1970s, early 1980s, and late 1990s, as well as after Bush's 2000 victory. As in the health insurance field, there has also been a major decline in employer support for retirement protection—and, in tandem, a major privatization of risk.

As Figure 2.5 shows, employer pension contributions have significantly decreased as a share of compensation since the 1970s. (Benefits, however, have continued to rise, as workers covered in the past enter retirement.) Like the decline in private health insurance, the fall in pension contributions is symptomatic of the broader reversals in the economic outlook of less-educated workers. The likelihood that a worker's employer will offer a pension plan decreases dramatically with income, as does the probability that a worker will actually be included in a plan (Silverman and Yakoboski 1994: 8). This disparity is growing more pronounced: Between the early 1980s and the mid-1990s, the value of pension benefits to current workers dropped in every income group, but by far most rapidly among the lowest paid workers (Pierce 1998). In addition, tax breaks for private pensions and other retirement savings options increasingly favor better-paid employees, for whom the value of tax exemptions and the likelihood and generosity of private protections are greatest. Current Treasury data show that two-thirds of the nearly $100 billion in federal tax breaks for subsidized retirement savings options, including Individual Retirement Accounts (IRAs), accrue to the top 20 percent of the population, while only 12 percent accrue to the bottom 60 percent (Orzag 2000).

Although the post-1970s economic transformation deserves the lion's share of responsibility for these forms of drift and conversion, its impact has been deeply mediated by politics. The tax and deficit battles of the 1980s signaled the beginning of an ongoing tug-of-war between two increasingly homogenized and polarized parties, with Republicans seeking to create and liberalize individual

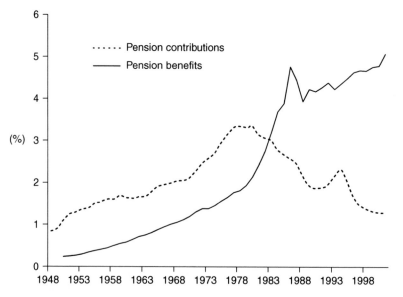

Figure 2.5 Pension contributions and benefits, as a less share of compensation, 1948–2001
Source: Author's calculation from National Income and Product Accounts.

retirement options and Democrats fighting to place new restrictions on existing pension tax subsidies and limit the top-heavy skew of individual accounts. The overall thrust of policy has nonetheless been in the more conservative direction— toward the expansion of tax-favored plans and toward the loosening of restrictions both on eligibility for them and on the purposes for which they can be used.

The path of IRAs illustrates the overall pattern. Included in the 1974 ERISA legislation as a retirement savings device available only to workers without private coverage, IRAs were expanded and made available to all workers in the early 1980s. Though saddled with new eligibility restrictions during the loophole-closing Tax Reform Act of 1986, IRAs were subsequently liberalized again, permissible uses of the accounts were broadened to include education and housing expenses, and a new plan—called the 'Roth IRA' after its chief sponsor, Republican Senator William Roth—was created that would require account holders to pay taxes up front and then avoid all future taxes on their accounts (including estate taxes). Since, at the time, the vast majority of Americans already had incomes low enough to establish traditional IRAs, the main effect of these changes has been to make tax-favored accounts even more available and attractive to upper-income households.

The story of so-called 401(k) plans is different but similar (the full story can be found in Hacker 2002: 164–72). 401(k) plans are defined-contribution plans that operate under section 401(k) of the tax code—a provision added with little debate in 1978, apparently to clarify the status of certain types of profit-sharing plans that had been under Treasury Department scrutiny. In 1981, a private benefits expert pressed the IRS to rule that the provision extended to pension plans in which workers voluntarily put aside their own wages, much as in an IRA. The Reagan IRS agreed, and corporate sponsorship of 401(k) plans exploded. In 2001, as part of President George W. Bush's tax reduction plan, Republicans successfully pressed for further dramatic liberalization of 401(k)s and IRAs and the creation of 'Roth 401(k)s' similar to Roth IRAs.[11]

Though virtually unnoticed by political analysts, the explosive growth of 401(k) plans and IRAs over the past decade represents one of the most important developments in the political history of US pension policy. During the 1980s, contributions to IRAs, 401(k)s, and Keogh plans for the self-employed rose dramatically (Venti and Wise 1997: 85). By 1994, contributions to 401(k)s exceeded contributions to all other types of plans combined, and they continue to grow (Scheiber and Shoven 1999: 355). Not surprisingly, the assets of 401(k)s and IRAs have expanded at a breathtaking pace, as Figure 2.6 indicates.

Behind this transformation lies a new conception of pensions, for these retirement accounts have few of the characteristics of either Social Security or older defined-benefit plans. Unlike traditional pensions, these accounts are voluntary for individual workers. Participants have a significant degree of control over investment choices, and benefits are often paid as a lump sum upon employment separation or achievement of a specific age and, increasingly, can be accessed for purposes besides retirement. Because these accounts are voluntary, many younger and poorer employees who are offered them choose not to participate or

66   *J. S. Hacker*

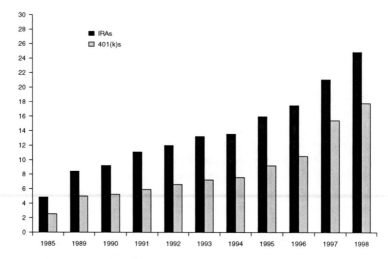

Figure 2.6 IRA and 401(k) plan assets, as a percentage of GDP, 1985–98

Source: US Census Bureau, *Statistical Abstract of the United States* (Washington DC: US GPO, 1999), tables 851 and 852; IRA and 401(k) information for 1997 and 1998, from Investment Company Institute, *Mutual Funds and the Retirement Market in 2002* (Washington DC: Investment Company Institute, 2003), figures 5 and 13, available at http://www.ici.org. Historical GDP data from Congressional Budget Office. *The Budget and Economic Outlook: Fiscal Years 2004–2013* (Washington DC: CBO, 2003, appendix F, table 11).

contribute little. The risk of poor investment decisions or bad financial luck falls entirely on participants—as became painfully clear in the wake of the recent stock market downturn.[12] And most lump-sum distributions are not spent on a retirement annuity or rolled over into other retirement savings vehicles (Bassett, Fleming, and Rodrigues 1998).

Another characteristic that IRAs and 401(k) plans share is their attractiveness to higher-income workers. Because eligibility, participation, and contributions all rise dramatically with income, highly paid workers account for a disproportionate share of total 401(k) contributions. As Figure 2.7 shows, for upper-income workers, private 401(k) holdings and traditional pension assets already dwarf the amount that these workers are legally entitled to receive from Social Security. Indeed, if 401(k) assets continue to grow as in the past (a seemingly dubious assumption at the moment), it will be just a quarter century before the majority of workers receive the majority of retirement income from 401(k) plans. By this time, as the figure demonstrates, the top 20 percent of workers on the income ladder will receive six times as much from 401(k) plans as from Social Security. Even partial movement in this direction would represent a sweeping shift of risk from organized providers, both public and private, to individuals and their families.

The strength of the stock market in the 1990s obviously helps explain the enthusiasm for individualized investment accounts. But the shift must also be seen as rooted in linked economic and political developments of the

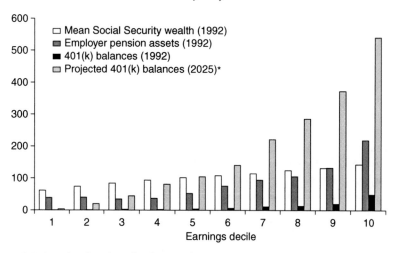

Figure 2.7 Actual and projected retirement income streams, 1992, 2025 (in thousands of 1992 dollars)

*If 100 percent of accounts in assets, assuming historical rates of return on assets and past trends in eligibility and contributions.

Source: James A. Poterba, Steven F. Venti, and David A. Wise (1998). 401(k) Plans and Future Patterns of Retirement Savings. *AEA Papers and Proceedings* 88: 2, 182–3.

past two decades. By the 1980s, defined-benefits pension no longer offered the attractions to employers that they had in the more stable employment climate of the 1950s and 1960s, with its strict managerial hierarchies and large unionized manufacturing firms. Nor, as Social Security's tax-to-benefit ratio grew less favorable, did employers have a strong incentive to set up integrated plans whose expense would be partially offset by the federal program.

No less important, however, are the underlying political motives that lie behind the expansion of private accounts. For years, conservatives despaired of ever effectively challenging Social Security. Even at the height of Reagan's influence in the early 1980s, the conservative push for reform was quickly crushed by the weight of past programmatic choices (Pierson 1994). These past defeats, however, fostered a new awareness on the part of conservative critics that Social Security could only be fundamentally reformed if there existed a 'parallel system' of private individual accounts that could eventually be portrayed as a viable alternative to the public program (Butler and Germanis 1983: 551, 553). Conservatives therefore retooled their strategy to encourage private retirement savings through ever more flexible and individualized means, acclimating Americans to private accounts and layering the institutional infrastructure for a full-fledged private system on top of the core public program of Social Security. Moving away from the traditional conservative call for cuts and income-testing, they increasingly stressed the positive-sum benefits of privatization—a message that capitalized on Social Security's declining position and the increased familiarity with private accounts to promise a pain-free transition away from an imperiled and antiquated system.

The motives for this approach have been carefully analyzed by Stephen Teles (1998), who argues that 'conservatives have slowly built up counter-institutions, counter-experts, and counter-ideas . . . [in] an attempt to solve the political problem of social security privatization'. The core of this strategy, Teles concludes, was to 'carve out a competing policy path, one that would slowly undermine support for Social Security and preserve the idea of privatization for the day when it was politically ripe' (Teles 1998: 14–15). This is *layering* par excellence.

Whether this strategy will yield its ultimate prize remains a very open question. As President George W. Bush has already learned, the reluctance of elected politicians to consider plans for even partial privatization of Social Security is overwhelming—all the more so, in light of the recent federal budgetary turnaround. The difficulty of reforming mature pay-as-you-go-pension systems, which stems from the powerful expectations and huge accumulated fiscal commitments they embody, stands out as the ultimate example of programmatic path dependence (Weaver 1998).

Nonetheless, the daunting barriers to conservative-backed reform should not blind us to the significant change that has already occurred. As corporations and individuals have shifted to more individualized plans, the explicit links between the public and private systems have steadily eroded, undermining some of the self-reinforcing mechanisms that previously secured Social Security's privileged position. Once tightly integrated with a program that offered a tremendous deal to all, private plans now increasingly stand alone—a constant reminder to the well-paid workers most likely to benefit from them that Social Security's weakened fiscal position (and redistributive benefit formula) precludes the high returns that similarly situated workers earned in the past, or that their own private retirement accounts earned during the recent boom. And most American employers have lost their direct stake in the program's health, as their own plans have broken off from the public pension core around which they previously revolved. These transformations are perhaps most visible in the changing balance of public and private pension benefits—a balance that, as Figure 2.8 shows, tilted toward the private side of the scale for the first time in the 1980s. Whatever else the end of Social Security's reign as the prime provider of retirement income foretells, it clearly signals a major privatization of risk.

Rethinking retrenchment

In the end, then, the conventional story about retrenchment appears only half right. The path dependence of large-scale social welfare interventions is undeniable. Yet the *character* of path dependence has varied greatly across different programs and policy domains. In some, such as Social Security, path dependence has implied relative stability both in formal policies and their outcomes. In others, such as employer-provided benefits and some state-based programs, formal policies have

Figure 2.8 Occupational pension and old-age insurance benefits, as a share of combined benefits, 1950–2001

Source: Private and public occupational plan data calculated from National Income and Product Accounts; Social Security data include only old-age and survivors insurance benefits and come from Social Security Administration (SSA), *Social Security Bulletin Annual Statistical Supplement* (Washington DC: SSA, 2002), table 4.A.5.

been relatively stable but outcomes have not. A critical explanation for this difference is that policy departures in these latter areas could occur without active policy change, because formal policy structures created opportunities for unilateral (or near-unilateral) action by the administrators, sponsors, or providers of benefits. At least as important as active policy conversion of this sort, however, are politically rooted failures of public action—which retrenchment studies, focused as they are on large-scale policy reform, have largely failed to examine. Even as the scope of risk protection provided by the American social welfare framework eroded in crucial domains, policy responses intended to close the growing gap caused by policy drift were repeatedly stymied.[13]

By no means is this the last word on recent trends in American social protection. The need for comprehensive data on the ground-level effects of risk-protection policies is pressing, and scholars have only started to move toward assembling the types of evidence that might allow more conclusive answers.[14] More studies of specific policy areas must be done, examining not only trends in social risks affecting workers and families, but also varying welfare state responses to these trends. Nor, I want to stress, is the foregoing intended as a refutation of research on welfare state retrenchment that shows that big programmatic reforms have been rare. My point is not that public social programs and policies in the

United States have been radically scaled back, but that, for a variety of reasons, their ability to achieve the goals embodied in them has noticeably weakened. This is an argument that, while not-infrequently advanced, has not been intensively interrogated, and its elaboration and refinement could go a long way toward reconciling the conflicting views that continue to characterize the burgeoning body of research on welfare state reform.

The experience of the United States suggests the considerable utility of this shift in focus, demonstrating a general pattern that I have described as 'privatization of risk without privatization of the welfare state' (Hacker 2004). Although public social programs have indeed largely resisted the political and economic onslaught of recent decades, efforts to update them to changing social risks have failed (*drift*), their ground-level operation has shifted in directions at odds with their initial goals (*conversion*), and new policies that subvert or threaten them have been put in place (*layering*). The result has been a significant erosion of the American framework of social protection, despite the absence of many dramatic instances of policy reform. Since the American experience is widely considered to be the strongest evidence of welfare state resilience in the face of fierce and ongoing conservative opposition, this itself is a notable finding. But it also carries lessons for our understanding of the process of welfare state restructuring in other nations, and for the character, cause, and consequence of policy reform more generally.

The erosion of shared risk in the American social welfare system presents, in extreme form, a transformation taking place in many affluent democracies (Esping-Andersen 1999). Based on the US case, three reasons for the disjuncture between the aspiration of risk protection and the reality appear crucial. The first is the cause highlighted by Esping-Andersen and others: the rise of new or newly intensified risks, which have strained the capacity of existing social welfare frameworks. This, however, is mostly an argument about the effects of exogenous shocks. To the extent that it concerns the politics of reform, its focus is explaining welfare state responses to external challenges. Yet I have highlighted two key respects in which the gap between risks and policies grows directly out of the politics of welfare state restructuring. First, while the literature on retrenchment has focused on active legislative reform, considerable evidence suggests that changes in policy purposes and operation have occurred even in cases where formal policy structures have been relatively stable. Conversion of this sort is especially likely, I have argued, when policies lack powerful support coalitions and when program structures embody principal–agent relationships that leave substantial control over the delivery of benefits to institutions and organizations other than the elected authorities charged with establishing basic policy rules.

Why change of this form has been mostly in the direction of restricted protection is an important question. In the case of subnational policymaking bodies, there are of course the well-known constraints on redistributive spending that states face due to interstate competition for capital and skilled labor (Peterson 1981). But the changing orientation of front-line policy actors, such as caseworkers, also shows up as crucial in existing research (e.g. Levy and Michel 2002), and much more needs to be done to understand the diversity of state responses. In the case of employment-based benefits, the reasons for the retreat from inclusive risk protection may appear far more obvious. Yet it was employers, after all, who constructed the extensive private systems of risk socialization that they are now so busy dismantling. Their abandonment of the old order appears to reflect not just the rising cost of past approaches and economic changes that have undermined the value of private benefits for corporate strategies, but also the absence of effective ideological or political counterweights in either the halls of government or the private sector. The weakening of organized labor may not imperil the welfare state, but in the world of private benefits, the precipitous decline of American unions does seem to matter greatly.

The second cause of risk privatization that is endogenous to the politics of reform is precisely the fierce assault on public social programs that Pierson (1994, 1996) and others have seen as ultimately so ineffectual. My reason for highlighting conservatives' ability to reframe the debate over social policy and block new initiatives is not that I wish to equate these dimensions of accomplishment with the large-scale reforms that retrenchment studies have searched for (and found mostly lacking). Although I believe that US conservatives have been more successful than received scholarly wisdom acknowledges in layering onto existing programs self-reinforcing incremental reforms that could prompt more fundamental changes down the line, my essential argument is simply that, in a context where social risks are changing and policy drift is ubiquitous and consequential, *conservatives have not had to enact major policy reforms to move toward many of their favored ends.* Merely by delegitimizing and blocking compensatory interventions designed to correct policy drift or ameliorate intensified risks, opponents of the welfare state in the United States have gradually transformed the orientation of social policy. The struggle over the welfare state has not simply been concerned whether programs will be cut or scrapped; it has also concerned the degree to which social policies will uphold long-standing goals and adapt to the world around them. We vastly understate the strength of the welfare state's opponents if we do not see the extent to which they have succeeded in this latter debate.

As I have argued, this 'second face' (Bachrach and Baratz 1962) of conservative influence exposes an important soft spot in retrenchment scholarship. Retrenchment studies have argued that fragmented constitutional structures, such as the United States', have very different implications in the era of retrenchment than they did in the era of expansion: The same institutional fragmentation and multiple veto points that once hindered the passage of large-scale social programs now present an effective barrier to conservative attempts at retrenchment (Pierson 1994; Huber and Stephens 2001; Swank 2001). Yet this argument does not go far enough in acknowledging the conditional character of institutional effects. In the United States since the late 1970s, conservatives have had two central projects—cutting back existing policies and preventing new initiatives or the updating of existing ones—and while institutional fragmentation has indeed hindered the former project, it has facilitated the blocking activities that are the central strategic element of the latter. Furthermore, a strong argument can be made that US institutional fragmentation, though it has created multiple veto points, has also created multiple 'venues' (Baumgartner and Jones 1993) in which conservatives can pursue their aims. And fragmentation has also hindered efforts by defenders of existing programs to undo the policy drift and parallel policy paths that result.

More generally, as we shift our gaze beyond episodes of large-scale retrenchment to take in processes of welfare state adaptation (or failures of adaptation, as the US case seems to be), the political struggles that we find bring together the 'old' and 'new' politics of the welfare state in interesting ways. In the battle to scale-back existing programs, we see the new politics writ large: the perilous obstacle course of institutional veto points, public loss aversion, and mobilized welfare state constituencies. Yet when we begin to consider the ways in which welfare states have responded to shifting constellations of risk and the weakened ability of established systems of social provision to cope with them, we see more affinities between present political struggles and those that lay behind the welfare state's rise. There is good reason to believe, for example, that the power of leftist parties and organized labor—and of emergent pro-welfare state forces like feminist coalitions—are quite important in determining whether and how welfare states adapt to new social realities. And, as just discussed, there is also good reason to believe that the political-institutional factors that help explain the size and scope of existing social welfare frameworks have effects similar to those that they had in the past on contemporary efforts to upgrade existing policies. The crucial difference between the past and the present—and here the 'new politics' indeed looms large—is that current struggles take place in the shadows of massive systems of social provision, which pervasively shape both the challenges and the opportunities that today's leaders confront.

If this argument is on the mark, then a crucial priority for work on welfare state reform is to better specify the relationship between processes of path dependence and sources of institutional change. Promising theorizing along these lines has appeared in recent years, much of it advanced by historical-institutional scholars, including Pierson himself (see, in particular, Thelen 1999, 2003; Mahoney 2000; Pierson forthcoming). These scholars have increasingly stressed that path dependence does not preclude change but instead systematically conditions it. This argument has begun to correct the strong tendency in previous historical-institutional research to privilege stability in description and explanation and therefore treat institutional change as exogenous. What is emerging is a more variable and dynamic conception of path dependence, which not only embodies a more precise specification of the factors that encourage path dependence, but also sees certain kinds of institutional changes as internally generated. In this view, institutional or policy frameworks that are path-dependent exhibit strong continuities over time, but those continuities emerge out of the dynamic behavior of agents within an evolving matrix of incentives and constraints that facilitates some changes even while hindering others.

The progress of welfare state reform suggests the considerable value of this turn in historical-institutional theorizing. The US social welfare framework is scarcely 'locked in', and yet there can be no denying the political struggles that now surround it have been profoundly conditioned by the legacies of past choices. The evidence is most striking in the realm of large-scale public social programs, which are typically characterized by the full roster of factors that theorists associate with path dependence—large set-up costs, sizable organized constituencies, long-lived commitments (Arthur 1988; North 1990; Pierson 2000; Hacker 2002: 52–8). Yet while path dependence has been most evident with regard to public programs, the concept is at least equally relevant to the study of policies designed to encourage and bolster private social benefits (such as tax expenditures for employment-based health insurance), which have resisted cutbacks at least as effectively as public social programs, even as their costs have grown (Hacker 2002). These policies have survived and thrived not only because of their low visibility, but also because, even more than public programs, their supporters extend beyond the circle of direct beneficiaries to include highly organized and resourceful sponsors and providers of benefits. In both the public and private realms of US social policy, therefore, change has been quite clearly bounded, just as work on path dependence would predict.

Yet path dependence has not meant stasis, and here we reach an important area of weakness in existing scholarship. Path dependence claims have mostly centered on explaining broad stability in institutional frameworks. Yet even relatively stable institutions may create highly unstable outcomes, depending on their character and context. Too often, as retrenchment studies suggest, claims about institutional stability slip without warning or reflection into claims about outcomes stability. This is a perilous conflation, particularly when—as in the retrenchment literature— the subject of study encompasses both institutional reforms (has the welfare state changed?) and institutional consequences (is the welfare state less progressive in its effects?).

More to the point, the ultimate subject of claims about path dependence is not institutional continuity as such but the forces that account for it, and these forces are themselves crucial sources of insight into the potential scope for institutional change. This contention owes much to Thelen's suggestion that theorists of path dependence who are interested in explaining change should try to identify the 'mechanisms of reproduction' that anchor enduring institutions, because these are also an institution's crucial points of vulnerability (Thelen 2003). Yet the issue is broader than this. Mechanisms of reproduction should not only help us identify points of vulnerability. Ideally, they should allow us to formulate expectations about the *character* of changes that are likely to occur.

The evolution of private social benefits in the United States provides a fertile field for the application of this strategy. As I have argued, policies encouraging and shaping private benefits have strong tendencies toward path dependence. As with large-scale public social programs, citizens have come to depend on private benefits, and powerful expectations, interests, and constituencies have arisen around them. This has simultaneously made certain changes extremely difficult (national health insurance, mandates on employers) *and* shifted the agenda for reform toward policies that attempt to work around or bolster existing workplace benefits (Hacker 2002). Yet the nature of path dependence in this realm is distinct. Because policies encouraging private benefits allow considerable discretion on the part of private actors, they allow substantial changes *within* the confines of existing policy. Furthermore, nongovernmental actors working within these often loose constraints do not have to engage in collective political action to achieve their ends. If they are able to overcome internal resistance, they can adopt changes unilaterally (on this general point, see Wood 2001: 374). As a result, private social benefits have proved extremely unstable even while the overall policy framework that governs them has been highly change-resistant.

Moreover, as we have seen, the role that private benefits play in a particular policy area—whether they serve as the core source of benefits, as in health policy, or as a supplementary source, as in pension policy—influences the reform strategies that opponents of the welfare state adopt in the precise fashion that a path-dependence framework suggests it should. When private benefits play a core role, opponents need only play defense, keeping new state interventions at bay and abetting externally caused policy drift. When private benefits are supplementary, however, much more active use of government power is required to encourage the expansion of private options and undercut public programs, as evidenced by conservatives' layering of new tax breaks onto existing policies in the pension policy area.

Using arguments about path dependence to probe the latitude for institutional change opens up two potentially fruitful avenues of research in work on welfare state reform. The first would take scholars deeper into the internal structure of programs, applying arguments about the policy effects of alternative political institutions to the program-specific decision procedures and relations of delegation through which formal policy decisions are translated into ground-level effects. The second avenue of research would press scholars to identify and conceptualize the specific sources of resilience enjoyed by existing systems of social protection. What is it that sustains a regnant social program? What kind of changes are likely and unlikely given these underlying bases of support and under what conditions? One means to connect these two approaches would be to think more seriously about the long-term strategies of those who seek to restructure social policies. As I have argued, there is good reason to think that insurgents will be cognizant of at least some of the constraints and opportunities that path dependence claims highlight, and that they will craft their strategies in response. That we see conservatives in the United States trying to construct alternative paths of policy by exploiting gaps between rules and effects and searching out vulnerabilities in existing programs is perhaps the best evidence that recent work on path dependence can illuminate our understanding of change as well as stability.

To this end, this chapter has outlined a general framework for studying policy change that suggests that the strategies chosen by opponents of existing policies are shaped by the relative costs of working within an existing policy framework to achieve their goals or of supplanting the framework through authoritative political change. This strategic calculation suggests that, in political settings that make authoritative change difficult, insurgents may not seek formal revision of policies whose operation and aims are highly convertible, but may instead work to alter such policies through active internal reform or the blocking of adaptation to external circumstances. Although I used this framework to illuminate the strategies of opponents of the welfare state—and, in turn, to question the conclusion that there has been limited retrenchment of US social policy—the argument has much broader applicability. Indeed, it suggests a novel solution to the old rational choice conundrum 'Why so much stability?' (Tullock 1981) that does not rest on ad hoc distinctions between institutions and outcomes (Riker 1980), or on claims about the inherent uncertainty of reform (Shepsle 1986). Rather, this framework suggests that choices about policy design are not equivalent to preferences regarding states of the world simply because policies can be used to achieve multiple ends. Policy reformers always face the fundamental question of whether the sacrifices to their aims that they must make to work within an existing policy structure outweigh the political costs of undertaking formal revision.

This framework is well supported by my in-depth analyses of pension and health policy. Faced with the high political costs caused by America's status-quo biased political institutions and the high conversion costs caused by rule-bound policies and powerful support coalitions, conservative opponents of the welfare state have turned to strategies designed to abet policy drift, eroding long-standing programs like Medicare by reducing tax revenues and blocking efforts to adapt existing policies to shifting social risks. When the support coalitions behind policies have proved weaker or the latitude for internal change greater, they have turned to strategies of internal conversion, changing policies' aims or operation without significantly changing their formal structure. The decline of private benefits and the use of waivers to retool social assistance programs each represent examples of such conversion. And when the political costs have declined in response to favorable electoral or political winds, they have successfully layered new policies, such as tax subsidies for individualized private benefits, on top of existing change-resistant programs. As the framework would suggest, layering has proved particularly important in pension policy, where the core public program of social protection, Social Security, has well-specified aims and clear lines of authority and enjoys powerful bases of support—and thus is highly resistant to the sort of internal conversion found in other policy areas.

The pursuit of theoretical advances should not, however, cause us to lose sight of the ultimate concern: the changing role of the welfare state in the lives of citizens. In the new climate of economic and family risks, the welfare state has had to run to stay still—to do more merely secure past gains. In the United States, it has not done more, and when we examine the broader framework of American social protection, a strong case can be made that it has done less. The scholarship on retrenchment has offered strong reassurance to those who believe the welfare state is an essential element of a just society. My analysis raises the possibility, however, that formal welfare state policies may turn out to be more resilient than the ideals embodied in them.

Notes

1. For helpful comments on earlier versions of this chapter, I thank Benjamin Cashore, Philip Manow, Kimberly Morgan, Paul Pierson, Kathleen Thelen, Wolfgang Streeck, and Kent Weaver, as well as participants in workshops at Brandeis University and Ohio State University. Nelson Gerew, Rachel Goodman, Pearline Kyi, Joanne Lim, Julia Sheketoff, and Tova Serkin provided able research assistance; Nigar Nargis helped develop the index of income volatility; David Jesuit, Vincent Mahler, and Timothy Smeeding kindly supplied me with unpublished data on income redistribution; and, finally, the Peter Strauss Fund, Yale Institution for Social and Policy Studies, and the William Milton Fund of the Harvard Medical School granted financial support.
2. On 'drift', see Douglas Rae's discussion of 'utility drift' in Rae, Douglas (1975). The Limits of Consensual Decision. *American Political Science Review* 69(4): 1270–94. Policy drift was also clearly recognized by Hugh Heclo in his classic *Modern Social Politics in Britain and Sweden*. Heclo, Hugh (1974). *Modern Social Politics in Britain and Sweden*. New Haven, CT: Yale University Press. Heclo writes of Swedish Pension Act of 1913 (p. 211): 'In large part, it was precisely because this basic framework remained unaltered in the midst of changing circumstances that the framers' intentions were unconsciously subverted. As noted throughout this volume, one of the easiest ways to change a policy is to fail to change a program to accord with the movement of events.' I am grateful to Kent Weaver for this citation.
3. In some respects, this chapter is an attempt to revisit Pierson's rather weakly explored arguments about 'systemic retrenchment'. For the most part, however, the changes I describe fall between systemic and programmatic retrenchment, involving the creation of new policies, internal changes that occur without formal revision, and erosion of programs in the face of external change.
4. To be fair to Pierson, he has acknowledged some of these limits. Pierson, Paul (ed.) (2001). *The New Politics of the Welfare State*. Oxford: Oxford University Press. Pierson, Paul (2002). A Quiet Revolution?: Long-Term Processes and Welfare State Restructuring. Paper read at Transforming the Democratic Balance among State, Market and Society: Comparative Perspectives on France and the Developed Democracies, May 17–18, at Center for European Studies. In response to claims that Britain did arguably experience a system shift in the 1980s, he has also conceded that he underestimated the extent of retrenchment there.
5. See in particular Paul Pierson (1994). *Dismantling the Welfare State?* Cambridge: Cambridge University Press, p. 5 ('[T]his study is . . . [about] changes in social programs. Changes in the welfare state have in most cases been less significant than substantial continuities in policy').
6. Thus Evelyne Huber and John Stephens, in their recent comprehensive study of welfare state growth and reform, limit their definition of retrenchment to policy changes that decrease the degree to which welfare states redistribute from rich to poor and from men to women, and changes in the redistributive and antipoverty effects of the welfare state are the only outcome measures that they consider. Evelyn Huber and John Stephens (2001). *Development and Crisis of the welfare State*. Chicago, IL: University of Chicago Press.

7. Indeed, the prominence of social insurance suggests that the welfare state is not simply a device for redistribution, but also, and perhaps more centrally, a response to weaknesses of private markets in covering certain risks. Baldwin, Peter (1990). *The Politics of Social Solidarity: Class Bases of the European Welfare State, 1875–1975.* Cambridge: Cambridge University Press; Barr, Nicholas (1998). *The Economics of the Welfare State*, 3rd edn. Oxford: Oxford University Press; Iversen, Torben and David Soskice (2001). An Asset Theory of Social Policy Preferences. *American Political Science Review* 95(4): 875–93; Moene, Karl Ove and Michael Wallerstein (2001). Inequality, Social Insurance, and Redistribution. *American Political Science Review* 95(4): 859–74.

8. 'Risk-individualization' might be a better description than 'risk-privatization', given that—in theory, at least—risks can be socialized under private as well as public auspices. Nonetheless, the process of shifting responsibility for social provision from collectivities onto citizens is typically referred to as 'privatization'; I see no reason to refrain from adopting that common usage here. Moreover, 'risk-individualization' is not entirely accurate as a description of these shifts either, for they push risks onto households far more than onto individuals. I am grateful to Kimberly Morgan for highlighting this concern.

9. Recognizing the shortcomings of cross-sectional data on redistribution, some scholars have begun to turn to an alternative source of evidence on social welfare effects: panel studies of income dynamics. Burkhauser, Richard V. and Greg J. Duncan (1991). United States Public Policy and the Elderly: The Disproportionate Risk to the Well-Being of Women. *Journal of Population Economics* 4: 217–31; DiPrete, Thomas A. and Patricia A. McManus (2000). Family Change, Employment Transitions, and the Welfare State: Household Income Dynamics in the United States and Germany. *American Sociological Review* 65(3): 343–70; Goodin, Robert E., Bruce Headey, Ruud Muffels, and Henk-Jan Dirven (1999). *The Real Worlds of Welfare Capitalism.* Cambridge, UK: Press Syndicate of the Cambridge University Press. These are studies that repeatedly interview the same families and individuals over many years—in the case of the longest such study, the US Panel Study of Income Dynamics, over more than thirty years. Unfortunately, only a small handful of studies attempt to use panel income data to analyze the effects of welfare states. Moreover, although this research is longitudinal, it does not at present allow for assessments about change over time (the only exception is the preliminary findings reported shortly). Even those who have limited their attention to the US data have lumped together all the years that they analyze. This prevents any conclusions about the change in income dynamics over time, or the extent to which public policies have contributed to it.

10. In all these figures, we assess variability in income against the baseline over-time trend in family income, so general income gains are factored out of these findings.

11. Among other changes, the legislation more than doubles IRA contribution limits, increases 401(k) limits significantly, and indexes both to inflation—all revisions of particular benefit to high-income workers.

12. The spectacular collapse of Enron in 2001 highlights another risk: the potential for massive losses that arises when accounts are invested too heavily in the stock of the employer sponsoring a plan.

13. Ironically, the best example of policy updating is welfare reform, which translated the increasing expectation that mothers should work into an elimination of the entitlement to cash benefits for poor parents.

14. Along with Nigar Nargis, I am currently in the process of putting together a data set based on the PSID that I hope will allow more detailed statistical analyses of the changing risk-protection effects of public and private social transfers. For access to our preliminary findings, see my website: http://pantheon.yale.edu/~jhacker.

References

ADEMA, WILLEM and MARCEL EINERHAND (1998). *The Growing Role of Private Social Benefits*. Paris: Organization for Economic Cooperation and Development.

ARTHUR, W. BRIAN (1988). Self-Reinforcing Mechanisms in Economics. In: D. Pines (ed.), *The Economy as an Evolving Complex System*. Reading, MA: Addison-Wesley.

BACHRACH, PETER and MORTON S. BARATZ (1962). The Two Faces of Power. *American Political Science Review* 56(3): 942.

BALDWIN, PETER (1990). *The Politics of Social Solidarity: Class Bases of the European Welfare State, 1875–1975*. Cambridge: Cambridge University Press.

BARR, NICHOLAS (1998). *The Economics of the Welfare State*, 3rd edn. Oxford: Oxford University Press.

BASSETT, WILLIAM F., MICHAEL J. FLEMING, and ANTHONY P. RODRIGUES (1998). How Workers Use 401(k) Plans: Their Participation, Contribution, and Withdrawal Decisions. *National Tax Journal* 51(2): 263–89.

BAUMGARTNER, FRANK R. and BRYAN D. JONES (1993). *Agendas and Instability in American Politics*. Chicago, IL: University of Chicago Press.

BLACKBURN, MCKINLEY L., DAVID E. BLOOM, and RICHARD B. FREEMAN (1990). The Declining Economic Position of Less Skilled American Men. In: G. Burtless (ed.), *A Future of Lousy Jobs? The Changing Structure of U.S. Wages*. Washington DC: The Brookings Institution.

BONOLI, GIULIANO, VIC GEORGE, and PETER TAYLOR-GOOBY (2000). *European Welfare Futures*. Cambridge, UK: Polity Press in association with Blackwell Publishers Ltd.

BURKHAUSER, RICHARD V. and GREG J. DUNCAN (1991). United States Public Policy and the Elderly: The Disproportionate Risk to the Well-Being of Women. *Journal of Population Economics* 4: 217–31.

BUTLER, STUART, and PETER GERMANIS (1983). Achieving Social Security Reform: A 'Leninist' Strategy. *Cato Journal* 3(2): 547–56.

CAMPBELL, ANDREA LOUISE (2003). *How Policies Make Citizens: Senior Political Activism and the American Welfare State*. Princeton, NJ: Princeton University Press.

—— and KIMBERLY J. MORGAN (2002). The Political Mechanisms of Risk Pooling: Long-Term Care in Germany and the United States. In: *ISPS Health Policy Seminar*. New Haven.

CBO (1997). *For Better or for Worse: Marriage and the Federal Income Tax*. Washington DC: Congressional Budget Office.

CLAYTON, RICHARD and JONUS PONTUSSON (1998). Welfare-State Retrenchment Revisited: Entitlement Cuts, Public Sector Restructuring, and Inegalitarian Trends in Advanced Capitalist Societies. *World Politics* 51(1): 67–98.

CLYMER, ADAM (1995). Of Touching Third Rails and Tackling Medicare. *New York Times*, 27 Oct: 21.

DiPRETE, THOMAS A. and PATRICIA A. McMANUS (2000). Family Change, Employment Transitions, and the Welfare State: Household Income Dynamics in the United States and Germany. *American Sociological Review* 65(3): 343–70.

Domestic Policy Council, White House (1993). *Health Security: The President's Report to the American People*. Washington DC: Government Printing Office.

ECKSTEIN, HARRY (1975). Case Study and Theory in Political Science. In: F.I. Greenstein and N.W. Polsby (eds.), *Handbook of Political Science*. Reading, MA: Addison-Wesley.

ELLWOOD, DAVID T. and CHRISTOPHER JENCKS (2001). The Growing Difference in Family Structure: What Do We Know? Where Do We Look for Answers? Cambridge, MA: John F. Kennedy School of Government, Harvard University.

ELVING, RONALD D. (1996). *Conflict and Compromise: How Congress Makes the Law*. New York: Simon & Schuster.

ERIC (2003). *Who We Are* ERISA Industry Committee (ERIC) [cited September 19, 2003]. Available from http://www.eric.org/public/who/overview.htm.

ESPING-ANDERSEN, GOSTA (1999). *Social Foundations of Postindustrial Economies*. New York: Oxford University Press.

—— (1990). *The Three Worlds of Welfare Capitalism*. Princeton, NJ: Princeton University Press.

FamiliesUSA (2003). *Going Without Health Insurance*. Washington DC: Families USA Foundation.

GABEL, JON R. (1999). Job-Based Health Insurance, 1977–1998: The Accidental System Under Scrutiny. *Health Affairs* 18(6): 62–74.

GAO (2000). *Unemployment Insurance: Role as Safety Net for Low-Wage Workers is Limited*. Washington, DC: United States General Accounting Office.

GIDRON, BENJAMIN, RALPH M. KRAMER, and LESTER M. SALAMON (1992). *Government and the Third Sector: Emerging Relationships in Welfare States*. San Francisco, CA: Jossey-Bass.

GILBERT, NEIL (2002). *Transformation of the Welfare State: The Silent Surrender of Public Responsibility*. New York: Oxford University Press.

GOODIN, ROBERT E., BRUCE HEADEY, RUUD MUFFELS, and HENK-JAN DIRVEN (1999). *The Real Worlds of Welfare Capitalism*. Cambridge, UK: Press Syndicate of the Cambridge University Press.

GOTTSCHALK, MARIE (2000). *The Shadow Welfare State: Labor Business and the Politics of Welfare in the United States*. Ithaca, NY: Cornell University Press.

GRAETZ, MICHAEL J. and JERRY L. MASHAW (1999). *True Security: Rethinking American Social Insurance*. New Haven, CT: Yale University Press.

GREENSTEIN, ROBERT and ROBERT SHAPIRO (2003). *The New Definitive Data on Income and Tax Trends*. Washington, DC: Center on Budget and Policy Priorities.

HACKER, JACOB S. (2002). *The Divided Welfare State: The Battle over Public and Private Social Benefits in the United States*. New York: Cambridge University Press.

—— (2004). Privatizing Risk Without Privatizing the Welfare State: The Hidden Politics of Social Policy Retrenchment in the United States. *American Political Science Review* 98(2): 243–60.

Health Insurance Association of America (1996). *Source Book of Health Insurance Data*. New York: Health Insurance Association of America.

HOWARD, CHRISTOPHER (1997). *The Hidden Welfare State: Tax Expenditures and Social Policy in the United States, Princeton Studies in American Politics*. Princeton, NJ: Princeton University Press.

HUBER, EVELYNE and JOHN D. STEPHENS (2001). *Development and Crisis of the Welfare State*. Chicago, IL: University of Chicago Press.

IMMERGUT, ELLEN M. (1992). *Health Politics: Interests and Institutions in Western Europe, Cambridge Studies in Comparative Politics*. Cambridge, UK: Cambridge University Press.

IVERSEN, TORBEN and DAVID SOSKICE (2001). An Asset Theory of Social Policy Preferences. *American Political Science Review* 95(4): 875–93.

JACOBS, LAWRENCE and ROBERT SHAPIRO (2000). *Politics don't Pander: Political Manipulation and the Loss of Democratic Responsiveness.* Chicago, IL: University of Chicago Press.

JACOBY, MELISSA B., TERESA A. SULLIVAN, and ELIZABETH WARREN (2001). Rethinking the Debates over Health Care Financing: Evidence from the Bankruptcy Courts. *New York University Law Review* 76: 375–417.

KORPI, WALTER and JOAKIM PALME (1998). The Paradox of Redistribution and Strategies of Equality: Welfare State Institutions, Inequality, and Poverty in the Western Countries. *American Sociological Review* 63: 677.

—— —— (2001). New Politics and Class Politics in Welfare State Regress: A Comparative Analysis of Retrenchment in 18 Countries 1975–1995. Stockholm: Swedish Institute for Social Research.

KREHBIEL, KEITH (1998). *Pivotal Politics: A Theory of US Lawmaking.* Chicago, IL: Chicago University Press.

KRONICK, RICHARD and TODD GILMER (1999). Explaining the Decline in Health Insurance Coverage, 1979–1995. *Health Affairs* 18: 30–47.

LEVY, DENISE URIAS and SONYA MICHEL (2002). More Can Be Less: Child Care and Welfare Reform in the United States. In: S. Michel and R. Mahon (eds.), *Child Care Policy at the Crossroads: Gender and Welfare State Restructuring.* New York City: Routledge.

LEVY, JONAH (1999). Vice into Virtue? Progressive Politics and Welfare Reform in Continental Europe. *Politics and Society* 27(2): 239–73.

LIPSKY, MICHAEL (1980). *Street-Level Bureaucracy: Dilemmas of the Individual in Public Services.* New York: Russel Sage Foundation.

LYNCH, JULIA (2000). The Age Orientation of Social Policy Regimes in OECD Countries. *Journal of Social Policy* 30(2): 411–36.

MAHONEY, JAMES (2000). Uses of Path Dependence in Historical Sociology. *Theory and Society* 29: 507–48.

MARMOR, THEODORE R. (2000). *The Politics of Medicare,* 2nd edn. London: Routledge & K. Paul.

—— JERRY L. MASHAW, and PHILIP L. HARVEY (1990). *America's Misunderstood Welfare State: Persistent Myths, Enduring Realities.* New York: Basic Books.

MEDOFF, JAMES L. and MICHAEL CALABRESE (2000). *The Impact of Labor Market Trends of Health and Pension Benefit Coverage and Inequality.* Washington, DC: Center for National Policy.

METTLER, SUZANNE and ANDREW MILSTEIN (2003). A Sense of the State: Tracking the Role of the American Administrative State in Citizens' Lives Over Time. Presented at the Annual Meeting of the American Political Science Association. Chicago, IL. April 3–6.

MOENE, KARL OVE and MICHAEL WALLERSTEIN (2001). Inequality, Social Insurance, and Redistribution. *American Political Science Review* 95(4): 859–74.

MOFFITT, ROBERT and PETER GOTTSCHALK (2002). Trends in the Transitory Variance of Earnings in the United States. *Economic Journal* 112 (March): 68–73.

MOON, MARILYN (1993). *Medicare Now and in the Future.* Washington, DC: Urban Institute Press.

NORTH, DOUGLASS C. (1990). *Institutions, Institutional Change, and Economic Performance.* New York: Cambridge University Press.

ORLOFF, ANN SHOLA (1993). *The Politics of Pensions: A Comparative Analysis of Britain, Canada, and the United States, 1880–1940.* Madison, WI: University of Wisconsin Press.

ORZAG, PETER R. (2000). Raising the Amount that can be Contributed to Roth IRAs: The Dangers in the Short Run and the Long Run. Washington, DC: Center on Budget and Policy Priorities.

PETERSON, MARK A. (1998). The Politics of Health Care Policy: Overreaching in an Age of Polarization. In: M. Weir (ed.), *The Social Divide: Political Parties and the Future of Activist Government*. Washington DC: The Brookings Institution.

PETERSON, PAUL E. (1981). *City Limits*. Chicago, IL: University of Chicago Press.

PIERCE, BROOKS (1998). *Compensation Inequality*. Washington, DC: Bureau of Labor Statistics.

PIERSON, PAUL (1993). When Effect Becomes Cause: Policy Feedback and Political Change. *World Politics* 45(4): 595–628.

—— (1994). *Dismantling the Welfare State? Reagan, Thatcher, and the Politics of Retrenchment*. New York: Cambridge University Press.

—— (1996). The New Politics of the Welfare State. *World Politics* 48(2): 143–79.

—— (2000). Increasing Returns, Path Dependence, and the Study of Politics. *American Political Science Review* 94(2): 251–67.

—— (ed.) (2001). *The New Politics of the Welfare State*. Oxford: Oxford University Press.

—— (2002). A Quiet Revolution? Long-Term Processes and Welfare State Restructuring. Paper read at Transforming the Democratic Balance Among State, Market and Society: Comparative Perspectives on France and the Developed Democracies, May 17–18, at Center for European Studies.

—— (forthcoming). *Politics in Time*. Princeton, NJ: Princeton University Press.

RAE, DOUGLAS (1975). The Limits of Consensual Decision. *American Political Science Review* 69(4): 1270–94.

REIN, MARTIN and ESKIL WANDENSJÖ (eds.) (1997). *Enterprise and the Welfare State*. Cheltenham, UK: Edward Elgar.

RIKER, WILLIAM H. (1980). Implications from the Disequilibrium of Majority Rule for the Study of Institutions. *American Political Science Review* 74: 432–46.

RITAKALLIO, VELI-MATTI. (2001). Trends of Poverty and Income Inequality in Cross-National Comparison. Syracuse, NY: Maxwell School of Citizenship and Public Affairs.

SCHEIBER, SYLVESTER J. and JOHN B. SHOVEN (1999). *The Real Deal: The History and Future of Social Security*. New Haven, CT: Yale University Press.

SCHICKLER, ERIC (2001). *Disjointed Pluralism: Institutional Innovation in the U.S. Congress*. Princeton, NJ: Princeton University Press.

SHAPIRO, ISAAC and ROBERT GREENSTEIN (2001). The Widening Income Gulf. Washington DC: Center on Budget and Policy Priorities.

SHEILS, JOHN and PAUL HOGAN (2004). Cost of Tax Exempt Benefits in 2004. *Health Affairs* (Web Extra).

SHEPSLE, KENNETH (1986). The Positive Theory of Legislative Institutions: An Enrichment of Social Choice and Spatial Models. *Public Choice* 50: 135–79.

SILVERMAN, CELIA and PAUL YAKOBOSKI (1994). Public and Private Pensions Today: An Overview of the System. In: N.S. Jones (ed.), *Pension Funding and Taxation: Implications for Tomorrow*. Washington DC: Employee Benefits Research Institute.

SKOCPOL, THEDA (1992). *Protecting Soldiers and Mothers: The Political Origins of Social Policy in the United States*. Cambridge, MA: Belknap Press of Harvard University Press.

—— (1996). *Boomerang: Clinton's Health Security Effort and the Turn Against Government in U.S. Politics*. New York: W.W. Norton & Co.

—— (2000). *The Missing Middle: Working Families and the Future of American Social Policy*. New York: W.W. Norton & Company.

SMEEDING, TIMOTHY M. and LEE RAINWATER (2001). Comparing Living Standards Across Nations: Real Incomes at the Top, the Bottom and the Middle. Syracuse, New York: Maxwell School of Citizenship and Public Affairs.

Stetson, Dorothy McBride and Amy G. Mazur (eds.) (1995). *Comparative State Feminism*. Thousand Oaks, CA: Sage.

Swank, Duane (2001). Political Institutions and Welfare-State Restructuring: The Impact of Institutions on Social Policy Change in Developed Democracies. In: P. Pierson (ed.), *The New Politics of the Welfare State*. New York: Oxford University Press.

Teles, Steven M. (1996). *Whose Welfare? AFDC and Elite Politics*. Lawrence, KS: University of Kansas Press.

—— (1998). The Dialectics of Trust: Ideas, Finance and Pensions Privatization in the US and UK. Paper read at Association for Public Policy Analysis and Management, October 29–31, at New York City.

Thelen, Kathleen (1999). Historical Institutionalism in Comparative Politics. *Annual Review of Political Science* 2: 369–404.

—— (2003). How Institutions Evolve: Insights from Comparative-Historical Analysis. In: J. Mahoney and Dietrich Rueschemeyer (eds.), *Comparative Historical Analysis in the Social Sciences*. Cambridge: Cambridge University Press.

Tsebelis, George (1995). Decision Making in Political Systems: Veto Players in Presidentialism, Parliamentarism, Multicameralism and Multipartyism. *British Journal of Political Science* 25: 289–325.

Tullock, Gordon (1981). Why So Much Stability? *Public Choice* 37: 189–205.

Uninsured, Kaiser Commission on Medicaid and the (2002). *The Uninsured: A Primer*. Washington DC: Kaiser Family Foundation.

Venti, Steven F. and David A. Wise (1997). The Wealth of Cohorts: Retirement Savings and the Changing Assets of Older Americans. In: J.B. Shoven (ed.), *Public Policy Toward Pensions*. Cambridge, MA: The MIT Press.

Warren, Elizabeth (2003). What is a Women's Issue? Bankruptcy, Commercial Law, and other Gender-Neutral Topics. *Harvard Women's Law Journal* 25.

Weaver, R. Kent (1996). Deficits and Devolution in the 104th Congress. *Publius* 26(3): 45–86.

—— (1998). The Politics of Pensions: Lessons from Abroad. In: R.D. Arnold (ed.), *Framing the Social Security Debate*. Washington DC: Brookings Institution Press.

—— (2000). *Ending Welfare As We Know It*. Washington DC: The Brookings Institution.

Wolff, Edward (2002). *Top Heavy: A Study of Increasing Inequality of Wealth in America*. New York: Twentieth Century Fund.

Wood, Stewart (2001). Labour Market Regimes under Threat? Sources of Continuity in Germany, Britain, and Sweden. In: P. Pierson (ed.), *The New Politics of the Welfare State*. New York: Oxford University Press.

Zedlewski, Sheila R. (2002). Are Shrinking Caseloads Always a Good Thing? Washington DC: Urban Institute.

3

Changing Dominant Practice: Making use of Institutional Diversity in Hungary and the United Kingdom

Colin Crouch and Maarten Keune

As discussed in the introduction to this volume, neo-institutional theory is generally better equipped to deal with continuity and stability than with discontinuity and change. Institutional configurations are often presented as a straightjacket from which endogenous actors cannot escape and which can only be seriously modified through external shocks. However, from time to time endogenous actors do make major and more or less sudden changes. It is by no means common; more often than not the central puzzle of a situation is why powerful, strategic actors do not change institutions which they recognize to be functioning in ways that do not suit their interests. That is why neo-institutionalism and path dependence are attractive as explanatory approaches. However, from time to time radical, rather rapid change is introduced by endogenous actors. Unless neo-institutionalism is simply to concede explanatory failure at such moments, it needs to be able to give its own account, consistent with its overall approach, which of course stresses the strength of institutions. Hence, in the present chapter we discuss how endogenous change can come about, given the constraints which neo-institutionalist and path-dependence theories have shown to restrict capacity for institutional innovation. In particular, how can actors change the core characteristics of a dominant, surrounding institutional system?

A key problem in this respect is that neo-institutionalist analysis often starts from an assumption of homogeneity, that is, it depicts the institutions of a society as highly systematic, with everything operating according to a single logic, with endogenous actors operating within a single action space. They thus have no possibility of changing in order to face new challenges for which the practices encouraged by their existing institutions do not equip them. For example, Hall and Soskice (2001) regard whole economies, and their attendant political institutions as well, as characterized by one of two modes of organization: the liberal market or the coordinated market. Firms in countries possessing the one form have no access to the instruments needed for the other. In such a case, change has to be exogenous—to both the local actors and to the theory itself.

Contrary to this assumption, in the following we lay particular emphasis on the need to accept that space must be left for elements that do not 'fit', that might actually contradict any overall system logic, or which are simply different, perhaps redundant. The presence of such elements causes a given institutional system to be heterogeneous. Indeed, the empirical analysis of any system should be expected to find examples of such heterogeneity, in varying degrees. Such 'deviant' elements, so easily rejected as mere 'noise' by dedicated system analysts, might occasionally provide the institutional raw material, or alternative action spaces, that innovative actors use.

Apart from accepting institutional heterogeneity, the present approach also abandons the singular focus on the constraining features of institutions since this is too limited to capture the complexity of social change. In line with the perspective of actor-centered institutionalism (Mayntz and Scharpf 1995; Scharpf 1997) we need further understanding of the role of agency and how it produces innovation, operating under the constraints of its institutional context, but simultaneously using the available (heterogeneous) institutional resources in a creative way.

Such a perspective is particularly important if we are to study endogenous capacity for change in the countries of central and eastern Europe. Their state-socialist institutional legacy is generally considered to have left them with nothing of any use in the twenty-first century market economy. In the following we therefore concentrate on a case of change and innovation in central Europe, in Hungary, which demonstrates the role of preexisting institutional diversity. However, we are not developing a 'special case' argument that applies particularly to 'post-communist exceptions'; we consider that our argument is generally applicable. Therefore we precede our account of the Hungarian case with a similar analysis from a country normally regarded as part of the core for neo-institutionalism: the United Kingdom. The purpose of setting this case alongside the Hungarian one is therefore *not* to invite a comparison between the two; but to show that a good theory can be applied in diverse contexts. The Hungarian case concerns a region, which, compared to the rest of the country and to most of the former state-socialist block, managed to make swift and endogenously driven change to local institutions. As in the case of the United Kingdom, we shall argue that this was facilitated by the inheritance of a heterogeneous local institutional environment, certain elements of which contradicted the dominant state-socialist institutional make-up of the country. Since this case is not so widely known as the first one we will dedicate more space to its empirical discussion.

In both cases actors were confronted by major blocks in the paths inherited from their immediate pasts, but have made what seem like radical innovations and started to adopt 'new' approaches. They would seem to be refutations of the power of institutional deadweight. However, these innovations were strictly speaking scientifically predictable: rather than involving completely disruptive Schumpeterian processes, actors worked creatively with institutional materials that were at hand within the empirical diversity of the various paths demonstrably available within their institutional legacies, but submerged by more dominant or more recent practices. The key terms here are the empirical diversity of the institutional legacies, and the tendency at any one time for some components of the diversity to be dominant or major and others subordinate or minor. The type of change we are dealing with here occurs when a previously subordinate or minor set of practices successfully supplants a dominant one. By 'successful' change we mean that such a shift in dominant practice has occurred, and that those pushing for the change have broadly achieved what they wanted. We do not imply any normative judgments, nor do we necessarily mean that the consequences of the change produce superior outcomes.

What the cases have in common is the importance of institutional heterogeneity in explaining rapid and profound change driven by endogenous actors. The mere existence of institutional heterogeneity cannot however stand alone as an explanation of how change is possible. Explaining alternative, subordinate institutional paths becoming dominant requires us to account for at least two other phenomena which tend to lock actors into particular forms of behavior and create institutional rigidities: power relations and the learning curve. Both these factors are frequently argued to create rigidities and to make endogenous change difficult if not impossible.

Power relations create rigidities because all actors within a particular context become more expert at pursuing those courses of action which favor powerful interests, and this process in itself further advances the position of those interests. Potential rivals to the dominant group not only lack the power to make a challenge, but also lack expertise and the possibility of convincing others that alternative actions are practically viable. This is a theoretical account of the strength of conservatism. Interests and experience alike develop around existing systems and seek to maintain and strengthen them and block possible changes, even if the existing system is failing to deliver results. In such cases, a path continues to be followed by rational actors even though it does not produce general positive returns, because it does generate insider rewards for powerful interests.

This brings us to the importance and difficulty of acquiring the knowledge needed to operate institutions. Complex policy practices cannot be simply executed with complete competence by anyone wishing to do so. Repeated practice of complex social repertoires brings increased expertise. The experienced perform more effectively than the inexperienced, at least until a point is reached where increased practice brings only small rates of further return. This is the reasoning that lies behind the sociopsychological concept of the learning curve. It fits well with path dependence theory and other theories that predict the reinforcement of an action by the practice of it. If, every time one among a number of alternative actions is practised, the actor acquires increased competence in practising it, the more likely will the actor be to choose that action next time round.

But two further assumptions are needed for the possibility of endogenous change to be excluded from such a situation. First, the actors' environment is homogeneous in the sense that all institutions within this environment require the same kind of behavior, giving them access to no alternatives. Second, all other actors known to and sharing interests with these actors, and who might therefore have been expected to indicate alternatives, are trapped within the same kinds of institution. If we relax these assumptions in order to model an institutional environment that contains a small and identifiable range of diversity, we can model endogenous change and not just rigid continuity of behavior. In the simplest case we need only envisage a situation in which there are two modes of actions available. One is the more frequently used, and benefits from the self-reinforcing effects of the learning curve and power relations; but the other maintains a presence. For example, actors may operate in two action spaces, a dominant one and a minor one, the dominant mode being used in the dominant spaces, and the minor in the minor spaces. Or actors in the dominant space may have easy access to other actors who operate in minor spaces. While the dominant actors will not be able to switch practice at will to the minor mode, they will have more possibilities of accessing this mode than actors in truly monotonic environments.

Such forms of institutional diversity may appear to the dominant actors to constitute inefficiencies, redundant capacities. An actor able to use only one approach in all situations has far lighter learning and expertise requirements than one who has to learn several different approaches. And borrowing approaches from others involves various transaction costs. We should therefore expect rational but myopic actors to *prefer* to maintain in their repertoire only the 'one best way' that they initially found. This would, for example, be the case of a multinational corporation which has developed a mass production system using unskilled labor, and which takes this system to every new country where it invests. It does not want to know that the workforce in a particular country has some skills that would enable the job to be done more efficiently using different means.

Sometimes, however, institutional rigidities do not enable such actors to do this, but impose enduring redundant capacities on them. Such actors are required to have diversified repertoires. (For example, the multinational may be required to participate in a national training system, the improved labor skills resulting from which it does not use.) In the short term this may constitute an inefficiency. However, in the event that change is one day needed, the redundant capacity may enable such actors to do so rapidly.

This example illustrates change related to the learning curve; the actor finds it easier to acquire expertise in the use of a procedure if that procedure exists as a minor mode elsewhere within the actor's environment. Similarly, in the case of power relations, we can predict change if there is a shift of power away from those identified with the dominant procedure to those associated with the minor one. We shall now illustrate these points by a discussion of the two cases.

The British neoliberal turn

That a major change in power relations took place in the United Kingdom during the 1980s is clear to all observers, and is the main explanation usually deployed to explain the institutional changes that then occurred in that country. Far less noticed—because of the prevailing tendency among analysts to see national systems as coherent and monotonic at any one period of time—is how those implementing change were able to draw on existing patterns within the society to solve problems of expertise and learning.

During the late 1970s it was common for observers of British political institutions to see the country as fixed in a highly unsuccessful set of macroeconomic institutions. (Major examples of such arguments were Beer 1982 and Middlemas 1979). A legacy of postwar corporatism had survived in a set of institutions which gave a considerable role to trade unions and employers associations, but neither these nor governments had either the will or the structures to make these institutions function in a way that produced sustained positive outcomes (Crouch 1977). Most attempts at reform concentrated on trying to make British institutions more closely pursue neo-corporatist stability. There was a long record of this, starting with attempts at incomes policy in the early 1960s, and culminating in the attempted social contract of 1974–9 (Crouch 1977; Middlemas 1979, 1986–91). However, none of these attempts had more than a temporary success. Meanwhile macroeconomic policy continued, with rather greater achievements to its name, along a Keynesian path (Shonfield 1965; Stewart 1972, 1977; Middlemas 1986–91). Governments used fiscal policy to keep levels of unemployment and inflation at low levels. However, whenever these objectives came into serious opposition, there was recourse to incomes policy and similar forms of restraint to try to ensure that increased demand produced by action to reduce unemployment did not lead to a general rise in prices; but these attempts ran into the problem that British interest organizations did not easily behave in a neo-corporatist way. British Keynesianism, unlike the Scandinavian variety, was not intrinsically linked to neo-corporatist industrial relations, though it came to depend on them.

British policymakers were deeply embedded in a Keynesian approach and its neo-corporatist correlates. Even though the latter rarely produced effective results, policymakers who had been operating it since around 1940 were unable to switch even when it was clearly failing.

By the 1980s there had been a dramatic change in policy of a kind that very few 1970s observers, anticipating a continuation of the policy path, had predicted: industrial relations institutions of employers and employees alike had lost their public-policy role; Keynesian policy had been abandoned; there was no longer a commitment to maintain low unemployment through direct government action. Control of the supply of money had replaced unemployment reduction as the main concern of macroeconomic policy. By the 1990s several other European countries had begun to adopt elements of this new policy, but the United Kingdom has been the case where the changes started first, moved fastest, and proceeded furthest.

This is a good example of major policy change. It is clear that Keynesianism had initially delivered returns. British wartime and postwar decisionmakers learned how to practise these policies, which in turn reinforced the position of certain sets of interests. When, by the end of the 1960s, decisionmakers realized that the policy mix was no longer delivering success, they nevertheless continued to try to use it. However, by 1976 the Labour government had made some initial steps toward monetarist policies. When that government fell in 1979 its Conservative successor embarked on an initially still gradual but thoroughgoing reversal of the entire trajectory of neo-corporatism and Keynesianism. By the mid-1980s the United Kingdom had completely changed path.

Accounting for the change: the role of existing legacies

Any account of changes in the British power structure during this period will include certain major factors: the British government was in considerable debt to the International Monetary Fund and had to accept certain exogenous policy terms imposed on it; the Labour Party, which by the mid-1970s had become the partisan guardian of what was earlier a Keynesian consensus, formally split for the first time since 1931; and the trade union movement suffered bitter divisions and also a major political defeat in the mining strike of 1984–5. Peter Hall has also pointed to certain initially unintended long-term institutional changes caused by a series of reforms in competition and credit control in the early 1970s (Hall 1992: 99–106; 1993). These made British policy exceptionally vulnerable to short-term evaluation by the financial markets, giving the interests associated with them a power to break the Keynesian paradigm (Hall 1992: 108–9).

Hall sees the case as showing how institutions, as well as hindering change, can assist it (1992: 106–8), provided they take a certain form. Here the relevant form was the centralization of power in the British political and mass media systems. He also points out how the initial social learning which fostered the introduction of monetarism took place in powerful structures outside the state but was able to influence it. He argues that this demonstrates the weakness of state-centric theories that look at the logics of action embedded in political institutions alone to find explanations of government policy change (1993: 288). The impetus came from the party-political (as opposed to government) system, from within the Conservative Party, and these groups engaged in a successful power struggle to oppose the paths familiar to both the public administration and the rest of the political system, including other parts of the Conservative Party.

But the point that is essential to be noted is that the UK system had been, even during the postwar period, a complex hybrid between Keynesianism and a *laissez faire* approach inherited from earlier periods. Neo-corporatist Keynesianism never dominated the whole British political economy. An important part of the British mid-century compromise was a strong division of labor between sectors covered by the compromise and those excluded or exempted from it. Among the latter was the financial sector. This did in fact take a corporatist form; the City of London was not just corporatist in the analogous sense in which that term is used in contemporary analysis; it *was* (and is) a medieval corporation, and possessed everything that implied in terms of highly articulated collective organization and political access. It comprised in fact a set of some of the purest markets bounded by an instance of the purest corporatism. Nevertheless, it stood outside the terms of the Keynesian compromise. The latter was concerned mainly with two sectors of the economy: the production of goods (and services concerned with their distribution) and public services. The first was at the heart of the Keynesian cycle linking employment and consumption; the second provided the channels through which the public spending that powered the system was spent, and provided further employment. Employer and employee interests within production, distribution, and public services enjoyed positive-sum interests within this framework. And the productive industries and public services were the main sectors represented by trade unions.

The investment and securities sector stood largely outside this. Historically it had played only a small part in the financing of manufacturing. Its activities were mainly located offshore and it had little connection to the economic life of the geographical and political territory of the United Kingdom. With the exception of frontline banking and insurance, the sector was also weakly unionized. Its main interest in the British economy was in ensuring that the pound sterling, in which it conducted much of its business, was a stable currency, and that UK economic and financial policy would provide a stable basis for the operations of a global financial sector. City interests were therefore particularly averse to inflation and would always favor monetary stability over full employment. And, unlike industrial capitalism and some other sectors, British finance capitalism never became embedded in the rest of the British society.

Despite this, the sector was usually extremely powerful within that society; it was in a way its absentee landlord. Even in the period of foreign exchange controls and regulated capital movements, finance had mobility, and would move out of the country if it did not provide a favorable environment, while the City's earnings made a positive contribution to the country's balance of payments. Although firms in manufacturing and other nonfinancial sectors might occasionally criticize the low profile of the City in providing them with their own investment finances, they also welcomed the opportunity to make offshore investments and to liquidize their assets through the City institutions. Also, within its highly organized, corporatist network, the City incorporated the UK central bank, the Bank of England, itself. This in turn enjoyed a special relationship with the Treasury, the most powerful ministry in the government. The sector therefore had a 'sponsoring ministry' considerably more significant than did, say, the agricultural sector. British financial interests therefore enjoyed a combination of autonomy from the UK economy and polity and a highly influential role within both.

There was therefore a very strong division of labor and of perspectives within the British postwar compromise; it was a compromise that allocated different interests a role in different sectors; it made fewer demands on them to come to terms with each other within a sector. The Keynesian part of British political

economy did not make claims on the scope of the City, and the latter largely
tolerated the Keynesian policy framework. They certainly clashed from time to
time over the relative importance of currency stability and full employment, but
the *modi operandi* of the two remained distinct.

By the 1970s, when the parameters of the Keynesian system were proving
increasingly difficult to sustain, the City was also at one of its weakest moments.
It had become highly marginal to the British economy; new share issues contributed a very small proportion of investment finance. Just as it had happened
during the recession of the 1930s, there was political debate over whether the
City was serving national interests. The sector was also in a period of internal
uncertainty. The web of informal understandings, personal friendships, and
family links that had sustained it for centuries as a kind of industrial district were
being strained by the early stages of internationalization.

By the early 1980s a series of major institutional innovations were to propel
the City to a new global importance. The so-called 'big bang' of reform brought
together a liberalization of capital movements, a shift from an informal, private
corporatist regime to a state-directed one, and the possibilities of a new technology. Further, the processes described by Hall (1992, 1993), whereby government
became increasingly dependent on the willingness of financial institutions to
accept its policies, further strengthened the City's role. All this prepared it to play
a major role in the new ascendancy of share markets that characterized the global
economy of the 1990s.

The monetarist, non- (pre-, anti-, post-) Keynesian practices that came to
dominate during this period had always been the policy preference of the financial
sector; the secondary neoliberal path had run alongside the dominant Keynesian
one throughout the postwar period. British political elites had made available
to them this alternative action space; therefore abandonment of the Keynesian
model did not present any profound problems to them.

Conclusions: the UK case

That the United Kingdom was the first and remains the most thoroughgoing
example of a turn from neo-corporatism and Keynesianism toward monetarism
and neoliberalism in western Europe seems amply explained. The neo-corporatist
component of the former model had not in practice been successfully pursued;
and the power balance that sustained it and the Keynesian model had collapsed
and had been replaced by a very different configuration. In terms of the two
phenomena identified above—power relations and learning curve—the former
requirement for change was clearly satisfied. Increasing returns now flowed to a
UK policy system that pursued a neoliberal path, whereas the former model had
been delivering decreasing returns for some time.

As Hall shows, there was also considerable effort at the level of policy learning.
Neoliberal academic economists and 'think tanks' supported by the power interests who would gain from the change, articulated monetarist policy models that

could replace Keynesian mechanisms. Measures of increase in the money supply were developed to replace the indicators used by the Keynesian approach. These provided technical solutions to the problem of how to govern the economy with different targets from those relating to the relationship between employment, inflation, growth, and currency stability. (In practice they played a mainly talismanic role in policy steering. Governments adopted whatever definition of monetary targets their policies seemed able to achieve. The debate over what rate of monetary expansion would produce what level of inflation was never resolved. All that was necessary was that the political and economic elites had a frame of reference that suited their preferences, could be presented publicly, and gave them some strategic orientation.)

Local development policy in a Hungarian region[1]

From 1949 to 1989, Hungary belonged to the state-socialist world, characterized by features like the one-party state, almost exclusive state ownership of means of production, and a deep entrenchment in the international economic structure of the state-socialist block. State socialism in Hungary was not an immovable object, and institutional change took place during those forty years. Policymakers initially concern with institutionalizing the centralized Stalinist model with its exclusive concern with industrialization (Kornai 1992; McDermott 2002). Growing dissatisfaction among the population led to the 1956 uprising, brutally suppressed by the Soviet army. The political dominance of the party was reconfirmed by these events. However, from the 1960s onwards many economic institutions associated with the Stalinist model became subject to gradual reform, as policymakers searched for ways to improve productivity and living standards to avoid social unrest. Among them were a gradual decentralization of economic decisionmaking and responsibility for performance from the center to the enterprise level, strengthening the autonomy of enterprise managers; the legalization of certain forms of private economic activities; and the beginning of borrowing on international markets to finance growth and consumption. The country started to import Western technology, and stepped up exports to Western countries. It did so to a much more important extent than most other state-socialist countries. These reforms were however gradual, and they took place within a state-socialist context. Indeed, they were attempts to prop up a slowly stagnating economic system instead of attempts at changing the system itself.

Since the collapse of state socialism in 1989, a much more dramatic process of institutional innovation has taken place. The renewed (but not always new) national political elite embarked on a quest to build 'Western style capitalism', posing privatization, macroeconomic stabilization, and liberalization of prices and trade as policy priorities. Also, all post-socialist Hungarian governments, whatever their political persuasion, have posed foreign direct investment (FDI) as the main economic policy tool to restructure and modernize the national economy (Neumann 2000). In addition, the 1990s saw an accelerated appreciation of the role of local and regional institutions and policymaking, following from attempts at political, administrative, and fiscal decentralization, often explicitly modeled on practices in the European Union (Keune 2001).

It is within this context that local political and economic actors have been confronted with the predicament of how to adapt to this new situation which, from their point of view, can largely be modeled as a rapidly changing external environment. Here we will discuss this process of adaptation in the region of Győr, one of the traditional industrial centers in Hungary, located in the north-west of the country, close to the Austrian and Slovak borders. This region has managed this process of adaptation in a relatively successful way in the past fifteen years or so in comparison with most other Hungarian regions as well as other Central and Eastern European (CEE) regions. Hence, it does not constitute an example of a general Hungarian (or CEE) experience, but an uncharacteristic case with its own dynamics. We shall analyze the responses of local elites to the post-1989 challenges and discuss how they have innovated local economic development policy. In particular, we will highlight that their successful response can largely be seen as an endogenous one, built on the heterogeneous institutional profile of the region.

State socialism in Győr: an example of multiple action spaces

The region of Győr consists of the City of Győr and surrounding municipalities and has a population of around 200,000. It became one of the key industrial centers of Hungary in the late nineteenth and early twentieth centuries, mostly due to an influx of FDI from Austrian companies and banks specializing in engineering, textiles and clothing, and food processing. Several of today's major firms in Győr were established by foreigners at that time, often largely oriented toward export to the West, and the region became the country's bridgehead with the West. The institutionalization of state socialism after the Second World War and the subsequent nationalization of industry profoundly changed the local economy. Production became concentrated in a few, very large enterprises, decisionmaking was largely transferred to the central planning organs, and exports were redirected toward the East. The 'Iron Curtain' severed earlier connections between the region and the West and the reluctance of the center to invest in the Western border regions transformed it into a disadvantaged outpost during the 1950s.

This did not last for long. Already in the late 1950s and early 1960s central investment in the local industry increased substantially. Then, when economic and political reforms started in the 1960s, local enterprises regained much of their decisionmaking authority, and the importance of enterprise managers rapidly increased. Also, when export to the West received renewed importance, Győr slowly regained its earlier role as a bridge between Hungary and the West. Crucial here was the fact that a number of state-owned companies that had previously solely produced for state-socialist markets, began to establish supplier relations with western European and American producers. In Győr this renewed cooperation with the West was of much higher importance than in the rest of the country. A host of official and personal contacts developed between Westerners and local individuals and institutions, including local government authorities and managers of state-owned companies. Hence, as the result of changes in central policy, local actors effectively became involved in two quite different action spaces following quite distinct institutional logics. The dominant action space continued to be the state-socialist political economy in which local actors interacted with the center, with other state-owned enterprises, and with the other state-socialist countries. Much less salient, but growing in importance, was the other, minor action space of interaction with capitalist actors and markets, and largely following capitalist practices. These two action spaces, or parallel paths, coexisted for several decades in the region, making it a good example of a heterogeneous institutional system.

Coinciding with this integration into Western commodity chains, as well as the increased enterprise level autonomy, in the 1980s a relatively young, professionally oriented, and dynamic managerial stratum began to head the major local state-owned companies, which developed close connections with a number of Western firms. Together with the local political elite they formed a tight informal group. As the state-socialist economy was stagnating, this coalition considered further integration in the Western capitalist economy, including foreign investment, to be the best means to foster local economic growth as well as their own political or economic interests. Such integration also seemed feasible considering the continuous economic reforms implemented by the center. Hence, in anticipation of economic reforms—though not, of course, in anticipation of the surprising collapse of state socialism as such—a series of initiatives were started to prepare the region for increased contact and exchange with the West. It was in the late 1980s that the city council and local enterprises cooperated with Austrian investors to establish the Győr Industrial Park, the first industrial park in Hungary. Also, in the late 1980s, the first joint ventures with Western enterprises were set up in the region. In addition, a considerable expansion and upgrading of vocational training took place, emphasizing 'new' subjects like business administration, tourism, and Western languages. Also, the start of preparations for the Vienna–Budapest motorway and the reconstruction of the Vienna–Budapest railway, largely the competency of the state, initiated an improvement of Győr's infrastructure. Local managers and public officials alike saw these changes in education and infrastructure, including the industrial park project, as key conditions for the renewal of the local industrial base and for further integration into the Western economy. All this contributed to further strengthening of the second action space.

Also in the 1980s, in line with national developments, and locally spurred by the growing inflow of Western tourists, small-scale private activities started to emerge in the region, often in the shadow economy. To some extent we could consider these to constitute a third action space since its logic was again different from the other two. However, it remained small in scale until 1989.

A change in dominant practice: power, policies, and inheritance

In 1990, with the turn to capitalism in the former state-socialist block, two principal views on how to orient local development policy in Győr emerged. One centered on the vision of a rapidly growing, innovative small and medium-size enterprise (SME) sector, including a prominent role for the small private sector that had developed in the late 1980s, considered to be one of the potential sources of revitalization of the local economy (Rechnitzer 1993: 75–103). This view was supported by the coalition of center–right political parties that governed Győr between 1990 and 1994 after winning the first free local elections. However, the early 1990s demanded crisis management and left only limited space for a comprehensive SME promotion policy. Also, initially, in conformity with the optimistic market philosophy underlying much of economic policymaking in those days, a spontaneous emergence of large numbers of new, productive SMEs, without much particular public assistance, was anticipated (Gábor 1997). For local government, innovation in local economic development policy thus meant principally its own withdrawal from the economic sphere. An exception was that it promoted the use of the industrial park by innovative SMEs. However, although many new small enterprises emerged, the industrial park remained largely unused, the SME sector did not manage to generate large-scale economic renewal and it failed to become the economic motor of the region. It was plagued by inexperience, lack of capital, and faced great difficulties in becoming competitive in the increasingly open economy.[2] Also, the widespread expectation of a rapid incorporation of local SMEs into the supplier chains of Western companies did not materialize. In addition, the shadow economy experience accumulated by local small entrepreneurs in the state-socialist 1980s, turned out to be much less valuable in the turbulent and capitalist 1990s.

Meanwhile, the former political elite, in coalition with the managers of the (former) state enterprises and a number of highly placed individuals in public institutions, now firmly promoted FDI as the sole feasible basis for future economic development. The leaders of the socialist party (MSZP), that is, the former ruling party now in opposition, made FDI central to their political platform and proposed a number of measures to foster FDI inflow. Managers, using their earlier developed contacts with the West, often actively (and successfully) tried to find a 'proper' foreign investor to buy their firm or for other types of financial involvement.[3] In a similar fashion, public institutions made efforts to attract foreign investment. For example, the local employment office started to offer incoming FDI companies assistance in finding appropriate employees and to organize training courses to adapt their profiles to the needs of the companies. It also offered detailed overviews of empty production sites available for investment projects and of the availability of labor in the different municipalities of the region. Using long-standing official and personal contacts with the neighboring Austrian Burgenland region, this information was regularly provided to the Chamber of Commerce and Industry of Burgenland, complemented by assurances that local institutions would assist foreign investors in all possible ways.

It was this second view that got sustained by developments in the local economy in the early 1990s. While state enterprises were in crisis following the collapse of the state-socialist block, and small enterprises had great difficulties in becoming productive, FDI started to pour into the region, making use of the contacts with local managers and of the services of local public institutions. First, foreign SMEs, mostly Austrian, established plants in neighboring villages, often using personal contacts in the process. Second, several large local companies were sold to foreign investors, including General Electric and United Biscuits, again often after active use by managers of their contacts with Western enterprises, developed before 1989. In 1993, FDI received an enormous boost with the arrival of Audi in the region, which subsequently attracted a number of supplier companies and drew the attention of other foreign companies. Since then, numerous other foreign investors have established greenfield project (e.g. Philips, AMOCO, VAW). They have: acquired local manufacturing enterprises or public services (e.g. the regional gas company); participated financially in large local (domestically owned) enterprises; set up large retail outlets (Spar, Tesco, and Metro); or participated in infrastructural development.

As a result the region has fared much better than most of the rest of the country. The initial economic crisis of 1990–3, with an 18.2 percent decline in national GDP and of almost 30 percent in employment, was shorter and much less profound in Győr.[4] What is noteworthy is that, while most of the country was still struggling to get back on its feet in the mid-1990s, Győr started to boom. Since then the region has enjoyed virtual full employment; indeed, it suffers from a shortage of labor.

The apparent success of the 'FDI path' as well as the support of the large enterprises were important factors for the victory of the socialist party in the 1994 local election. The party included many of the same political figures as the ruling party of the late 1980s. (For example, the pre-1989 Secretary of Economic Affairs of Győr became the new mayor and has remained in this position until today.) It argued that indeed FDI had shown it could do the job SMEs were not able to do, saving enterprises and jobs through privatization and creating many new ones through greenfield investments. The region has subsequently presented itself as a favorable FDI location, offering well-educated but cheap industrial labor, a good geographical location with good infrastructural characteristics, and local institutions used to dealing with foreign enterprises and willing to attend to their needs. Local public institutions became more and more geared toward the provision of conditions and public services favoring the inflow and expansion of FDI projects. Such support comprises the further development of infrastructure, often tailored to the particular needs of foreign investors; subsidies to local public transport to facilitate commuting by workers; a dramatic increase in public education and the adjustment of profiles and curricula to the needs of foreign investors; tax holidays; further development of the industrial park, now offering plots and services to large greenfield investors; specialized and subsidized assistance from the Employment Office in selection and training of workers; and others. This policy package has successfully contributed to sustaining the stream of incoming capital and foreign enterprises establishing in the region. In early 2004, the industrial park in the region was almost full and Győr is one of the main motors of the rapid economic growth in Hungary.

Moreover, as important as attracting FDI, the region's policies have played an important part in the expansion of foreign investment projects. A good example is again Audi. Originally it came to Győr to assemble a limited number of engines, importing the parts from Germany and again exporting the assembled engines. Ten years later Audi Győr assembles about half of all the engines of the entire Volkswagen Group of which Audi is a part, assembles cars (the Audi TT models), produces a variety of auto parts, and has launched a R&D center. It has built close relationships with a wide variety of local institutions, which have helped it to make this expansion possible. It cooperates closely with the local university in R&D and employs a number of its engineers and other graduates. Audi set up long-term programs with local vocational schools, offering resources and training places in exchange for adaptation of curricula to its needs, aiming to attract skilled workers. The company has benefited from a number of infrastructural developments, including road connections with supplier companies and the development of a small airport in the neighborhood, which allows for flights connections to Audi headquarters in Germany on a daily basis. It also gets continuous assistance from the local Employment Office in satisfying its recruitment needs.

In this way, the region has made a relatively swift and successful change in dominant practice. Before 1989 the national state-socialist economy was clearly dominant and the participation of the region in the global capitalist economy was a subordinate action space. Since 1989 the latter has become the dominant action space, and the region operates within this with relative ease and success. Győr has been able to do this in such a short time because it could build on the institutions, resources, and capabilities developed in and inherited from the subordinate pre-1989 pattern. This allowed local elites to draw on experiences and action patterns that fit the post-1989 global capitalist economy.

This does not mean that this shift has been unproblematic or uncontested. Indeed, the rapid reindustrialization has faced difficulties and opposition. One problem is that the region faces a shortage of labor, which forces it to organize commuting from as far away as 80 km on a daily basis. Other problematic features are, for example, the limited R&D content of FDI in the region; the fact that local SMEs are only weakly integrated into the supplier chains of FDI companies; and that local wages and incomes do not seem to catch up with Western ones. Moreover, recently a number of important FDI companies, in particular but not exclusively those that mainly employ low-wage–low-skilled labor, have closed down their operations in Hungary to move to more profitable countries like Ukraine or China. This has also happened in Győr where much of the textile industry and food industry, abundantly present in the 1990s, have relocated. Even though the region has had no problem compensating for these movements by attracting FDI in engineering and electronics, these developments have shown its vulnerability to decisions made in distant headquarters and have raised questions about the stability of the local economy.

To some extent therefore the FDI path is contested, even though nobody seriously challenges its achievements. A number of prominent local leaders and institutions continue to advocate an alternative SME-focused development strategy. They include local center–right political parties, academics, and the local Chamber of Commerce and Industry. The local SMEs themselves, often through the Chamber which acts as their representative, have repeatedly voiced their discontent with the lack of support for their sector in, for example, access to capital, technology transfer, or inclusion in supplier chains. They claim that they are treated in a disadvantageous way compared to foreign investors, in particular where taxes are concerned. Another discontent is that voiced by workers in FDI companies. They increasingly claim that their productivity levels are equal to their Western colleagues, but that this is not reflected at all in their salary level. But although both these groups have created a strong local polemic, they have not been able to convert this into a challenge to the coalition of large enterprises, local government, and local public institutions.

A comparative perspective

To underpin the above claims concerning the role of local institutions it is useful to compare processes of institutional innovation in other Hungarian regions. Whereas, for example, retail FDI has spread throughout Hungary, the peculiarity of developments in Győr, and the basis of its success, is the concentrated inflow of manufacturing FDI, often oriented toward export.[5] One of us has recently compared Győr with Szabolcs–Szatmár–Bereg, for long the country's poorest region located in the East of the country (Keune with Kiss and Tóth 2004). Szabolcs–Szatmár–Bereg was historically an agricultural region, which during the state-socialist era depended, much more than did Győr, on large central investment programs for its industrialization. The region had been largely excluded from integration with Western economies before 1989 and therefore had not developed the same FDI-favorable resources as Győr. Local institutions had had little knowledge of how Western companies operated; local elites had had few contacts with Western elites; and local policies had not been geared toward strengthening integration into the capitalist global economy.

As a result, after 1989 local institutions and individuals in Szabolcs–Szatmár–Bereg were ill-equipped to face the challenges of the new capitalist era. Faced with a deep economic crisis and a lack of investment resources, local elites tried to mimic the FDI strategy followed by Győr. However, they did so not only in a less favorable geographical location but also without the FDI-favorable institutions, experience, and innovative capacities of Győr. Following from this lack of capacities and understanding of the newly dominant action space, the region's competitive strategy was largely based on low costs, that is, low-wage costs compared to the national average, and fiscal incentives. As could be expected, this strategy has proved to be insufficient and manufacturing FDI was almost absent during the 1990s. Its presence remains limited today (Keune with Kiss and Tóth 2004).

The lack of success of this innovation attempt led Szabolcs–Szatmár–Bereg to fall back on a strategy with which it had historically been far more familiar: securing state resources for economic development. During the state-socialist era, building on its position as the country's poorest region, local elites had developed ample expertise in lobbying the center for financial and investment support. After 1989 they put these capabilities to good use, not in their dealings with economic actors, but with the post-socialist state. They have been able to get a much higher-than-average share of central development funds (Keune with Kiss and Tóth 2004). Unlike Győr, however, this does not represent a successful replacement of dominant practice, but rather a successful adaptation of old practices to a new context.

Conclusions: local development in Győr

In the 1990s, local policymakers in Győr made what seemed radical innovations in local economic development policies, in the context of the collapse of state socialism and the turn to capitalism in Hungary. In a very limited time period it successfully reshaped itself from a region dominated by state-owned, COMECON-oriented enterprises, to one dominated by private enterprises and foreign investment coming from the West.

Certainly national developments assisted this process. One has been the central importance given to foreign investment by the national governments during the 1990s. Second is the process of political and administrative decentralization taking place as part of the transformation of the country's political economy, making local governments and local public institutions more important players in economic development. Third was the process of economic decentralization during the 1970s and 1980s, as well as the way the privatization process was regulated in the early 1990s, which opened the possibility for enterprise managers to control the privatization of 'their' enterprises and personally benefit from this process.

But we have also seen Győr's regional specificity within the national framework. While during the state-socialist era the main action space within which its actors were involved was clearly the COMECON-oriented economy, as early as the 1960s the region had become increasingly and unusually involved in the Western capitalist economy as well. Although this remained a subsidiary path, it resulted in the accumulation of diversified experiences and expertise, most importantly in a growing familiarity with capitalist practices, as well as contacts in the West, which could usefully be employed after 1989.

When state socialism collapsed, a coalition of managers, the former local political elite, public institutions, and enterprise managers advocated an FDI-based development path. This coalition has been able to dominate local economic development policy throughout the 1990s, the only exception being the 1990–4 local government, which was formed by the competing pro-SME coalition. Hence, it has had the power to impose the FDI-oriented development path. In addition, building on its experience in the subsidiary action space under state socialism, it had the knowledge, experience, and contacts to make this path a success and had relatively little need for learning. The abandonment of state socialism in favor of capitalism did therefore not present a similarly profound problem to this coalition than it has to those in other regions in Hungary and around CEE that have attempted similar innovations in local development policy. To the ruling elites in Győr, systemic change involved a change in dominant practice, bringing to the fore the previously secondary development path of the region. Their response to the demise of state socialism was to a large extent an endogenous one.

General conclusions

It is part of the implicit claim of neo-institutionalist theory—as indeed of all analytical sociology—that it embodies abstract underlying principles of social structure and action which can be applied across different substantive fields. It is therefore appropriate to test the capacity of these approaches through two case studies—the British neoliberal turn and economic reconstruction in Győr—that concern very different issues and contexts and involve different kinds of actors. Different though their empirical referents are, these studies both demonstrate the possibility of innovation and changes in paths by endogenous actors, and the capacity for an amended neo-institutionalist analysis to model these.

Social science can account for cases like this while remaining within the range of predictability, provided it is prepared to model adequate empirical complexity within the examples it studies. Both our cases show how power relations and the learning curve, while intrinsic to the establishment and maintenance of strong continuities, can also help explain how change takes place. In both cases subsidiary possibilities remained in existence alongside previously dominant ones: the neoliberal approach of the British financial system alongside postwar Keynesianism; cooperation with Western capital in Győr alongside state social-ism. In neither case were these particularly 'hidden' subsidiaries. What is more remarkable is that, despite their relative prominence while being subsidiary, their strong contradiction of the previously dominant counter-models continued for a lengthy period. Complex social arrangements can tolerate a considerable amount of internal tension.

This last point raises a new set of questions. First, given the strength of the many arguments in the literature which predict institutional homogeneity, how is it possible for institutional heterogeneity to persist over time? This directs our attention to 'insulation' mechanisms, sub-institutions, divisions of labor, which limit the antagonistic interaction of distinct parts. An insistence on the internal unity of specifically *national* systems prevents us from searching for such mech-anisms and therefore limits the ambitions and potential achievements of the analytical project. The next stages of neo-institutional analysis would do well to develop concepts and theories of these, what they might be, how they might operate. In doing so, there will be strong temptations to resort to a reinforced functionalism, which can be avoided by also specifying the limits to the range of mechanisms of this type.

Second, what are the kinds of linkages which might serve to short-circuit these forms of insulation, making possible those forms of innovation which take the form of interinstitutional borrowing of the kind considered here? This requires a theory of linkages and potential linkages which is in fact already required by the assumptions of tendencies toward homogeneity of neo-institutionalism, but rarely spelt out in theoretical detail.

Third, we have shown the important role of endogenous actors in shaping responses to exogenous shocks. In the Hungarian case there is little doubt that external developments have been a main trigger for change, that change has been rapid, and that it has involved foreign elements. Also in the United Kingdom, the oil price shocks were external factors testing the Keynesian approach to destruction. But response was possible to the shocks because internal actors had acquired experience in less prominent elements of the totality of paths that in reality had long been part of the overall empirical cases. This is a general mechanism through which institutions sometimes change, the dominant practice being replaced, but not by an entirely exogenous one. The fact that endogenous elements are useful for the new situation then reduces the learning curve and makes immediate action or rapid response possible.

Finally, one needs to assess the following possible objection to the argument made above concerning enduring heterogeneity. 'In the end' an orthodox neo-institutionalist might argue: the incongruence between the logic of the UK financial sector and that of Keynesianism had to be resolved. The UK economy is *essentially* a neo-liberal one; the Keynesian and neo-corporatist components were temporary, undigested, bolted-on additions, developed to deal with the exigencies of World War II and immediate post-war reconstruction, but which always remained 'alien' to the underlying logic of the system. And once this incongruity was cleared away, the British economy began to function better than before.

And 'eventually Hungarian society could no longer contain an externally oriented economic sector closely linked to western capitalism within a closed Soviet-oriented state socialism. That is why the system collapsed'.

To appraise this kind of argument requires resolution of a number of epistemological questions. When, in the social sciences, can we decide that the kind of historical resolution implied by arguments of the style 'in the end' has arrived? Do we know, how can we know, whether the United Kingdom and Hungary in the 2000s have reached points of historical completion, whereas in the 1960s to 1990s they were in a period of uneasy transition? Can we, indeed, speak of ends to history? What are the limits to mutual tolerance between incongruent institutions in complex, functionally differentiated societies? Should we expect greater 'success', innovation, capacity for adaptation from social formations which have 'resolved' such tensions and can therefore realize fully the unimpeded rationality of a particular end, or from those which retain their internal contradictions and thereby a continuing capacity to avoid complete dependence on a particular path?

The next stage of development of neo-institutionalist analysis might also try to develop a set of theoretical arguments for resolving these questions—or at least for demonstrating awareness that some of its current assumptions leave them begging.

Notes

1. This section is to a large extent based on Keune and Tóth (2001).
2. As in the rest of the country, many small-scale activities were established; however, initially they were often above all an alternative to unemployment and oriented toward consumption instead of growth (Laky 1996; Gábor 1997).
3. This formed part of the phenomenon of 'spontaneous privatization' occurring around the country, in which enterprise managers, through a variety of constructions, became private owners of state enterprises or sold them to other (Hungarian or foreign) enterprises or private persons under advantageous conditions. Spontaneous privatization was made possible by several legal changes during the 1980s and later by a series of lacunas in the competencies and functioning of the central State Property Agency, established in 1990 to control the privatization process (Stark and Bruszt 1998).
4. Large regional differences have been one of the striking characteristics of economic development in Hungary since 1989 (Fazekas and Ozsvald 1998; Keune and Nemes Nagy 2001). For details on the comparison between Győr and the rest of Hungary, see the statistical appendix in Keune and Nemes Nagy (2001).
5. A related question here is whether the rapid and sustained inflow of FDI into Győr has been simply the result of the fact that the region is on the one hand strategically located close to the Austrian (and until recently the European Union) border. While undoubtedly this has been a factor aiding its attractiveness to foreign investors, the region easily outperformed the rest of the Hungarian regions bordering on Austria, while the two other regions with a high concentration of FDI, Székesfehérvár and Budapest and surroundings, are much further away from the border. Against explanation by geographical location alone is also the fact that, during the 1990s, Győr also attracted much more FDI than the Czech regions bordering Austria or Germany, even though these are geographically much more to the West. Some of these regions may have started to catch up with Győr after 2000, but that substantial time lag only underlines the latter's capacity to make a swift change.

References

BEER, S.H. (1982). *Britain Against Itself: The Political Contradictions of Collectivism.* London: Faber.

CROUCH, C. (1977). *Class Conflict and the Industrial Relations Crisis.* London: Heinemann.

FAZEKAS, K. and OZSVALD, É. (1998). Transition and Regional Policies: The Case of Hungary. In: M. Keune (ed.), *Regional Development and Employment Policy. Lessons from Central and Eastern Europe.* Budapest and Geneva: ILO.

GÁBOR, I. (1997). Too Many, Too Small: Small Entrepreneurship in Hungary—Ailing or Prospering? In: G. Grabher and D. Stark (eds.), *Restructuring Networks in Post-Socialism. Legacies, Linkages and Localities.* Oxford: Oxford University Press.

HALL, P. A. (1992). In: Steinmo et al. (eds.), The Movement from Keynesianism to Monetarism: Institutional Analysis and British Economic Policy in the 1970s, q.v., pp. 90–113.

—— (1993). Policy Paradigms, Social Learning and the State: The Case of Economic Policymaking in Britain. *Comparative Politics* 25(3): 275–96.

—— and SOSKICE, D. (eds.) (2001). *Varieties of Capitalism: The Institutional Foundations of Comparative Advantage.* Oxford: Oxford University Press.

KEUNE, M. (2001). Local Development, Institutions and Conflicts in Post-Socialist Hungary: An Overview. In: M. Keune and J. Nemes Nagy (eds.), *Local Development, Institutions and Conflicts in Post-Socialist Hungary.* Budapest: ILO.

—— and NEMES NAGY, J. (eds.) (2001). *Local Development, Institutions and Conflicts in Post-Socialist Hungary.* Budapest: ILO.

—— and TÓTH, A. (2001). Foreign Investment, Institutions and Local Development: Successes and Controversies in Győr. In: M. Keune and J. Nemes Nagy (eds.), *Local Development, Institutions and Conflicts in Post-Socialist Hungary.* Budapest: ILO.

—— with KISS, J. P. and TÓTH, A. (2004). Innovation, Actors and Institutions: Change and Continuity in Local Development Policy in Two Hungarian Regions. *International Journal of Urban and Regional Research* 28(3): 586–600.

KORNAI, J. (1992). *The Socialist System: The Political Economy of Communism.* Princeton, NJ: Princeton University Press.

LAKY, T. (1996). *Labour Market Report 1995.* Budapest: Hungarian Foundation for Enterprise Promotion.

MAYNTZ, R. and SCHARPF, F. (1995). Der Ansatz des Akteurzentrierten Institutionalismus. In: R. Mayntz and F. Scharpf (eds.), *Steuerung und Selbstorganisation in Staatsnahen Sektoren.* Frankfurt am Main: Campus.

McDERMOTT, G. (2002). *Embedded Politics. Industrial Networks and Institutional Change in Postcommunism.* Ann Arbor, MI: The University of Michigan Press.

MIDDLEMAS, K. (1979). *Politics in Industrial Society: The Experience of the British System since 1911.* London: A. Deutsch.

—— (1986–91). *Power, Competition and the State*, 3 vols. Basingstoke, UK: Macmillan.

NEUMANN, L. (2000). Decentralized Collective Bargaining in Hungary. *The International Journal of Comparative Labour Law and Industrial Relation* 16(2): 113–28.

RECHNITZER, J. (1993). Innovációs pontok és zónák választási irányok a térszerkezetben' [Innovative sectors and points in the regional structure]. In: Gy. Enyedi, (ed.), *Társadalmi-területi egyenlőtlenségek Magyarországon* [Social and regional inequalities in Hungary]. Budapest: KJK.

SCHARPF, F. (1997). *Games Real Actors Play. Actor-centred Institutionalism in Policy Research.* Boulder, CO: Westview Press.

SHONFIELD, A. (1965). *Modern Capitalism: The Changing Balance of Public and Private Power.* London: Oxford University Press.

STARK, D. and BRUSZT, L. (1998). *Post-socialist Pathways. Transforming Policy and Property in East Central Europe.* Cambridge: Cambridge University Press.

STEWART, M. (1972). *Keynes and After.* Harmondsworth: Penguin.

—— (1977). *The Jekyll and Hyde Years: Politics and Economic Policy since 1964.* London: J. M. Dent.

4

Redeploying the State: Liberalization and Social Policy in France

Jonah D. Levy

France has long been paired with Japan as the archetypal state-led political economy (Shonfield 1965; Cohen 1977; Katzenstein 1978; Zysman 1983; Hall 1986).[1] For decades, French planners aggressively manipulated an array of policy instruments—from trade protection, to subsidies, to cheap credit, to exemption from price controls—in an effort to accelerate the pace of economic moderniza- tion. French authorities channeled resources to privileged groups, favoring investment over consumption, industry over agriculture, and big business over small. They also 'picked winners', both specific sectors, such as coal and steel in the reconstruction era and nuclear power and telecommunications in the 1970s, and specific firms, the so-called 'national champions', multinational corporations anointed as France's standard-bearers in the battle for global economic leader- ship. When national champions did not exist, French planners constructed them through a series of state-sponsored mergers; when national champions lacked capital, the planners financed them through cheap capital and guaranteed state markets; and when national champions were deficient in technology, state-run labs performed research for them, transferring cutting-edge solutions in com- puters, nuclear power, high-speed trains, and digital telecommunications switches (Cohen and Bauer 1985; Cohen 1992).

Beginning in 1983, French policy took a new direction. Confronted with double-digit inflation, rising trade and budget deficits, stagnant investment, and a currency crisis that threatened to push the French franc below the minimum exchange rate allowed by the European Monetary System (EMS), Socialist President, François Mitterrand opted to reverse his government's voluntarist tack. A leftist administration that had been elected just two years earlier on a campaign to intensify *dirigisme* began instead to dismantle *dirigisme*.

Today, virtually nothing remains of the institutions and practices associated with the *dirigiste* model. Planning, sectoral industrial policies, and ambitious *grands projets* have been abandoned; the vast majority of nationalized companies have been privatized; credit, price, and capital controls have been lifted; restric- tions on layoffs and temporary and part-time employment have been eased; and a macroeconomic orientation emphasizing inflationary growth coupled with large devaluations has given way to one of the lowest inflation rates in Europe and a strong franc, culminating in European Monetary Union (EMU). By all accounts,

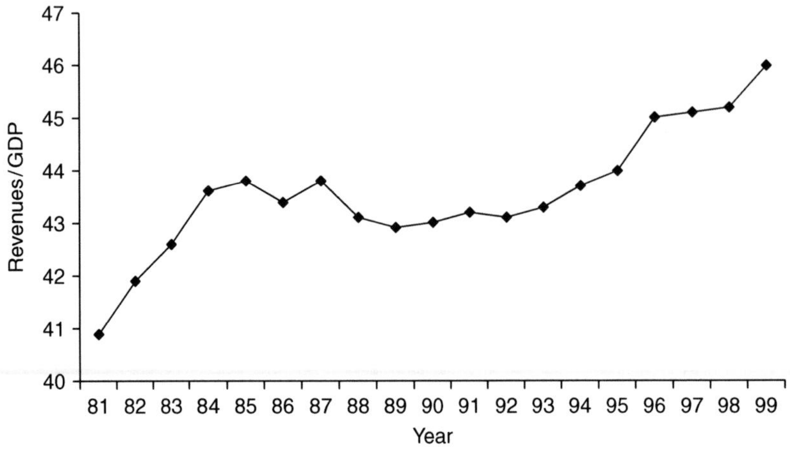

Figure 4.1 Total French tax revenues as a percentage of GDP, 1981–99
Sources: OECD (2000*b*); Ministry of Finance (2001).

France has become a much more market-oriented political economy, whose performance rests on the calculations of profit-seeking businesses, as opposed to state technocrats.

The rollback of *dirigisme* is only part of the French story since 1983, however. French governments have also launched a number of expensive new programs, notably in labor markets, social protection, and the promotion of small business. State authorities have sought to facilitate market-led adjustment by tendering benefits to potential victims of industrial restructuring and channeling resources to innovative small firms. The French government may not be pouring billions of francs (or euros) into industrial policy, but it is still spending plenty. As Figure 4.1 reveals, government revenues, which totaled 42.6 percent of GDP in 1983, at the height of Socialo-Communist voluntarism, have continued to rise in the ostensibly less interventionist post-*dirigiste* period, reaching 46 percent of GDP in 1999 (OECD 2000*b*; Ministry of Finance 2001). French social and labor market expenditures now approximate Scandinavian levels. Thus, not only has the post-*dirigiste* French state failed to shrink; by some measures, it has grown bigger than ever.

The reforms of the past twenty years have redefined the fundamental purposes of state policy. The traditional *dirigiste* strategy of directing capital while excluding and neglecting labor has been abandoned. State authorities are striving instead to facilitate market-led adjustment while pacifying and demobilizing potential victims of this process. In a sense, the *dirigiste* state has become the social anesthesia state.

The transformation of France's statist model is perhaps best understood as a process of *institutional redeployment*. State intervention has been redeployed on behalf of new objectives. This redeployment has involved elements of what the editors of this volume term 'institutional conversion' and 'institutional layering'

(Chapter 1), even if the process as a whole is not reducible to either. At the most basic level, the French state has been converted from a market-directing to a market-supporting role. That said, whereas conversion entails changing the purposes of existing institutions, in the French case, some state institutions have been dismantled, while others have been created. Recent changes also evoke elements of institutional layering, in that new institutions have been added to the old. In the case of the French state, however, many old instruments of state intervention have been discredited and cleared away entirely, while new interventionist tools have been forged to take their place.

My chapter is divided into five sections. The section titled 'The dismantling of *dirigisme*' traces the elimination of the key features of the *dirigiste* model following the 1983 U-turn. The section 'Post-*dirigiste* state intervention' describes some of the most prominent new state activities. The section on 'The roots of redeployment' identifies the political, economic, and institutional forces that have driven state intervention. The section on 'The social anesthesia state' describes the achievements and limitations of the new state intervention, situating this intervention in cross-national perspective. The Concluding section considers the implications of the French experience for our understanding of path dependence and change.

The dismantling of *dirigisme*

The 1983 U-turn touched off a range of reforms that struck at the core of the *dirigiste* model (Cohen 1989; Hall 1990; Schmidt 1996; Levy 1999, 2000). These changes, inaugurated cautiously by the Socialists from 1983 to 1986, were amplified when the right returned to power under a neoliberal banner from 1986 to 1988, and confirmed and completed by subsequent governments on both sides of the political spectrum. Four sets of changes figured most prominently.

The first change concerned macroeconomic policy. For much of the postwar period, French authorities stimulated the economy through a combination of deficit spending and lax monetary policy, with much of the money flowing to industry (Zysman 1983; Hall 1986; Loriaux 1991). The effects of the resulting inflation on competitiveness were negated by periodic 'aggressive devaluations' that not only compensated for price differentials with France's trading partners, but also conferred a temporary advantage on French producers, albeit at the expense of worker purchasing power.

The Socialists broke with this strategy in 1983. Under the so-called *franc fort* policy, the French franc was informally anchored to the Deutschmark. Since devaluations were no longer an option (let alone 'aggressive devaluations'), France would gain the edge through 'competitive disinflation', that is, by running a rate of inflation lower than that of its trading partners. Toward this end, Keynesianism demand stimulus gave way to austerity budgets, wage indexation was abandoned, and most important, monetary policy was tightened, with real interest rates ranging from 5 to 8 percent for over a decade (Fitoussi 1995). Since the early 1990s, the French inflation rate has been among the lowest in western Europe, while the balance of trade, after nearly twenty years in the red, has registered steady surpluses.

The second set of reforms pertained to France's public enterprises. In 1982, the left nationalized twelve leading industrial conglomerates and thirty-eight banks. When combined with the Liberation-era nationalizations carried out by General de Gaulle, this latest program, costing 47 billion francs, placed thirteen of France's twenty largest firms and virtually the entire banking sector in state hands (Stoffaës 1984). Public enterprises received tens of billions of francs in subsidies, but were pressured to expand employment and invest in areas deemed strategic (if not profitable) by the government.

The 1983 U-turn brought a fundamental shift in the government's relationship with the public enterprises. Nationalized companies were released from their planning targets and instructed to focus instead on profitability. While slashing capital grants and subsidies, the left offered no resistance when public enterprises closed factories and withdrew from strategic sectors. This shift in public-sector management set the stage for the right to launch a campaign of privatizations upon its return to power in 1986. Before the privatization process was interrupted by the 1987 stock-market crash, thirteen financial and industrial groups had been sold off, netting 84.1 billion francs to the French treasury (Zerah 1993: 183). Since 1993, a second round of privatizations has been conducted by governments of both the right and the left, reducing the once-vast holdings of the French state to little more than energy production, public transportation, and some weapons manufactures.

The third major policy shift after 1983 was the abandonment of state efforts to steer private industry. The guiding spirit of this change was that firms would receive less government assistance, but would be subject to fewer restrictions, so that they could raise the necessary resources by their own means (Hall 1990). The hefty budgets for bailouts of loss-making companies, sectoral industrial policy programs, high-tech *grands projets*, and subsidized loans quickly dried up, triggering a wave of bankruptcies. As a counterpoint, however, French business gained a number of new freedoms. The deregulation of financial markets, initiated in 1985, enabled firms to raise funds by issuing equity, reducing their dependence on state-allocated credit. The removal of price controls in 1986 allowed companies to reap the full benefits of successful competitive strategies. The elimination of capital controls in the late 1980s facilitated the expansion of production abroad and gave managers an 'exit' option if domestic conditions were not to their liking. Taken together, these and other reforms helped boost corporate profitability from 9.8 percent of value added in 1982 to 17.3 percent in 1989 (Faugère and Voisin 1994: 32).

The revival of corporate profits was also fueled by a fourth set of developments, the reform of France's system of industrial relations (Groux and Mouriaux 1990; Howell 1992a, Howell 1992b; Labbé and Croisat 1992). State authorities de-indexed wages and lifted a number of restrictions limiting managerial prerogatives, most significantly, the administrative authorization for layoffs (the requirement that layoffs of ten or more employees for economic reasons receive the approval of an inspector from the ministry of labor). They also expanded the scope of workplace bargaining. In a context of high unemployment and weak and divided trade unions, French employers were able to use this new bargaining arena to introduce labor market flexibility largely on their terms. Studies of initial firm-level deals revealed that most accorded no compensation to employees in return for acceptance of greater flexibility and that up to one-third of these agreements actually violated French labor law. Not surprisingly, much of capital's gain in the post-1983 period would come at labor's expense. From 1982 to 1989, the share of value added received by capital increased from 24.0 to 31.7 percent, surpassing the levels of the early 1970s (Faugère and Voisin 1994: 28–9).

The reforms since 1983 have left no *dirigiste* stone unturned. Looking across the wealthy democracies, one would be hard-pressed to find any country that moved so far away from its postwar economic strategy as the France of François Mitterrand and Jacques Chirac. But there is more to the French story than the roll-back of *dirigisme*. State authorities have also launched a number of new programs.

Post-*dirigiste* state intervention

If the practices and institutions associated with *dirigisme* have been dismantled with astonishing speed and thoroughness, the same cannot be said of the French state. On the contrary, state spending and taxation have increased somewhat in the post-*dirigiste* period, as new initiatives have been launched in such areas as labor market policy, social protection, and the promotion of small- and medium-sized enterprises (SMEs). This section describes each of these new state activities in turn.

Labor market programs

French labor market policy has developed in a number of directions. State intervention centered initially on early retirement, a strategy designed to square the circle of 'job loss without unemployment' (Daley 1996). French authorities recognized the need for companies to be able to restructure in order to restore profitability and competitiveness, but such restructuring would not come at the expense of the workforce. Rather, government programs would permit employees over the age of 55—or, in some cases, 50—to retire at close to full pension.

The expansion of early retirement to accommodate and humanize restructuring began under the Giscard presidency. Between 1974 and 1980, the number of early retirees more than tripled from 59,000 to 190,400 (DARES 1996: 100). The left tripled the figure again to over 700,000 workers in 1984. Such measures were expensive, costing as much as 1 million francs per retiree, but they were assumed to be temporary. Officials expected that once French firms restructured and the economy recovered, job creation would begin anew, and early retirement programs could be wound down. Employment creation has remained sluggish, however, and the number of participants in early retirement programs has held steady between 450,000 and 600,000 since the mid-1980s. The effects of early retirement on the French labor market are striking. Today, fewer than one worker in three is still employed at age 60, and France's labor force participation rate for men aged 55–64 is among the lowest in western Europe, at just over 40 percent (Scharpf and Schmidt 2000: 350).

With the return to recession and rising unemployment in the early 1990s, center-right governments deployed a second labor market strategy. The right's efforts focused on the reduction of labor costs, particularly at the low end of the wage spectrum, where a relatively generous minimum wage (6,800 francs per month) and heavy social security charges (roughly 50 percent of wages) are said to dissuade job creation. In 1994, Gaullist Prime Minister, Edouard Balladur attempted to create a subminimum wage for youths 20 percent below the legal minimum, before retreating in a hailstorm of protest. Subsidies and tax breaks for low-wage hires proved less controversial. Under Balladur, employers hiring low-wage workers were exempted from family allowance contributions, while a program inaugurated in 1995 by Balladur's Gaullist successor, Alain Juppé provided subsidies of 5,000–15,000 francs for jobs paying less than 1.3 times the minimum wage.

The center-left government of Lionel Jospin added two further labor market initiatives during its tenure from 1997 to 2002. The first was a youth employment program, the *Programme Emploi Jeunes* (PEJ), which occupied some 350,000 young people. The PEJ was targeted at youths with no significant work experience. In contrast to previous state-sponsored, make-work projects, the PEJ provided full-time employment for an extended period (five years). The government hoped that this extended tenure would enable participants to acquire the skills and experience necessary to secure permanent employment once the subsidies ran out. Under the highly generous terms of the PEJ, the state paid 80 percent of the minimum wage and all social security contributions, leaving only 20 percent of the minimum wage to the charge of the employer. Employers in the private sector were barred from participating, however. Fearful that private companies would substitute subsidized hires for existing personnel, the government restricted the PEJ to nonprofit and public organizations. The PEJ was expensive, costing some 35 billion francs, although some of the money was recovered from other youth employment programs that were terminated.

The second high-profile measure by the Jospin government was the reduction of the workweek from 39 to 35 hours. Although conservative critics and the national employer association denounced the reform as a job-killer that would force companies to lay off workers as a result of higher labor costs, the government took a number of measures to assuage business concerns. The reform was phased in over a five-year period, giving employers time to adjust and to extract wage concessions from employees as the price for shorter working hours. Employers were also allowed to introduce considerable flexibility into work schedules, which can now vary considerably from week to week. Finally, the government

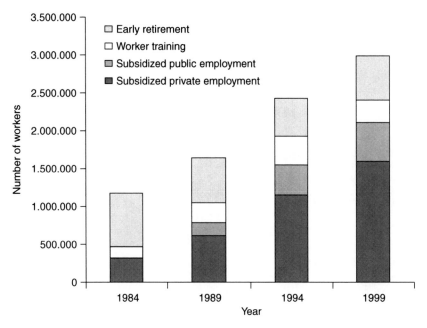

Figure 4.2 Number of French workers in public labor market programs
Source: DARES (1996, 2000).

tendered significant subsidies to companies that signed collective bargaining agreements reducing work time. The subsidies are greatest at the bottom of the pay scale (21,500 francs per year for a minimum-wage hire), declining gradually to 4,000 francs for jobs paying more than 1.8 times the minimum wage. The cost of the reform is estimated at 110 billion francs, although again, part of the money is being shifted from other programs, notably the Balladur and Juppé government's subsidies for low-wage hires.

Looking at labor market policy globally, Figure 4.2 reveals that the number of French workers enrolled in some kind of public labor market program has expanded two-and-one-half-fold in the post-*dirigiste* period—rising from slightly under 1.2 million in 1984, at the height of industrial restructuring, to nearly 3 million in 1999 (DARES 1996; DARES December 2000).[2] This total is in addition to the 2 million French workers who are formally unemployed. Aggregate spending on labor market policy has shown a similar increase, expanding from slightly over 2 percent of GDP in the mid-1980s to 4.2 percent of GDP in 1999. Today, France spends as much on labor market intervention as Sweden, the Mecca of active labor market policy.

Social protection

The French state has been equally prominent in the social policy arena (Levy 2000). Once classified as a 'welfare laggard', Figure 4.3 reveals that France has

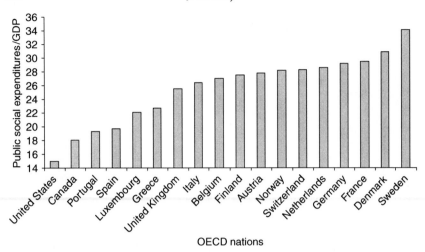

Figure 4.3 The 1998 Public social expenditures as a percentage of GDP, select OECD nations
Source: OECD (2002*b*).

developed the largest welfare state outside Scandinavia, exceeding even Germany laboring under the costs of unification. French welfare spending rose from 21.3 percent of GDP in 1980 to 26.5 percent in 1990, to 29.5 percent in 1998 (OECD 2002*b*). The two largest welfare programs, pensions and health care, have both experienced significant growth since the early 1980s. Spending on pensions increased from 7.7 percent of GDP in 1981 to 9.8 percent in 2000 (Ministry of Finance 2001: Statistical Annex, table VII.2). France's pay-as-you-go pension system is among the most generous in the world and, in contrast to most other countries, it has experienced only limited retrenchment measures in recent years (Charpin 1999; Myles and Pierson 2001). French health care spending increased from 7.4 percent of GDP in 1980 to 9.6 percent in 1998, as France passed Austria, Belgium, Denmark, Holland, and Sweden to become the number two spender in the European Union (EU), behind Germany (OECD 2000*a*: table A7). The French health care system is not without problems, but thanks in part to this increased commitment of resources, the French system was rated the planet's best by the World Health Organization.

French authorities have not only expanded existing social programs; they have also launched new ones. In 1988, the Socialist government of Michel Rocard, established a national social safety net or guaranteed income, the *revenu minimum d'insertion* (RMI), for all adults over the age of 25. The RMI replaced a patchwork of local and targeted social assistance programs that had left large segments of the population uncovered, notably the long-term unemployed and persons suffering from psychological problems, alcoholism, and/or chemical dependency. Benefits are available on a means-tested basis to all citizens and long-term residents over the age of 25. The RMI provides a monthly allowance of 2,500 francs along with the promise of support services to help 'insert' (the 'I' in 'RMI') recipients back into society and, in some cases, into a job.[3] Claimants are also eligible for housing allowances and free health insurance. Although the 'insertion' dimension of the RMI remains underdeveloped, the program does provide nonnegligible financial assistance to some 1 million of France's neediest citizens, at an annual cost of 25 billion francs.

The Jospin government launched two new social programs. The *couverture maladie universelle* (CMU), which began operating in 2000, makes health care available free of charge to low-income groups. The CMU originated with a pledge by the Juppé government in 1995 to extend public health insurance to the 200,000 French citizens (0.3 percent of the population) who lacked such coverage. The Jospin government honored Juppé's pledge, but also addressed the far greater problem of access among those who actually possess heath insurance. France's public health insurance reimburses just 75 percent of the costs of medical treatment on average (Join-Lambert, Bolot-Gittler et al. 1997). Although 85 percent of the population reduces co-payments by subscribing to a supplementary insurance, for the remaining 15 percent, low reimbursement rates tended to place all but emergency medical treatment out of reach. The CMU greatly attenuated this problem by providing free supplementary health insurance on a means-tested basis to an estimated 5 million people at a cost of some 10 billion francs annually.

In 2002, the Jospin government created a new welfare entitlement, the *aide personnalisée à l'autonomie* (APA), which helps defray the costs of in-home assistance for the elderly. Like the RMI, the APA replaced a locally variable program, the *prestation spécifique de dépendance* (PSD), which had been established by the Juppé government in 1997. The APA provides up to 7,000 francs per month, depending on the severity of the incapacity and the financial resources of the claimant, for home-assistance expenses. Some 800,000 elderly citizens are expected to benefit from the APA, as against 135,000 for the PSD, at a cost of 23 billion francs per year.

The commitment to expanding France's welfare state extends beyond partisan lines. The RMI was established by a unanimous vote of the French parliament. While it is true that governments of the left enacted the CMU and APA, in both cases, the left built upon earlier initiatives of the right. Moreover, Gaullist President Jacques Chirac was elected in 1995, thanks to a campaign that stressed the need for heightened state intervention to heal France's 'social fracture' and renew the 'Republican pact' between state and citizen.

An interesting feature of French political discourse is that the same distrust of market forces and faith in state guidance that animated *dirigiste* industrial policy can now be found in social policy. Jacques Chirac would have never dreamed of calling for a new round of nationalizations or a revival of sectoral planning. Yet it was entirely legitimate, even electorally savvy, for him to call for intensified state intervention in the social arena. This kind of redirection of the sphere of legitimate state intervention can be seen in the third area of intensified activism, the promotion of SMEs.

Promotion of SMEs

While winding down industrial policy programs for the 'national champions', state authorities have developed an array of instruments to promote SMEs (Levy 1999). The guiding principle of these programs is to encourage SMEs to 'make leaps', to accelerate the pace of their development. State subsidies of up to 50 percent or success-conditional loans are available for a variety of risky ventures, including: integrating composite materials or electronics into existing products; developing new products; computerizing production operations; and hiring managers and engineers. All of these actions are designed to usher SMEs to a new stage in their development, whether in the form of new products, new production processes, or a new management structure.

State authorities see no contradiction between their claim to have moved beyond *dirigisme* and the multiplication of public programs and tax credits, costing some 100 billion francs annually, in support of SMEs. Part of the reason is that they regard SMEs as more needy than the national champions, as more susceptible to various forms of market failure. Large firms and conglomerates possess the financial and managerial resources to think strategically; they do not require government programs to assist them in these tasks. By contrast, many SMEs lack the resources or know-how to act strategically. The various measures proffered by state agencies have been devised with the idea of addressing traditional weaknesses or problems confronted by SMEs: a limited awareness of new process and product technologies; underdeveloped managerial structures; a lack of capital and access to bank loans. French officials believe that small, well-targeted programs can help SMEs overcome these obstacles, bolstering what has traditionally been a weak segment of France's economy.

State authorities reject the *dirigiste* label for a second reason. In their view, the character of SME promotional policies is very different from past *dirigiste* methods. State officials are no longer picking winners and forcing firms to merge; they are merely trying to create a supportive environment for private managers. They are not imposing competitive strategies or planning targets, but rather underwriting the strategies developed by small businesses. Moreover, many of the tools of intervention operate through private consulting companies, as opposed to state technocrats. Thus, the new SME policies are more market-conforming, more respectful of private initiatives than traditional state intervention.

For all these changes, though, the underlying assumption behind the policies toward SMEs is that the heads of small firms do not fully understand their own interests and that the state must encourage (and, in the process, become quite involved in) such desirable practices as: investment in risky innovation; improvements in quality control methods; the introduction of new materials into products; modernization of plant and equipment; use of sophisticated software; hiring of managers and engineers. Nor is coercion entirely absent from the relationship. While state officials are not telling private managers what to do, they are paying 20–50 percent of the costs for them to do certain things. Ironically, it could be argued that at no point in French history has the state meddled in so many firms and in so many prerogatives of management as under today's ostensibly post-*dirigiste* regime.

This section has shown that despite the discrediting of France's postwar *dirigiste* model, a number of expensive new state interventions have emerged in the years since 1983. The French state may be different from the past, but it is not smaller. The next section explains why state intervention has proven so resilient in France.

The roots of redeployment

France's political system has remained very receptive to state intervention in the years since the 1983 U-turn. Three sets of forces have driven this new intervention: (1) the terms of party competition; (2) the pressures and fall-out associated with economic liberalization; and (3) the limited capacity of non-state actors.

The terms of party competition

Two characteristics of French party competition that have fueled continued state activism are the nature of the dominant party of the right, the Gaullist Rally for the Republic (RPR),[4] and the vulnerability of incumbent governments.

Like many other European countries, France lacks a strong self-avowed liberal party. But in France the dominant party of the French right, the RPR, is not only not neoliberal but also statist. This is a striking departure from most European countries, where Christian Democrats are generally the main conservative party. Christian Democracy shares to some extent the neoliberal aversion to concentrated state power (Kersbergen 1995). For French Gaullists, by contrast, the state has tended to be the first resort, arguably the only resort. Thus, during the quarter century prior to Mitterrand's election as president in 1981, it was the French right, not the left, that ran France's *dirigiste* model, and it was the Gaullist party that gave the clearest expression to the *dirigiste* vision. The party's founder, General Charles de Gaulle saw the state as the agent of modernization and the general will. An enlightened, interventionist state would lead French business where markets feared to tread, overriding France's cautious, traditional elites to restore the country to greatness. State intervention was associated not just with industrial modernization, but also with restoring France as a great power in the international arena in general, and reducing its dependence on the United States in particular. De Gaulle's reign as president from 1958 to 1969 marked the heyday of *dirigiste* policymaking—of voluntarist industrial policy, 'national champions', and advanced-technology *grands projets*. For many Gaullists, even today, an activist state is a core component of their ideology.

In the post-*dirigiste* period, Gaullists no longer embrace industrial policy, but as before, Gaullist ideology holds that protecting France from pernicious US influences, from a race to the bottom in social standards and convergence on a neoliberal minimum, requires state activism. It is, therefore, no coincidence that a Gaullist, Jacques Chirac campaigned for president in 1995 on a program of intensified state intervention to heal France's 'social fracture' and restore 'social cohesion'. From a Gaullist perspective, the expansion of state intervention is not merely a social imperative, but a geopolitical imperative, a measure of France's capacity to preserve its sovereignty and identity in an increasingly integrated, interdependent, and US-influenced world.

Beyond these goals, the Gaullist movement associates state intervention with maintaining social order. This concern was not a founding feature of Gaullist ideology, but rather a legacy of the near-revolution that rocked France in May 1968 and led to Charles de Gaulle's resignation from the presidency the following year. Many leading figures in the Gaullist party, including Chirac and Balladur, were junior government officials in May 1968. This scarring, formative political experience has made both Chirac and Balladur extremely reluctant to confront popular protests. In a country with a relatively new and contested constitution and a long tradition of revolutionary politics, concern for social order has invariably trumped concern for fiscal prudence. Time and again, French leaders (to be fair, leaders from all parties, not just the Gaullists) have responded to protests with policy concessions—new spending programs, protection from competition, or the withdrawal of proposed liberalizing reforms (Berger 1981; Cohen 1989; Levy 2000).

Gaullism, then, is not a garden-variety conservative party. Its founding ethos emphasizes state intervention as the key to rapid economic development and the breaking of American hegemony. Its transformation, stemming from the events of May 1968, has made Gaullist leaders willing to pay almost any price to limit protest and preserve order.

Along with the specificities of French conservatism, state activism has been driven by more mundane electoral considerations. Over the past twenty-five years, French governments have been exceedingly vulnerable. Each of the last three presidencies has included one period of 'cohabitation', that is, of a president and parliament from opposite sides of the political spectrum (1986–8, 1993–5, 1997–2002). Indeed, since 1986, France has experienced cohabitation as often as not (nine years out of eighteen). What is more, the sitting prime minister has lost seven consecutive national elections dating from 1981 (1981 presidential and legislative elections, 1986 legislative, 1988 presidential and legislative, 1993 legislative, 1995 presidential, 1997 legislative, 2002 presidential). With such a tenuous hold on power, leaders of all political stripes have felt keen pressure to respond to popular demands for state protection and resources.

Economic liberalization

France's break with *dirigisme* eliminated a number of interventionist policies, but it also created pressures for new kinds of state intervention. As described above, the dramatic expansion of early retirement opportunities played a critical role in facilitating market-driven industrial restructuring. Instead of protecting jobs through bailouts of uncompetitive companies, French authorities allowed firms to reorganize, while protecting worker income streams through early retirement. Early retirement helped salve the left's guilty conscience, but more important, it effectively demobilized France's working class, undercutting trade union capacity to mount resistance to industrial restructuring. The vast majority of French workers were more than willing to quit smelly, physically taxing, alienating jobs, to receive 90 percent of their previous wages without having to report to work. The political dynamics involved in early retirement were almost the mirror image of those in Germany, as analyzed by Trampusch (Chapter 8). In Germany, unions aggressively used early retirement to offload adjustment expenses onto the state. In France, by contrast, the unions opposed early retirement, viewing it as a retreat from the state's commitment to promote employment through Keynesian demand stimulus and industrial policy. Early retirement marginalized French unions, preventing them from mobilizing their members against industrial restructuring. Thus, the recourse to early retirement was not simply a social strategy, but also an economic strategy—a fundamental prerequisite for carrying out much-needed industrial restructuring.

Government policies were deployed not only to facilitate the movement away from *dirigisme*, but also to palliate the perceived limits or failings of economic liberalization. The restoration of corporate profitability and competitiveness in the mid-1980s did not bring about an appreciable reduction in unemployment. Consequently, beginning with the Rocard government in 1988, French authorities adopted a much more interventionist approach to labor markets. The Rocard government expanded active labor market policies, notably training programs, public internships, and subsidies for hard-to-place youths and the long-term unemployed. The number of beneficiaries of government measures had already risen from 450,000 in 1984 to 850,000 in 1989, but it would more than double during the next five years, reaching 1,900,000 in 1994 (DARES 1996: 100). In the latter year, while France counted 3.1 million workers officially unemployed, another 2.5 million citizens benefited from some kind of labor market measures (early retirement, subsidized employment, training programs, and public internships). In the 1990s, center-right governments expanded employment subsidies, while the left multiplied public internships. The 35-hour workweek was also presented as a job-creating measure (although this claim was hotly disputed).

The persistence of mass unemployment has led French authorities to innovate in the area of welfare policy as well as labor market policy. France's Bismarckian welfare state was constructed on the basis of social insurance, as opposed to social assistance (Palier 1999). In other words, benefits are tendered, not as a matter of right, to all citizens (social assistance), but in return for contributions, primarily payroll taxes, paid previously to the social security system (social insurance). Prior to the 1970s, the distinction between social insurance and social assistance was of little practical significance, since conditions of full employment enabled virtually all workers and their families to meet the requirements for obtaining coverage.

With the spread of unemployment, part-time employment, and temporary employment, however, French workers are often unable to accumulate sufficient social security contributions to qualify for insurance benefits. Aggravating the problem, surging rates of divorce and out-of-wedlock births have made it less likely that women and children will be covered under the insurance of a 'male breadwinner'. Thus, a large and growing segment of the population—the long-term unemployed, part-time and temporary workers, the intermittently employed, and many single or divorced parents and their offsprings—has found itself unprotected by the traditional system of social insurance (see Palier, Chapter 5).

A number of social initiatives have been designed to plug the holes in France's Bismarckian, insurance-based system. The RMI offers basic income support to adults who have exhausted or failed to qualify for unemployment insurance. The CMU provides supplementary health insurance for citizens not covered by employers. French authorities have also redirected France's program of family allowances toward poverty relief. The broad trend, since the early 1970s, has been toward the 'socialization of family policy': 'horizontal redistribution' between childless workers and families with children has given way to 'vertical redistribution' between the wealthy and the poor (Lenoir 1990; Commaille 1998). The primary vehicle for this change has been the development of means-tested programs. Originally, family allowance payments were made according to the number of children, with no reference to income levels. Since the early 1970s, however, French authorities have added a number of means-tested benefits—including housing allowances, child-care subsidies, and income supplements for single parents—to assist struggling families. The share of family allowance spending subjected to means-testing has risen from 13.6 percent in 1970 to over 60 percent today. Thus, if French social protection has been expanding, the new social programs reflect a liberal, market-conforming logic, as Palier notes (Chapter 5), and are less generous and secure than traditional, Bismarckian benefits.

France's break with *dirigisme* in the 1980s provided a dual impetus to state intervention. The *promise* of liberalization induced authorities to commit vast resources to the transition process, to the alleviation of social pain and political resistance, in the expectation that a more flexible labor market would quickly generate enough jobs and make such costly transitional measures unnecessary (or, at least, much less necessary). The *disappointments* of liberalization, the continuing high levels of unemployment not only made it impossible to wind down supposedly transitional early retirement measures, but drove new spending in the form of active labor market programs and social assistance programs. In short, 'de-dirigisation' and welfare state expansion were two sides of the same (very expensive) coin.

Institutional incapacity outside the central state

State activism has been driven not only by political and economic logics, but also by an institutional logic. As Tocqueville lamented over 150 years ago,

French authorities have long concentrated power in the central state, while weakening or, at least, neglecting societal and local institutions. This orientation figured especially prominently in the postwar *dirigiste* model. Under the logic of *dirigisme*, state authorities needed to be free to pursue the general will, unimpeded by conservative, self-serving, particularistic interest groups. The 'strong' French state rested upon a 'weak' set of societal and local organizations.

In the post-*dirigiste* period, this strategy has come back to haunt French policymakers—an outcome that I have labeled 'Tocqueville's Revenge' (for an extended treatment, see Levy 1999). Time and again, French authorities have attempted to devolve economic and social functions to actors outside the central state, who were deemed more flexible, efficient, and democratic. Yet in each instance, the organizations in question have been too weak and divided to handle these new responsibilities. As a result, pressures for intervention have bounced back into the state arena, spawning new forms of state activity.

We can observe this pattern across a number of areas. As the state withdrew from detailed industrial relations, French authorities hoped that unions, employers, and works councils would work together to upgrade training, launch apprenticeships, and expand flexibility. As it withdrew from industrial policy, French authorities hoped that investment banks would nurture long collaborative relations with industry, what the French call *banque-industrie*, taking an equity stake, providing capital in hard times, and financing risky long-term development. As French authorities became less enamored of 'national champions', they looked to provincial policy networks to nurture local districts of SMEs with guidance, technology, and capital. And as French authorities sought to move away from micro-managing the health care system, they hoped that the medical profession could organize responsible cost control. In each case, however, the historic domination of state authorities had marginalized, weakened, and distorted the strategies of the very institutions called upon to assume critical responsibilities in place of the state. The problem was compounded by the limited scope of institutional reforms in the 1980s. The arrival of a leftist government in power for the first time in decades offered a chance to shuffle the institutional deck, and several reforms did create new opportunities for societal and local institutions. Still, most of these reforms were passed during the initial ultra-*dirigiste* phase of the Mitterrand years and were geared more toward second-left, *autogestionnaire* themes of participation and democratic expression than toward economic coordination. As a result, the reforms did not tend to give societal and local institutions the powers that they needed.[5]

The weakness and inexperience of French institutions between state and market—whether historically predetermined or the result of the timidities and contradictions of the 1980s—scuttled successive attempts on the part of the state to hand over traditional state responsibilities and obligations to societal institutions and associations (Levy 1999). Consequently, state authorities have come under tremendous pressure to salve pressing problems. With neoliberal deregulation politically contested and German-style association-based solutions institutionally unavailable, state authorities have found themselves on the front line. In response, the French state has re-intervened on a large scale. In industrial relations, for example, to cushion French workers against a one-sided, employer-driven deregulation, state authorities have both spent and reregulated. Official unemployment, high as it is, has been limited by massive spending on early retirement, subsidized hires, and government internships. On the regulatory front, the government has imposed modest restraints on layoffs—more consultation, better severance packages—and a less modest requirement that firms move to a 35-hour workweek.

The financial arena has likewise seen extensive state intervention. When French banks neglected low-margin SMEs, the government created a series of specialized credit channels, providing billions of francs of subsidized loans, which were eventually merged into a bank for the development of SMEs. When French banks refused to assist troubled 'national champions', the state injected 10–20 billion francs in Renault, Air France, Thomson, Bull, and the SNCF (Société Nationale des Chemins de Fer Français), respectively. And when Crédit Lyonnais, the leading proponent of the *banque-industrie* strategy, experienced an un-German financial collapse, the government committed over 90 billion francs to a rescue package.

In the provincial arena, with local authorities unable to mount coherent, well-funded programs in support of SMEs, the state has stepped into the void. As noted above, state authorities have created a number of special lending channels, culminating in the SME Development Bank, as well as programs that encourage SMEs to integrate new technology, launch new products, or upgrade managements' structures. State authorities have also bolstered their organizational presence in the provinces, shifting personnel and resources downward, in order to be able to respond quickly to the demands of local business. Most of the small-business programs are administered by so-called 'deconcentrated' agencies associated with the Ministry of Industry: the National Agency for the Valorization of Research (ANVAR), the Agency for the Development of Applied Production Technology (ADEPA), and the Ministry of Industry's own field services, the Regional Directions of Industry, Research, and the Environment (DRIRE). The French use the word 'deconcentration' to denote a shifting of power *within* the state, from Parisian ministries to provincial branch offices—in contrast to 'decentralization', which entails a transfer of power *away* from the state, to independent, elected local authorities.

Finally, in health care, the failure of a negotiated approach to cost control has given way to a decidedly top-down approach. In 1995, the Juppé government, a government of the right, enacted what has come to be known as the 'nationalization' of the French health care system. Juppé's reform, which required an amendment to the French constitution, subjects the health care budget to a parliamentary vote. His hope was that by imposing an annual budget from above, rather than accommodating a series of autonomous spending decisions from below, the government would be able to better limit spending. The Juppé plan also tightened administrative controls on hospitals and proposed to reward or punish physicians by adjusting fees annually, from one region to the next, according to each region's success in meeting government spending targets. The Jospin government continued along these lines, levying penalties on medical professions and pharmacists who exceeded public targets. Recurrent government meddling prompted the French employer association to withdraw from the health care administration board, arguing that there was no sense in participating in a system where the government called all the shots.

The social anesthesia state: achievements and limitations

If state activism remains a prominent feature of France's political economy, the goals and instruments of that intervention have changed dramatically. Post-*dirigiste* state intervention differs in two important ways from its *dirigiste* antecedents. The first is in the relationship to the private sector. Instead of seeking to impose specific industrial strategies on firms, state initiatives have been geared toward providing an enabling environment, especially for small business: subsidies for innovation, market prospecting, and investment in new technologies; resources for training and low-skill hires; and early retirement programs that permit firms to downsize without provoking worker resistance. All of these state programs have expanded the options available to companies, while leaving the initiative in private manager's hands. They have been market-conforming more than market-directing (see Palier, Chapter 5 on welfare policies in particular).

The other distinctive feature of the new state intervention concerns the losers of economic liberalization. In its original form, the *dirigiste* model shifted resources from consumption to investment, limiting real wages and social spending. By the 1970s, however, the losers of economic modernization had been mobilized, and state resources were used increasingly to block change—to bail out uncompetitive firms, thereby preventing layoffs and plant closings. The more recent state intervention reflects a strategic shift. The concerns of modernization's losers have been addressed, but not by blocking economic reform. Rather, under what I would call a 'social anesthesia' strategy, public resources are mobilized to pacify and demobilize the victims and opponents of market-led adjustment. Many of the most expensive new policies in France over the past twenty years have reflected this social anesthesia logic: early retirement, guaranteed minimum income, need-based supplementary health insurance, employment subsidies, and public internships. The social anesthesia mission has also bolstered the enabling environment strategy. Whereas the *dirigiste* state sought to steer the market, the social anesthesia state underwrites market-led, privately determined adjustment strategies by pacifying, dividing, and demobilizing potential opponents.

Seen in a comparative light, the social anesthesia strategy has much to recommend it. Over the past twenty years, the leading exemplars of state-led economic development have experienced profound crisis. Japan's statist system, once the object of envy and fear among Japan's trading partners, is now blamed for the country's decade-long period of economic stagnation. In the wake of the 1998 financial meltdown in East Asia, the Korean offshoot of the Japanese model has been recategorized as 'crony capitalism'. The roots of these statist crises evoke the French experience of the 1970s and early 1980s: a less hospitable international environment; the erosion of conservative hegemony, making it difficult for state authorities to ignore the demands of labor, while channeling resources to big business; a diversion of industrial policies from economic modernization, as concerns about unemployment lead officials to preserve jobs at almost any cost.

If the roots of statist crisis are similar across France, Japan, and Korea, only France has been able to extract itself from this crisis. The contrast to Japan is especially illuminating. Despite over a decade of economic stagnation and the discrediting of state guidance in the eyes of the population, Japanese authorities have been able to implement only limited, partial, liberalizing reforms, at best (for an analysis of the changes that have taken place, see Vogel, Chapter 6). Part of the reason is a reluctance of state authorities to cede traditional powers. In addition, the Japanese political system, with its weak governing coalitions, is ill-suited to the task of enacting sweeping, controversial reforms like liberalization packages. But perhaps of greatest importance is the fact that Japan lacks a French-style social safety net (Miura 2002*a*, Miura 2002*b*; Levy, Miura et al. forthcoming). Japanese authorities are spending vast amounts propping up debt-laden banks which are propping up, in turn, debt-laden companies because were those banks and their customers to shut down, millions of Japanese workers would lose their jobs, and Japan has no social safety net to take care of them. As Mari Miura has argued, in Japan, employment itself is the main instrument of social protection.

State spending has increased dramatically in Japan as in France, from around 30 percent of GDP in the late 1980s to nearly 40 percent of GDP today (OECD 2002*a*). Indeed, Japan's public debt is now the highest in the OECD, at some 140 percent of GDP, exceeding the debt of traditional fiscal laughing-stocks like Italy. Whereas France's social anesthesia spending has enabled the country to break with dysfunctional statist policies and reap the benefits of market-led adjustment, Japan has little to show for its spending. The expansion of state outlays has served to delay economic adjustment, rather than facilitate it. Put crudely, social anesthesia permitted France to dismantle dysfunctional, diverted *dirigisme*. In Japan, by contrast, the problems of diverted *dirigisme* remain, while the fiscal resources that could have supported a French-style, social anesthesia path of adjustment have been squandered on a succession of bank bailouts and unsuccessful stimulus packages.

France's social anesthesia state is not without problems and risks, however. The first is that recurrent state intervention will reinforce the Tocquevillean problem of a demobilized and irresponsible associational landscape. French interest groups have little incentive to organize and bargain with each other if the state is calling all the shots. Recently, the French employer association withdrew from the national health insurance board, arguing that the board's corporatist principles of operation were rendered moot by recurrent government meddling. Moreover, lacking partners and buffers, state authorities often find themselves on the front line, as every aggrieved party in French society—from displaced workers, to uncompetitive farmers, to overworked truckers—turns to the state for relief. In an extreme example, workers in a factory slated for shutdown occupied the factory and threatened to dump toxic chemicals into the river unless the state (not the company) dispatched a labor official to negotiate a better severance package!

A second problem of the social anesthesia strategy is that it is very expensive. Many social initiatives, such as generous early retirement programs, were envisaged as temporary. Workers would be pensioned off, companies would restructure, then job creation would resume anew, and early retirement programs could be wound down. Instead of winding down, however, social anesthesia programs have been preserved. What is more, new initiatives—such as a guaranteed minimum income—have been added, as mass unemployment has claimed new victims. While one can certainly sympathize with the effort to protect the poor and vulnerable, the cost of these programs has pushed the French state to the limits of its taxing capacity and, critics argue, undermined competitiveness and job creation.

A third problem is that social anesthesia is largely passive; it pays people not to work. If this represents an improvement over bailing out uncompetitive companies in order to prevent layoffs, one can imagine better uses for the money. Once again, a comparative perspective is revealing. Social democratic countries like Sweden spend as much or even more than France on social programs, but the social democratic approach is centered around the so-called 'work line', the notion that every adult should be employed (Titmuss 1987; Esping-Andersen 1990; Huber and Stephens 2001). As a result, passive measures tend to be limited, with much of the spending concentrated on 'active' measures that facilitate employment, such as education and training, relocation assistance, and low-cost public child care. Under the 'active' or 'social investment' model, there is an economic pay-off beyond simply keeping displaced workers from protesting and blocking layoffs. France's social anesthesia strategy offers few such benefits, few if any gains in human capital and employment. Bringing the two cross-national comparisons in this section together, one can say that French state spending has brought greater economic gains than Japanese spending (not to mention French spending in the 1970s and early 1980s), but that it is still a far cry from the Swedish, social democratic, social investment/workline model.

The fourth problem of the social anesthesia strategy is that the anesthetic appears to be wearing off. A minimum income of $500 per month may be acceptable as a stop-gap, but not as a way of life. In the long run, the RMI is no substitute for social integration through a steady job, for upward social mobility. Many of the supposed beneficiaries of social anesthesia policies harbor great bitterness toward a government that offers them meager allowances and a succession of dead-end internships and substandard part-time or temporary jobs. This dissatisfaction probably cost Lionel Jospin the presidency in 2002, as leftist voters flocked to three different Trotskyist parties, preventing Jospin from qualifying for the run-off election with President Chirac. This dissatisfaction has also helped fuel the rise of the xenophobic, racist National Front of Jean-Marie Le Pen, which has become the number one party by far among both blue-collar workers and the unemployed.

For all its limitations, the social anesthesia state has enabled France to jettison dysfunctional *dirigiste* industrial policies, to create a competitive, productive, export-oriented, and reasonably dynamic economy, while limiting the social fall-out. Looking toward the future, French authorities are unlikely to depart in any dramatic way from the social anesthesia approach. France does not have a neoliberal political party. French voters have little love for economic liberalism, and President Chirac is not known for swimming against popular opinion. Moreover, having been burned in 1995, when his government launched a bold plan to overhaul the health care and pension systems, only to have this plan dissolve in the face of massive protests, Chirac is proceeding with great caution. The government is attempting to reduce health care and pension outlays, but through limited, gradual reforms, rather than any kind of 'big bang'.

The one area where significant change may yet occur is in the area of labor market policy. There is widespread agreement that French labor market policy is heavily tilted in a passive direction and that more could be done to increase labor market participation. A number of actors have mobilized around this theme. The French employer association, the Movement of French Enterprises (MEDEF), has engaged the unions in a series of negotiations to increase incentives and opportunities for unemployed workers to accept jobs. The government has voiced a desire to scale back costly early retirement programs and has also phased out many make-work, public internships. Under the Jospin premiership, a number of tax reforms were enacted to reduce poverty traps among low-wage workers, including the introduction of a modest version of the US Earned Income Tax Credit. Should France's fiscal picture improve, an extension of such policies might appeal to a government eager to show its social side, its concern for, in the words of the prime minister, *la France d'en bas* (the France below, at the bottom). This interest in labor market activation has been bolstered by external factors: the EU's Employment Strategy, which has been accepted by all member states, including France, sets a target of 60 percent labor force participation by the year 2010, with a 50 percent goal for older workers.

Conclusion: implications of the French experience

This chapter has shown that notwithstanding the repudiation of the *dirigiste* model and the growing constraints of globalization and European integration, state activism has remained a prominent feature of France's political economy. My explanation has emphasized political, economic, and institutional factors.

Politically, France has been a case of liberalization without liberals. It is not just parties on the French left that feel ambivalent about liberalization, but also a French right marked by the Gaullist-statist heritage and a deep concern for social order. Economically, France has been a case of state-led liberalization, with state authorities deploying new instruments first to make economic liberalization politically acceptable and then to compensate for its limitations. Finally, institutionally, France has been a case of 'Tocqueville's Revenge'. The inability or unwillingness of state authorities to rebuild long-neglected societal and local institutions has left the French state on the front line. Lacking buffers to deflect demands for economic assistance or social protection, French authorities have found themselves intervening on a massive scale.

My point is not that France has failed to change in the years since 1983. On the contrary, France has experienced significant liberalizing reform. The *dirigiste* model has been dismantled, the market unleashed, and French competitiveness greatly enhanced. Still, the move toward the market has not been accompanied by a shrinking of the state, but rather by a redeployment of state energies to new arenas—labor markets, social protection, and the promotion of SMEs.

France's experience since 1983 offers three main insights into the changing place of the state. The first is that dismantling specific policies or tools associated with a particular statist framework is not the same thing as dismantling that framework itself. State intervention can morph and migrate. While voluntarist industrial policy has become a thing of the past in France, labor market and welfare expenditures have grown to near-Scandinavian proportions. For this reason, in gauging institutional change, it is important to examine what is new, not just what is old. If we confine our investigation to existing forms of state intervention, to the question of whether these forms are surviving or being undermined, we may be committing the analytic equivalent of searching for the key under the lamppost. In the French case, such an investigation would yield the erroneous conclusion that the state has become a nonfactor, that it has been scaled back, rather than redeployed.

The second lesson is that shifting paths requires a positive action as well as a negative action—the forging of a new mode of economic and social regulation to replace the old. This lesson is reflected in both the achievements and limitations of France's post-*dirigiste* transformation. In terms of the achievements, French authorities were able to extricate themselves from a dysfunctional statist system—an accomplishment that Japanese authorities can only regard with envy—because they developed a social anesthesia strategy to accompany the move to the market. In terms of the limitations of the French transformation, French authorities have been unable to reduce demands on the state because they failed to invest in societal institutions between the state and the market. The underdevelopment of intermediate societal associations and institutions for economic coordination has left the French state on the front line, greatly complicating the task of reducing social spending. Put in more general terms, the lesson is that without a new institutional order, there will always be pressures and opportunities to resurrect elements of the old.

The third lesson of the French experience is that to the extent that globalization or European integration necessitates changes in state intervention, national responses may take the form of a redeployment of the state, as opposed to a shrinking of the state. This vision not only stands in contrast to strong globalization claims about convergence, but also to path-dependent analyses emphasizing the persistence of long-established arrangements. French authorities have not perpetuated postwar *dirigiste* arrangements; they have dismantled these arrangements. There has been real change. At the same time, the French state has not shrunk, as the logic of globalization would anticipate. Between *plus-ça-change* continuity and globalization-driven convergence, France may be on a third path—where old forms of state intervention have been discredited and cleared away, but new forms have emerged in their place. Borrowing from Schumpeter, we might conceive of this redeployment path as a kind of 'institutional creative destruction'.

Notes

1. In addition to members of the workshop on Continuity and Discontinuity in Institutional Analysis, I wish to thank the following for their comments and suggestions on earlier drafts of this chapter: Stephen Cohen, Peter Hall, Ellen Immergut, Bruno Palier, T. J. Pempel, Nicolas Véron, and John Zysman.
2. Figure 4.2 also suggests that French labor market expenditures have become more 'active' over the years, encouraging recipients to work ('active'), rather than to withdraw from the labor market ('passive'). Whereas the number of employees in passive early retirement programs declined slightly from just over 700,000 in 1984 to less than 600,000 in 1999, subsidized jobs in the private sector expanded from 320,000 to 1.6 million, subsidized jobs in the public sector from 8,000 to 509,000, and positions in training programs from 143,000 to 298,000.
3. Although job placement is one of the objectives of the RMI, the program has no employment search requirement. For many recipients—older, unskilled workers or persons suffering from psychological problems, alcoholism, and/or chemical dependency—employment is a remote possibility, at best. In addition, the RMI has been criticized for creating poverty traps. A claimant who accepts a low-wage, part-time job can lose as much in benefits as he or she earns in wages. Even for a full-time, minimum-wage position, the effective tax rate is estimated to exceed 60%. Bourguignon, F. and Bureau, D. (1999). *L'Architecture des prélèvements en France: Etat des lieux et voies de réforme*. Paris: La Documentation Française.
4. Following the 2002 presidential election, a new party of the right was created, the Union for the Presidential Majority (UMP). The Gaullist RPR and most of the UDF were absorbed by the UMP, which is dominated by the Gaullists.
5. For instance, the Auroux laws mandated workplace bargaining, but left France's anemic labor movement without the capacity to negotiate with employers on an equal footing. Privatization gave French financial institutions an equity stake in industrial enterprises, but the banks were squeezed as both lenders and borrowers by policies of financial market liberalization and were, therefore, in no position to engage in risky, long-term investments. The Defferre laws freed French local authorities from heavy-handed state controls, but gave them little extra money and failed to rationalize a distinctly un-Cartesian provincial landscape, marked by a proliferation of overlapping local initiatives. Finally, the government conferred official recognition on MG-France, but did little to bolster this organization against its rivals in the medical profession.

References

BERGER, SUZANNE (1981). Lame Ducks and National Champions: Industrial Policy in the Fifth Republic. In: William Andrews and Stanley Hoffmann (eds.), *The Fifth Republic at Twenty*. Albany, NY: SUNY Press, pp. 160–78.

BOURGUIGNON, FRANÇOIS and BUREAU, DOMINIQUE (1999). *L'Architecture des prélèvements en France: Etat des lieux et voies de réforme*. Paris: La Documentation Française.

CHARPIN, JEAN-MICHEL (1999). *L'avenir de nos retraites*. Paris: La Documentation Française.

COHEN, ELIE (1989). *L'Etat brancardier: Politiques du déclin industriel (1974–1984)*. Paris: Calmann-Lévy.

—— (1992). *Le Colbertisme 'high tech': Economie des Telecom et du Grand Projet*. Paris: Hachette.

—— and BAUER, MICHEL (1985). *Les grandes manoeuvres industrielles*. Paris: Belfond.

COHEN, STEPHEN (1977). *Modern Capitalist Planning: The French Model*. Berkeley, CA: University of California Press.

COMMAILLE, JACQUES (1998). La politique française à l'égard de la famille. *Regards sur l'actualité* (January): 12–24.

DALEY, ANTHONY (1996). *Steel, State, and Labor: Mobilization and Adjustment in France*. Pittsburgh, PA: University of Pittsburgh Press.

DARES (1996). *40 ans de politique de l'emploi*. Paris, Direction de l'Animation de la Recherche, des Etudes et des Statistiques.

—— (December 2000). La politique de l'emploi en 1999. Paris, Direction de l'Animation de la Recherche, des Etudes et des Statistiques. 52.2.

ESPING-ANDERSEN, GØSTA (1990). *The Three Worlds of Welfare Capitalism*. Princeton, NJ: Princeton University Press.

FAUGÈRE, JEAN-PIERRE and VOISIN, COLETTE (1994). *Le système financier français: Crises et mutations*. Luçon, Nathan.

FITOUSSI, JEAN-PAUL (1995). *Le débat interdit: Monnaie, Europe, pauvreté*. Paris, Arléa.

GROUX, GUY and MOURIAUX, RENÉ (1990). Le cas français. *Les syndicats européens à l'épreuve*. Geneviève Bibes and René Mouriaux. Paris, FNSP: pp. 49–68.

HALL, PETER (1986). *Governing the Economy: The Politics of State Intervention in Britain and France*. New York: Oxford University Press.

—— (1990). The State and the Market. In: Peter Hall, Jack Hayward, and Howard Machin (eds.), *Developments in French Politics*. London, UK: Macmillan, pp. 171–87.

HASSENTEUFEL, PATRICK (1997). *Les médecins face à l'Etat: Une comparaison internationale*. Paris: Presses de la Fondation Nationale des Sciences Politiques.

HOWELL, CHRIS (1992a). The Dilemmas of Post-Fordism: Socialists, Flexibility, and Labor Market Deregulation in France. *Politics and Society* 20(1): 71–99.

—— (1992b). *Regulating Labor: The State and Industrial Relations Reform in Postwar France*. Princeton, NJ: Princeton University Press.

HUBER, EVELYNE and STEPHENS, JOHN (2001). *Development and Crisis of the Welfare State: Parties and Policies in Global Markets*. Chicago, IL: University of Chicago Press.

JOIN-LAMBERT, MARIE-THÉRÈSE, BOLOT-GITTLER, ANNE, DANIEL, CHRISTINE et al. (1997). *Politiques sociales*. Paris: Presses de la Fondation Nationale des Sciences Politiques.

KATZENSTEIN, PETER (ed.) (1978). *Between Power and Plenty: Foreign Economic Policies of Advanced Industrial States*. Madison, WI: University of Wisconsin Press.

KERSBERGEN, KEES VAN (1995). *Social Capitalism: A Study of Christian Democracy and the Welfare State*. New York: Routledge.

LABBÉ, DOMINIQUE and CROISAT, MAURICE (1992). *La fin des syndicats?* Paris: L'Harmattan.

LENOIR, RÉMI (1990). Family Policy in France since 1938. In: John Ambler (ed.), *The French Welfare State: Surviving Social and Ideological Change*. New York: New York University Press, pp. 144–86.

LEVY, JONAH (1999). *Tocqueville's Revenge: State, Society, and Economy in Contemporary France*. Cambridge, MA: Harvard University Press.

—— (2000). France: Directing Adjustment? In: Vivien Schmidt (ed.), *Welfare and Work in the Open Economy: Diverse Responses to Common Challenges*. Oxford: Oxford University Press, pp. 308–50.

—— MIURA, MARI, and PARK, GENE (forthcoming). Exiting *Etatisme*? New Directions in State Policy in France and Japan. In: Jonah Levy (ed.), *The State after Statism: New State Activities in the Age of Globalization and Liberalization*.

LORIAUX, MICHAEL (1991). *France after Hegemony: International Change and Financial Reform*. Ithaca, NY: Cornell University Press.

Ministry of Finance (2001). *Projet de loi de finances pour 2002*. Paris: Ministry of the Economy, Finance, and Industry.

MIURA, MARI (2002a). *From Welfare through Work to Lean Work: The Politics of Labor Market Reform in Japan*. Ph.D. Dissertation, Department of Political Science, University of California, Berkeley (unpublished).

—— (2002b). *Playing without a Net: Employment Maintenance Policy and the Underdevelopment of the Social Safety Net*. Annual Meeting of the American Political Science Association, Boston, MA, August 29–September 1.

MYLES, JOHN and PIERSON, PAUL (2001). The Comparative Political Economy of Pension Reform. In: Paul Pierson (ed.), *The New Politics of the Welfare State*. Oxford: Oxford University Press, pp. 305–33.

OECD (2000a). *OECD Health Data*. Paris: OECD.

—— (2000b). *Revenue Statistics, 1965–1999*. Paris: OECD.

—— (2002a). *Economic Survey: Japan*. Paris: OECD.

—— (2002b). *OECD Statistics Database: Total Social Expenditures*, URL: http://oecdnt.ingenta.com.

PALIER, BRUNO (1999). Réformer la sécurité sociale: Les interventions gouvernementales en matière de protection sociale depuis 1945, la France en perspective comparative. Institut d'Etudes Politiques de Paris.

SCHARPF, FRITZ and SCHMIDT, VIVIEN (eds.) (2000). *Welfare and Work in the Open Economy: From Vulnerability to Competitiveness*. Oxford: Oxford University Press.

SCHMIDT, VIVIEN (1996). *From State to Market? The Transformation of French Business and Government*. New York: Cambridge University Press.

SHONFIELD, ANDREW (1965). *Modern Capitalism: The Changing Balance of Public and Private Power*. Oxford: Oxford University Press.

STOFFAËS, CHRISTIAN (1984). *Politique industrielle*. Paris: Les Cours de Droit.

TITMUSS, RICHARD (1987). Welfare State and Welfare Society. In: Brian Abel-Smith and Kay Titmuss (eds.), *The Philosophy of Welfare: Selected Writings of Richard Titmuss*. London: Allen & Unwin, pp. 141–56.

ZERAH, DOV (1993). *Le système financier français: Dix ans de mutations*. Paris: La Documentation Française.

ZYSMAN, JOHN (1983). *Governments, Markets, and Growth: Financial Systems and the Politics of Industrial Change*. Ithaca, NY: Cornell University Press.

5

Ambiguous Agreement, Cumulative Change: French Social Policy in the 1990s

Bruno Palier

The French welfare system is characteristic of those 'immovable objects' (Pierson 1998) often found in Continental Europe. As in the German and other Continental European cases, French social policies are usually considered to be not only the most in need of reform, but also the most difficult to change (Esping-Andersen 1996; Scharpf, Schmidt 2000; Pierson 2001). The resistance to change demonstrated by welfare programs is commonly analyzed as a consequence of path dependence phenomena (Pierson 1998, 2000). Most of what has happened in French social policy since the 1980s can be related to the field of path dependence (blockages, strikes and demonstrations, limited and difficult cutbacks; Palier 2000). One can argue that it is the institutional design of the French welfare system that explains why it is so difficult to change (Bonoli and Palier 2000). However, the data on welfare state development in France also show that a series of deep, even transformative changes have occurred, emerging first in the late 1980s and manifesting their full impact and significance during recent years (Palier 2000, 2001*a*, 2002). These changes can be said to be both incremental and transformative. In this chapter, I will try to analyze in detail the kind of political processes that lead to such changes, and the type of policy development that leads to a gradual transformation of the French welfare system. The argument is that it is mostly through 'layering' that the French social welfare system has been changed.

Most of the instruments used in the French welfare system clearly reflect the Bismarckian tradition of social insurance: entitlement is conditional upon a contribution record; most benefits are earnings-related; financing is provided mainly by employers' and employees' contributions; and the social partners are greatly involved in the management of the system. The usual goal assigned to social policy in France is income maintenance (rather than poverty alleviation, activation, or redistribution). Despite (or beside) this tradition, during the last twenty years, new policies have emerged which incorporate new goals and new instruments. These policies are *Revenu Minimum d'Insertion* (RMI minimum income),

An earlier version of this chapter has been presented at the Center for European Studies, Harvard University. I would like to thank all participants in the discussion as well as Peter Gourevitch, Colin Hay, Bernard Manin, Paul Pierson, Charles Sabel, Kathy Thelen, Wolfgang Streek, and especially Peter Hall for the helpful comments and encouragement.

Couverture Maladie Universelle (CMU, universal health insurance), *Contribution Sociale Généralisée* (CSG general social contribution), *Loi de Financement de la Sécurité sociale* (LFSS Social Security Budget Act) and, less obvious for the moment, trends toward activation in employment policies, and the development of fully funded individualized pension plans or funds (Palier 2002).

Confronted with the growing number of jobless, young, or long-term unemployed, governments have created new benefits since the late 1980s. Through the development of new social policies and the development of minimum income benefits, especially the RMI, part of the French social protection system is now targeting specific populations by using new means-tested benefits with reference to a new goal (to combat social exclusion). Similarly, in 2000, a new scheme called CMU (*Couverture Maladie Universelle*) was created to provide the poorest with free access to health care, and to offer free complementary health insurance to those who cannot afford it. This new scheme is means-tested.

Since the late 1980s, governments of different political orientations have implemented contribution exemptions for employers to encourage job creation. In order to generalize this movement of lowering labor costs by reducing the level of social contributions paid by the employers, governments have progressively replaced some contributions with taxation. A new tax was created in December 1990: the CSG to replace the social contribution. It is used to finance noncontributory benefits.

In order to enable governments to implement their reforms, new instruments have been invented to reinforce the autonomy of the state within the system for social protection. These reforms have mainly been implemented since the Juppé Plan of 1995. The most important reform is the adoption of a constitutional amendment (in February 1996), making the French parliament responsible for passing a new social security budget every year. For the first time in France, the parliament is taking part in the debate on the *Sécurité sociale* budget, which before was not seen as being part of the state budget.

All these new policies promote new goals (poverty alleviation, universal access, and tax funding for health care, activation—rather than workers' income maintenance) and involve new policy instruments (such as targeted social benefits instead of contributory benefits; financing by taxation instead of social contribution; decisionmaking and management by the state instead of by the social partners; conditional employment programs instead of 'passive' compensatory unemployment benefits; fully funded pensions instead of pay-as-you-go schemes).

These changes, while gradual, are nonetheless highly significant because, although they take a form rarely analyzed within the literature on welfare state developments (Palier 2001*b*), their cumulative impact over time implies a major shift in social policy orientation. To use a notion associated with the literature on changes in policy, these changes could also be characterized as 'third order changes' (Hall 1993) since they all involve a change in the instruments and in the goals of social policy.[1] The existence of these changes presents a dual puzzle for the literature. They are puzzling for most of the historical institutionalist literature since this approach, mainly focused on path dependence processes, does not expect major change to occur outside of critical juncture (Thelen 1999). However, these third-order changes in social policy are slow-moving, incremental, and only 'cumulatively transformative',[2] therefore also puzzling for the literature on policy change since paradigmatic changes in policy are usually conceived of as explicit and abrupt (Hall 1993).

Gradual but profound changes of the sort we can observe in French social policy are not really expected by comparative historical institutionalism. These approaches tend to emphasize path dependence and continuity along the policy lines originally chosen. 'Once actors have ventured far down a particular path, however, they are likely to find it very difficult to reverse course' (Skocpol and Pierson 2000: 10). If recent works on welfare state development recognize that some changes have occurred, they usually conclude that reforms have had a limited impact on the structure of the different welfare states, not threatening but preserving the very nature of each system. Since the recent studies identify three main types of reforms, each of them associated with one of the three welfare regimes, reforms are seen as merely reinforcing the logic of each welfare system (Esping-Andersen 1996; Scharpf and Schmidt 2000; Pierson 2001). Therefore, reforms that imply structural changes of the welfare system are not really expected, nor sufficiently analyzed, by the current literature.

Admittedly, some recent pieces of work in historical institutionalism emphasize the possibility of slow-moving changes that may bring about structural transformations of the welfare state or of any other kind of sticky institution (Pierson 2003). However, the changes mentioned here are macro-social changes (such as demographic changes like ageing, or changes in public opinion) or economic changes (such as a shift from an industrial to a service-based economy) which may, in the long run, force institutions to change. If the macro-social and economic transformations are the 'real' exogenous causes of policy changes, analyzing these macro transformations does not provide us with an understanding of the political process through which policies are actually changed. Analyzing the impact of globalization, ageing, social changes, etc. on welfare states may explain why welfare states change, but certainly neither when nor how they change; these questions require an analysis of the political processes through which such change is actually negotiated.

When the political processes are the focus of the analysis, they are generally understood as leading to resilience, to continuity rather than to change. Most of the arguments of 'the new politics of the welfare state' (Pierson 2001) are indeed meant to explain why and how political factors and processes lead to continuity through increasing returns mechanisms (Pierson 2000). However, as Thelen puts it, 'Increasing returns arguments tell only part of the story; they are better at articulating the mechanisms of reproduction behind particular institutions than they are at capturing the logic of institutional evolution and change' (Thelen 2003). Welfare state development has too often been conceptualized as an evolutionary process where inertia of institutions prevails. We still need a theory of how social policy changes (radically), which analyzes the political process through which transformative reforms are elaborated, adopted, and implemented.

The literature on changes in public policy might of course be of help. As already mentioned, one can characterize some changes in French social policy as third-order changes. The second puzzle here is that the third-order changes in French social policy do not occur in the same way as the paradigmatic changes in British macroeconomic policies. Hall (1993) demonstrated that changes in economic policies in the United Kingdom occurred explicitly, that they were present in political debates, that their adoption was dependent on electoral competition, and that their implementation was quite abrupt and rapid. As will be shown below, it is clear that the new French social policies were elaborated through reference to the previous ones. However, it is also clear that the choice of a measure was less the result of electoral competition showing clear cleavages than of an ambiguous agreement involving almost all the actors affected by the measure. They were also introduced incrementally, and developed by governments from both sides of the political spectrum. Instead of a brutal, explicit paradigmatic revolution, I see a progressive, slow-moving transformation, the new social policy paradigm becoming clearer and clearer as new policies expand. Thus, if the result of the new policies appears to be a deep transformation, it is only through an incremental development that the changes occurred. These changes clearly belong to the ones identified by Kathy Thelen and Wolfgang Streeck: incremental in their processes, resulting in a gradual transformation of the whole welfare system.

In brief, the political development of third-order changes in French social policy cannot be understood in the same way as third-order changes in British macroeconomic policies. Here again, there is still the need for an adequate theory of continuity *and* (transformative) change in social policy. In order to contribute to this theory, I will systematically compare the political processes through which the reforms leading to the RMI, the CMU, the CSG, and the LFSS have been conceived, elaborated, adopted, and implemented (and I will also make brief references to activation and pension funds, but in a less systematic way).[3] I will try to generalize some common pattern that the comparison of the processes highlights, thus sketching the political mechanisms through which gradual but cumulatively transformative changes occur in social policy.[4] In order to produce an analytical grid for comparing the different processes that lead to the above-mentioned changes in social policy, I will rely on Jones' classical approach to public policy (Jones 1970). Jones differentiates several sequences in the policymaking process: emergence and diagnosis of a problem (agenda setting), elaboration of alternatives, decision, and implementation. I will compare each of these four phases in the different cases of social policy change, and show what is similar in each of these cases.

This 'systematic process analysis' serves as a base for generalizing about when and how significant changes have occurred in French social policy over the past two decades. Each sequence is characterized by a similar trait. The main findings are:

1. *Diagnosis of failure.* Path-shifting reforms are possible when there is a common agreement that the new problem to be dealt with is due to former policy failure and/or that old policies are not able to deal with the new problems.

2. *Elaboration of alternatives in opposition to past policies.* New programs or measures are elaborated in opposition to former programs. Policymakers are mainly focused on creating new ways of doing that are the opposite of what they were doing before, instead of dealing directly with the new problem.

3. *Decision based on an ambiguous agreement.* New measures are accepted by a wide range of different groups (political parties, administrations, trade unions, employers and others) who agree on the new measure, but for different reasons and with different interests. They share neither a common vision of the reforms nor the same interest in the measures. During the decisionmaking process, the measure which is selected from the alternatives is the one which is able to aggregate different visions and interests.

4. *An incremental, but cumulatively transformative, implementation.* The new measures are introduced at the margin, as if their purpose were only to fix or complement the system, but they develop to become very important, causing a shift in the whole welfare state trajectory. This type of change is to be associated with the ones conceptualized as 'layering' by Kathy Thelen and Wolfgang Streeck in their introductory chapter. Indeed, the addition of new policies to the existing welfare system and the interaction of the two have prompted a change in the overall trajectory of the welfare state. This chapter is therefore aimed at deepening the understanding of one way through which institutions change, namely layering.

In the rest of the chapter, I will detail the content of the four mechanisms producing institutional change through layering. In the conclusion, I will discuss the possible generalization of these findings. The first and the third points above can be understood as defining the conditions under which social policy has changed in France, and the second and the fourth as defining rather *how* such changes have been occurring. Even if it is difficult to generalize from a single country case, I will discuss the conditions under which these four characteristics of the policy process might be seen as political conditions for both the selection and the sustainability of the path-shifting reforms of welfare systems.

A shared diagnosis of policy failure

During the 1980s and early 1990s, the political debates on social policy issues raised 'new problems': social exclusion and long-term unemployment, burden of nonwage costs due to high levels of social contribution affecting firms' competitiveness, crisis in the management of the system, demographic ageing, etc. If these problems are initially termed 'new problems', they can also be analyzed as the consequence of past policies and as evidence of inefficiencies in the existing welfare system.

Before implementing new path-shifting policies, French governments developed path-dependent policies that tended to follow the pathways determined by existing social insurance institutions. As shown elsewhere (Palier 2000, 2001a, 2002), to tackle the initial financial difficulties encountered by the social security system in the mid-1970s, governments first chose to increase resources (i.e. social contributions) instead of reduce social expenditure. In a second stage, constrained by European requirements as well as by the economic recession of the early 1990s, governments implemented some cutbacks in health care coverage, in unemployment benefits and in pensions. These retrenchment measures are typical of social insurance: reduction in social expenditure is secured through stricter requirements for receiving social benefits, that is, by strengthening the link between the amount of contribution and the level of the benefits (through changing the calculation formula and/or introducing stricter entitlement rules).

However, all these measures had spillover effects at the time. The plans to balance the social security budget increased the level of social contributions. Retrenchment policies contributed to restricting access to unemployment benefits, therefore leaving more people with no right to social insurance. Such policies thus increased social exclusion. Meanwhile, the retrenchment measures triggered large and noisy demonstrations. As expected in a conservative corporatist welfare system, these reforms were difficult to implement, being accompanied by a lot of demonstrations and strikes, with trade unions vigorously opposing and trying to block the main changes. In the eyes of experts, politicians, employers, and increasingly, trade unions, the social protection system was producing more and more failures. The accumulation of these spillover effects changed their view of the role of the social protection system in the economic, social, and political regulation of France, from a positive to a negative role. During the 1990s, new diagnoses of the difficulties started to spread and become legitimized, suggesting that the system was not a victim of the crisis, but one of the causes of the social, economic, and political difficulties experienced in France. These diagnoses were elaborated and progressively shared within government commissions appointed specifically to produce reports on various social protection problems. Within these commissions (especially at the *Commissariat général du Plan*)[5] experts, high-ranking civil servants, employers, and employee representatives were involved.

Throughout the various reports produced during the 1980s and the 1990s, signed by almost all the actors involved in social protection, social insurance was perceived as being the cause of economic, social, and political problems on three counts. It was held that the contributory nature of most social benefits reinforces social exclusion, that the burden of social contribution prevents job creation, and that joint management of the system by the social partners engenders irresponsibility and a management crisis in the system.[6]

Since the late 1970s, France has seen a significant increase in unemployment. The social insurance system set up in 1945 was not made to tackle mass unemployment. This predominantly contributory system is unable to deal with those who have never been involved in the labor market or who have been removed from it for long periods. Because they have not contributed to social insurance, or because they are not contributing any more, the young unemployed or the long-term unemployed have no access to social insurance rights. During the 1980s, the number of 'excluded people' kept on increasing so that, by the late 1980s, this had become one of the most pressing social issues. Intense mobilization from civil society (NGOs coping with poor and excluded persons), supported by socio-logists,[7] accused the welfare state, based as it was on social insurance, of being unable to cope with this phenomenon; they claimed that new benefits were needed. The RMI was specifically designed and created to cope with the problem of social exclusion.

The system was also said to be producing unemployment. In France, 80 percent of social protection was financed through employment-related contributions. The burden of social contribution was increased during the 1980s. For a long time, employers were saying that the level of contributions was too high. Their discourse was relayed by economists and politicians in the early 1990s, when European integration was perceived as increasing competition within the single market. The argument was that social insurance contributions inhibited job creation since they were having a direct impact on the cost of low-skilled labor. Consequently, the weight of the '*charges sociales*' became a central issue in the French debate. Every report on the financing of the French social protection system underlined the necessity to lower labor costs by decreasing the level of social contribution.[8] Economic surveys could not demonstrate that France had overall higher labor costs than its European counterparts, but the idea that low-skilled job creation was limited due to the high level of social insurance spread to all political parties, as is shown by the various policies of social contribution exemption on low-paid jobs that developed after 1986.[9] The CSG was created to compensate for the exemptions of social contribution.

The management arrangement was also subject to severe criticism. In 1945, the management of the social insurance system was given to the social partners in the name of democracy (*démocratie sociale*) and in order to avoid bureaucratization and the subordination of social policy efficiency to purely budgetary considera-tions. With the increasing importance of budget control during the 1980s and 1990s, the devolution of the management of social insurance to the social partners became problematic: the government accused the social partners of having hijacked the social security funds, of abusing their position within the system at the expense of the general good, and of not accepting their responsibility for containing cost increases. The strongest opposition to change came not from political confrontation, but from trade unions and social mobilization when governments tried to implement important reforms. Within the governmental sphere, the social partners' involvement in social insurance was considered to be a source of inefficiency whereas the state would do better to contain expenditure increase. The social partners also criticized the lack of clear responsibility in the system. They usually accused the state both of failing to accept its own respons-ibility and of preventing them from autonomously managing the system. The LFSS was created so that a clear (and so-called democratic) orientation could be decided by the representatives of the nation for the benefit of the social security system.

In recent analyses of the problems encountered by Bismarckian welfare systems, the causes of the difficulties were held to be the very characteristics of these systems (contributory benefits, financed by social contribution, managed by the social partners). Meanwhile, all the bases of the Keynesian compromise that supported the whole system from 1945 to 1975 were undermined: protection of the workers did not support social integration anymore but led to social exclusion; the system was not contributing to economic growth anymore but rather impeding it due to its funding mechanisms; the *démocratie sociale* was not sustaining social peace, but was leading instead to demonstrations and blockages. Certainly, the basic institutional settings of the French social protection system began to cumulate a number of problems, preventing important reforms, and causing economic and social difficulties. These analyses supported a change in political discourses and agenda around the late 1980s/early 1990s: from rescuing the *Sécurité sociale*, the aim of governmental intervention came to transform it.

Traditional path-dependence arguments usually see the weight of past policies as positively reenforcing existing institutions and programs. But the weight of the past can also lead to rupture if the past is seen as a bad thing. In France, existing social policies have been progressively perceived as unable to deal with new social problems (such as social exclusion or demographic ageing, since PAYGo systems are said to be more sensitive to demographic ageing than fully funded schemes). Worse still, they are perceived as helping to reenforce the problems (social insurance excludes people, social contribution increases nonwage costs, management by the social partners impede an effective decision). Finally, measures following the line of the past (retrenchment by increasing the link between contribution and benefits) appeared to have negative consequences (e.g. increased inequalities, exclusion, and higher social contributions).

If 'events or processes occurring during "critical juncture" emerge as crucial' (Skocpol and Pierson 2000: 10), we could add that negative diagnoses (or 'critical conjectures') of past policies contribute to change the course of policies. The past can lead to innovation instead of reproduction through an accumulation of failures. Actors can then become convinced that the past should be changed. However, the condition is not only that a new diagnosis criticizing the past policies emerges, but also that this diagnosis is shared by most of the actors involved in the policymaking process.

As long as certain crucial veto players (Tsebelis 1995) can provide another interpretation of the same problem, there is no common diagnosis, and no possibility of going further. For instance, during the 1970s and the 1980s, the social security deficit was understood in two different ways. Governments, experts, and economists analyzed it as a consequence of decreasing resources (lower growth rates leading to smaller wage increases and a rise in the number of inactive or unemployed people who pay no contributions) and rising expenses (more unemployed people, higher demand for health and old-age provision). For them, the solution was either to increase resources (social contributions) or cut expenditures. However, trade unions had a different interpretation. They claimed that the deficit was due to the state using the social insurance funds to finance noncontributory benefits (such as the minimum income for the elderly who are poor or for lone parents). For the defenders of the social insurance system, the 'undue charges' (*les charges indues*) explained the deficit that could be removed if the state paid for its own welfare policies (national solidarity benefits implying vertical redistribution). From the trade union perspective, the deficit did not justify reductions in the level of the contributory benefits for which workers had paid through their contributions. As long as all the trade unions claimed that the state was responsible for the deficit (and not economic and social trends), no retrenchment policies could be passed, nor could further reforms be implemented. It was only when the government in 1993 started to finance noncontributory minimal pensions through taxes (Balladur Reform of Pension, see Bonoli 1997) and in 1994 voted a law obliging the state to compensate for any social contribution exemption that the trade unions' argument became irrelevant, obliging them to join the other actors (government, MPs, experts) in the dominant analysis of the social insurance deficit.

An important element that allows diagnosis of failure to lead to change in policy is that most of the actors involved (experts, politicians, employers, unions) share the idea that the old policies cannot work anymore, either because they are unable to cope with the new problems, or because they produce new problems themselves. The shared sense of policy failure is essential for gathering people on an alternative track of policy. It can take a long time before a majority of the actors involved agree on the diagnosis of the problem. As long as the problem is not perceived in the same way, it is difficult, if not impossible, to change the course of action. In French social policy, the first measures taken by governments during the 1980s, therefore, were the creation of large commissions in charge of analyzing the problems and producing reports, where all the actors involved worked together until they shared the same view of the cause of the problems. This negative perception of the past is a precondition for deep reform; it also channels the way in which the new reforms are elaborated.

Opposing the past

The second striking feature of all the processes through which path-shifting reforms have been developed is that they have all been conceived with negative reference to the past. In our cases, the elaboration of alternatives in public policies was less driven by a problem-solving approach than by the will to solve the problems created by past policies. Alternative policies are directed more at reversing or altering old policies than they are at directly attacking the problem itself.

The problem of social exclusion and the potential solutions to it have been the subject of several government reports in France. When thinking of measures to combat social exclusion, experts have usually sought measures that would not reproduce the inefficiencies and perverse effects that social insurance had provoked.[10] Since the early 1980s 'reinsertion' policies have been proposed. These policies are conceived in contrast to the traditional features of social insurance, underlining the inadequacy of the former system. While the social insurance system has been traditionally geared toward employees, the new policies target the most disadvantaged or socially 'excluded'. Rather than treating all sorts of situations with the same instruments, social reinsertion policies are geared toward specific groups and are designed according to local needs. That is why reinsertion policies are characterized by a high degree of devolution to local authorities. In addition, unlike the social insurance system which treats social risks separately (old age, sickness, unemployment), reinsertion policies address a whole range of relevant social problems in an integrated manner, so that housing and vocational training are now included in the field of social policy.

An important debate on the financing of social protection has developed in France since the mid-1970s. This debate is mainly fueled by experts through their reports. One can identify three different periods in this debate. From 1945 to 1974, the main debate was about the role that the state budget should play within the financing of social protection. Two main objectives were proposed: to increase resources and to improve the redistributive capacity of financing and spending. Although the unions claimed that the state should pay for noncontributory welfare, they did not want the system to become mainly tax-financed since they would then lose their role within the system. Therefore, no substantial changes occurred during this period and social contributions continued to play a major role in the funding of the French social protection system. From 1974 to 1981, the debate changed and became oriented more toward economic efficiency than toward redistributive capacity. Seventeen reports on financing were published between 1974 and 1982 (Dupuis 1989). They all emphasized the negative impact of contributions on employment. Before 1981, various reports favored a new 'social' indirect tax (VAT). However, employers could not accept this solution since it would have increased the price of goods and therefore would have had negative consequences for firms. Experts were looking for a solution that would not reproduce the problem of social contribution, that is, increasing nonwage costs on firms. After 1982, all the main reports suggested that the new forms of financing should affect households rather than firms. A new tax, which would be earmarked and proportional to all income, was proposed (Dupuis 1989: 29). A new tax was created in December 1990: the CSG, originally designed to replace the social contribution scheme that had hitherto financed noncontributory benefits. Its features are dissimilar to both social contribution and income tax. Unlike insurance contributions, it is levied on all types of personal income: not just wages (even the lowest ones), but also capital revenues and welfare benefits. Unlike income tax in France, CSG is strictly proportional and earmarked for non-contributory welfare programs.

The choice in favor of new modes of organizing the system has also been built in opposition to the past. In 1945, all the important actors involved in the creation of the system agreed that it should not be given to either the state or to private insurance companies. They favored a corporatist management of the system, allocating a major role to employers and to employees' representatives. The arguments for this solution were based on a distrust of the state and parliamentary democracy and a belief in the necessary role of intermediary institutions. The participation of the workers in the management of the social protection system was termed *la démocratie sociale*, the aim of which was to guarantee the social and political integration of the workers within the society, as well as promote collaboration between workers and employers. However, the fact that three types of actors (state, employers, employee representatives) were involved progressively appeared to all three actors to be an obstacle to efficient decisionmaking. Therefore, after years of contesting who should govern social security, all the actors wanted to 'clarify responsibilities' and, in order to avoid the blurred mix of responsibility that characterized the former system, agreed to give some power to the parliament, as long as the social partners continued to play a part within social insurance funds.[11]

The elaboration of new policies always took a long time, during which the different actors met to discuss the problems and offer their solution. This consultation processes also had the effect of creating an apparent consensus of many actors for the new measures, which have since been implemented.

An ambiguous agreement

As detailed interviews of the actors involved show (Palier 2002), and as confirmed by the use of the new instruments by governments of every complexion since their adoption, a large majority of those concerned with social protection problems agreed with the new measures which brought about structural changes (RMI, CMU, CSG, LFSS, etc.). No change could have occurred without the consent of a broad majority of the different actors involved in the field of social protection. However, precise analysis of the different positions which actors adopted toward the new measures shows that they agree on the same measure, but for very different—often contradictory—reasons.

All these reforms have been made in the name of the distinction between insurance and assistance (referred to as 'national solidarity'—*solidarité nationale*—in French). Trade unions wanted this rationalization in order to preserve their domain of social insurance, whereas governments and civil servants anticipated receiving more responsibilities in social protection through these changes, at the expense of the social partners. The RMI was seen by the left as a means of proposing money and social aid (vocational training, for instance) through the contract, while the right saw in the contract a counterpart to the money. The left supported the CSG because it was a fairer tax than social contribution for employees, whereas the right supported it as a means of lowering social charges for the employers. Civil servants supported the CSG because it encouraged state control over the expenses financed by this new tax, whereas employers and unions argued that it would allow the social partners to preserve the purity of social insurance, since noncontributory benefits would be financed by taxes. Politicians and civil servants wanted the parliament to be empowered in order to weaken the social partners, whereas the latter saw this reform as a means of forcing the state to assume and discharge its core responsibilities in this area.

An important element for the acceptance of a new measure seems to be its capacity to aggregate different—and even contradictory—interests, based on different, and sometimes contrasting, interpretations of the consequence of implementing the new instrument. In order to introduce significant changes to a conservative corporatist welfare system, there is a need to secure consent from multiple actors with quite different interests and situations. In our cases, agreement on new policies was secured from an aggregation of actors, each of whom had a different conception of and interest in the policy. The political dynamic is not one in which a large number of people (majority, median voters . . .) acquire the same 'new' interest in a 'new' policy, but rather one in which policy appeals to actors with varied interests.[12] Paradoxically, it seems that the fact that the same measure can be interpreted differently and aggregate different interests is a necessary condition for its selection.

Structural changes in social policy are achieved through ambiguous measures rather than via a clear ideological reorientation. This development is quite different from explicit paradigmatic change which is the object of political conflict and debate. The ambiguous agreement is based on a common acknowledgment of past policy failure, on a common will to oppose the past and on an agreement on new, but polysemic, measures. It is not based on a common, explicit, new, and coherent vision of the world (a new paradigm). These new measures have first been introduced at the margin of the system, in a very incremental and gradual way.

Incremental, but cumulatively transformative

All the new measures that we are studying here have first been introduced at the margins of the social protection system and have been gradually extended. Their development has often led to a change in their meaning within the system. They are first introduced to 'complete' or repair the existing system, but they gradually become the base for a new type or logic of social protection within that system. The interplay between the new policy and the existing system has meant, progressively, a change in the overall trajectory of the system. The detailed analysis of the development of new social policies in France tells us how 'layering' can lead to structural and profound changes.

When it was created, the new RMI benefit was supposed to be delivered to between 300,000 and 400,000 people. Already by December 2001, however, almost 1.2 million people were receiving the RMI. Including spouses and children of recipients, 3.5 percent of the French population was involved. Beside the RMI, France has now seven other social minimum incomes. More than 10 percent of the French population is currently receiving one of these minima. This means that, through the development of new social policies and the development of minimum income benefits, part of the French social protection system is now targeting specific populations by using new instruments (means-tested benefits delivered according to need, financed through state taxation, and managed by national and local public authorities), through reference to a new logic (to combat social exclusion instead of to guarantee income and status maintenance). The use of this new repertoire of social policy has also been extended to health care with the creation of a specific health care scheme for the poorest members of society (*Couverture maladie universelle*).

The development of targeted benefits aimed at poverty alleviation within the French social protection system has imported the logic which goes with it and which was virtually absent in France before. Traditionally in the liberal welfare states, these benefits are accused of creating a dependency culture and unemployment traps. By the late 1990s, more and more analyses in France were underlining the fact that people receiving social minima, especially the RMI, were losing money and social benefits if they took up a part-time job paid at the minimum wage level.[13] At first, people receiving the RMI who found a job were allowed to collect the RMI and their new wage (if very low) for a while (initially three, then six months) so that they did not lose out when getting a job. Moreover, in order to improve the incentives to go back to the labor market, in 2001 the Jospin government created a tax credit called '*Prime pour l'emploi*', which is a negative income tax for low-paid jobs. Hence, both a totally new rhetoric (unemployment trap, work disincentive) and a totally new type of social policy instrument (working family tax credit) have been imported in the wave of the development of measures aimed at poverty alleviation in France.

Very recently, this trend toward activation can also be discerned in social insurance. In 2000, the social partners signed a new agreement reforming the unemployment social insurance, which eliminated the digressive element of the unemployment insurance benefit while creating a new individualized contract for job seekers so that they are accompanied in their search for jobs (the *Plan d'aide et de Retour à l'Emploi*—Pare). The social partners who signed this new convention explicitly agreed on the idea that unemployment insurance benefits should not only compensate for the loss of income, but also encourage people to find a new job. Welfare reforms in France now include activation as part of their main goal, initiating a U-turn from 'welfare without work strategy' (Esping-Andersen 1996) to an employment-friendly restructuring of the system. This attempt to render the system more employment-friendly has also supported the shift in financing.

In the early 1990s, the CSG appeared to play a marginal role in the system. When it was introduced, the CSG was levied at 1.1 percent of all incomes. In 1993, the Balladur government increased the CSG to 2.4 percent of income. In 1995, the Juppé plan set it at 3.4 percent of income, and since 1998 the rate is 7.5 percent, replacing most of the health care contribution paid by the employees. The CSG now provides more than 20 percent of all social protection resources and represents 35 percent of the health care system's resources.

The introduction of this earmarked tax has facilitated a shift in the financing structure of the system toward increased state taxation. This new instrument has two main consequences, which imply a partial change in the logic of the system. First, since financing does not just come from the working population, the CSG breaks the link between employment and entitlement. Access to CSG-funded

benefits cannot be limited to any particular section of society. The shift in
financing is thus creating the conditions for the establishment of citizenship-
based social rights, especially in health care, where a new scheme, the *Couverture
maladie universelle*, was created in 2000. Second, this shift in financing means less
legitimacy for the social partners to participate in the decisionmaking and
management of the provisions financed through general taxation since, in France,
there exists a fairly strong normative perception according to which joint management by employers and employees is only acceptable if schemes are financed
through employment-related contributions (Bonoli and Palier 1996). In this
respect, a shift toward taxation constitutes pressure for a transfer of control from
the social partners to the state. This evolution corresponds to more important
political changes which have occurred since the mid-1990s in the distribution of
power within the system.

The difficulties in containing social expenditure are partly interpreted by
French politicians and civil servants as a consequence of the lack of state control
over the system. Therefore, some reforms have been implemented in order
to empower the state within the system, at the expense of the social partners' position. New instruments have been invented to reinforce the autonomy of the state
within the system. The most important reform is the adoption of a constitutional
amendment (in February 1996) asking the French parliament to vote a social
security budget (LFSS) each year. The use of the new parliamentary competence
helps the government to control the social policy agenda: instead of having always
to legitimize their intervention in a field originally belonging to the realm of labor
and employers, with the institutionalization of a parliamentary vote, they are now
able to regularly plan adaptation measures, especially cost-containment ones. This
new instrument also introduces a new logic of intervention: instead of trying to
find resources to finance social expenditure which is demand-driven by the
insured, the vote of a *loi de financement* implies that a limited budget should be
allocated to social expenditure. As most of the social benefits are still contributory, it is impossible to totally define a priori a limited budget, but governments
are engaging with this new logic, and the French parliament is now voting in new
instruments designed for this purpose, such as limited global budgets for the
hospitals and for ambulatory doctors, along with ceilings and rates of growth for
social expenditure.

In each of the cases analyzed here, instead of trying to replace existing social
programs that are usually well defended (even if they are criticized), governments
have created a new layer of policy on the edge of the core system. Introducing this
policy at the margin avoids objections from the major defenders of the core system,
either because they do not feel concerned by the new measure (RMI is not intended
for the salaried workers whom trade unions have traditionally defended) or
because they believe that these new measures help them to defend the very nature
of social insurance (tax funding of noncontributory benefits) or because the measures are targeted at those least able to protest (the low-skilled were the first to have
their income exempted from social contribution, and they were also the first to be

targeted by activation policies). As in other case of layering, policymakers 'worked around opposition (by constituencies created by existing institutions) by adding new institutions rather than dismantling the old' (Thelen 2003). However, 'new developments do not push further in the same direction but rather alter the over-all trajectory of policy and politics' (Thelen 2003). The new measures have slowly expanded to the extent that they imply a structural change for the whole system.[14]

These structural reforms have all contributed to revising the original Bismarckian nature of the French social protection system—moving instead toward state-run, tax-financed logics, and practices—in the area of health care, family benefits, and poverty alleviation. The traditional way of providing social protection in France has been fiercely criticized and destabilized in its bases, the new instruments designed to cope with the structural difficulties of the French social system subscribe to a logic very different from the previous Bismarckian/Christian-democratic one. After several years of implementation, one can see that these reforms are not marginal, but affect an important propor-tion of the population and an important share of the financing, and have given the state more opportunity to intervene in the system. These changes have led to the conclusion that the system is currently being dualized.

In fact, a double dualization is underway. First, all reforms tend to separate two worlds of welfare within the French social protection system. The first one is the enduring sphere of social insurance (mainly old age and unemployment insurance), where professional solidarity is central. In these domains, benefits are still acquired through work, but with greater reference to the level of contribution than before. The second world of welfare is called 'the realm of national solidarity', which includes health care, family benefits, and policies designed to combat social exclu-sion. Here, the benefits can be either universal or means-tested; they are financed out of taxation and the state plays a more important role than before. But there is also a second dualization going on which separates the French population into two different groups: one is made up of the people who are still able to rely on social insurance (complemented by a number of private schemes) to provide for their (still generous) social protection, and another comprises a section of the population (10–15 percent of it) which only relies on targeted minimum benefits.

Conclusion: when and how path-shifting changes in social policy occur

We have seen that changes in institutions and logics in French social policy come about less through an explicit and radical ideological change than through a change in the policy instruments. The systematic tracing of the political processes through which social policies in France have been fundamentally revised over time reveals four specific conclusions. First, the elaboration and implementation of new recipes depends on a shared diagnosis of past policy failure. Second, recipes are conceived against the backdrop of how things were done in the past, not necessarily as a result of programmatic reorientation and agreement. Third, reforms are in fact often passed and implemented on the basis of an ambiguous agreement. Fourth, these recipes are implemented in an incremental way, encapsulating new ways of doing and new ways of thinking, which develop and whose significance is only revealed over time, with the expansion of the programs and the growth in their constituencies.

This type of policy change, although a structural (or third-order) change, is quite different from the paradigmatic changes that occurred in British economic policy, as Peter Hall analyzed them. This difference might be linked to the difference in the policy domain. Macroeconomic policymaking is a relatively technical field, while social policy is less technical. Therefore, it may be harder to say there is something like a social policy 'paradigm'—at least in the full Kuhnian sense of the term.[15] One could add that Continental welfare systems are among the most resilient institutions and therefore cannot be changed without broad agreement on what ought to be done.

Thus, social policy change could occur in France when there was a common sense of failure of past policies, and when new recipes that could aggregate different positions in their favor were elaborated. This means that change may occur not merely when economic or social conditions change (external chock), but also when the existing policies are perceived as unable to cope with the new economic or social environment. This perception is based on the experience of failure (the inability of social insurance to deal with mass unemployment, for instance), on the exhaustion of alternative interpretations, and on the socialization of the various actors, who begin (perhaps for different reasons) to converge on a similar diagnosis of policy failure. Agreement is also important for the adoption of an innovative measure. This agreement can, however be deeply ambiguous, as is any kind of majority formation in politics.

The mechanisms through which cumulative transformative reforms are elaborated and developed (in short, how policy changes) is closely linked to the existing institutional configuration. Where change emanates from a shared perception of past policy failure, new measures are frequently conceived in opposition to the past. However, in the case of French social policy these new measures have not been implemented as an abrupt, total replacement of existing institution, but much more as marginal complements to the existing system, which have then developed alongside and in interaction with that system. Their development, interacting with the existing institution, as we have seen, can gradually effect an overall change in the system of social protection. This evolution of social policy institution can be dramatic, while still based on a relative consensus—deeply transformative in its impact, though incremental in nature.

Notes

1. We can identify three distinct kinds of changes in policy . . . First, [a change in] the levels (or settings) of the basic instruments. We can call the process whereby instrument settings are changed in the light of experience and new knowledge, while the overall goals and instruments of policy remain the same, a process of first order change

in policy . . . When the instruments of policy as well as their settings are altered in response to past experience even though the overall goals of policy remain the same, [changes] might be said to reflect a process of second order change . . . Simultaneous changes in all three components of policy: the instrument settings, the instruments themselves, and the hierarchy of goals behind policy . . . occur rarely, but when they do occur as a result of reflection on past experience, we can describe them as instances of third order change.   (Hall 1993: 278–9)

2. To use James S. Liebman and Charles Sable's terms (2002).
3. All the empirical evidences on which this chapter is based can be found in Palier (2002).
4. I try to follow here the research strategy proposed by K. Thelen, who reminds us that Elster defined 'mechanisms [as] frequently recurring ways in which things happen' (Elster quoted by Thelen 2003).
5. More than fifty reports were produced in France during the 1980s and the 1990s. For an analysis not only of their content but also of the process of their production (see Palier 2002). These reports are listed on pages 437–9.
6. The three arguments are analyzed in detail respectively in chapters 6–8 of Palier (2002).
7. See especially Paugam (1991).
8. All these reports have been analyzed by Dupuis (1989).
9. Palier (2002: Chapter 7).
10. See Schwartz (1981), Dubedout (1983), Bonnemaison (1983).
11. Interviews of actors expounding these arguments can be read in Bonoli and Palier (1996).
12. I owe this formulation to my exchanges with Peter Hall.
13. See reports from *conseil d'analyse économique*, as well as parliamentary debates on *lois de lutte contre l'exclusion sociale* in 1998 and 1999.
14. The best illustration of this kind of progressive change is given by Paul Pierson and John Myles when they show how an initially marginal introduction of a ceiling in tax benefits expanded so that negative income tax became a central social policy in the Canadian welfare system (Myles and Pierson 1997).
15. As P. Hall has pointed out to me.

References

BONNEMAISON, GILBERT (1983). *Prévention, répression, solidarité*. Paris: La Documentation Française.

BONOLI, GIULIANO (1997). Pension Politics in France: Patterns of Co-operation and Conflict in Two Recent Reforms. *West European Politics* 20(4): 160–81.

BONOLI, GIULIANO and PALIER, BRUNO (1996). Reclaiming Welfare. The Politics of Social Protection Reform in France. In: *Southern European Society and Politics*, 1(3) Winter: 240–59.

—— —— (2000). How do Welfare States Change? Institutions and their Impact on the Politics of Welfare State Reform. *European Review* 8(2): 333–52.

DUBEDOUT, HUBERT (1983). *Ensemble, refaire la ville*. Paris: La Documentation Française.

DUPUIS, JEAN-MARC (1989). *La réforme du financement de la protection sociale, inventaire bilan*. LERE, rapport pour la Mire, convention no 310/88.

ESPING-ANDERSEN, GØSTA (ed.) (1996). *Welfare States in Transition, National Adaptations in Global Economies*. London: Sage.

GOUREVITCH, PETER (1986). *Politics in Hard Time*. Ithaca, NY: Cornell University Press.

HALL, PETER A. (1993). Policy Paradigm, Social Learning and the State, the Case of Economic Policy in Britain. *Comparative Politics*, April: 275–96.

HECLO, HUGH (1974). *Modern Social Politics in Britain and Sweden*. New Haven, CT: Yale University Press.

JONES, CHARLES O. (1970). *An Introduction to the Study of Public Policy*. Belmont: Duxbury Press.

LIEBMAN, JAMES S. and SABEL, CHARLES F. (2002). Emerging Model of Public School Governance and Legal Reform: Beyond Redistribution and Privatization. Working paper.

MYLES, JOHN and PIERSON, PAUL (1997). Friedman's Revenge: The Reform of 'Liberal' Welfare States in Canada and the United States. EUI Working Paper RSC No. 97/30, European University Institute.

PALIER, BRUNO (2000). Defrosting the French Welfare State. *West European Politics* 23(2): 113–36.

—— (2001*a*). Reshaping the Social Policy Making Framework: France from the 1980s to 2000. In: Taylor-Gooby (ed.), *Welfare States Under Pressure*. London: Sage, pp. 52–74.

—— (2001*b*). Beyond Retrenchment: Four Problems in Current Welfare State Research and One Suggestion how to Overcome them. In: Jochen Clasen (ed.), *What Future for Social Security? Debates and Reforms in National and Cross-National Perspective*. The Hague: Kluwer Law International, pp. 105–20.

—— (2002). *Gouverner la Sécurité sociale, les réformes du système français de protection sociale depuis 1945*. Paris: PUF.

—— and BONOLI, GIULIANO (2000). La montée en puissance des fonds de pension. *l'année de la régulation* 4: 71–112.

PAUGAM, SERGE (1991). *La disqualification sociale. Essai sur la nouvelle pauvreté*. Paris: PUF.

PIERSON, PAUL (1998). Irresistible Forces, Immovable Objects: Post-industrial Welfare States Confront Permanent Austerity. *Journal of European Public Policy* 5(4): 539–60.

—— (2000). Increasing Returns, Path Dependence, and the Study of Politics. *American Political Science Review* 94(2): 251–67.

—— (2003). Big, Slow-Moving, and . . . Invisible: Macro-Social Processes in the Study of Comparative Politics. In: James Mahoney and Dietrich Rueschemeyer (eds.), *Comparative-Historical Analysis in the Social Sciences*. New York and Cambridge: Cambridge University Press.

SCHARPF, FRITZ W. and SCHMIDT, VIVIEN A. (eds.) (2000). *From Vulnerability to Competitiveness: Welfare and Work in the Open Economy*, 2 vols. Oxford: Oxford University Press.

SCHWARTZ, BERTRAND (1981). *L'insertion professionnelle et sociale des jeunes*. Paris: La Documentation Française.

SKOCPOL, THEDA and PIERSON, PAUL (2000). Historical Institutionalism in Contemporary Political Science. Paper for the APSA meeting, Washington.

THELEN, KATHY (1999). Historical Institutionalism in Comparative Politics. *The Annual Review of Political Science*, 2.

—— (2003). How Institutions Evolve: Insights from Comparative-Historical Analysis. In: James Mahoney and Dietrich Rueschemeyer (eds.), *Comparative-Historical Analysis in the Social Sciences*. New York and Cambridge: Cambridge University Press.

TSEBELIS, GEORGE (1995). Decision Making in Political Systems: Veto Players in Presidentialism, Parliamentarism, Multicameralism and Multipartism. *British Journal of Political Science* 25(3): 289–325.

6

Routine Adjustment and Bounded Innovation: The Changing Political Economy of Japan

Steven K. Vogel

To understand how the Japanese model of capitalism is changing, we can usefully begin by examining how it is *not* changing, and why. Given Japan's dismal economic performance after 1990, many Japanese opinion leaders concluded that the Japanese economic model was no longer viable.[1] Japan would have to abandon its outmoded institutions—including the main bank system, lifetime employment, interfirm networks (*keiretsu*), and close government-industry ties—and embrace the liberal market model. Yet Japan has not done so. Why not?

To unravel this puzzle, we must first recognize that market systems are embedded in a complex web of laws, practices, and norms (Polanyi 1944; Fligstein 2001). This implies that the process of liberalizing markets—just as much as the process of constraining markets—involves the transformation of laws, practices, and norms. Scholarship on the varieties of capitalism sometimes employs language that suggests that the Japanese model is more embedded in institutions than the American model. Yet an American-style external labor market is not any less embedded than a Japanese-style internal labor market; and an American equity-based financial system is not any less embedded than a Japanese credit-based system. This means that for Japan to shift toward the liberal market model, it would not simply have to dismantle existing institutions but also create new ones. And a full conversion would involve changes at all levels of the system: laws, practices, and norms (Table 6.1).

For Japan to become a liberal market economy, it would have to make a transition roughly analogous to the historical transition to market society in western Europe, the creation of market institutions in developing countries, or the transition to a market system in post-Communist countries.[2] The transition would not be as fundamental, because Japan already has the basic institutions of a market system in place—such as a legal system that protects property rights and a modern financial system—but Japan's transition would resemble these others in that it would entail a complex process of building market institutions.

For example, those Japanese workers who enjoy lifetime employment guarantees are not 'commodified' in the sense that employers can buy and sell their labor on the free market.[3] Japan lacks an external labor market for permanent employees

Table 6.1 What would it take to turn Japan into a liberal market economy?
Selected examples from labor and finance

Government policy	Corporate behavior
Labor	
Laws	Practices
Labor market reforms	Layoff workers when necessary
Changes in case law doctrine	Do not favor new graduates over mid-
Corporate governance reform	career hires
Pension reform	Shift from seniority to merit-based pay
Lift holding company ban	Introduce stock options
Norms	Norms
The government should not use regulation	Companies should not preserve
to preserve employment	employment at the expense of profits
Net result: An active external labor market	
Finance	
Laws	Practices
Financial reforms	Sell off cross-held shares
Banking crisis resolution	Banks make lending decisions and price
Corporate governance reform	loans on the basis of risk
Pension reform	Corporations choose banks on
Tax reform	the basis of price
Lift holding company ban	Banks stop lending to insolvent firms
Norms	Norms
The government should not protect banks	Companies should maximize
or manipulate financial markets	shareholder value
Net result: A market for corporate control	

(*shain*) at large corporations. To cultivate such a market, the Japanese government would have to reduce legal restrictions on dismissal, cultivate organizations to match employers with workers, promote portable pension plans, and expand unemployment insurance. It would probably also have to revise financial regulations, accounting standards, and commercial law to encourage firms to be more responsive to shareholders and less beholden to their workers. Corporations would have to renegotiate their basic agreements with their workers and redesign their systems of employee representation. Workers would have to become less loyal to their employers, employers would have to become less protective of their workers, and there would need to be sufficient numbers of employers looking for workers and workers looking for new employers to provide sufficient 'liquidity' in the market.

We can think of institutional change as that occurring when an exogenous shock pushes actors to reassess the balance between the costs and benefits of the status quo. But institutional change is a function of the nature of this shock plus the incentives and constraints built into the existing system. This means that even when the shock is big enough to impose change, preexisting institutions still shape the substance of change. In the Japanese case, preexisting institutions leave an especially heavy imprint on the trajectory of change due to the stability of the actors in the system. In the corporate arena, very few large firms enter or exit the system, so change comes via the incremental reform of existing firms rather than via their replacement by new firms with radically different practices. In the political arena, the same economic ministries collaborate with the same ruling party to dominate the policy process, so the primary arena of decisionmaking does not shift, for example, from the bureaucracy to the judiciary or from the national government to local authorities. We shall find, therefore, that outside forces—such as foreign companies bringing new business practices or foreign governments promoting policy reforms—play a critical role in institutional change. Japanese business and government leaders lost confidence in their own institutions in the 1990s, so they have been especially vulnerable to outside influence.

In this chapter, I develop a simple model of institutional change, and apply it to recent developments in two core components of the Japanese model, the labor relations and financial systems. I seek to describe and explain patterns of corporate restructuring and policy reform, and analyze variations across companies and across policy issue-areas. In the conclusion, I separate out three different levels of change—routine adjustments, bounded innovations, and fundamental breaks— and identify how the Japanese case fits within the framework of this volume.

For our purposes, the forces for change outlined below comprise the exogenous shock, and the Japanese model itself constitutes the incentives and constraints that shape the response to this shock. Some observers have concluded that Japan is experiencing a partial convergence toward the liberal market model or a 'hybridization' between the Japanese and the American models. This language can be misleading, however, because it implies that preexisting institutions are simply acting as friction impeding fuller liberalization or convergence. I contend that these institutions shape the trajectory of change in a much more active way. They not only impede certain types of institutional changes but also *enable* other types of institutional innovation. One could view Japan as doubly constrained: it cannot maintain its existing economic system due to the forces for change, and it cannot converge on the liberal market model due to the logic of its own existing institutions. But these dual constraints are themselves the major drivers of institutional innovation (see Table 6.2).

The Japanese model: forces for change

Before shifting to the model of institutional change, let us briefly review the core features of the Japanese system, and outline the forces for change. For present purposes, we can define the Japanese model as a constellation of institutions (including political institutions, intermediate associations, financial systems, labor

Table 6.2 If Japan is not turning into a liberal market economy, then how is it changing?
Selected examples from labor and finance

Current adjustments	Future possibilities	Future non-possibilities
Labor		
Restrain wages	Use holding company	Preserve existing system
Terminate nonregular workers	structure to differentiate tiers of workers	Shift to LME model
Increase share of nonregular workers in workforce	Enhance internal labor markets	
Introduce merit-based pay systems		
Shift 'lifetime' employment guarantee from company to corporate group		
Finance		
Renegotiate/reinforce main-bank ties	Use holding companies to create 'virtual' ventures	Preserve existing system
Sell off cross-held shares	Use employee ownership/ stock options to promote stable shareholding	Shift to LME model
Reform corporate boards		
Introduce stock options		
Restructure main-bank relationships around reorganized corporate groups		

relations systems, and interfirm networks) linked together into a distinct national system of economic governance. Japan is similar to other coordinated market economies (CMEs) such as Germany, and different from liberal market economies (LMEs) such as the United States, in that it fosters long-term cooperative relationships between firms and labor, between firms and banks, and between different firms. And the state and intermediary associations play a critical role in establishing and maintaining the framework for private-sector coordination (Aoki 1988; Hall and Soskice 2001).

The postwar Japanese labor relations system combined a grand bargain of wage moderation in exchange for employment security with firm-level pacts that promoted labor-management cooperation. Labor unions were organized primarily at the enterprise level, rather than at the sectoral level, giving managers and workers a strong incentive to collaborate to raise productivity more rapidly than other firms in the same sector. Large Japanese firms cultivated channels to incorporate labor into the management process and to facilitate communication between managers and workers. They fostered the loyalty of their core workers by offering 'lifetime' employment, by tying wage increases primarily to seniority, and by offering firm-specific benefit programs such as non-portable pension plans.

They fostered internal labor markets by promoting personnel transfers within the firm, while impeding external labor markets by restricting most hiring to recent graduates. They retained considerable flexibility with a starkly tiered system of permanent employees, who enjoyed job security and full benefits, combined with various categories of nonregular workers, who may work did not enjoy the same level of wages, security, or benefits.[4]

Japan's financial system centered on bank lending rather than equity finance. The Japanese government actively directed the allocation of credit through government financial institutions and private banks. The government insulated the market from international capital flows, segmented financial institutions into distinct niches (securities houses, insurance firms, and various types of banks), and heavily regulated the financial sector to prevent market entry and exit. Firms cultivated long-term relationships with their 'main' banks. The main banks would provide their clients with a stable line of credit at favorable rates, monitor the clients' performance, and aide the clients in the case of financial distress. The firms, in turn, would conduct a large and stable share of their borrowing and transaction business with the main bank. The firms and their main banks often shared ties with a common industrial group, and solidified their relationships by cross-holding shares. This allowed firms to keep a large proportion of their shares in stable hands, insulating them from outside shareholders and all but eliminating the risk of hostile takeover.

The Japanese economic system confronted two fundamental challenges: internationalization and the economic crisis. The increase in trade and capital flows between nations broke down the relative insulation of the Japanese market. The growing mobility of capital and corporate activity not only undermined the government's ability to control corporate behavior, but also encouraged it to reform policies to prevent capital or corporate flight. Capital mobility allowed firms to exit from long-term relations with workers by shifting to foreign suppliers or moving production abroad, and it permitted large corporations to shift from domestic borrowing to global equity financing. Domestic companies were exposed to new patterns of behavior as they move abroad, and domestic markets are infiltrated by foreign companies that did not behave according to local norms. Meanwhile, scholars, journalists, financial analysts, and other opinion leaders argued that Japan should conform to 'global standards', which they equated with American standards. And the US government, other national governments, and international organizations such as the World Trade Organization (WTO) pressed Japan to lower trade restrictions, reduce domestic barriers to competition, and shift toward international regulatory standards. In addition, Japan experienced a long-term appreciation of the yen, especially in the late 1980s and early 1990s, which increased pressure on corporations to cut costs to compete in international markets.

Most critically, Japan confronted a sharp decline in economic performance, with a prolonged period of stagnation and a full-fledged financial crisis. This generated enormous political pressure for reform, with the ruling

Liberal Democratic Party (LDP) and the opposition competing to propose solutions to the crisis. It strained core institutions of the Japanese model such as the long-term employment system and the main-bank system by forcing firms to cut costs. And it undermined the legitimacy of the postwar model. Japanese opinion leaders began to openly question the merits of their own economic system and to view the American model more favorably.

The Japanese economic crisis was not a purely exogenous shock, of course, for the institutions of Japanese capitalism played a role in the crisis. The experts continue to debate whether the crisis was due more to specific policy failures or to structural problems inherent in the Japanese model itself, but only policy failure can account for the abrupt shift from economic success in the 1980s to failure in the 1990s.[5] Many of the core institutions of the Japanese model—such as 'lifetime' employment or the main-bank system—are neither as beneficial as popularly believed in the 1980s nor as detrimental as popularly believed today. Hence it would be more accurate to suggest that the economic crisis undermined Japan's labor relations and financial systems than to claim that the labor and financial systems brought down the economy.

Understanding institutional change

Here I build on insights from the New Institutional Economics (NIE), the Varieties of Capitalism (VOC) literature, and economic sociology to outline one perspective on institutional change, and apply it to Japan today (Williamson 1985; Aoki 1988; North 1990; Fligstein 2001; Hall and Soskice 2001). Let us view the Japanese model of capitalism as a system of incentives and constraints. That is, actors within these systems (firms, banks, unions) use institutions such as the lifetime employment system, the main-bank system, and interfirm networks to reduce transaction costs. Then they incorporate these institutions into their cost–benefit calculus as they adapt to new circumstances. Corporations will only abandon their stable partners—such as labor unions, banks, or other corporations—when the efficiency gains from doing so outweigh the cost of forgoing future benefits from cooperation with these partners. And in most cases, the marginal increase in efficiency does not justify the large fixed cost of undermining these relationships. This perspective not only helps to explain why the Japanese model has been slow to change, but it also helps to explain *how* it has been changing.

In many cases, we can account for the resilience of these institutions equally well in economic or sociological terms. That is, we can describe the logic with reference to rationality or legitimacy, interests or norms. If we want to understand why a Japanese firm might be reluctant to layoff workers, for example, we might suggest that the firm is calculating the cost savings against the potential damage to its cooperative relationship with the remaining workers. Or we might conclude that it is simply adhering to prevailing norms of acceptable firm behavior. The concept of reciprocity offers some clues as to how a rational calculus and an adherence to norms might blend in practice, for relationships of reciprocity have both a rational and a normative element. Japanese managers feel that they benefit from long-term relationships of reciprocity with workers, banks, and other firms, but they also have normative commitments to these relationships.

We can attempt to incorporate norms into a cost–benefit framework by thinking in terms of broadening circles of rationality. In the first circle, for example, a manager would simply calculate the estimated costs of financing with the firm's main bank versus the costs with a foreign investment bank. If the competitor were less costly, he would abandon the main bank. In the second circle, however, he would weigh the cost savings against the potential damage to the long-term cooperative relationship with the main bank. And in the third circle, he would further broaden the calculus to include possible costs beyond the main-bank relationship, such as damage to the firm's reputation or strains in relationships with workers, other business partners, intermediary associations, or the government. The first circle represents a simple economic calculus; the second adds institutional factors along the lines of the VOC approach; and the third incorporates broader normative commitments.[6]

One could argue that this model is still too rationalistic: it views the Japanese model as a system of incentives and constraints rather than a system of norms.[7] Actors facing new circumstances do not rationally calculate costs and benefits so much as they fall back on preexisting norms and routines (Powell and Dimaggio 1991). They may respond more to the diffusion of norms than to shifts in incentives. For example, foreign firms or domestic opinion leaders might introduce new ideas, altering the prevailing discourse about corporate adjustment or policy reform, and thereby shifting actors' judgments about what constitutes an appropriate response.

I develop the model here in three stages.

1. *The micro level (logic).* At the firm (micro) level, the forces for change outlined above translate primarily into increased pressure to cut costs. As Japanese firms strive to cut costs, however, they are constrained from laying off workers, abandoning their main banks, and cutting off stable suppliers by the logic of the Japanese model itself. Their options for adjustment are limited by legal and regulatory constraints, such as laws governing the dismissal of workers, and their preferred strategies for adjustment within these legal constraints are shaped by their preexisting relations with workers, banks, and other firms.

We can view a company's options in terms of 'exit' and 'voice' (Hirschman 1970). The Japanese system differs from the liberal market model in that it imposes greater constraints on exit from business relationships, but it also has more fully developed channels for voice within these relationships. This is no accident, of course, because actors who are constrained from exit have a greater incentive to cultivate mechanisms for voice. So when Japanese firms confront tougher competition or a weaker economy, they are more likely to exercise voice than exit.

This simple model already gives us some hints about the substance of corporate adjustment. Japanese companies will not abandon their workers, their banks, and their suppliers, but they will renegotiate the terms of their relationships with these partners. They will not lay off workers, but they will demand wage restraint or greater flexibility in deploying workers. They will not abandon their main banks, but they will press the banks to hold down lending rates or to offer more sophisticated financial instruments. In short, companies will strive to adjust as much as possible without undermining these relationships, and they will try to leverage the benefits of these relationships to ride out their problems.

We can fill out the substance of this pattern by building on more specific knowledge of the Japanese model. For example, the proposition (above) that Japanese firms will leverage the benefits of their relationships does not mean much until we specify what these benefits are. In the case of labor relations, we know that large Japanese companies offer employment security to their core workers in exchange for wage moderation and labor cooperation in raising productivity. So in an economic downturn, we would expect them to press for further wage restraint or to redouble efforts at labor–management collaboration. For bank relations, we know that companies remain loyal to their main banks in exchange for an enhanced level of service plus insurance that the bank will extend credit or otherwise bail out the company if necessary. So in hard times, we would expect them to demand extra services or to cash in on this insurance.

2. *The macro level.* At the national (macro) level, the Japanese government is also constrained from moving toward the liberal market model. Just as firms' preferred business strategies reflect the incentives and constraints of the Japanese model, so do their preferences on policy reform. There is a micro logic to macro preferences. Firms derive comparative institutional advantage from the institutions of Japanese capitalism, such as the labor relations and financial systems, so they have to weigh the expected efficiency gains from policy reforms against the possible costs of undermining these institutions.

Political economy models typically deduce industry policy preferences from their (macro) position within the economy (Frieden and Rogowski 1996). For example, they expect employer interests to differ from worker interests in fairly predictable ways across different national contexts. In contrast, the VOC approach pushes us to look at the micro-level determinants of policy preferences (Hall and Soskice 2001; Thelen 2001). In this view, the degree of harmony or discord between employer and worker interests, for example, depends on the specific market institutions in a given sector or a given country. In Japan, market institutions modify industry preferences for liberal reforms: fewer firms advocate reform than one would otherwise expect, and those firms that do advocate it are more ambivalent than one would otherwise expect.[8] As a result, Japanese government leaders are likely to move cautiously on reforms, and to design reforms to preserve the core institutions of the Japanese model as much as possible.

3. *Micro–macro interaction.* Thus the Japanese model generates relatively predictable patterns of corporate adjustment and government reform. But the

actual trajectory of change over the longer term is complicated by the fact that the two levels interact. As the government enacts policy reforms, these reforms create new opportunities and constraints for further corporate adjustment. And as firms adjust to new challenges, these adjustments modify firms' policy preferences and thereby affect future policy reforms.

Patterns of corporate adjustment

Let us now see how the model outlined above plays out by looking at recent developments in labor relations and finance.

Labor relations

Japanese firms have responded to increased pressure to cut costs in remarkably predictable ways, given the enormous diversity across sectors and companies. Unlike their American counterparts, they have made considerable efforts to reduce costs without laying off workers. We can understand this in terms of the model sketched out above: firms and workers have a long-term relationship of reciprocity, and this relationship has both a rational and a normative component. So when a Japanese firm considers laying off workers, it does not simply weigh the benefit of reducing operating expenses versus the cost of shrinking the workforce, but also assesses how this decision might impair its ability to mobilize remaining workers to enhance productivity. And it considers the broader implications for its reputation: the impact on its ability to recruit new workers in the future, and on its image among business partners and consumers.

Nissan's 'Revival Plan' of 1999 was one of the most aggressive restructuring schemes in recent Japanese history, yet even Nissan managers did not consider laying off workers. They carefully assessed how cost-cutting measures would affect the firm's reputation. One manager describes the decision to close a plant as follows: We had to take into account the union; the local community, including local businesses and suppliers, and our image overall. Some of the stakeholders resisted because they felt this would hurt us in the long run, after we recover. But the larger problem concerned our image with the broader public. The Murayama plant closure was featured on the front page of the news, so this really hurt our reputation. Our image among college students, our potential recruits, dropped considerably.[9]

Instead of laying off Murayama plant workers, Nissan transferred most of them to other plants, left a few at the plant site for a transitional period, and offered a generous early retirement program to those who preferred to retire rather than to move to a new location. The Nissan managers appeared to calculate within all three of the circles of rationality outlined above: they considered immediate costs, the longer-term potential cost of diminished comparative institutional advantage, and the broader potential cost of a damaged reputation.

Precisely because Japanese managers are so reluctant to undermine good relations with workers, they have focused extra effort on reducing nonlabor costs. They have called on their banks to obtain more credit or reduce financing costs, and they have worked with suppliers to cut procurement costs. And they have leveraged their relationships with workers to enhance productivity, rather than simply striving to reduce costs.[10] When they have sought to reduce labor costs, however, they have done so in a roughly predictable sequence of steps, with layoffs as the last step in the chain: (1) reduce overtime, (2) reduce bonuses, (3) reduce new hires, (4) restrain wages, (5) transfer workers to affiliates, (6) reduce nonregular workers by not extending contracts, (7) offer a voluntary early retirement program, and (8) layoff workers. A 2002 Japan Institute of Labor survey reports that 81.6 percent of companies used natural attrition as a means of reducing the workforce, 76.9 percent reduced new hires, 34.2 percent offered early retirement programs, and only 6.9 percent laid off workers.[11] NEC (NEC Corporation-originally Nippon Electric Company but official name changed to NEC Corporation), for example, reduced its worldwide workforce (of 150,000) by 14,000 from 1999 through 2001 without any domestic layoffs. It achieved these cuts by natural attrition (5,000), sales of divisions (3,500), early retirement (1,500), transfers to affiliates (500), closure of plants abroad (3,000), and not extending contracts of nonregular workers (most of the remaining 500).[12] When it sold divisions, it negotiated with the buyer to maintain workers at the facility and to offer them comparable terms.

Many firms have enhanced their flexibility further by increasing the proportion of nonregular workers in their workforce. As a result, the share of part-time workers steadily increased from 11.1 percent of the workforce in 1990 to 12.8 percent in 1995 and 17.7 percent in 2000.[13] Many firms have also shifted from seniority wages to more merit-based pay schedules, but pay differentials remain small compared to Western firms. Some have conveniently used merit pay as cover for wage reductions, by introducing a new compensation system and reducing bonus payments at the same time.

Japanese firms have gone beyond the confines of the existing system, however, by shifting the employment guarantee from the firm to the corporate group. In the past, Japanese firms used corporate networks as channels for reemploying workers after retirement. Then they extended this practice by transferring workers to affiliated companies as an alternative to layoffs. In fact, some companies diversified with precisely this goal in mind: to create subsidiaries and affiliates that could employ excess workers. In many cases, the home company either pays the employee's salary in full or makes up the difference between the employee's salary at the home company and the lower salary at the affiliate. More recently, some companies have been making up for less than the full difference, or simply offering a one-time bonus at the time of transfer.

Finance

As Japanese firms seek to reduce costs and bolster profits, they naturally try to lower financing costs. In the 1980s, many large corporations moved away from reliance on bank loans, but they renegotiated their relationships with their main banks rather than abandoning them. Even the most competitive export firms continued to borrow from their main banks during this period as a way of maintaining the relationship. And the banks sought new ways to retain the loyalty of their best customers, such as mediating strategic alliances or providing information on overseas markets. Meanwhile, the banks strengthened their ties with medium-sized firms in order to compensate for business lost from the larger companies. Japanese banks were not universal banks, and therefore the gradual shift from borrowing to equity financing posed a serious threat to their business. Not surprisingly, they lobbied to enter the securities business, gaining the right to underwrite debt through separate subsidiaries in 1992. They have since leveraged their main-bank relationships to seize a substantial share of the corporate bond market. As the economic crisis deepened, however, some firms actually reinforced their ties with their main banks because poor bond ratings forced them to shift back from equity financing to borrowing. And while the banks' ability to bail out the firms diminished, the firms' reliance on the banks' generosity only increased. 'We are moving back to older ways now', conceded one retail executive. 'When things are tough, the capital markets will not take care of you. So we ask our banks for support.'[14]

Since the 1990s, banks and firms have made some major adjustments in their relationships. Japanese bankers describe an elaborate ritual in which the banks and their main-bank clients renegotiate terms. The guiding principles are twofold: prior consultation and reciprocity. If a bank wants to sell shares of a company, for example, it consults the company first. As a result, it can expect to lose a proportionate share of the company's banking business. Likewise, a company that shifts some of its banking business to other financial institutions can expect the bank to divest some shares. In either case, the bank does not divest all of its shares, and the company does not completely drop the main bank, so the long-term relationship continues. As banks vie for underwriting business, a similar logic applies. The banks expect their favored clients to give them the largest share of this business, but the client companies do so on the condition that the banks offer terms, expertise, and a menu of financial instruments nearly comparable to the top securities firms.

Banks have continued to play a role in corporate restructuring, yet they have been much less capable of providing funds given their own problems. When banks intervene to help firms in crisis, they do so in accord with the principles of reciprocity described above. That is, they gauge their commitment to a firm in terms of the level of cross-ownership and the firm's loyalty as a banking customer. In the 1990s, bank loyalty to corporate clients became a major barrier to the resolution of the nonperforming loan (NPL) crisis. The banks continued to lend to insolvent borrowers rather than to call in the loans, so the overall volume of NPLs simply ballooned.

Variations across firms

Within these basic patterns, firms vary considerably in the level and nature of adjustment. The most striking variation comes between partially foreign-owned firms, which have been much more likely to test the limits of prevailing norms, and others, which have been more hesitant to undermine relations with workers, banks, suppliers, or other business partners. We can examine these differences by looking at how three foreign-owned firms have restructured, and comparing this to their own restructuring efforts before foreign investment and to comparable firms within the same sector. I define 'restructuring' here to include a wide range of measures associated with cutting costs and raising returns: reducing the workforce, cutting wages, selling off business units, selling off cross-held shares, selling off other assets, reforming corporate boards, introducing stock options, adopting merit-based pay systems, switching to lower cost suppliers, and shifting to lower cost methods of financing.

Nissan and Shinsei Bank have been pioneers in assaulting traditional Japanese business practices, both through their own behavior and through their role in reshaping the public debate. Nissan had been languishing for years, steadily working away at reducing costs by suppressing wages and closing facilities but not fundamentally shifting its strategy. Then Renault invested, and incoming President Carlos Ghosn stunned the company and the nation with his audacious Revival Plan in 1999. Nissan closed its Murayama plant, but buffered workers from the impact of this move (as noted above). It aggressively restructured its relations with suppliers, selling off shares in most of its affiliated suppliers and shifting to a more cost-based approach to procurement. Ghosn transformed from public enemy No. 1 in 1999 to a national hero by 2002, as he met his own ambitious goals for returning Nissan to profitability.[15] Meanwhile, Toyota executives have reaffirmed their long-term commitment to their workers, and have strengthened ties with core suppliers.

The Long-Term Credit Bank (LTCB) engaged in some cautious cost-saving measures throughout the 1990s, but it had such a huge burden of NPLs on its books that it could not save itself from bankruptcy in 1998. The government nationalized the bank and then sold it to a US investment group, Ripplewood Holdings. The new bank, Shinsei (meaning 'rebirth' in Japanese), did not have to resort to layoffs, for almost 2,000 of 3,800 employees quit voluntarily. The new management team introduced a ruthlessly meritocratic promotion system that seeks to weed out employees who do not meet performance targets. 'Our shareholders set percentage targets for reducing these employees', reports one personnel manager, 'but we haven't been able to meet them'.[16] Shinsei has put top priority on maximizing returns by moving out of unprofitable business lines and concentrating on the most lucrative niches. It has infuriated government regulators and stirred public ire for cutting off insolvent borrowers rather than rolling over loans to these borrowers. At the same time, however, Shinsei has won over some admirers for devising a radically different business model and quickly generating profits. In contrast, Mizuho, Japan's largest financial group, has been more cautious in restructuring despite facing a much more dire financial situation. It has reduced personnel and branches at a gradual pace, and it has failed to reduce its exposure to NPLs because it continues to refinance insolvent borrowers.

Seiyu, a major supermarket chain, faced a financial crisis in 1997 stemming from its nonbank subsidiary, and subsequently launched a major restructuring program. It reduced permanent employees from 10,000 to 7,000 over five years, closed 41 stores, and reorganized and sold off numerous affiliates. But Seiyu has begun an even bolder transformation since announcing an alliance with Walmart in March 2002. Walmart took advantage of recent reforms in corporate law to schedule a series of options to increase its ownership stake from 6.1 percent initially to 66.7 percent by 2007. Walmart and Seiyu formed a joint task force to scrutinize options throughout 2002, and began implementing their 'integration' program in January 2003. Seiyu introduced a comprehensive program to educate its workers in Walmart's philosophy and its personnel evaluation system. It then proceeded with further reforms, including a drastic streamlining of corporate headquarters, the adoption of a US-style corporate board with outside directors, the introduction of a voluntary retirement program that removed 1,500 permanent employees in 2004, and a sharp reduction in the ratio of managers (mostly permanent employees) to salespeople (mostly temporary employees). It also launched new types of team-led negotiations with suppliers to reduce purchasing costs.[17] Meanwhile, Mitsukoshi, a leading department store chain, announced a restructuring scheme in 1999 that closely mirrors that of Seiyu before the Walmart investment. It reduced permanent employees by cutting new hires and offering a voluntary early retirement program, it increased the share of temporary workers in the workforce, and it streamlined its procurement system.[18]

These case studies imply that Japanese firms' approach to restructuring is powerfully shaped by normative commitments and/or social ties, because foreign owners adopt dramatically different strategies from their Japanese counterparts under similar circumstances. 'The previous managers faced the same choices and made similar calculations', reports an advisor to Nissan top management, 'but when push came to shove they could not pull the trigger. They were too bound by the web of human relations'.[19] The cases also show the limits on how far foreign firms can stretch the system, however, for all three have been extremely sensitive to employee concerns, avoiding layoffs, and they have carefully renegotiated relations with their domestic business partners.

Ahmadjian and Robinson (2001) have conducted a quantitative analysis using the Nikkei Needs database that confirms the basic findings from these case studies. They find that foreign ownership was the most important factor (controlling for firm performance) determining the degree of Japanese firms' downsizing as defined by reductions in workforce. They also find that smaller, younger, and lower-reputation firms were more likely to downsize. They note that these effects diminished from 1990 to 1997, and conclude from this that firms may have become less reluctant to downsize over time. That is, firms may have broken through social constraints via a 'safety in numbers' effect. It is also possible, however, that firms that resisted or delayed downsizing in the early 1990s simply gave in as the economic crisis continued.

Patterns of policy reform

Japanese firms' choices are limited not only by informal constraints, such as commitments to long-term relationships, but also by the formal laws and regulations that underlie the Japanese model. So any substantial transformation of the model requires policy reform. As Peter Gourevitch (1996) has noted, the microinstitutions of capitalism rest on macro (political) foundations, and thus major reforms to these institutions must survive the political process. Yet just as the microinstitutions of the models themselves affect firms' preferred strategies for adjustment, these institutions also shape firm preferences on policy reform.

Labor market reform

Commentators blame rigid labor markets for high labor costs, decreasing competitiveness, and high unemployment. Given the cost pressures they face, one would expect Japanese employers to favor labor deregulation, which should give them access to a wider pool of workers at a lower cost. Politically, one would expect the battle over labor deregulation to pit firms, employer federations, and the LDP against workers, union federations, and the opposition parties. Yet in fact firms have been highly ambivalent about labor market reforms, fearing that reforms might undermine the advantages of the labor relations system. Moreover, firm preferences have been aggregated through employer federations and political parties that represent opponents as well as advocates of reform.

Employers have not proposed any wholesale change in the employment system, but only piecemeal reforms to give firms more flexibility coupled with more active adjustment polices and new protections for workers. The government has moved forward with modest deregulation measures in the context of a government-wide deregulation movement that began in the 1980s and has accelerated since 1993. In 1997, it amended the Equal Employment Opportunity Act to remove some special protections for female workers, such as those governing overtime and nighttime work. Then in September 1998, it revised the Labor Standards Law to give employers more flexibility with employment contracts and overtime pay, but it coupled this with increased regulation of termination notices, working conditions, and overtime hours.

The Japanese government is also limited in its ability to reform the labor market because the system has become embedded in case law that cannot be overturned easily via legislation. The Japanese courts have developed a case law doctrine that deters employers from dismissing workers. The legal system gives employers considerable flexibility to manage human resources within the firm, by transferring employees to subsidiaries or increasing work time, for example, while sharply constraining their ability to hire and fire workers (Yamakawa 1999).

In July 1999, the government revised the Worker Dispatching Law and the Employment Security Law to give employers greater freedom in dispatching workers, to allow private companies to provide employment placement services, and to increase legal protection for job seekers. 'The unions opposed the liberal-ization of dispatch workers', recalls one Labor Ministry official, 'but many employ-ers had their doubts as well. They wanted to preserve a system in which they keep the best people forever'.[20] The government has made modest adjustments in wel-fare provisions for unemployed workers, but it has not made a broader shift toward a full-fledged safety net. It revised the Employment Labor Insurance Law in April 2000 to increase insurance premiums for employers and to give priority to benefits for those who lost jobs due to restructuring or bankruptcy. It contin-ues to rely more on government policies and private-sector practices that main-tain employment than on policies to support those who lose their jobs.

The government has made some progress on many of the pieces of legislation that could potentially shift Japan toward a more open labor market (see Table 6.1). It has loosened labor standards and it has begun to promote the infrastructure for a more active external labor market, including private employment agencies. It has enacted corollary reforms in a wide range of areas, such as finance, corpo-rate governance, pensions, and tax reforms. Yet the government has been cautious in crafting the detailed terms of these reforms. More critically, corporations and employees have not changed their practices sufficiently to generate an effective external labor market.

Financial reform

One would expect Japanese firms to advocate financial and corporate governance reforms designed to make equity markets operate more efficiently because this would reduce financing costs and stimulate financial innovation. But many man-agers have worried that financial reforms might undermine the advantages of close working relations with their banks. They count on these banks for preferential access to credit at special rates, a wide range of free services such as providing informa-tion and brokering business alliances, and assistance in the event of a financial crisis. They also value the freedom to hide profits and losses or to manipulate reporting to smooth out earnings over time, so they are reluctant to embrace financial reforms that would bring stricter requirements for information disclosure. Despite the firms' reservations, however, the government has moved forward with substantial financial reforms in the face of the forces for change outlined above.

Some of the biggest banks favored more rapid liberalization in the 1980s, but moderated their demands because they recognized that it could threaten other financial institutions with whom they have strong long-term working relationships. They also understood that articulating demands too strenuously could jeopardize their relationship with the Ministry of Finance. The ministry moved very delib-erately, packaging elaborate political compromises between the various groups within the financial sector (city banks, securities houses, insurance companies, regional banks, credit associations, cooperatives) (Vogel 1996: 93–117). With the financial crisis and the widespread loss of faith in the ministry in the 1990s, however, the political pressure for reform increased substantially.

In response, Prime Minister Ryūtarō Hashimoto proposed a 'Big Bang' reform in which the government would liberalize foreign exchange restrictions; open up the mutual fund, pension, and trust markets; deregulate brokerage commissions; allow banks, securities houses, and insurance companies to enter each other's lines of business through holding companies; and delegate some of the ministry's supervisory duties to a new finance agency. Even so, the Big Bang did not represent a complete break with past patterns of financial regulation, as the government phased in these measures gradually while paying special attention to the impact on domestic financial institutions. Moreover, the government gained leverage over the financial sector as a result of the banking crisis. It played a major role in allocating funds to banks in crisis, monitoring troubled banks' behavior, and orchestrating the reorganization of the financial sector.

Japan also has a large public-sector component within its financial system, representing about one-third of total savings, that strongly resists reform. The bureaucracy has allied with powerful LDP politicians to fight back calls for reforming the postal savings system. Prime Minister Junichirō Koizumi finally began to push through his long-anticipated reform program in 2002, but was forced to pare down his proposals considerably. The government reorganized the postal service as a public corporation in a July 2002 reform bill, and Koizumi vowed to press forward with privatization.

The Japanese government has made progress on corporate governance reform despite considerable ambivalence within the private sector. The Ministry of Finance and the Financial Services Agency have gradually phased in a shift toward market value-based accounting. They introduced consolidated reporting in 1999, and then market valuation of equity portfolios in 2000. They had committed to these reforms before many businesses or unions grasped the full ramifications. 'The accounting change was not a change in legislation, so we did not know about it', protests one labor union leader. 'The ministry discussed it with the accountants, and with the Ministry of International Trade and Industry (MITI). When we realized what was up, we got mad. We argued that this would constrain long-term investment and undermine competitiveness.'[21] Many firms feared that accounting reforms would make it more difficult to manipulate return on equity figures, to smooth out earnings over time, to ignore contingent or unfunded liabilities, or to camouflage the cross-subsidization of business operations (Shinn 1999). The banks strongly opposed market valuation because this would decimate their reported financial results. Meanwhile, both the Federation of Economic Organizations (Keidanren) and the LDP proposed measures to allow corporations to restructure their cross-shareholdings without causing the stock market to collapse or allowing outside shareholders to buy up the shares.[22] Yet these measures violate the very purpose of market-oriented corporate governance reform: to facilitate stock market adjustments and corporate contests for control (Shinn 1999: 10–11). In 2003, LDP party elder Tarō Asō and colleagues proposed legislation that would suspend some of the key accounting reforms for several years.

The government also passed a series of reforms to facilitate corporate restructuring and to give companies a wider range of options for corporate governance. It lifted the ban on holding companies in 1995, allowed companies to distribute stock options in 1997, and revised the Commercial Code to facilitate corporate spin-offs in 2000. In 2002, it passed further revisions of the Commercial Code: it strengthened the auditing system, allowed new corporate structures with more outside directors, and limited corporate liability in shareholding suits. Keidanren successfully argued that the new corporate structures should be optional, not mandatory. As of 2003, only 1.3 percent of companies in a national survey reported that they would adopt a US-style board structure while 83.5 percent stated that they had no plans to do so, and many prominent executives stated a preference for the Japanese structure (*Nikkei Weekly*, May 19, 2003: 12).

Variations across policy issue-areas

It is much more difficult to assess variation in the degree of policy change than variation in the level of corporate restructuring. Nonetheless, it is important to try to discern patterns of change and continuity in the policy arena precisely because there has been a combination of major reforms in some areas and deadlock in others. Many scholars have argued that the Japanese political system has become stuck since the 1990s, unable to enact vital reforms (Curtis 1999). Yet even a cursory review of legislative activity demonstrates that the Japanese political system has delivered extensive and substantial reforms. Japan overhauled its electoral system in 1994 and completely reorganized the bureaucracy in 2000. It pushed through a series of reforms designed to transform state–society relations, including the Administrative Procedures Act of 1993, the Non-Profit Organization Act of 1998, and the Information Disclosure Act of 1999. It has enacted major changes in accounting, corporate governance, and financial regulation. Yet the government was more cautious in those areas most critical to economic recovery: fighting deflation and resolving the NPL crisis.

Among the reforms reviewed above, Japan has moved more boldly with financial reforms than with labor reforms. The crisis was more severe in finance than in labor, the government authorities experienced a greater loss of legitimacy, and foreign political pressures and international market forces were more powerful. Hashimoto pushed through the financial Big Bang at a moment when both the Ministry of Finance and the financial sector had experienced such a severe loss of face that they were in no position to resist. The government has made some of the boldest reforms in accounting and corporate governance, two areas that are relatively far removed from the political process ('stealth' reforms) yet particularly vulnerable to arguments that Japan must adjust to 'global standards'. In accounting, the authorities made some critical changes via agency decree, thus avoiding the legislative process altogether. In corporate governance, MITI and the Ministry of Justice quietly collaborated, along with Keidanren. In contrast, the government has moved much more gingerly in areas where reforms would entail a broad public debate, such as tax and welfare reforms.

If reform is in fact moving more quickly in finance and corporate governance than in labor, this then raises the question of how tightly the different parts of the Japanese system are linked. Masahiko Aoki (1994) stresses that national systems of economic governance incorporate labor, financial, and political systems that complement each other (institutional complementarity), so it is difficult to change one part of the system without affecting the whole. For example, firms may only be able to make long-term commitments to their workers because the financial system shields them from shareholder demands for short-term profits. If this is true, then will more competitive financial markets force Japanese firms to abandon their long-term commitments to their workers? To date, changes in finance have put additional pressure on companies to reduce costs and raise returns, but they have not forced firms to abandon the core features of the labor-relations system.

Future prospects

Since the 1990s, Japanese firms have engaged in substantial restructuring and the Japanese government has enacted major policy reforms, yet these adjustments have been conditioned by the preexisting labor and finance systems. So how do we make sense of this combination of change and continuity? We can take a first step by making an analytical distinction between three levels of change: routine adjustment, bounded innovation, and fundamental breaks. In practice, it is tricky to differentiate between these levels of change because routine adjustments can cumulate into substantial revisions over time, and substantial revisions can cumulate into radical breaks.

Japanese firms have certain built-in mechanisms of adjustment in an economic downturn including negotiating for wage restraint, not renewing contracts of temporary workers, collaborating with workers and suppliers to cut production costs, or asking their banks to extend credit or to bail them out. So exercising these options does not represent a change in the system. Some adjustments, however, have the potential to cumulate into substantial change over time. For example, Japanese firms are *downgrading* their ties to banks and other firms by selling off cross-held shares. This represents a standard mechanism of adjustment during an economic downturn, but it has real consequences for the level of mutual obligation between the firms in the short term, and it could lead to the erosion of ties between firms over the longer term. To date, Japanese firms have negotiated with the other party prior to selling off shares and have carefully calibrated the level and timing of sales depending on the specific nature of the relationship.

Meanwhile, banks are *differentiating* their corporate clients into distinct tiers. They are strengthening main-bank relations with smaller companies, reinforcing main bank relations with larger companies that are having financial problems, and loosening main-bank relations with the stronger multinationals. Bank 'relationship managers' used to have a relatively uniform set of conditions for main-bank clients. Increasingly, however, they classify corporate clients into a wider range of possible relationships, depending on the company's size, financial status, and management philosophy. The strongest multinationals have all opted out of the main-bank system, so if this tier expands then the main-bank system will be that much less salient to the economic system as a whole.

Japanese companies have also been *borrowing* foreign practices in form while retaining their own standard practices at the same time. For example, most major Japanese firms have adopted some form of merit-based pay system, but most have kept pay disparities within a narrow range, and many have in fact deployed these systems as camouflage for wage restraint. Likewise, some companies have begun to adopt US-style corporate boards, but they remain reluctant to cede real control to outside directors.

Japanese government ministries have been *converting* to new roles. The major ministries, and especially MITI, have demonstrated a remarkable knack for reinventing themselves.[23] MITI officials helped to orchestrate the bureaucratic reorganization that gave them a new name (the Ministry of Economy, Trade and Industry, or METI) and broader responsibilities, including the right to comment on overall economic management by absorbing functions from the former Economic Planning Agency. MITI shifted goals from promoting exports, to promoting investment abroad, to promoting investment in Japan; and it has moved from classic industrial policy to promoting deregulation, cultivating market infrastructure, and facilitating corporate restructuring. Despite all of this, METI retains the old MITI's basic orientation: a commitment to promoting Japanese industry, a tradition of working closely with the private sector, and a fierce determination to preserve its own authority.

In terms of the language employed in the introduction to this volume, we might view differentiating among corporate clients and borrowing foreign practices (above) as types of *layering*, and ministries converting to new roles as a case of *conversion*. These adjustments will constitute cases of major institutional change to the extent that firms outside the main-bank system outweigh those within it, firms borrow foreign practices in substance as well as in form, and ministries reorient themselves in fundamental and not simply tactical ways.

Now let us look at *bounded innovation*, meaning institutional innovation shaped by preexisting institutions (see Table 6.2).[24] By shifting the employment guarantee from the firm to the corporate group, Japanese corporations are not only downgrading the status of lifetime employment but also redefining the role of corporate groups. Pressed by the dual constraints of economic competition and preexisting labor market institutions, Japanese firms have come up with an innovative solution that allows them to cut labor costs without violating their commitment to stable employment. This solution not only builds on preexisting institutions—corporate networks—but also transforms them in the process.

Likewise, by allowing financial institutions to cross business lines (such as banking, securities, and insurance) via holding companies, the government set the stage for the redefinition of the main-bank system and the reconfiguration of corporate groups. As the finance industry shifted from a segmented system to universal banking via holding companies, the main banks responded by trying to leverage main-bank ties in the investment banking business. They have only partially succeeded, however, because underwriting debt does not require the kind of close working relationship involved in standard bank lending, and the organizational separation of banking and securities subsidiaries complicates this strategy. The big banks have reorganized Japan's main industrial groups—which used to be based on a 'one set' principle of one commercial bank and one major company per industrial sector—by merging with partners from other corporate groups (e.g. Sumitomo Bank and Sakura Bank). The bank mergers have fostered other corporate mergers across the same groups, thus creating recombined corporate groups (Career Development Center 2001).

In May 2003, the government launched the Industrial Revitalization Corporation (IRC), which offers a creative approach to addressing the NPL crisis by building on the main-bank system. The government allocated 10 trillion yen in deposit insurance funds to the IRC to turn around troubled borrowers. Government officials designed the IRC to resolve a specific failure of the main-bank system. That is, the main banks tend to roll over loans to troubled borrowers because they judge that this is less costly than allowing the borrowers to fail, and they have an obligation as the main bank to support these borrowers. Yet they do not have the resources to restructure these borrowers on their own, and the other lenders (especially nonbanks) do not want to participate in restructuring because they have much less stake in the companies' survival. The IRC resolves this dilemma by purchasing the nonbank lenders' share of the NPLs, and then working together with the main bank to reorganize the company.

These examples illustrate the logic of bounded innovation. Corporate and government reforms go beyond routine adjustments to the point where they generate substantial institutional change, yet the trajectory of change is still shaped by the preexisting institutions. So then what would constitute a real break in the system? In practice, as noted above, it is difficult to distinguish incremental change from a fundamental break because the former can easily cumulate into the latter. For our purposes, however, I have suggested that a preference for voice over exit mechanisms represents a defining feature of the Japanese system. By that definition, we have not yet encountered a fundamental transformation of the system. Japanese firms continue to favor voice mechanisms over exit with their workers, banks, and suppliers. We could proclaim a break in the labor relations system, for example, if Japanese firms were to shift from an internal labor market model, hiring fresh graduates and transferring them internally, to an external labor market model, hiring mid-career employees and actively poaching from other firms. Likewise, we could declare a break in the financial system if Japanese firms were to develop a full-fledged market for corporate control in which investors buy and sell firms on the open market (Table 6.1).

Looking toward the future, we should expect this pattern of routine adjustment plus bounded innovation to continue. We cannot predict the precise form it will take, but we can engage in some informed speculation because we know that existing institutions close off certain options and favor others. By lifting the ban on holding companies, for example, the Japanese government has opened up new possibilities for institutional change that are consistent with the logic of the Japanese system. Most countries already have pure holding companies, but this option could solve Japan-specific problems in distinctive ways. For example, it could help companies to extend their practice of using interfirm links and diversification to manage labor costs without layoffs. They could differentiate wages, benefits, and levels of job security across the various companies within the holding company structure. Likewise, holding companies may be able to foster a functional substitute for venture capital by funneling investments into virtually autonomous subsidiaries with their own compensation structures and accounting systems.

Japanese firms might also enhance internal labor markets rather than shifting toward external ones. Specifically, they could start to make internal labor markets work more like real markets and less like a centrally controlled rotation system. The NEC personnel division has engaged in some early experiments in this direction. It encourages all employees to post a curriculum vitae on the firm's internal network, specifying not only their qualifications but also their preferences for future job assignments. Then it asks managers to regularly screen through these files. It allows managers and employees much greater freedom to arrange their own job matches. In addition, NEC has redefined its lifetime employment guarantee as 'lifetime career support'. In practical terms, this means that the NEC personnel division supports its permanent employees in finding new positions within the firm, within the corporate group, and outside the group as well.[25]

Yet another possibility would be for Japanese firms to use employee ownership and stock options to stabilize ownership rather than to give employees and managers performance incentives. They could compensate for reductions in cross-held shares within the corporate group by increasing shares held by employees and managers. This would give them a way to adjust to the changed financial climate without increasing their vulnerability to pressure from outside shareholders.

By looking at the interaction of policy reforms and corporate restructuring in this way, we begin to see both the strengths and the limits of the model presented here. By focusing on how preexisting institutions shape the trajectory of change, we can go quite far in explaining the distinctive Japanese pattern of corporate adjustment and policy reform over the short to medium term. We can also show how adjustments at one period of time reshape possibilities and constraints for change at a later time. But we cannot predict the long-term evolution of these institutions because government reforms and corporate adjustments interact and cumulate into broader institutional change over time.

Notes

1. This chapter builds on Vogel (2003). The author thanks Kenneth Haig, Yasuyuki Motoyama, Keith Nitta, Gene Park, and Masaya Ura, for their valuable research assistance.
2. On the parallels between these other types of market transition, see Chaudhry (1993).
3. Their status differs fundamentally from Swedish workers, for example, who are 'de-commodified' in the sense that the government guarantees their livelihood even if employers do not hire them (Esping-Andersen 1990).
4. Nonregular workers include 'temporary' workers that often work full time in skilled positions (*paato*), true part-time workers such as students (*arubaito*), and dispatch workers or agency temps (*haken shain*).
5. Posen (1998) represents the former view, and Katz (2003) the latter.
6. Granovetter (1985: 505–6), for example, defends the assumption of rationality but expands it to focus more on social structure.
7. Of course one could also refine the model by incorporating a more explicitly political analysis. See Knight (1992) on the theoretical argument, and Vogel (2001) on the German and Japanese cases.
8. Moreover, these preferences are aggregated in the political arena in a manner that further moderates demands for liberal reform (Vogel 2001).
9. Interview, January 15, 2002, Tokyo.
10. Tabata (1996) offers a fascinating case study of how Japanese auto unions worked with management to reduce costs and increase productivity.
11. Japan Institute of Labor (2002).
12. NEC corporate documents.
13. Government of Japan, annual census data.
14. Interview, January 23, 2002, Tokyo.
15. I introduce here initial findings from a larger research project that includes in-depth case studies of restructuring efforts by ten companies, plus a quantitative analysis of patterns of restructuring throughout the economy.
16. Interview, March 26, 2002.
17. Interview with Seiyu executives, January 23, 2002, Tokyo.
18. Interview with senior executive, Mitsukoshi, January 24, 2002, Tokyo.
19. Interview, January 15, 2002.
20. Interview, March 25, 2002, Tokyo.
21. Interview with Tadayuki Murakami, Assistant General Secretary, Japan Trade Union Confederation (Rengō), March 27, 2002, Tokyo.
22. Keidanren merged with the Japan Federation of Employers' Associations (Nikkeiren) in 2002, forming the Japan Business Federation (Nippon Keidanren).
23. Johnson (1989), 183–6; Elder (2003).
24. Margaret Weir (1992) employs the concept of 'bounded innovation' somewhat differently, arguing that institutions can narrow the range of ideas that are likely to influence policy over time.
25. Interview, January 21, 2002, Tokyo.

References

AHMADJIAN, CHRISTINA and PATRICIA ROBINSON (2001). Safety in Numbers: Downsizing and the Deinstitutionalization of Permanent Employment in Japan. *Administrative Science Quarterly*, 46: 622–54.

AOKI, MASAHIKO (1988). *Information, Incentives, and Bargaining in the Japanese Economy.* Cambridge: Cambridge University Press.

—— (1994). The Japanese Firm as a System of Attributes: A Survey and Research Agenda. In: Masahiko Aoki and Ronald Dore (eds.), *The Japanese Firm: Sources of Competitive Strength.* Oxford: Oxford University Press, pp. 11–40.

Career Development Center (2001). *Kigyō gurūpu to gyōkai chizu* [Corporate Groups and Industry Charts]. Tokyo: Takahashi Shoten.

CHAUDHRY, KIREN (1993). The Myths of the Market and the Common History of Late Developers. *Politics and Society* 21(September): 245–74.

CURTIS, GERALD (1999). *The Logic of Japanese Politics.* New York: Columbia University Press.

ELDER, MARK (2003). METI and Industrial Policy in Japan: Change and Continuity. In: Ulrike Schaede and William Grimes (eds.), *Japan's Managed Globalization.* Armonk, NY: M. E. Sharpe, pp. 159–90.

ESPING-ANDERSEN, GØSTA (1990). *The Three Worlds of Welfare Capitalism.* Princeton, NJ: Princeton University Press.

FLIGSTEIN, NEIL (2001). *The Architecture of Markets: An Economic Sociology of Twenty-First Century Capitalist Societies.* Princeton, NJ: Princeton University Press.

FRIEDEN, JEFFREY and RONALD ROGOWSKI (1996). The Impact of the International Economy on National Policies: An Analytical Overview. In: Robert O. Keohane and Helen V. Milner (eds.), *Internationalization and Domestic Politics.* Cambridge: Cambridge University Press, pp. 25–47.

GOUREVITCH, PETER (1996). The Macropolitics of Microinstitutional Differences in the Analysis of Comparative Capitalism. In: Suzanne Berger and Ronald Dore (eds.), *National Diversity and Global Capitalism.* Ithaca, NY: Cornell University Press.

GRANOVETTER, MARK (1985). Economic Action and Social Structure: The Problem of Embeddedness. *American Journal of Sociology* 91(November): 481–510.

HALL, PETER and DAVID SOSKICE (eds.) (2001). *Varieties of Capitalism: The Institutional Foundations of Comparative Advantage.* Oxford: Oxford University Press.

HIRSCHMAN, ALBERT (1970). *Exit, Voice and Loyalty: Responses to Decline in Firms, Organizations, and States.* Cambridge, MA.: Harvard University Press.

Japan Institute of Labor (2002). *Jigyō saikōchiku to koyō ni kansuru chōsa hōkokusho* [Survey Report on Restructuring and Employment].

JOHNSON, CHALMERS (1989). MITI, MPT, and the Telecom Wars: How Japan Makes Policy for High Technology. In: Chalmers Johnson, Laura D'Andrea Tyson, and John Zysman (eds.), *Politics and Productivity: How Japan's Development Strategy Works.* Cambridge: Ballinger.

KATZ, RICHARD (2003). *Japanese Phoenix: The Long Road to Economic Revival.* Armonk, NY: M.E. Sharpe.

KNIGHT, JACK (1992). *Institutions and Social Conflict.* Cambridge: Cambridge University Press.

NORTH, DOUGLASS C. (1990). *Institutions, Institutional Change and Economic Performance.* Cambridge: Cambridge University Press.

POLANYI, KARL (1944). *The Great Transformation: The Political and Economic Origins of Our Time.* Boston, MA: Beacon Press.

POSEN, ADAM (1998). *Restoring Japan's Economic Growth.* Washington DC: Institute for International Economics.

POWELL, WALTER and PAUL DIMAGGIO (eds.) (1991). *The New Institutionalism in Organizational Analysis.* Chicago, IL: University of Chicago Press.

SHINN, JAMES (1999). Corporate Governance Reform and Trade Friction. Paper for the Study Group on U.S.–Japan Economic Relations, Council on Foreign Relations, March, Washington.

TABATA, HIROKUNI (1996). Gurobaraizeeshon to jidōsha sangyō—jidōsha sōren no sangyō seisaku. [Globalization and the Auto Industry: The Autoworkers Union's Industrial Policy.] Institute of Social Science Discussion Paper J-52, June.

THELEN, KATHLEEN (2001). Varieties of Labor Politics in the Developed Democracies. In: Peter Hall and David Soskice (eds.), *Varieties of Capitalism: The Institutional Foundations of Comparative Advantage*. Oxford: Oxford University Press, pp. 71–103.

VOGEL, STEVEN (1996). *Freer Markets, More Rules: Regulatory Reform in Advanced Industrial Countries*. Ithaca, NY: Cornell University Press.

—— (2001). The Crisis of German and Japanese Capitalism: Stalled on the Road to the Liberal Market Model? *Comparative Political Studies* 34(December): 1103–33.

—— (2003). The Re-Organization of Organized Capitalism: How the German and Japanese Models are Shaping their Own Transformations. In: Wolfgang Streeck and Kozo Yamamura (eds.), *Germany and Japan: The Future of Nationally Embedded Capitalism in a Global Economy*. Ithaca, NY: Cornell University Press, pp. 306–33.

WEIR, MARGARET (1992). Ideas and the Politics of Bounded Innovation. In: Sven Steinmo, Kathleen Thelen, and Frank Longstreth (eds.), *Structuring Politics: Historical Institutionalism in Comparative Analysis*. Cambridge: Cambridge University Press, pp. 188–216.

WILLIAMSON, OLIVER (1985). *The Economic Institutions of Capitalism*. New York: Free Press.

YAMAKAWA, RYŪICHI (1999). The Silence of Stockholders: Japanese Labor Law from the Viewpoint of Corporate Governance. *Japanese Labor Bulletin* 38(November): 6–12.

7

Change from Within: German and Italian Finance in the 1990s

Richard Deeg

It hardly needs to be stated that there have been tremendous changes in the European political economy over the last two decades. But just how profound are these changes? To put it in more theoretic terms, are we simply witnessing a period of relatively rapid evolution along old institutional trajectories (paths), or are we in fact witnessing a critical historical juncture that is launching nations onto new trajectories? How can we determine when an existing institutional path or trajectory is ending and being replaced with a new one? How does such a process take place? How can we distinguish between institutional innovation within an existing trajectory and a switchover to a new trajectory or path?

In this chapter, I explore these questions and illustrate my theoretical arguments by examining the pattern of institutional change in the German and Italian financial systems.[1] I draw on recent theoretical work on path dependency and institutional change to identify the mechanisms of institutional reproduction and institutional change in the two cases. The cases suggest that path dependency, or self-reinforcing positive feedback mechanisms, can be used to help explain the observed pattern of institutional innovation. Yet the cases also suggest that path dependency theory can be enhanced through further theoretical modifications.

The empirical focus of this chapter is on the financial system—understood to include the banking system, securities markets, and elements of the corporate governance system—which occupies a central position within the institutional complex of a national political economy. Thus fundamental changes in the financial system have direct and significant consequences for the nonfinancial sector. However, in this chapter, I deal only with the financial system and do not attempt to generate an account of change in the entire economy.[2] Studying the financial sector also enables us to see how economic and political actors respond jointly to incentives for change in a given institution or institutional complex. This is so because much of institutional change and reproduction in the financial sector is predicated on coordinated responses by actors outside the sector, notably but not exclusively in the form of government regulation.

I will argue that the German financial system has initiated a new path or trajectory by bifurcating in two heterogeneous subsystems or subregimes. One subregime encompasses banks and firms continuing to operate in the traditional regime, while the other encompasses banks and firms who are now operating under a new regime. In both subregimes we see a hybridization process in which many of the institutions of the old path continue as before, some old institutions are transformed to new purposes (conversion), and new institutions are introduced (layering) (Thelen 2003). Yet in one subregime institutional change is sufficiently radical to generate a new 'logic', as a result of which the incentive structures for key actors and patterns of strategic interaction among them within the sector have changed substantially.

The Italian case is less clear-cut. The Italian financial system as a whole has undergone many of the same formal institutional changes as the German system, though only in the banking system narrowly defined is there clear off-path institutional change. Since efforts to transform Italian finance began much later than in Germany, this may just mean that Italy is in an earlier stage of transition and will, like Germany, move onto a new path. On the other hand, comparison of the German and Italian cases suggest that both were subjected to more or less the same exogenous 'shocks', yet their respective financial systems changed in notably different ways and to notably different degrees. This reminds us that endogenous factors, which I will discuss in greater detail, matter to outcomes, and this is why Italy may continue to evolve in an on-path fashion.

My particular conception of a path and off-path change may diverge from that commonly assumed by other theorists of path dependence. But if one were to take the position that a new path can only be constituted by complete, radical change— as most theorists apparently do—then the concept is of rather limited use. If one were to take the position that a switch to a new path can only result from discontinuous change ('exogenous shocks'), that is, wars, revolutions, conquest, or natural disasters, then we would find relatively few cases to study (see also North 1991: 90–1). Assuming this was so, in my view it can only lead to one of two conclusions. The first is that, for all practical purposes, there is no true path change, that is, everything just evolves along its given path, and hence the concept of a path is tautological. The second is that a switch to a new path is always (or nearly so) an evolutionary process. I will, as already suggested, argue the second position.

Institutional stability and change

In a recent work Paul Pierson (2000*a,c,d*) has elaborated an enticing theory of path dependence which is more complete and precise than that typically found in social science. Pierson (2000*a*: 74–7) argues that a path-dependent historical or temporal process is one characterized by a self-reinforcing sequence of events. Path dependence constitutes a particular kind of historical process with a number of distinctive characteristics. First, *when* a particular event happens in a sequence it is very important, because 'small' events early in a sequence can have disproportionately large effects on later events. Second, during the early stages of a sequence—what can be understood as the critical juncture—things are relatively open or permissive but get more restrictive as one moves down a path. Third, as one moves further down the path change becomes 'bounded', that is, 'previously viable options may be foreclosed in the aftermath of a sustained period of positive feedback, and that cumulative commitments on the existing path will often make change difficult and will condition the form in which new branchings will occur (Pierson 2000a: 76)'. Path dependence thus involves three phases: the first is the critical juncture in which events trigger a move toward a particular path out of at least two possibilities; the second is the period of reproduction, that is, the period in which positive feedback mechanisms reinforce the movement along one path; and finally, the path comes to an end when new events dislodge the long-lasting equilibrium. Thus, for Pierson every path begins and ends with a critical juncture, or what has also been frequently referred to as a punctuated equilibrium, marked by specific triggering events.

Mahoney takes this point a step further by arguing that these initial events must be *contingent* in that they cannot be explained by prior events or initial conditions (Mahoney 2000: 507–8). This does not mean that events are completely random or without antecedent causes, but they are either events too specific to be explained by prevailing theories, such as the assassination of a political leader, or they are large random events like natural disasters (Mahoney 2000: 513). 'Analysts may also treat an outcome as contingent if it contradicts the predictions of a particular theoretical framework specifically designed to account for this outcome (Mahoney 2000: 514).' The contingent nature of initial events is a necessary and logical element of such a conception of path dependency, but I will suggest in my analysis that this condition is too restrictive theoretically and empirically difficult to sustain.

One of the most important contributions of Pierson to recent institutionalist debates is his effort to specify mechanisms of institutional reproduction, or, put simply, what keeps things moving along the same path. Borrowing from economics, Pierson argues that a specific path is promoted via positive feedback mechanisms or the realization of *increasing returns* to moving along this path (Pierson 2000a,b). A variety of feedback mechanisms could be at work here. One possibility is 'large set-up or initial costs'; once actors make a large investment in a particular institution they have an incentive to continue it in order to recover those costs. Another possibility is 'learning effects', that is, over time actors operating within the institutions that define a particular path become more adept and knowledgeable and use this to enhance the efficiency of the institutions. A third mechanism is 'coordination effects', in which the benefits accruing to one set of actors from engaging in a particular activity grow when other actors adapt their behavior to it. A related mechanism is 'adaptive expectations'. This is operative when actors *expect* other actors to adopt a particular option, so they themselves adopt that option in order not to be left behind.

Mahoney lumps the four mechanisms together into a 'utilitarian' explanation of institutional reproduction (Mahoney 2000: 516–18). It is based on the assumption that actors choose particular institutions and choose to reproduce them as long as they see it in their interest to do so, and this determination is based on a cost–benefit analysis of alternative choices. To it Mahoney adds other mechanisms of institutional reproduction, like the exercise of 'political authority' or 'power' in favor of a particular path. 'Legitimacy' can also produce positive feedback, since often acceptance among actors of something as legitimate or appropriate encourages others also to accept it as such.[3]

Important for my analysis is also the argument that it is not only single institutions that are subject to positive feedback effects, 'but configurations of complementary institutions in which the performance of each is affected by the existence of others (Pierson 2000a: 78)'. Complementarity among institutions can generate high increasing returns to the extent that the effectiveness of each is enhanced by the existence and functioning of the others. Financial systems fit this description since they are composed of a broader institutional complex involving, for example, banks, insurance firms, stock exchanges, corporate governance regimes, accounting regulations, tax laws, etc.

One of the glaring (and surprising) gaps in this debate is that no one has attempted to explicitly define, let alone theorize, when one is no longer on the old path. How do we know when change is 'bounded change' within the old path, or when change is the start of a new path? Indeed, it seems obvious that if we cannot make a clear distinction between change within a path and change to a new path, then the concept itself is rather useless. Moving forward on this issue starts with a definition of institutions, a working definition of a path, and a 'measurable' conceptualization of path change. I will follow Hall (1986: 19) that institutions are 'the formal rules, compliance procedures, and standard operating practices that structure the relationship between individuals in various units of the polity and economy'. Of particular interest in this chapter is path dependency and change in institutional systems or regimes, that is, a configuration of institutions that are collectively structuring a specific sphere of activity. In this chapter, I argue that the *path* of an institutional system is not synonymous with the particular institutions which constitute it at a given point in time, but with the logic generated by their interplay, that is, the typical *strategies, routine* approaches to problems, and *shared decision rules* that produce predictable patterns of behavior by actors within the system (this draws on Zysman 1994). When actors are confronted with new situations, they will resort to these strategies, routines, and decision rules. Even if many institutions in a system change dramatically, so long as the logic of the system is preserved, this change represents on-path change. Conversely, even though many institutions in a system might remain unchanged over a period of time, changes in other institutions might be sufficient to generate a new logic and thus off-path change. This conception of path change draws our attention away from formal institutions and toward the behavior of actors.

Financial systems, for instance, are often divided into two types exhibiting different logics. In *market-based* systems the logic is characterized by arms-length, deal-based interactions among firms. Relationships are more likely to be based on explicit, contractually determined exchange and obligations. Banks reduce their market risks by maintaining distance with clients, limiting their financial exposure to a given firm, and minimizing risk through diversification of exposures. Banks and other financial institutions often prefer to be pure financial intermediaries between savers and borrowers, carrying little risk themselves. Borrowing from Hirschman (1970), we might call this a *logic of exit*: financial firms limit their obligations to an individual firm to make exiting from the relationship relatively easy.

In *bank-based* systems, by comparison, longer-term, reciprocity-based interactions prevail. Relationships are more likely to involve implicit obligations and trust. Banks reduce their market risks through closeness to clients as maintaining a higher financial exposure places the bank in a position to monitor and influence client firms' management. Specifically, through mechanisms such as board seats and equity investments, banks gain the inside information necessary to manage their credit risks. This we might call a *logic of voice*: financial firms cooperate with clients and use their leverage over them to improve the relationship (see also Beyer 2002).

Starting from this conception of a path, I will advance three theoretical claims through an examination of institutional change in the German and Italian financial systems:

1. *Endogenous change.* The first claim is that, contrary to the theory of path dependence which asserts that only exogenous change can move actors off a current path, an exogenous shock is *not* the only way fundamental (off-path) institutional change is initiated. Endogenous sources of change include actions undertaken by actors within an institution or institutional system that result directly from mechanisms of path reproduction.[4] With this definition it becomes essential to identify these mechanisms exactly and show how their gradual, 'natural' evolution over time can lead to changes which undermine or alter these very mechanisms. Increasing returns may thus cease to increase or even turn into decreasing returns. This, in turn, induces actors to seek institutional changes that will either restore the old path (possibly through non self-reinforcing mechanisms of institutional reproduction, like power) or move to a new path. A logical corollary to this claim is that an event sequence involving a move to a new path may not necessarily follow from a contingent event, yet may nonetheless be driven by path-dependent increasing returns processes.[5]

2. *Path dependency as a mechanism of change.* Positive feedback or self-reinforcing mechanisms are usually viewed as mechanisms of institutional reproduction or stability. But they can also be mechanisms of change. The two cases examined later show how increasing returns to a new institutional path may gradually displace the old path. As self-reinforcing effects become stronger for a new path they weaken the self-reinforcing effects of the old and may, eventually, tip the balance in favor of the new. Another possibility is that the old path gets bifurcated in that the system develops into two heterogeneous subregimes operating on different logics—one on the old logic, the other on a new one. Each path may be stabilized by self-reinforcing mechanisms. Of course not all instances of off-path change occur through self-reinforcing or path-dependent processes.

3. *Cultivation of increasing returns.* This leads to my third theoretical claim: that increasing returns to social and political institutions must often, or perhaps normally, be cultivated by actors as they do not happen automatically. While this point is not necessarily inconsistent with much of the literature, it has not received sufficient attention. Cultivation takes the form of mobilization in the political arena on behalf of policy or regulatory change. It also takes the form of organizing collective action, often for the purpose of coalition building. Here power and ideas enter crucially into the institutional change process. If change in the financial system were simply a result of actors finding the most efficient institutional solution, then a simple functionalist explanation would suffice. But if, for instance, we take the fundamental choice confronting actors in the German and Italian financial systems between adapting the existing system or converting to a market-based system, the most efficient choice is not obvious. In the abstract neither system is clearly superior to the other, and the consequence of choosing one over the other is highly uncertain: sticking with the old could be slow demise, while choosing the new may be sudden death. In such situations actors deploy power, ideology, or both to promote their favored outcomes. As institutional change moves in a direction sought by key actors, we should see a declining need for cultivation as other actors independently adapt their behavior to reinforce the new path. In other words, over time positive feedback effects must become strong enough to become self-reinforcing.[6]

In the two case studies to follow, we shall see that endogenous factors are very important in explaining the extent of change in the German case, as well as the different degrees of change in the two cases. Similarly, the cases demonstrate the importance of cultivation by actors, showing in particular that broader and more concerted cultivation in Germany explains why a path change occurred here but not in Italy. Finally, in both cases increasing returns effects contribute to explaining change yet they appear to be weaker in Italy than in Germany. This difference is ascribed to the absence of endogenous pressures for change in Italy and weaker efforts at cultivation.

The German case

If the German financial system is not unambiguously suboptimal, why do they change it? How do they manage to do this if there are strong positive feedback effects that ought to keep Germans on the same path? My answer starts with the assertion that key actors come to see their interests as diverging from the existing path because of decreasing returns to them within it; first as a result of endogenous developments in the path and, later, exogenous changes. The movement to a new path in Germany may have begun small, in some sense, but it cannot be traced back to a single contingent event. Rather, it is a cumulative result achieved through an evolutionary process—*mostly* intended by actors—that is eventually driven forward by self-reinforcing mechanisms in what can be viewed as a critical juncture, that is, the mid-1980s to late 1990s. Paradoxically, it turns out that self-reinforcing mechanisms can be observed at work in simultaneously preserving the old path and promoting a new one. This is possible because the old system 'bifurcates' in a sense; part of the system (mostly comprised of smaller banks and firms) continues to evolve along the old trajectory—that is, on-path change—while another portion (mostly involving large banks and firms) develops a significantly new institutional path. Yet both parts remain constituent pieces of the German financial system and the evolution of each is conditioned by that of the other. In more theoretical terms, the operative mechanism of institutional change is bifurcation: because many actors continue to prefer the old system (path), actors seeking major institutional change achieve their aims by carving out a distinct subregime.

The existing path

It virtually goes without saying that the banking industry is widely recognized as a key ingredient of German industrial success. Much studied and debated is the historically close relationship between large banks and firms (e.g. Edwards and Fischer 1994). This relationship rests on several institutions and patterns: First, in comparative perspective German firms have not relied much on equity markets for external finance, instead relying on bank loans. Second, large banks frequently have substantial equity stakes in large firms (and vote shares of others they hold on deposit), giving them a voice in firm management. Moreover, ownership in large German firms tends to be concentrated in the hands of a few long-term share-holders, primarily families, other large nonfinancial firms, and, to a lesser extent, financial firms. And third, bank representatives have historically sat on a wide range of corporate supervisory boards, placing them in an unparalleled position to monitor and influence management. It has frequently been argued that this system lends certain comparative advantages to German firms, in particular the ability to rely on 'patient capital' and focus on long-term expansion rather than share price maximization (Porter 1992). Historically, small- and medium-sized enterprises (SMEs) have eschewed the stock market and instead relied heavily on long-term relations and loans from savings and cooperative banks (Vitols 2000).

The institutional path of the German system embodies an overall *logic of voice* with long-term cooperation founded on expectations of mutual reciprocity (see also Zysman 1983). Market actors following this logic seek to reduce risks and increase their own economic gains through cooperation. Following my earlier conceptualization of a path's logic, we can identify three dimensions of actor behavior that follow from this logic. First, the key institutions (formal rules) governing the financial system are developed through a consensual bargaining process involving the associations of the three major banking groups. When other groups' interests were affected, they too participated but the pattern of bargaining did not change. The *shared decisionmaking* system was therefore a corporatist (consensual) rule-making one within a tight-knit policy community. The state's role in this process was largely to act as mediator and codifier of privately negotiated agreements, that is, establishing the statutory framework to govern extensive self-regulation by industry actors (Lütz 2000: 152–5).

The second dimension of the system's logic is reflected in the market strategies of individual actors. In the 'insider control' character of German corporate governance, insiders—major shareholders such as large banks, insurance firms, corporations, and families—control the strategies and decisions of large German firms (relatively free of the influence of stock markets or small shareholders; Vitols 2000). This system rested on the corporate *strategies* of these insiders. The strategy of large commercial banks, for instance, focused on cultivating industrial development and competitiveness through a system of broadly negotiated industrial change (Zysman 1983). Part of this strategy involved investment in maintaining strong networks (both capital and human) among larger firms and the cultivation of long-term relationships with corporate customers. Another prominent strategic behavior is 'group competition' in which the savings and cooperative banks, through various kinds of cooperative strategies within their associational structures, attempt to compete as a group against the large commercial banks in all segments of financial business. This system meant that the *routine response* of corporate actors to common challenges—and frequently to challenges or problems facing an individual firm—typically involved some significant collective response.

As with any complex set of institutions, there are many mechanisms that reinforced this system. One key *mechanism of reproduction* was the increasing returns accruing to the system as a whole due to the complementarity of institutions. For example, the strong, long-term links between banks and nonfinancial firms were connected to the specific organizational strategies of each, that is, reliable sources of long-term finance encouraged firms to develop business strategies with long-term investment horizons. This, in turn, created an interest on the part of nonfinancial firms in maintaining the existing financial system. Furthermore, the weakness of equity markets in Germany reinforced the reliance on bank loans as the key source of external finance. Relatively strong competition in commercial loan markets and state lending ensured competitively priced loans for firms, thus further encouraging heavy reliance on bank loans. The bankruptcy laws also encouraged bank borrowing over equity issues (Sauvé and Scheuer 1999: 70–7).

The insider system of corporate governance embodied another key mechanism in the form of *coordination gains*. Major gains include protection from unwanted takeovers, useful information about general industrial developments, and the assurance of reward for long-term success of the firm rather than the achievement of short-term financial targets. This insider system also encouraged a stakeholder approach to the management of German corporations, that is, firms were managed not only in the interest of owners but also other stakeholders such as employees, suppliers and customers, and society at large.

A final mechanism of reproduction was the relative parity and stable distribution of *power* among the three key banking groups. Parity meant that no single group could dominate the establishment and change of the rules. Stability rested on the fact that each banking group is economically significant, has powerful allies in the economy and the political party system, and draws from independent sources of *legitimacy*. This stable power distribution undergirded the consensual rule-making pattern and the cooperative logic of the system more generally.

The change to a new path

In line with my first theoretical claim, the process of moving to a new institutional path for the German financial system began endogenously. Key actors within the system, notably the large commercial banks, began to gradually see their interests as diverging from the status quo. They sought to confront their competitiveness problems in the 1970s through market strategies, but they ultimately started to focus on changing the higher level institutions or rules that govern the financial system as a solution to their problems. The internationalization of financial markets—an exogenous force—ultimately became a powerful source of pressure for change, but it did so only after endogenous developments initiated the movement to a new path.[7] Thus the internal dynamics of the system led to developments that altered the interests of key/central actors who initiated a series of institutional changes designed to serve their interests. This case suggests that a 'critical juncture' can emerge (at least partly) out of normal processes of change inside a path (also Schwartz 2001).

That said, the initial movements in the 1970s and early 1980s toward a new path might not have been consolidated but for the growing impact of internationalization on the interests and preferences of domestic actors. The initiation of the Single Market process in 1987 really becomes the vehicle through which the internationalization of financial markets begins to strongly impact domestic German developments. Nonetheless, change toward a new institutional path in Germany still required intensive cultivation by actors—in the late 1980s and early 1990s. Increasing returns effects become readily observable only in the 1990s, notably in the wake of the crucial decision at Maastricht in 1991—which can be understood as an intensification of the process begun by the SEA (Single European Act)—to establish monetary union a decade hence.

Left at this, my explanation could probably be viewed as entirely consistent with the Pierson (2000*d*) conception of path dependency, as he suggests that path-dependent processes are all based on such a threshold model in that a small event or movement acts as the trigger, that is, pushes a cumulative variable above a threshold point that unleashes more dramatic off-path change. While one could construct a plausible argument that the SEA was a contingent event, for this kind of path-dependent argument to work one has to assume that in the absence of the triggering event the cumulative variable would not move above the hypothetical threshold on its own. But the internationalization of financial markets—the cumulative variable of interest here—would clearly have continued to cumulate and sooner or later would have come to have similar determinative force over

Table 7.1 Market share of loans to firms and manufacturing industry by bank group (% of total)

Year	Commercial banks	Big banks*	Savings banks	Cooperatives
Firms				
1968	35.4	15.7	31.3	12.9
1970	36.2	16.0	32.3	12.3
1972	36.7	15.4	33.2	12.9
1974	35.0	14.9	34.1	13.6
1977	31.8	13.2	34.6	15.1
1982	30.1	11.9	36.7	17.4
1986	27.0	10.7	35.9	16.1
Manufacturing industry				
1968	52.9	28.3	24.6	10.8
1970	54.6	29.6	24.7	10.4
1972	54.2	28.2	26.1	11.3
1974	53.2	28.4	25.8	12.2
1977	48.5	25.1	27.9	14.9
1982	38.8	18.2	33.2	17.5
1986	39.3	18.8	31.8	18.4

* Big banks are a subset of the commercial bank category. Loans to firms include the self-employed and mortgage loans on commercial property.

Source: Deutsche Bundesbank, *Statistische Beihefte zu den Monatsberichten der Bundesbank, Reihe 1, Bankenstatistik nach Bankengruppen* (various years); and Deutsche Bundesbank, *Deutsches Geld- und Bankwesen in Zahlen, 1876–1975* (Frankfurt: Deutsche Bundesbank and Paris: Banque de France, 1976), tables 1.10 and 2.05. Percentages are authors own calculations.

domestic institutional changes. Thus, we find evolutionary change within a path that ultimately becomes a new path (marked by increasing returns) but without an *indispensable* triggering, contingent event.

The 1950s and 1960s represent the postwar equilibrium phase for the German financial system. The large commercial banks grew and profited primarily from their close association with large industrial firms, though they also began to rapidly expand retail banking business during the 1960s. As can be seen in Table 7.1, in the late 1960s and early 1970s loan market shares among the bank groups were relatively stable. But beginning with the 1974 recession a rapid shift from the commercial to savings and cooperative banks can be observed. The shift is particularly stark in the category of loans to manufacturers—along the mainstay of commercial banks and especially the big three banks. With this shift the benefits (returns) to the major banks of the old path began to decline, thereby touching off a gradually intensifying search for institutional changes.

This shift can be attributed to two general endogenous developments. The first is the new aggressiveness and success, beginning in the late 1960s, of the savings and cooperative banks in commercial lending (see also Deeg 1999: 47–55).

The second was the decline in borrowing by large firms that were the primary customers of the big commercial banks. Even though the late 1970s and early 1980s involved extensive economic restructuring, large firms as a whole decreased substantially their financial dependence on the banking system because they were able to self-finance at higher rates. Commercial lending by banks was further undermined by the expanding banking activities of many large nonfinancial firms, including lending to other enterprises.[8] The declining benefits to the banks of the existing system were likely further depressed by a steady and significant rise in corporate bankruptcies since the mid-1960s: This occurred despite the insider position of banks—resting on equity holdings, board seats, and proxy voting of shares held on deposit—which presumably gave them sufficient information and leverage to minimize such risks (Beyer 2002).

The decline in bank borrowing by large firms represents an endogenous factor because the reproduction of the existing path of the German financial system depended on a close, capital-based relationship between banks and firms. As this relationship began to change, the ability of the system to reproduce itself began to erode. It is also endogenous because in Germany dependence on bank borrowing reflected the preferences of the banks and industrial firms, that is, it was not a consequence of state-imposed restrictive regulations, as was the case in many 'repressed' financial systems such as France or Japan. In many of these systems bank borrowing by large firms also declined in this period but as a result of exogenous changes in state policies.[9]

This rapid decline in lending touched off a search by large commercial banks for a new, long-term market strategy. One response of these banks was to lend more aggressively to small- and mid-sized firms. While they had some success in this effort, it was not enough. By the early to mid-1980s the big commercial banks determined that their best opportunities lay in financial activities related to capital markets, most importantly underwriting and trading. This shift in strategy coincided with rising concern among banks over growing competition from foreign financial institutions and centers. This concern became quite powerful in the wake of the sweeping liberalization of the London securities industry (the 'Big Bang') and the SEA, both of which occurred in 1986.

Given these endogenous and now increasing exogenous pressures, the large banks launched a concerted effort in the late 1980s to promote Germany's 'underdeveloped' securities markets through financial product innovation and market liberalization. Because German investors could not be expected to increase their demand for securities as rapidly as the banks needed, the strategy soon came to rest importantly upon wooing foreign institutional investors (Lütz 1998). Despite a firm belief in the effectiveness of the traditional German regulatory regime for capital markets, the pro-reform coalition found itself increasingly compelled to adopt many of the Anglo-Saxon market regulations and norms demanded by these investors (Deeg and Lütz 2000). Yet it is important to stress that when these exogenous pressures became important in Germany the big German banks were already moving in this direction.

The chief movers behind the reforms were a 'Frankfurt Coalition'—the big three commercial banks and the DGZ bank (acting on behalf of the savings bank sector). The coalition drew steady support from the Land government of Hesse (home to Frankfurt, Germany's financial capital), the association of foreign banks, and with somewhat less conviction, the Bundesbank (Lütz 2001). During the 1990s many large nonfinancial firms also became supporters of efforts to cultivate the development of securities markets. No longer relying on bank loans for external funds, many firms instead preferred to see modern capital market products in Germany that could increase their financial flexibility (Deeg 1999: 88). But developing German securities markets required much more than a few liberalization measures. One of the main challenges confronting the Coalition was the costly and fragmented structure of the German stock exchange system. Thus in 1986 the Coalition began what turned into a long-term campaign for reorganizing the stock exchange system. Early efforts focused on developing electronic trading as a means to overcome institutional fragmentation. Amendments to the German stock exchange law in 1989 opened the door to the new German Futures Exchange in 1990. This same year also saw the passage of the first of four Financial Market Promotion Laws subsequently promulgated. All of these omnibus laws contained numerous and wide-ranging statutory additions and amendments intended to stimulate the supply and demand of securities. The 1990 law, for instance, eliminated various taxes considered hindrances to securities trading (see Deeg 1999; Ziegler 2000; Cioffi 2002; Goyer 2002; Jackson 2003).

Efforts to develop and promote securities markets in Germany became even more intense and focused in the early 1990s as the momentum for capital market integration and monetary union in Europe accelerated. But more importantly the German state itself now took an intense interest in these issues. The state was motivated by the fact that in international bodies engaged in financial market integration (the Basel Committee, International Organization of Securities Commissions, and the European Union (EU) itself) it was severely disadvantaged by its dearth of statutory authority and regulatory control over its own securities markets. The Germans feared that their inability to shape the terms of international financial market integration would severely handicap Germany economically (Lütz 1998). Thus in early 1992 the German Finance Ministry launched its *Finanzplatz Deutschland* campaign (Finance Center Germany).

One of the first successes of this campaign was the long-sought reorganization of the stock exchange system into a publicly traded company, the Deutsche Börse AG, in 1993 (Lütz 1998). The next success was the Second Financial Market Promotion Law in 1994 that harmonized the content and form of German regulation with international norms and EU directives. It also moved Germany away from the traditional self-regulation of securities markets and exchanges with the creation of an independent Federal Supervisory Office for Securities Trading. The new state agency, modeled after the American SEC (Securities and Exchange Commission), was charged with enforcing a new legal ban on insider trading and newly stringent information reporting requirements by issuers of securities and traders. The push for greater openness and transparency in reporting by public companies and in the markets represented a dramatic break with the past. It is also a good example of North's argument that changes in informal institutions often lag formal institutional change. This has certainly been true regarding German attitudes toward corporate openness and transparency in business deals and market transactions. However, over the course of the 1990s the new norms of transparency and openness clearly spread.

By the second half of the 1990s the need for reformists to cultivate institutional changes was declining, as the campaign for developing securities market achieved broad support and momentum among business, the public, and the political parties. This did not, of course, mean there were no significant disagreements over the details of specific reform initiatives. For example, the 1998 Law on Control and Transparency in Enterprises (*Gesetz zur Kontrolle und Transparenz im Unternehmensbereich, KonTraG*) was perhaps the most controversial reform legislation in the last five years. The law sought to support the growth of securities markets by increasing corporate transparency, management accountability, and protection for minority shareholders.[10] Not all of the initial proposals were embraced by the large banks and firms, but the Free Democractic Party (FDP), then coalition partner with the Christian Democratic Union (CDU) in government, pushed hard for the measure and gained support from the opposition Social Democratic Party (SPD) (and the unions as well). The FDP and SPD were motivated in particular by a desire to strengthen the ability of capital markets to put pressure on firms, that is, to undermine what they saw as excessive concentration of corporate power (Cioffi 2002; Höpner 2002). What this episode suggests is that self-reinforcing mechanisms were now quite strong—banks and financial firms had unleashed a process of institutional change toward a new market-oriented financial system that at times went even further in this direction than they preferred.

Since coming to power in late 1998, the SPD has been an aggressive pro-market reform party and one that has on occasion taken the initiative ahead of the large banks and firms. The SPD sees these as part of a strategy to modernize and revitalize the German economy and a strategy that realizes a long-standing aim of the part—the deconcentration and 'democratization' of corporate power. Bolstered by the tremendous surge in stock markets in the late 1990s and the spectacular success of the *Neuer Markt*, a new electronic exchange for fast-growing technology firms introduced in 1997, the SPD guided numerous key reform efforts during its first term in office. In 1998 the Third Financial Market Promotion Law was passed. Also in 1998, a law to facilitate equity issues (*Kapitalaufnahmeerleichterungsgesetz, KapAEG*) was promulgated which, among other things, allows German firms to balance their books using the more transparent international (IAS) or American accounting standards (US-GAAP: Luetz 33).[11] The SPD put together a neo-corporatist commission (Cromme Commission) to develop a corporate governance codex. Published in 2001, the codex seeks to encourage firms to adopt 'good' corporate governance practices (with a strong emphasis on minority shareholder interests).

While the German government was criticized for vetoing the European Commission's takeover directive in 2001, its own takeover law passed that same year is among the more liberal takeover laws in Europe. Finally, in 2002 the corporate governance codex—while it already had broad support—was given more authoritative status through the Corporate Sector Transparency and Publicity Act (TransPuG; Höpner 2002).

The late 1990s became the time when many of the reform efforts of the 1980s and early 1990s finally congealed and began to have a significant impact on the behavior of financial firms, large corporations, and German retail investors. It can be understood as marking the end of the critical juncture period during which the direction of institutional change was uncertain. Indeed, by this time the emergence of a subregime—a new path—becomes apparent. The new subregime follows a market logic, that is, an emphasis on shareholders, profits, and arms-length relationships. Most importantly, the cooperation and collective responses to market challenges of the old path is supplanted by individual responses and, increasingly, with more competition among firms as a market for corporate control slowly emerges. To put it in more theoretical terms, the gains from coordination have been eroding and along with this the ability of the old path to sustain itself. This change was stoked further by more general changes in the managerial strategies of many large German firms. For example, in the 1990s several large German firms began internationalizing their investor base (in part by listing on the New York Stock Exchange which better positioned them to make acquisitions in the United States). As a result the shareholder base of numerous large German firms has become more widely dispersed and internationalized, thus weakening domestic shareholder control and bank connections. Like the United States, institutional investors (e.g. pension funds and investment funds) and their preferences have become increasingly important in Germany.[12]

The internationalization of the investor base of many large German firms (and the big commercial banks too) is connected to a growing emphasis by such firms on shareholder value, that is, managing the company so as to maximize return on equity (as manifested in share prices and dividends; Jürgens et al. 2000: 15). In the past, German firms often focused more on expansion of the firm's revenues and market share while profitability, though important, was not the driving force of managerial decisions. This conventional focus was sustained by the fact that most large firms have been controlled by insiders who did not usually pressure management to pursue profit maximization as the foremost goal.[13] In this kind of shareholder-oriented (market and regulatory) environment corporate managers also face more pressure to sell-off divisions or close operations more quickly than they would have in the past if they are not generating sufficient return (Höpner 2000).

Relationship banking, that is, a mutual emphasis on a long-term relationship between a firm and its main bank(s) is being replaced by more market-based, transaction-oriented exchanges—from the logic of voice to the logic of exit. Since the 1970s, but especially during the 1990s, large German banks have generally reduced the size of their equity stakes in individual nonfinancial firms.[14] First, the banks were interested in reducing their exposure to the risks associated with large equity stakes in other firms. Second, like other large German firms, the banks are focusing on maximizing their own returns on equity and believe that many of their long-held equity investments 'locked up' in traditional relationships could be more profitably employed in other ways (*The Economist*, August 14, 1999; *New York Times*, August 13, 1999). As part of its broad program to modernize corporate Germany, in 2000 the Federal Government passed a Corporate Income Tax Law that made the sale of long-term equity stakes held by large firms and banks in other firms tax free after January 1, 2002 (Lang, Mayhew, and Shackelford 2001). It is widely expected that a large-scale restructuring of the German corporate world will occur in coming years. Already banks and firms have accelerated their sell-off of big industrial shareholdings (Höpner 2001; Beyer 2002). This new direction represents a radical break from the old path in which banks and other large firms were long-term shareholders providing 'patient' capital and protecting firm management from unwanted outside influences and takeovers.

Along with reducing their holdings, banks have been curtailing their traditional role in corporate governance, that is, the institutions and practices that regulate property rights and control of firm managers. In 1974 banks held 20 percent of the supervisory board seats in the 100 largest firms; by 1993 this percentage had shrunk to 6.3 percent.[15] All of the above changes mean that banks are playing much less of a monitoring role in large German nonfinancial firms, that is, creating managerial stability but also ensuring accountability. This role is presumably being taken over by the market.[16]

In sum, large banks in Germany have dramatically altered their strategies. They have tied their future prosperity to the growth and success of securities markets and a more open system of corporate governance. Their actions led to the emergence of a new subregime that adheres to a different logic than the old regime, thus constituting a new path. For example, firms in the new subregime are responding to current challenges by disentangling with each other (e.g. selling equity stakes): under the logic of voice of the old path they would have 'banded' together to confront problems in the market. Smaller banks, on the other hand, remain mostly rooted in the traditional system because smaller firms continue to rely on them. This system has also undergone noteworthy changes, especially through institutional layering. But these changes have been largely consistent with the cooperative or voice logic of the old path. As for nonfinancial firms, the pressures to adopt shareholder value and an 'Anglo approach' to corporate governance are significant but must be differentiated. As in the banking system, firms appear to be bifurcating between the relatively few yet very large firms that, for various reasons, embrace shareholder value and operate within the new subregime, and the greater number of firms who have shunned or only made weak efforts to adopt the shareholder approach (Jürgens et al. 2000; Ziegler 2000; Höpner 2001).

This points to the fact that even within the new subregime there are many institutions that were part of the old path. Social partnership, for example, is firmly rooted in Germany and organized labor has been an active participant in the transformation into shareholder capitalism (Vitols 2000; Höpner 2001: 20). More generally, there is little evidence that any broader move to shareholder capitalism requires a reduction or elimination of worker participation institutions in Germany, and there appears to be little political interest in explicitly weakening these institutions (Ziegler 2000: 212). Many large German firms, even those that are emphasizing shareholder value, continue to believe that the interests of other stakeholders—employees, customers, and society in general—must still be balanced against shareholder interests.[17] What ultimately matters is the fact that the interplay of new and old institutions within the market-oriented subregime generates a different logic and thus represents a new path.

The Italian case

Similar to Germany, the Italian banking system is shared mostly among three types of banks; commercial (joint-stock), savings (and other public banks), and cooperative banks. But here much of the similarity ends. The central hallmark of the Italian postwar financial system was the heavy presence of the state. Public ownership was extensive; first through the Treasury that controlled several of the largest banks, and second through communal governments that controlled the extensive savings bank sector. Public banks accounted for the large majority of banking sector assets, deposits, and loans (Aiello, Silipo, and Trivieri 2000: 28). Many banks were highly politicized in terms of board appointments and credit decisions and often viewed by public authorities as having a public interest rather than market function. Restrictive regulation and segmentation of the financial system severely restrained competition ('The Transformation of . . . 1997'). The banking system was very decentralized, thus leaving Italy with relatively small, localized banks in international terms. Beside smaller firms in industrial districts, banks, and firms generally did not have close, long-term relations of the German type.

To a certain degree, postwar Italian capitalism can be divided into three models with banks having a distinctive role in each. The first is the state-dominated model. From the early 1930s onward the Italian state controlled a substantial portion of industrial capital—notably through its holding company, IRI (Institute per la Ricostruzione Industriale). The second model or part of the economy was that of large, private firms. Such firms are comparatively few in Italy, though they are quite significant. Most of them, despite their large size, are family controlled (e.g. Fiat by the Agnellis).[18] Most of these firms were part of intricate interfirm networks cemented by alliances and strategic shareholdings. Pulling many of the strings in this system from the 1960s onward was Mediobanca, the Milan-based investment bank headed by Enrico Cuccia. The third model is that of small- and medium-sized (mostly family-owned) firms. Indeed, the Italian economy distinguishes itself from other advanced industrial economies by the high proportion of output accounted for by such firms, many of which are organized in industrial districts.[19]

By international standards, debt finance by nonfinancial firms has been comparatively high while equity finance was low. A very high percentage of external debt is to banks, and a very high percentage of bank debt by firms is short-term (OECD 1995: 70–2). This is due largely to the fact that only special credit institutes were allowed to do medium- and long-term lending, and their lending was largely directed toward state-owned firms ('The Transformation . . .' 1997: 595; Amatori and Colli 2000: 12). As a result, few ordinary banks had the expertise to do long-term lending. The very large bond market has been overwhelmingly dominated by government debt.

Similar to Germany, the finance and corporate governance system of the large-firm private sector fit an insider rather than an outsider model, that is, followed a logic of voice. It was a system of corporate control dominated by private, informal arrangements and norms of reciprocity. Relationships were long-term and rested on cooperation for mutual gain. Many key industrial and finance decisions were made within a negotiated—and very opaque—set of personal relationships. Private firms, especially family-owned, sought to minimize state interference rather than engage in a corporatist process as found in Germany (Segreto 1997). Perhaps partly for this reason the private-sector corporate network was even more tightly connected than in Germany. Reflecting this logic, share ownership in Italy is highly concentrated. In the early 1990s, the top five largest shareholders in a large firm held, on average, 87 percent of its shares; more than half of listed firms were majority controlled by a single owner (OECD 1995: 60–1). The stock market itself was, not surprisingly, very narrow with just a relatively small number of firms accounting for most of its capitalization and turnover. Cross-shareholdings are extensive and frequently take the form of a pyramidal structure which enables one firm to control several others using relatively small direct equity stakes. With the notable exception of Mediobanca, since the 1930s banks have not had equity stakes in nonfinancial firms and therefore do not perform a monitoring role in corporate governance. This is due in part to the relatively small size of banks compared to the large nonfinancial firms and by tight restrictions on commercial banks holding equity and sitting on boards of nonfinancial firms (OECD 1995: 73). Thus most big companies face little external control/monitoring from either banks or the stock market.

The logic of the banking system per se and the state-owned corporate sector was a *logic of hierarchy* or authoritative control. Competition was suppressed in the banking sector in favor of the authoritative direction of capital along political and regional lines. The financial system changed relatively little during the postwar era and was reproduced largely through the exercise of state power and authority. While other mechanisms of reproduction, such as legitimacy, sunk costs, and the like were at work, the process of change in the 1990s certainly affirms that the state's role was the most determinative within the financial system.

The path to change?

At first blush it appears that major changes in the Italian financial and corporate governance systems began in the 1980s. Large Italian firms entered the 1980s with high debt loads and, unable to sufficiently self-finance or borrow, turned to the equity market. The number of listed firms soared from 138 in the beginning of the decade to 217 by its end, while market capitalization rose from about 6 to 14 percent of GDP (Amatori and Colli 2000: 12; Aguilera 2001: 17–18). But this expansion of the stock market did not signify a major transformation of Italian finance and corporate governance. Most of the newly listed companies were spin-offs from the large industrial holding groups. This enabled them to raise new capital while retaining ultimate control over these firms through pyramidal or cascading shareholdings (and the generous use of nonvoting shares). Thus even in 1987 the nine largest industrial holding groups (mostly family-controlled) accounted for nearly all of the market's capitalization (Amatori and Colli 2000: 14). A central node and organizing force of this system—known as the 'Northern Galaxy'—was Mediobanca and its leader, Enrico Cuccia. While formally controlled by the three largest (and state-owned) banks in Italy, Mediobanca called its own shots. The institutional linkages among these firms were augmented by voting syndicates that protected them from hostile takeover and entrenched incumbent management and major owners (and trounced upon minority shareholder rights; McCann 2000: 19–21). Thus Italy entered the 1990s with its traditional model intact while substantial change was already underway in Germany.

The current transformation of the Italian financial and corporate governance systems, therefore, really begins in the early 1990s. The central object and instrument of this transformation has been the privatization of state-owned banks and firms. There were both internal and external pressures for change. Internally, the state's finances were in shambles due to massive public debt. Huge losses by state-owned firms added both to the debt and the declining legitimacy of state ownership. The Lira was pummeled out of the European Monetary System (EMS) and forced to devalue. The economy was in recession. The bribery scandal and demise of the Christian Democratic Party in 1992/3 no doubt added further impetus for major change. But all of these internal or domestic pressures for change were exogenous to the financial and corporate governance systems. Externally, the Single Market was nearing completion and Italian firms, especially banks, were unprepared for an integrated market. The Maastricht Treaty and its implications for stricter government finances added further pressure on Italy to get its finances in order.

Thus, at the beginning of the decade Italian reformers—mostly in the Bank of Italy and the Treasury—set out to overhaul Italian capitalism through privatization and the modernization of the financial system, including the revival of the stock market and the dispersion of corporate ownership in Italy (Amatori and Colli 2000: 24–6). Unlike Germany, then, in Italy the main actors cultivating institutional change were in the state. More generally, liberalizing reforms have been taken under the auspices of center–left governments during the 1990s responding to EU pressures but also utilizing these to unblock barriers to domestic reform.

The first key step in the state's strategy for promoting major change was to create new private-sector actors—notably privatized state banks—who would be committed to the state's strategy and themselves cultivate further institutional change. Partly for this reason the emergence of positive feedback effects came much later (and were less strong) in Italy. Furthermore, one of the key differences between the two cases is that large Italian firms and banks (such as they existed), unlike their German counterparts, were not early advocates of the development of a more open, Anglo-style financial and corporate governance system. Two factors appear to be important in explaining this difference. First, Italian firms were generally much less internationalized than German firms. Second, the interlocking networks in Italy were tighter and, by all appearances, continued to serve the interests of the firms participating in them. In other words, there was little incentive for large Italian firms to change the system and the single most potentially powerful actor for change—Mediobanca—was firmly committed to the old path from which it continued to profit. Another difference to Germany is that pressures for change are largely exogenous in the Italian case. Italy does not enter a critical juncture, that is, a period in which more than one path becomes viable, until the early 1990s. Once the critical juncture was initiated by European integration, the door was opened for certain actors to promote with success substantial change in the Italian financial system.

Sustained regulatory change and a program for systematic reform of the Italian financial system began in 1990 with the Amato law. Heavily shaped by EC directives, the law was promoted by the Bank of Italy and supported by most Italian banks. One of its most important elements was the conversion of all banks to joint-stock corporations. This paved the way for public banks (about eighty banks, mostly savings banks) to be privatized (which started in 1993) and thereby open up the banking industry to consolidation (though most public banks remained under public control through the vehicle of foundations which held the newly issued shares).[20] It was clearly passed in anticipation of financial market integration in Europe and the fear that large foreign banks would overrun much smaller Italian banks unless the latter consolidated extensively (Bank of Italy 1995: 174). In 1992 the government began laying the groundwork for the privatization of other state-owned firms with the transformation of all state holding into stock companies held by the Treasury. A second 1994 law was crucial in setting more specific rules for the allocation of shares and corporate governance. In this law the government aimed for broader share ownership in privatized firms while attempting to retain strategic influence through golden shares, the creation of noyeux durs, and the right of the Treasury to veto mergers or takeovers (Amatori and Colli 2000: 26).

The next major reform step was the comprehensive Banking Law passed in 1993. Like the Amato Law, it was heavily shaped by the need to transpose EC directives into Italian law, including the bank passport provisions, which significantly increased access of foreign financial institutions to Italy. This sweeping reform bill also reflected the desire among Italian financial officials to create a mixed- (or universal) banking system resembling that of Germany with its close, long-term relations between banks and firms (Cesarini 1994). Toward this end, the law ended decades of enforced market segmentation by permitting ordinary banks to issue bonds and extend medium and long-term credit, as well as to acquire stakes in nonfinancial firms.The Italian banking industry did not embrace many of these changes (at least in the early years), especially those intended to stimulate securities markets (Onado 1996: 100).

While there were further regulatory reforms during the mid-1990s, the most powerful source of change was the sweeping privatization program that included the major banks controlled by the Treasury. Because declining interest rates and state deficits (in order to qualify for European Monetary Union (EMU)) dramatically reduced the attractiveness of state bonds to Italian investors, shares in privatized state firms became an attractive alternative investment and thus a central driving force of the stock market's expansion in the late 1990s. Adding to the momentum, in late 1997 the Italian Stock Exchange (Borsa Italiana) was privatized. The Borsa, in turn, became a vocal proponent of further securities market reform and development (along with CONSOB, the securities market regulator, and the Treasury). Building on this momentum, but also frustrated by the persistence of concentrated control over Italian firms (even newly privatized ones) in 1998 the Treasury succeeded in guiding the passage of the Consolidated Law on Financial Intermediation (aka Draghi Law or Reform: Amatori and Colli 2000: 42–3). The overall goal of the Law is to make a significant push toward further modernization and development of the equity market through, among other things, improved protection for minority shareholders (including shareholder agreements), greater transparency of firms and market transactions (strict regulation of insider trading), increasing the number of IPOs (Initial Public Offerings), and a 'better' system of corporate governance in general. CONSOB was given considerable formal power to carry out this agenda. Similar to the German Finanzplatz Deutschland campaign, the Treasury created a committee named the 'Italian Financial Centre' to promote and coordinate further initiatives on the development of the market (Draghi 1998). The 1998 law was followed by the creation of self-conduct code for good corporate governance in 1999 drafted by university, business, and government representatives. In 1999 the Borsa also opened its own high-tech exchange, the Nuovo Mercato, and in 2001 a new exchange (STAR) for 'old economy' SMEs.

In sum, a decade and more of reform brought substantial change to the Italian financial system and Italian capitalism more generally. But what does this all add up to? On the one hand, the capitalization (as did turnover) of the main exchange soared from 18.6 percent of GDP in 1995 to 70.2 percent of GDP at the end of 2000.[21] While much of this rise was due to share price appreciation, a significant amount of new equity was also issued during this time (mostly from privatizations).[22] Italian retail investors clearly also found much greater enthusiasm for investing in stocks. Though, as everywhere, that enthusiasm has been dampened (at least temporarily) by the end of the boom.[23] In Italy, as elsewhere, institutional investors have also become more important.[24] The growth of institutional investors is widely viewed as prerequisite to the sustained development of equity markets and, more broadly, to an equity culture.[25] Liquidity of the main exchange also improved and the market has broadened; as late as the mid-1990s the top five business groups accounted for 70 percent of the Milan exchange's capitalization (Pradhan 1995), but by mid-2000 the top five accounted for just under 40 percent of the market's capitalization (Euromoney, June 2000: 181).

On the other hand, for all these indicators of a significant growth in securities markets and plans by the state to further strengthen them, it is not clear just how much Italian capitalism has so far changed. First, there appeared to be little change in firm financing patterns (Deeg and Perez 2000). Second, the efforts to expand the stock market had mixed success. The total number of firms listed on the main exchange increased only slightly during the 1990s (from 225 firms in 1987 to 237 at the end of 2001: www.borsaitalia.it). As elsewhere, the Internet/telecoms mania helped push up the Nuovo Mercato and stimulate excitement among Italians for stock trading.[26] But the bursting of the bubble has dramatically slowed new listings on the exchange and its capitalization has plummeted.

There has been some increase in ownership transparency, but insufficient evidence to suggest that the intricate networks of shareholdings linking large private Italian firms have changed all that much. While concentration is declining by some measures, the use of shareholder agreements to control firms has grown, thus ensuring that insider control over firms remains high (Amatori and Colli 2000: 37–8; Aguilera 2001: 14).[27] There is, as yet, no open market for control over firms (Aguilera 2001: 13). Even though Olivetti managed to takeover Telecom Italia in a hostile bid during 1999 in accordance with the new institutional framework—which many interpreted as a sign that Italian capitalism had definitely changed—it occurred in a thoroughly Italian fashion: Olivetti used an elaborate pyramidal holding structure to gain control of Telecom while owning just 3.2 percent of its shares (Amatori and Colli 2000: 49; McCann 2000: 57)! Further demonstrating the vitality of the old system, two years later Pirelli and Benetton joined together to take control of Olivetti (and indirectly Telecom Italia) using complex investment vehicles and cascading holdings that shortchanged small investors and was viewed as destroying shareholder value ('Keeping it in the Family'. *Financial Times*, July 31, 2001; Philip Webster, 'Pirelli takeover of Olivetti destroys value, prompts concern on debt'. AFX Europe, July 31, 2001). Furthermore, the new corporate governance code and transparency rules are still eschewed by the vast majority of listed Italian firms (not to mention unlisted firms) and CONSOB remains a weak enforcer of the new rules (Financial Times, 404; April 5, 2001; Onado 1996). In short, in Germany we saw the new logic of exit evidenced by the deliberate reduction of linkages (directors seats, equity holdings, etc.)—creating more 'distance'—among firms in response to new market challenges. In Italy we see instead a reshuffling of alliances and linkages in response to market challenges, but no systematic reduction of such: The logic of voice prevails.

Where there has been a move to a new institutional path is in the banking system narrowly understood (i.e. commercial and retail banking outside of securities markets) where the logic of (state) hierarchy has been replaced by a competitive market logic. As an owner, the state no longer dominates; in 1992 public-sector banks controlled 70 percent of bank industry assets, by the end of 1999 this was down to 12 percent (Bank of Italy 2000: 190). Many banks now considered private, including some larger ones, are still controlled by foundations which, in turn, are controlled by communal governments. Since foundation-controlled banks have grown through mergers, the influence of public bodies on the banking system remains substantial.[28] Nonetheless, even banks with significant public ownership (and cooperatives) are rapidly changing organizations. Instead of emphasizing support for social and political objectives, virtually all banks have been radically restructuring their operations and organizations, innovating new products, cutting costs, and making efficiency and profitability primary objectives. From the mid-1990s onwards the banking system has undergone a process of rapid consolidation that has been guided to a significant degree by the (sometimes heavy) hand of the Bank of Italy (The Banker, February 2001; Wilson, Ted. 'Middle Layer Hots Up in Italy.' *Acquisitions Monthly*, May 31, 2002; McCann 2000: 59). In mid-2002 the Bank announced that it considered the consolidation of banks on the national level essentially complete; the four largest banking groups—IntesaBCI, Sanpaolo-IMI, Unicredito, and Capitalia (formerly Banca di Roma)—now control about half of the sector's business ('Bank of Italy: Governor alludes to merger of MPS with BNL', *The Banker*, July 1, 2002).

This notwithstanding, where there does not appear to be off-path change is in the broader Italian finance and corporate governance system. Despite many formal legal and regulatory changes promoting corporate transparency and the role of securities markets, large Italian firms have not gone nearly as far as many of their European counterparts toward 'shareholder value' practices (see also Amatori and Colli 2000). Small shareholders and foreign institutional investors still view the Italian corporate governance system as too opaque and run through backroom deals by insiders.

The story of Mediobanca provides an excellent illustration of both what has changed in Italy and what has not. During the late 1990s, Mediobanca's position eroded as foreign investment banks made significant strides in gaining the business of major Italian firms. The wave of privatizations during the 1990s further bolstered foreign investment banks that were given significant business by the Italian Treasury, which feared that too much business for Mediobanca would strengthen the banks' influence rather than open up the Italian system. As Mediobanca's influence waned, the 'glue' holding the Northern Galaxy together weakened and a process of reshuffling alliances among member firms (and several newly privatized firms) began. Mediobanca's two most important shareholders—Capitalia and UniCredito—also became competitors. Capitalia, for example, expanded its own investment banking unit during 2002 by bringing in other large, influential Italian firms as shareholders (and allies), thus mimicking Mediobanca's own model of influence ('Capitalia throws down the gauntlet', *European Banker*, August 9, 2002). At the same time, IntesaBCI, Italy's largest bank and formerly supported by Mediobanca, announced a linkup with Lazard Italia—the nation's leader in M&A advising—in order to strengthen its own investment banking market power within Italy (Heather O'Brian, 'IntesaBCI, Lazard link in Italy'. *The Daily Deal*, September 10, 2002). Lazard had once been allied with Mediobanca. The struggle between the battered but still powerful Mediobanca and its own shareholders came to a climax in early 2003 when a group of banks, led by Unicredito and acting with the blessing of the Bank of Italy, were finally able to bring it under their control by ousting the long-time head of Mediobanca, Vincenzo Maranghi (Fred Kapner, 'An emerging generation of business leaders is promising to sweep away secrecy and cronyism'. *Financial Times*, April 7, 2003).

While it may be tempting to conclude that the occurrence of hostile takeovers and the rise of new challengers to Mediobanca are further proof that the very closed Italian system is beginning to open, at this point it still seems equally plausible that the assaults on Mediobanca spell not an end to the old system but more a reshuffling of who owns whom and who is allied with whom (see also McCann 2000). Nearly all major firms are still controlled by insiders through pyramids, shareholder alliances, voting pacts, and the like.

The four new Italian 'Big Banks' also embody this ambiguity over the direction of change. On the one hand, these banks have generally been public advocates of a new, market- and shareholder-oriented financial system and they have developed the investment banking capacities to participate in securities markets. On the other hand, these banks have become increasingly involved in the old insider corporate networks by taking equity stakes and making large loans to the same clients. For example, Unicredito and Banca Intesa are large lenders to Telecom Italia and Pirelli in which they also have significant equity stakes. Indeed, following the logic of voice, banks have become overexposed to telecommunications, energy, and media firms (Fred Kapner, 'BoI presses banks to limit certain exposures'. *Financial Times*, February 8, 2002). In short, the new big banks appear to be acting like German big banks used to act as much as they are acting like German banks do now: the Italian banks seem to be trying to follow both the logic of voice and logic of exit simultaneously. But these logics are opposed and they will be forced to choose at some point.

Even though the state has greatly reduced its role in the economy, like the French state, it continues to attempt to steer the direction of change by retaining—and deploying—strategic levers of influence such as golden shares or its authority to vet mergers and acquisitions. It is also very unclear as to how much the cultural norms (informal institutions) shaping the Italian political economy have changed, as even state reformers sometimes appear to favor evolution toward a German-style stakeholder capitalism rather than a more radical Anglo-American stakeholder mode (Draghi 1998: 351). Corporate leaders too, including many presumed proponents of change, appear much less convicted of the need for real change. Thus, in Italy the shape of a new path, or whether it is moving to a new path, is less clear. Even with many of the same institutional changes as adopted in Germany, the logic—that is, the strategic behavior, decisionmaking rules, and routine responses—of the Italian finance and corporate governance system has not clearly changed.

Comparing the cases

In Germany institutional change reaches a level whereby a distinctive subregime is created; a subregime that operates on a different logic than the previous financial system regime. In Germany's shareholder-oriented subregime, the logic of voice has been replaced by the logic of exit. In Italy many similar market-oriented institutions have been adopted but the logic of the old system has not been supplanted, nor has a distinct subregime emerged. One obvious indicator of this difference can be seen in the systematic and widespread disposal of cross-shareholdings and other large equity stakes by many of the key firms in Germany in order to free up capital to invest in core businesses—despite depressed share prices. Meanwhile, Italian firms continue to acquire major stakes in each other in order to build alliances and use as tools to outmaneuver rival domestic firms for control of other domestic firms. While some of these firms profess shareholder value, the effect of their actions is to sustain the old insider system of corporate governance. Going back to my earlier theoretical claim, what is common to both cases is the evidence that self-reinforcing or positive feedback effects have played an important role as mechanisms of institutional change: They are not limited to functioning merely as mechanisms of stabilization or reproduction.

First, the German financial industry has made huge *set-up* investments in the expansion of securities markets and the reorganization of the financial system around it. Much of this cost was incurred in the 1990s as the large German banks (and the savings and cooperatives too) began making huge investments in the requisite technology, organizational changes, and human capital for securities-related business. In Italy, in contrast, much of the banks' efforts and resources have been poured into domestic consolidation. While several of them have begun investing notable sums in developing investment banking and securities-related businesses, they began to do so just before securities markets began to take a nosedive. Thus they lag far behind their European competitors.

Learning effects are also evident. Well into the late 1990s even the big commercial German banks struggled with the new strategy. Their internal organization and culture was that of a commercial bank, not an investment bank, and the two cultures clashed for a long time. Put in another way, simply spending huge sums on the development of securities market-related business was in itself not enough to be successful. It took the banks many years to learn how to use these new capacities successfully. Italian banks, as one would expect, are at a much earlier point in this particular learning curve since they have only recently begun to make these same kinds of investments and efforts. There is, however, another dimension of learning in which most Italian banks have no doubt made substantial progress; that is, learning how to operate with a strong orientation to efficiency and profitability.

We also find *coordination effects* to be significant and quite essential to the development of the new German path. In the German case one can identify three axes of coordination which greatly facilitate the new path. The first axis is among the three major banking groups and individual banks. The goal of developing securities markets and benefits to actors who engage in them grow as other actors pursue this goal. While the increased attention to securities business by more and more banks increases competition among them, it has the effect of stimulating the growth of securities markets since each bank attempts to foster demand for its securities-related products and services. The second axis is between the suppliers and buyers of securities and capital market services, that is, between investors and issuers. That a balanced expansion of supply and demand is not automatic is readily evidenced by the fact that the growth of retail investment in shares by Germans—a key benchmark for the new strategy (and path)—did not really take off until the second half of the 1990s or roughly a decade after concerted reform efforts were initiated.[29] Once demand began growing rapidly all the previous reform efforts ensured that the system could supply it. The surprisingly rapid growth of the Neuer Markt is the prime example of this effect.[30] The third axis of coordination is that between market and political actors. During the 1990s key political actors (in the state and political parties) came to adopt the banks' capital market reform agenda as their own (Lütz 1998, 2001). As more and more political actors came to believe that Germany's economic success would increasingly depend on a more capital market-oriented economy, the pace and ease of reforms picked up.

In Italy we also find coordination effects pushing the system toward the new model though, again, the effects do not appear as strong as in the German case. First, there is a growing number of banks devoting resources to the development of securities markets. Without the same kind of national association structure and interbank cooperation that links savings and cooperative banks in Germany to national markets, however, smaller Italian savings and cooperative banks have developed comparatively little interest in promoting a financial system based on capital markets. Second, like Germany, there was successful coordination in the expansion of both the supply and demand for securities in Italy during the late 1990s. Increased supply came from privatized state firms while increased demand was stimulated by the decline of traditional investments in government debt. Finally, the relationship between market and political actors in Italy with regard to financial sector reform is much more muddled than in Germany. In Italy there is much less uniform commitment among banks and private firms—as well as key political actors—in promoting a capital market-based financial system.

Adaptive expectations are also in evidence. In Germany we see this first in the debates within the savings and cooperative banking sectors during the 1980s and early 1990s. Each of these groups contained within it many actors with varying commitment and interest in developing the capital market-related capacities of the group as a whole (Deeg 1999: 58–67). But changes within each group were driven forward by the generally undisputed belief that securities business would be ever more important and their competitors would pursue it; thus, they must be successful there too if they were to survive. Adaptive expectations are also quite evident in the arguments used by German and Italian reformists throughout the 1990s; namely, that Europe and the world were all moving toward greater market control and capital markets and, therefore, Germany and Italy must do likewise if they are to remain competitive. Indeed, in Italy reform appears to be driven overwhelmingly by the fear of losing out to international competition.

Finally, in both cases we find evidence of substantial increasing returns effects being generated by coordinated and correlated changes in a wide range of complementary institutions that together configure the financial system in the broadest sense. In other words, the push to develop capital markets reaches far beyond changes in financial product regulation or the structure and supervision of the stock exchanges. It encompasses myriad changes in tax, accounting, and corporate laws, ranging from those covering shareholder voting rights to the use of stock options and stock repurchases. The four Financial Market promotion laws in Germany and the Consolidated Law in Italy are perfect embodiments of this positive feedback mechanism.

To be clear, though, these positive feedback effects are generally broader in scope and stronger in the German than the Italian case. So, how do we explain these observable differences between the two cases? My answer comes back to two other key theoretical claims: cultivation and endogenous sources or pressures for change. Supporting my contention that increasing returns needed to be cultivated, at least in the initial phases, is the fact that the payoffs from early reforms were not that great, even in the German case. To fully realize these returns reformists needed to achieve a critical level of institutional changes before the 'take off'. Thus in Germany we find a decade of continuous reform before there are enough accumulated changes on the demand and supply sides of the capital markets that the returns to the new path start pouring in. In Italy the cultivation of increasing returns mechanisms has come later and with less conviction and comprehensiveness than in Germany. Why? In Italy private market actors generally saw no need for change. There were no Italian equivalents to the big German banks to press for change. Large, private industrial firms were also deeply engaged in the old path and did not press for change. Cultivation in Italy had to start with state actors who had to first create private market actors and invigorate or create new organizational actors who, in turn, would have an interest in cultivating institutional change. In a sense, exogenous pressures for change in Italy were 'endogenized' as the former were used to create these 'new' actors.

This also means that Italy originally lacked endogenous sources of change within its financial system. Italian state actors were responding in large part to exogenous pressures to change their finance and corporate governance systems: namely, European capital market integration and, more generally, global financial integration and competition. These were the same exogenous pressures Germany faced, yet we see a marked difference between the two cases in terms of broader systemic change. The key difference is that Germany started on this path to a new market-oriented financial system because of endogenous changes in its old path: Italy did not. Thus exogenous pressures alone cannot explain the timing, pace, direction, or the extent of institutional change. This also explains why, despite similar kinds and levels of formal institutional changes, the strength of increasing returns mechanisms and actual changes in behavior by market actors in Italy are not as far-reaching as changes observable in Germany.

Some broader lessons

In summary, I believe these cases yield several lessons that carry beyond them and can inform research on institutional change.

First, the cases showed that the end of one path and transition to another can be initiated by developments endogenous to the old path, that is, it is not necessarily the case that an exogenous force must disturb an equilibrium before a path change can occur. As a given institutional path evolves its very own mechanisms of reproduction can undermine itself. In the German case we saw how the evolution of competition in banking and erosion of large firm dependence banks set in train a series of events which led to further erosion of the path and emergence of a new one. Further, when a path switchover occurs gradually as a result (at least partially) of endogenous factors and without a contingent, triggering event, then there may be no obvious event or point in time when institutional change was no longer an on-path but an off-path change. Indeed, it may be that it is only possible to determine retrospectively and with considerable lag time that there has been a change to a new path. The comparison between the two cases also suggests that when endogenous and exogenous pressures for change combine, an off-path change is more likely.

The second lesson is that increasing returns mechanisms can also facilitate the movement from one path to another without being preceded by a collapse of the prior path.[31] Indeed, the cases suggest the possibility that, beside exogenous shocks, a path subject to increasing returns effects may be more likely dislodged when the factors pressing for change are themselves subject to increasing returns effects. In both cases we saw numerous institutional changes introduced by actors which, over time, became self-reinforcing to varying degrees. This pattern of change also reflected a hybridization process in both cases in the sense that new institutions—such as Anglo-style rules on corporate transparency—were introduced or altered (layering and conversion) which changed the behavior of market actors in significant ways. However, following my conception of a path as logic, in the Italian hybrid system the old logic still dominates and thus only in the German case does this hybridization process lead to an actual path change. Moreover, it does so via the formation of a subregime. While they may share certain institutions, the two subregimes are nonetheless distinct (and constitute two institutional paths) because each encompasses a broad range of complementary institutions which generate different logics of behavior. Under what conditions is this particular outcome more likely?

Path change via formation of a subregime appears to result from three general conditions: The first is that the old system or path continues to be functional for a large number of actors within it and these actors are sufficiently powerful to defend this path. The second condition is that other powerful actors no longer sufficiently benefit from the old path and are able to establish new institutions and cultivate positive feedback mechanisms. The final condition is that the two subregimes are minimally compatible in that actors within one are not immediately disadvantaged by the existence of the other and can choose, to a certain degree, which subregime within which to operate. Thus in Germany we see the preservation of the old path (logic) in the continuation of strong bank-oriented system—defended vigorously by political powerful savings and cooperative banks and the SME business associations—which is sufficiently adapted to maintain its functionality (e.g. by creating new forms of equity provision for SMEs which do not involve public listing). Meanwhile, the new path/subregime emerges alongside the old one through the efforts of the major financial and industrial firms. Small firms can choose the new subregime by, among other things, seeking a public listing. Large firms can remain in the old path by, among other things, sustaining concentrated ownership.

The third lesson is that increasing returns effects may not be automatic. Instead they may require 'cultivation' by actors in that they must continue to accrue institutional changes until sufficient returns from the new path can be realized and captured by actors. The necessity to cultivate returns is likely to be the case when actors are being confronted with choosing new institutions and the benefits of choosing new institutions may be unclear or when the promised benefits of these institutions will be enjoyed only if there is further institutional change. As self-reinforcing mechanisms become stronger, cultivation should be less necessary. However, even as a new path becomes self-reinforcing some cultivation is likely to be necessary to sustain that path since, as noted above, the mechanisms of path reproduction can deteriorate. Thus actors will need to adapt the institutions of the path over time in order to maintain it.

Finally, I have used these cases to develop and illustrate a concept of 'path' that rests on the notion of an institutional logic, that is, a path is defined by the logic (predictable strategies, routines, and share decision rules) generated through the operation of a given institution or institutional system. In the case of financial and corporate governance systems, I divided them into those with a logic of voice and those with a logic of exit. The two logics are opposed in a theoretical sense, but they are not mutually exclusive. All financial (or nearly any institutional system, for that matter) systems incorporate both possibilities, that is, firms who use voice with each other often still do have exit options. The crucial distinction is that in bank-based systems the logic of voice is dominant and exit serves as a secondary option. In market-based systems the converse holds. As Hirschman argued, the dynamics of each mechanism will lead institutions and systems to rely heavily on one or the other (Hirschman 1970: 120–6). Thus a clear distinction can be made between the two types of systems based on the logic of voice versus exit. This also helps us understand why, in the German case, the formation of subregime was attractive—it allowed for the two logics to operate within the national economy by creating semiautonomous systems. While my notion of a path as logic could (and inevitably will) be improved upon, I believe it advances the debates over path dependence and institutional change by providing at least an initial conceptualization of a path that can be applied in analyzing any set of institutional changes.

Notes

1. I would like to thank the following individuals whose comments on this and prior versions of this chapter were very helpful to me: Suzanne Berger, Andreas Broscheid, Michel Goyer, Hans-Willy Hohn, Susanne Lütz, Janice Bially Mattern, Hudson Meadwell, Jonas Pontusson, and Herman Schwartz. I would also like to thank the editors of this volume, Wolfgang Streeck and Kathy Thelen, as well as my co-contributors and especially Colin Crouch, for their probing comments and questions.
2. The 'national varieties of capitalism' literature rests on the premise that national economic models are constituted by a broad set of complementary and mutually reinforcing institutions such as labor market, financial, training, and innovation (e.g. Hall and Soskice 2001). While I believe that there is a fundamental element of correctness in this argument, the case explored in this chapter suggests (as have some others, e.g. Regini 2000) that the coupling among these institutions may be looser than is commonly argued. This opens the door to the possibility that the financial system can change to a new institutional path without the same necessarily being true of the entire political economic model.
3. On power and legitimacy as sources of institutional reproduction, see Mahoney (2000) and Clemens and Cook (1999). Schwartz (2001) argues that power is not a form of increasing returns and is, in fact, a far more potent source for path stability than increasing returns effects.
4. I am indebted to Andreas Broscheid for suggesting a definition along this line.
5. North (1991: 89, 100) makes a powerful argument that institutional change is almost always evolutionary and the result of thousands of accumulated marginal changes in formal and informal constraints. Schwartz (2001) makes a related point that the impact of seemingly small events usually depends on much bigger structural conditions.
6. The importance of cultivation notwithstanding, we should also recognize that the pursuit of specific institutional changes by particular actors may not always result in their intended outcomes, but the unintended effects may nonetheless reinforce (or stymie) the move toward a new path. Additionally, it should be noted that not all worlds are possible: what actors can achieve through cultivation will be constrained by a variety of institutional and other factors.
7. Internationalization is treated as an exogenous factor because German economic and political actors did little to promote it during the 1980s, that is, they were responding to changes they did little to bring about (see Deeg and Lütz 2000).
8. Deeg (1999: 85–6). To be clear, bank debt was not being replaced with either equity or corporate debentures, as equity finance remained very low throughout the 1970s and early 1980s and total corporate bonds outstanding actually declined quite dramatically (see Deutsche Bundesbank 1984, 1992).
9. I am indebted to Michel Goyer for suggesting this point. For more on repressed financial systems see Lukauskus (1994).

10. The law placed some limits on bank ownership of industrial capital and, most import-
    antly, abolished unequal voting rights in corporations. The law also allows German
    corporate managers to buy back their own shares and to pay their managers with share
    options; both are widespread practices in the United States but previously unknown
    in Germany. See Cioffi (2002) for more details.
11. To be clear, the SPD-Green government did not take power until late 1998, thus many
    of these legislative initiatives began well beforehand under the center-right govern-
    ment of Kohl. This makes clear that the movement toward a market-oriented system
    was not a narrowly partisan one.
12. Between 1990 and 1998 the investment funds' share of all German shares rose from
    4% to nearly 13%. See Jürgens et al. (2000) and Höpner (2001).
13. Compare Höpner (2000) and Edwards and Nibler (2000). Jackson (2003) shows that
    during the 1990s the proportion of shares held by 'stable investors' (banks, insurance
    firms, corporations, and the state) declined from 60.2% to 52.8%; while shares held
    by individuals, institutions, and foreigners—who are much more likely to actively trade
    shares—rose from 39.8% to 47.1%.
14. Aggregate equity holdings by banks have remained stable while insurance firms
    have increased theirs (Jackson 2003). By other accounts the number of significant
    bank-held stakes (5% or greater) rose during the first half of the 1990s (Bebchuk and
    Roe 1999).
15. See Lütz (1998). From 1990 to 1996 the number of chairs held by bankers in the forty
    largest corporations was steady, at around 40%; from 1996 to 1999 the number
    dropped to less than 25% (Höpner 2001: 5).
16. Though Jackson (2003) has argued that declining bank monitoring is not being
    replaced with capital market monitoring because no real market for corporate control
    has yet emerged in Germany and, while institutional investors promote 'good' corpor-
    ate governance practices in general, they are more likely to sell shares in a given firm
    than actively monitor management.
17. And a survey of top managers done in 2000 found that 72% put the interests of share-
    holders, employees, and the public interest on an equal footing, while only 7%
    espoused shareholder preeminence (Jackson 2003). Cioffi (2002: 26–7) has argued that
    the KonTraG—the first major reform of company law since the 1960s—did not alter
    the internal relations among corporate stakeholders because it upheld the key normat-
    ive principles of codetermination and stakeholder capitalism.
18. In the early 1990s, 50.8% of all private firm assets were held by families; this compares
    to 27% in France, 16.9% in Germany, and 13.3% in the United Kingdom (Cobham,
    Cosci, and Mattesini 1999).
19. The analysis in this chapter applies only to the state and large-firm private-sector
    models.
20. As of late 2001 only nine foundations had withdrawn completely from their banks and
    about one quarter of foundations continued to own at least 50% of their bank (The
    Economist, October 27, 2001: 70).
21. It slid back to 48.5% of GDP by the end of 2001 as a result of share price declines
    (www.borsaitalia.it).
22. In 1999, for example, 82% of new equity raised on the exchange was through privat-
    izations (Bank of Italy 2000: 178).
23. Equities and investment fund units rose from 38% of household assets in 1996 to 51% at
    the end of 1999—though, again, much of this rise was due to share price appreciation

(Bank of Italy 2000: 137)—but dropped to 36% by mid-2002 (Paul Betts, ' "BOTs" revert to old habits', *Financial Times*, August 12, 2002).

24. From 1990 to 1997 the value of financial assets held by institutional investors rose from 13.4% to 53.2% of GDP (Aguilera 2001: 22).

25. Assets under management as a percent of household assets rose from 9.8% in 1990 to 34.1% in 1999; but at the end of 1998, equities still represented only 19% of total institutional assets, leaving Italy well behind the United States and the United Kingdom (Bank of Italy 2000: 153–7).

26. Private equity and venture capital investment also soared at the beginning in 1998 (Financial Times, December 11, 2000).

27. Also, concentration dipped during 1997 and 1998 because of large privatizations but rose again significantly during 1999 and 2000. For example, for all listed companies the average holding of the top three shareholders equaled 59.6% of capital in 1996; this declined to 40.8% by 1998 but rose to 50.9% in 2000 (Aguilera 2001: 23).

28. Most of the major commercial banks count banking foundations—there were 89 in 2002—among their significant owners. Since the mid-1990s market reformers have made repeated efforts—with some success—to reduce the role of the foundations in the banking sector (Aiello, Silipo, and Trivieri 2000: 31–7).

29. From 1992 to 1999 the number of German adults owning shares (directly or indirectly) grew some 25%, with virtually all of this growth taking place during 1998 and 1999. Though at just under 13% of the population, Germany remains far behind countries such as the United States, the United Kingdom, and Sweden (Deutsches Aktieninstitut 2000).

30. From 1983 to 1996, an average of 16 companies went public *each year*; in 1998, 78 firms went public and in 1999, 167 firms went public; the vast majority did so on the Neuer Markt (Hutter and Leppert 2000).

31. This is a distinct claim from the prior one in that path changes do not necessarily exhibit increasing returns effects, that is, not all paths are created or stabilized by positive feedback—there are other mechanisms for institutional stability.

References

AGUILERA, RUTH V. (2001). Institutional Pressures Shaping Shareholder Value Capitalism and Corporate Governance in Italy and Spain. Unpublished manuscript (May).

AIELLO, FRANCESCO, DAMIANO BRUNO SILIPO, and FRANCESCO TRIVIERI (2000). Ownership Structure, Behavior and Performance of the Italian Banking Industry. Unpublished manuscript.

Bank of Italy (1995). *Annual Report for 1995*. Rome: Bank of Italy.

—— (2000). *Annual Report for 2000*. Rome: Bank of Italy.

BEBCHUK, LUCIAN ARYE and MARK J. ROE (1999). A Theory of Path Dependence in Corporate Ownership and Governance. *Stanford Law Review* 52: 127–70.

BEYER, JÜRGEN (2002). Deutschland AG a.D.: Deutsche Bank, Allianz und das Verflechtungszentrum grosser deutscher Unternehmen. MPIfG Working Paper 02/4, March.

CESARINI, FRANCESCO (1994). The Relationship Between Banks and Firms in Italy: A Banker's View. *Review of Economic Conditions in Italy* 48: 29–50

CIOFFI, JOHN W. (2002). Restructuring 'Germany, Inc.': The Politics of Company and Takeover Law Reform in Germany and the European Union. Institute of European Studies, Working Paper PEIF-1, University of California, Berkeley.

CLEMENS, ELISABETH S. and JAMES M. COOK (1999). Politics and Institutionalism: Explaining Durability and Change. *Annual Review of Sociology* 25: 441–66.

COBHAM, DAVID, STEFANO COSCI, and FRABIZIO MATTESINI (1999). The Italian Financial System: Neither Bank Based nor Market Based. *The Manchester School* 67(3): 325–45.

DEEG, RICHARD (1999). *Finance Capitalism Unveiled: Banks and the German Political Economy.* Ann Arbor, MI: University of Michigan Press.

DEEG, RICHARD AND SOFIA PEREZ (2000). International Capital Mobility and Domestic Institutions: Corporate Finance and Governance in Four European Cases. *Governance: An International Journal of Policy and Administration* 13(2): 119–153.

—— and SUSANNE LÜTZ (2000). Internationalization and Financial Federalism—the United States and Germany at the Crossroads? *Comparative Political Studies* 33(3): 374–405.

DEUTSCHE BUNDESBANK (1984). Business Finance in the United Kingdom and Germany. *Monthly Report of the Deutsche Bundesbank* 36(11): 33–42.

—— (1992). Longer-term Trends in the Financing Patterns of West German Enterprises. *Monthly Report of the Deutsche Bundesbank* 44(10): 25–39.

—— (1998). Entwicklung des Bankensektors und Marktstellung der Kreditinstitutsgruppen seit Anfang der neunziger Jahren. *Monatsbericht* 50(3): 33–64.

DEUTSCHES AKTIENINSTITUT (2000). Zahl der Aktionäre in Deutschland überschreitet 5 Millionen. DAI-Kurzstudie, 1.

DRAGHI, MARIO (1998). Corporate Governance and Competitiveness. *Review of Economic Conditions in Italy* 52: 341–57.

EDWARDS, JEREMY and KLAUS FISCHER (1994). *Banks, Finance and Investment in Germany.* Cambridge: Cambridge University Press.

FRANCO AMATORI, FRANCO and ANDREA COLLI (2000). Corporate Governance: The Italian Story. Unpublished manuscript (December).

GOYER, MICHEL (2002). Refocusing and Corporate Governance in France and Germany: The Centrality of Workplace Institutions. Presented at the Annual Meeting of the American Political Science Association. Boston, MA, August 28–September 1.

HALL, PETER (1986). *Governing the Economy: The Politics of State Intervention in Britain and France.* Oxford: Oxford University Press.

—— and DAVID SOSKICE (2001). *Varieties of Capitalism.* Oxford: Oxford University Press.

HIRSCHMAN, ALBERT O. (1970). *Exit, Voice and Loyalty: Response to Decline in Firms, Organizations, and States.* Cambridge, MA: Harvard University Press.

HÖPNER, MARTIN (2000). Kapitalmarktorientierte Unternehmensführung: Messung, Bestimmungsgründe und Konsequenzen. Paper presented at First Annual Meeting of the Research Network on Corporate Governance. Berlin, June 23–24.

—— (2001). Corporate Governance in Transition: Ten Empirical Findings on Shareholder Value and Industrial Relations in Germany. Max Planck Institute for the Study of Societies, Discussion Paper 01/5.

—— (2002). European Corporate Governance Reform and the German Party Paradox. Unpublished Paper, 25 November.

HUTTER, STEPHAN and MICHAEL LEPPERT (2000). Stock Offerings in Germany. *Corporate Finance* (May): 26–9.

JACKSON, GREGORY (2003). Corporate Governance in Germany and Japan: Liberalization Pressures and Responses During the 1990s. In: Wolfgang Streeck and Kozo Yamamura (eds.), *The End of Diversity? Prospects for German and Japanese Capitalism*. Ithaca, NY: Cornell University Press.

JÜRGENS, ULRICH, JOACHIM RUPP, and KATRIN VITOLS with BÄRBEL JÄSCHKE-WERTHMANN (2000). Corporate Governance and Shareholder Value in Deutschland. Discussion Paper of the Social Science Research Centre, Berlin, FS II 00–202.

LANG, MARK H., EDWARD L. MAYHEW, and DOUGLAS A. SHACKELFORD (2001). Bringing Down the Other Berlin Wall: Germany's Repeal of the Corporate Capital Gains Tax. Unpublished manuscript, January 21.

LUKAUSKAS, ARVID J. (1994). The Political Economy of Financial Restriction: The Case of Spain. *Comparative Politics* 27(1): 67–89.

LÜTZ, SUSANNE (1998). The Revival of the Nation-State? Stock Exchange Regulation in an Era of Globalized Financial Markets. *Journal of European Public Policy* 5(1): 153–68.

—— (2000). From Managed to Market Capitalism? German Finance in Transition. *German Politics* 9(2): 149–70.

—— (2001). *Der Staat und die Globalisierung von Finanzmärkten: Regulative Politik in Deutschland, Grossbritannien und den Vereinigten Staaten*. Habilitationsschrift, FernUniversität Hagen.

MAHONEY, JAMES (2000). Path Dependence in Historical Sociology. *Theory and Society* 29: 507–48.

McCANN, DERMOT (2000). The 'Anglo-American' Model, Privatization and the Transformation of Private Capitalism in Italy. *Modern Italy* 5(1): 47–61.

NORTH, DOUGLASS C. (1991). *Institutions, Institutional Change and Economic Performance*. Cambridge: Cambridge University Press.

OECD (Organization for Economic Cooperation and Development) (1995). *OECD Economic Survey: Italy 1994–95*. Washington DC: OECD.

ONADO, MARCO (1996). The Italian Financial System and the Challenges of the Investment Services Directive, *Review of Economic Conditions in Italy* 50: 89–103.

PIERSON, PAUL (2000a). Not Just What, but When: Timing and Sequence in Political Processes. *Studies in American Political Development* 14(Spring): 72–92.

—— (2000b). Increasing Returns, Path Dependence, and the Study of Politics. *American Political Science Review* 94(2): 251–67.

—— (2000c). The Limits of Design: Explaining Institutional Origins and Change. *Governance* 13(4): 475–99.

—— (2000d). Big, Slow-Moving, and . . . Invisible: Macro-Social Processes in the Study of Comparative Politics. Paper presented at Comparative Historical Analysis Workshop, November 10–11, Cambridge, MA.

PORTER, MICHAEL (1992). Capital Disadvantage: America's Failing Capital Investment System. *Harvard Business Review*, September–October: 65–82.

PRADHAN, MAHMOOD (1995). Privatization and the Development of Financial Markets in Italy. *Finance and Development* 32(4): 9–20.

REGINI, MARINO (2000). Between Deregulation and Social Pacts: The Responses of European Economies to Globalization. *Politics and Society* 28(1): 5–33.

SAUVÉ, ANNIE and MANFRED SCHEUER (eds.) (1999). *Corporate Finance in Germany and France*. Frankfurt: Deutsche Bundesbank and Paris: Banque de France.

SCHWARTZ, HERMAN (2001). Down the Wrong Path: Path Dependence, Markets, and Increasing Returns. Unpublished manuscript.

SEGRETO, LUCIAN (1997). Models of control in Italian Capitalism from the Mixed Banks to Mediobanca, 1894–1993. *Business and Economic History* 26(2): 649–61.

THELEN KATHLEEN (2003). How Institutions Evolve: Insights from Comparative-Historical Analysis. In: James Mahoney and Dietrich Rueschemeyer (eds.), *Comparative-Historical Analysis in Social Sciences*. Cambridge: Cambridge University Press.

The Transformation of Financial Markets (1997). *Review of Economic Conditions in Italy*, p. 51. Rome: Banco di Roma.

VITOLS, SIGURT (2000). The Reconstruction of German Corporate Governance: Reassessing the Role of Capital Market Pressures. Paper presented at First Annual Meeting of the Research Network on Corporate Governance, Berlin, June 23–24.

ZIEGLER, NICHOLAS (2000). Corporate Governance and the Politics of Property Rights in Germany. *Politics and Society* 28(2): 195–221.

ZYSMAN, JOHN (1983). *Governments, Markets, and Growth*. Ithaca, NY: Cornell University Press.

—— (1994). How Institutions Create Historically Rooted Trajectories of Growth. *Industrial and Corporate Change* 4(1): 243–83.

8

Institutional Resettlement: The Case of Early Retirement in Germany

Christine Trampusch

Introduction

This chapter examines the trajectory of early retirement policy in Germany from the 1950s to the present. The case provides valuable insights for scholars interested in the growth and retrenchment of the welfare state as well as those interested in the dynamics of institutional change.

The implicit model that informs a great deal of theorizing on the welfare state sees most advances in welfare state development as something which states (and often, specifically, left political parties in power) presided over, usually in times of relative prosperity (Huber and Stephens 2001), and which states (even under conservative governments) are now finding more resistant to change than previously thought (Pierson 1996; Myles and Pierson 2001). Indeed, Germany is often singled out as particularly reform-resistant, combining the usual entrenched constituencies and vested interests cited by Pierson with a political system that seems especially, if not uniquely, ill-suited to undertake reform (Scharpf 2000; Streeck 2003).

Against the backdrop to the conventional wisdom, the case of early retirement presents an instructive contrast—in terms of both the politics through which this program has grown and the trajectory of its reform. The growth of early retirement has been driven less by conscious design than by a dynamic one in which relatively small policy innovations undertaken before the mid-1970s (a period of relative prosperity) were massively expanded through their subsequent appropriation and widespread use in the late 1970s and 1980s (a period of economic decline) and after unification by the country's social partners, in an effort to address new problems.[1]

Overextension of early retirement ultimately drove its exhaustion. While theorists of the welfare state are right in emphasizing the forces militating against retrenchment, what has occurred instead in this case can be thought of as liberalization through institutional resettlement. Until the mid-1990s early retirement was regulated and financed mainly by government social policy (publicly financed

I wish to express thanks to Kathleen Thelen and Wolfgang Streeck for their support and critical remarks while preparing this chapter. For helpful comments on an earlier version of this chapter, I thank Jonah D. Levy as well as the other participants in the project workshop at Cologne in December 2002.

pension and unemployment insurance). Since the mid-1990s, however, funding and regulation of early retirement has been relocated and internalized in collective bargaining. Resettlement has pushed early retirement in a decidedly liberal direction by removing it from direct control of the state and of political parties and exposing it much more than before to the discipline of the market.

The case of early retirement policy contains important lessons for our understanding of institutional change. Hacker's analysis (Chapter 2) shows how health policy in the United States experienced creeping retrenchment ('drift') as employers reneged on previous social policy commitments and as active neglect by the government failed to close the resulting gap. In its growth phase German early retirement policy is the mirror image of this. It is a case in which employers and unions effected a massive expansion of a social policy by applying it to problems unanticipated by the policy's designers, with initial political tinkering only producing further unwanted extensions. What is similar to the dynamics Hacker identifies is that here too we find a pattern of change in which early, and at the time relatively minor, policy innovations have large downstream effects.

In terms of subsequent retrenchment and liberalization, the case of German early retirement exhibits a pattern of incremental change similar to many other cases in this book. Not overt retrenchment but institutional resettlement has rendered early retirement policy overall more market conforming. The shift from state sponsorship to collectively negotiated benefits has resulted in a narrowing of the scope of the policy (tied as it now is to a worker's status with respect to collective bargaining contracts, rather than being a matter of public policy and therefore social rights) and has also effectively forced unions and employers to internalize its costs.

The chapter proceeds in two stages. The first part describes the evolution of the policy of early retirement and charts the changing relations between the policy as originally designed and as actually practiced until the mid-1990s. It shows that the goals of the actors who introduced this policy were quite remote from the uses to which it was later put. Under changed economic conditions, the use by employers and unions of pension and unemployment insurance for early retirement placed a growing burden on the public budget and led to an increase in nonwage labor costs. The second part describes the crisis caused by the exhaustion of early retirement policy through its overextension in practice. It tracks the government's attempts to reform the system, and shows how the existence of an alternative institutional venue for financing and regulating early retirement policy—under the auspices of sectoral collective agreements—emerged even as the crisis of the public system grew more intense. Collective bargaining provided the alternative institutional context to which early retirement policy could be delegated as a solution to the crisis of the public system. In this case, then, liberalization did not result in the dismantling of early retirement but rather in its institutional resettlement to a venue that exposes the practice of early retirement to the discipline of the market. A brief comparison to the United States will underscore the significance of this shift in the German context.

Government social policy and the practice of early retirement
until the mid-1990s

Until the mid-1990s the German government regulated and financed early retirement mainly within the framework of pension and unemployment insurance (Ebbinghaus 2002: 173–4).[2] The roots of this can be traced all the way back to the economic crisis of 1929/30, when one of the last Weimar governments introduced provisions that allowed white-collar employees to retire at the age of 60 if they had been unemployed for at least one year (the '59 rule'). While all workers were exposed to unemployment in the Depression, income effects were especially pronounced for older white-collar employees, whose salaries (unlike their blue-collar counterparts) were linked to seniority.[3] In addition, growing numbers of unemployed white-collar workers strengthened their attempts to keep their status distance from blue-collar workers (Petzina 1986: 37). For both reasons, politicians and lawmakers in the parliament argued successfully on behalf of legislation that would allow older white-collars to exit the labor market early as an alternative to unemployment and its attendant negative income effects. The legislation was meant to expire at the end of 1933, but it was extended several times, both by the National Socialists and, later, by Germany's first postwar democratic government (Hockerts 1980: 356). Despite changed labor market conditions and low unemployment, the measure became 'politically irreversible' because its elimination would have eliminated a key status privilege of white-collar workers (Hockerts 1980: 356: fn. 118; Stolleis 2003: 176).

The first and most consequential postwar extension of this system occurred in 1957 under the conservative government of Konrad Adenauer, when the policy was expanded to cover blue-collar workers as well as white-collar employees. The Metalworkers' Union (IG Metall) and the Social Democratic Party (SPD) demanded this as part of their strategy to eliminate all status-based privileges that still existed in the pension system (Hockerts 1980: 320–425), while the governing Christian Democratic Union (CDU) was equally receptive to the idea. The CDU had an interest in cultivating its own working class base, especially on the eve of the 1957 parliamentary elections, when the issue was raised. In addition, Adenauer saw pension reform as a useful tool in the Cold War, as an opportunity to integrate West German society and to attract East Germans to it (Hockerts 1990: 103). The support of the Chancellor and segments of the CDU was sufficient to override the concerns of Labor Minister Anton Storch (CDU), who was skeptical about the need to introduce an unemployment pension for blue-collar workers, especially as these did not receive seniority pay.[4]

Equally important, the context in which the debate took place was one of rapid growth and full employment, indeed, if anything, of labor shortage. After a few years of postwar unemployment, mainly caused by the inflow of refugees and returning soldiers, the unemployment rate fell to below 1 percent during the 1960s. The only recession in this period (1966/7) was mild and was quickly followed by a return to tight labor markets. Unemployment rose to a peak of 2.1 percent in 1967, and was back to below 1 percent by 1969 (Bergmann, Jacobi, and Müller-Jentsch 1975: 344, table 5). The number of employees who retired under the 1957 legislation was therefore small: a total of 92,424 male employees in the entire period between 1960 and 1972 (VDR 2004, own calculation).

The operation of early retirement in this period made it popular with a wide and diverse constituency. Significant structural shifts (e.g. the decline of the coal industry) were accomplished with minimal social unrest, and early retirement played a key role in the management of this process.[5] Older workers engaged in physically demanding jobs in heavy industry could retire early on generous terms. This in turn opened up opportunities for younger workers in ways that made early retirement look like a positive-sum intergenerational deal. Employers could use it as a means to rejuvenate their workforces. The policy was widely seen as a particularly humane solution to structural adjustment, even if a few lawmakers worried about its misuse if economic conditions were to change.[6]

The alignment of interests that this produced set the stage for the extension of early retirement in 1972, under the country's first Social Democratic government. In the 1969 parliamentary election campaign, the Social Democrats had taken up the issue to 'gain the support' of the unions, and justified an extension of early retirement as a way to protect the health of older workers (Hermann 1988, 1990: 120; Hockerts 1992: 906). While previous legislation in 1957 had allowed older workers who became unemployed to exit the labor force at age 59 and begin to draw a pension, the 1972 legislation opened other avenues for workers to retire before the mandatory retirement age of 65, especially the so-called 'flexible retirement'.[7] Under the new law, workers with 35 years of employment could elect to retire at age 63, drawing full benefits as if they had retired at the regular pension age of 65. In this way, it was not just unemployed workers who became eligible for early retirement and could request flexible retirement on these terms. In practice, such requests were included in 'social plans' negotiated between works councils and employers, especially in declining industries such as coal, iron, and steel (Wenzel 1979; Casey 1992; Hemmer 1997). Such plans thus amounted in effect to mass retirement measures, under which some workers would be allowed to retire early under the new 'flexible retirement' option, others under the previous 'pension due to unemployment option' (the '59 rule'), and still others under new provisions for severely handicapped persons introduced by the 1972 law.[8]

The problem building up

The economic context shifted dramatically after the 1973 oil crisis, which brought soaring unemployment in Germany as elsewhere. Not the policy itself, but the extent of early retirement and its use by employers and works councils changed significantly in the new situation. After 1973 early retirement became the preferred solution for managing large-scale layoffs across a range of industries (Jacobs, Kohli, and Rein 1991: 190). In particular, the manufacturing sector quickly learned how to make use of early exit regulations to manage redundancies without social unrest (George 2000). Employees agreed to voluntary redundancy (that is, they agreed to become unemployed at age 59)[9] and began to draw unemployment pension after the lapse of unemployment benefits (which, at that time, were paid for a maximum of twelve months). Enterprises made this option attractive by topping up unemployment benefits with redundancy payments, sometimes up to 100 percent of previous earnings. Contributions of the 'pre-retirees' in unemployment to health and pension insurance were paid by the Federal Labor Office (Bundesanstalt für Arbeit).

Up to 90 percent of the costs of early retirement were borne by the welfare state (Blüm 1996: 8), leaving only the redundancy payments for firms to meet.[10] Social plans providing for early exit spread quickly during the employment crises of the 1970s and 1980s. In a recession and with layoffs inevitable, works councils were more than happy to facilitate the exit of older workers under the generous terms offered by the social security system. In fact they often found themselves under considerable pressure from older workers who wanted to retire under the existing provisions. Separate legislation in 1972 (the Works Constitution Act) had given works councils powerful rights in the negotiation of social plans (*erzwingbare Mitbestimmung*) and local labor leaders used these rights to pressurize employers to deal with redundancies through mass early retirement (Wenzel 1979; Casey 1992; Hemmer 1997).

The practice spread unevenly, however, as it was used mostly by big firms (Hoffmann 1996: 4).[11] As Mares (2003: 236–8) notes, large firms alone commanded the financial resources necessary to make it attractive for older workers to retire, by topping up unemployment benefits to match their previous wages. Smaller firms were normally unable to put together similarly enticing packages—not just for financial reasons but for organizational reasons, too. Early retirement became widespread in industries such as automobiles (Wenzel 1979; Casey 1992; Hemmer 1997). Mares (2003: 236) cites a study of the German Ministry of Social Affairs that showed that 'every second large firm had used the early retirement option'. From the perspective of the firms, it offered a welcome opportunity to offload most of the costs of downsizing onto the unemployment and pension systems.

The overall numbers of male workers exiting the labor force through early retirement grew dramatically in the 1970s and beyond (Figure 8.1). Starting in 1973 the inflow into the pension due to unemployment and the pension for severely handicapped persons increased steadily. More striking still, the new flexible retirement option created in 1972 proved immediately popular. Use of this measure peaked during the first oil crisis in 1973 when it was used for 121,154 employees and remained at a level of over 100,000 until 1976.

Exacerbating the problem by trying to solve it

In the 1980s, the use of pension and unemployment insurance for early retirement expanded further as a result of two additional developments—neither explicitly linked to early retirement, but both inadvertently fueling its expansion. The first

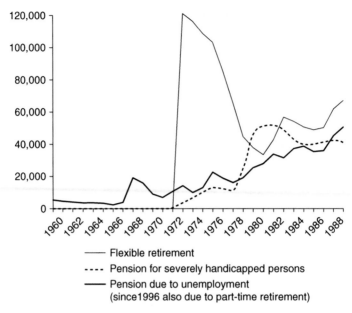

Figure 8.1 Early retirement in Germany: inflow of male employees between 1960 and 1989
Source: VDR (2004).

involved attempts by the government to solve conflicts among unions and to weaken the Metalworkers' Union. The second was in response to budget pressures produced by growing long-term unemployment.

The first development had its roots in a conflict among trade unions over working time reductions in response to unemployment. In the face of the steady increase in unemployment during the two oil crises, the two main manufacturing trade unions, the Metalworkers' Union (IG Metall) and the Chemical Workers' Union (IG Chemie), locked horns over this issue. On the surface, the conflict was over alternative models of working time reduction, with IG Metall advocating a reduction in weekly working hours (*Wochenarbeitszeitverkürzung*) and IG Chemie, along with other 'moderate' unions, calling for reductions in working time over the life course (*Lebensarbeitzeitverkürzung*; Schudlich 1982; Wiesenthal 1987). Behind the different models lay two different conceptions of the appropriate link between government policy and collective bargaining. IG Metall opposed any governmental intervention in collective bargaining and was unwilling to pay for an expansion of welfare with wage concessions, while IG Chemie and the moderates were willing to accept a link between welfare policy and wage bargaining and thus to help absorb the cost of early retirement with wage concessions (Wiesenthal 1987: 198).

The conflict came to a head in various yearly bargaining rounds in the early 1980s. In 1982, IG Chemie sought the creation of an industry-wide pension fund, to be financed out of a portion of yearly wage increases (Löwisch and Hetzel 1983: 13). Although unsuccessful in that year (Wiesenthal 1987: 198), IG Chemie remained clearly in favor of cutting working years, not hours, and was prepared to make concessions on wages to achieve this.[12] IG Metall, by contrast, formulated its wage policy with no consideration for social wage demands, in order to isolate their wage policy from government social policy and, by extension, from government income policies. To combat unemployment, IG Metall called for cuts in weekly working hours with no loss of pay, which it made its principal demand in the 1984 bargaining round.[13]

Employers feared the cost increases associated with IG Metall's model of weekly working time reduction and urgently appealed to the government to come to their aid (Streeck 2003: 6). In an effort to forestall a conflict in the metalworking industry and to reduce IG Metall's political power, the conservative government intervened on the side of IG Chemie and its alternative model, passing legislation supporting reduction of working life through collectively negotiated pension models (Naegele 1987; Wiesenthal 1987).

The Pre-Retirement Act of 1984 (*Vorruhestandsgesetz*) contained several provisions promoting early retirement, but made their use contingent on the existence of an industrial agreement governing industry-wide pension models. The law lowered the age of eligibility for early retirement to 58 and set the minimum benefit at 65 percent of the last gross income (with improvements possible through collective agreement). The benefit had to be paid by the employer but could be partly reimbursed at a level of 35 percent by the unemployment insurance fund if the pre-retiree was replaced with an unemployed person (Jacobs, Kohli, and Rein 1991: 194). The *Vorruhestandsgesetz* thus legalized and promoted a pre-retirement model regulated by collective bargaining, allowing the chemical industry to move ahead with its model.[14]

What the measure did not do, however, was remove weekly working time reduction from the agenda. IG Metall pressed on with its alternative model of weekly working time reduction in 1984 and, after a long strike, finally arrived at a deal with employers that combined a reduction in weekly working time with new possibilities for arranging working hours more flexibly.[15] The effects of weekly working time reduction with flexibility in metalworking drove a further expansion of early retirement, by sparking an intense wave of rationalization (Streeck 2003: 7). Higher personnel costs created the incentive and the innovative use of flexible working time schemes provided the means through which firms increased production by uncoupling an employee's personal working time from the firm's production schedule. Employees made redundant by the productivity increases caused by flexible working time arrangements were offered early exit. Since, unlike IG Chemie, IG Metall had refused to negotiate the establishment of collectively negotiated early retirement models, this was financed, as before, by public unemployment and pension insurance.

The second key development of the 1980s that contributed to the extensive and indeed growing use of unemployment and pension insurance was legislation to strengthen the link between benefits and contributions in unemployment insurance (*Äquivalenzprinzip*). As a result of three decisions by the Federal Government in 1984, 1985, and 1987, the duration of unemployment benefits for older unemployed workers was tied to the duration of compulsory insurance coverage and the age of the beneficiary, allowing older workers to draw unemployment benefit for a maximum of thirty-two months. Politically, the legislation was justified on grounds of restoring 'equivalence' in unemployment insurance, so that older workers who had contributed more were also entitled to more (Jacobs, Kohli, and Rein 1991: 193; Trampusch 2002). This was a goal with which parties across the spectrum were in agreement (see Trampusch 2002: 17–18).[16] In reality, the measure was introduced by the Finance Ministry, primarily to ease the financial burden on the federal budget of the country's means-tested 'unemployment assistance' (*Arbeitslosenhilfe*). With the increase in long-term unemployment in the 1980s, the costs of unemployment assistance had increased dramatically (Trampusch 2002: 52), and the idea of the reform was to shift some of the costs of this onto the unemployment insurance funds, which are financed by employer and worker contributions.[17] The measure did in fact consolidate expenditures for unemployment assistance (Trampusch 2002: 52).[18]

That is not all it did, however, for a side effect of the law was effectively to turn the previous '59 rule' into a '57 rule', as early retirement became even more attractive to firms. Now firms could retire employees at age 57. Workers could receive unemployment benefit in the form of *Arbeitslosengeld* for a period of thirty-two months, and then take advantage of the pension due to unemployment at the age of 60.[19] Whereas between 1960 and 1972 only a total of 92,424 male employees had made use of the '59 rule', between 1973 and 1990 the number of male employees who retired due to unemployment increased to a total of 527,093 (VDR 2004, own calculation), whereby more than a half of them retired after 1984. Some industries made early retirement by pension due to unemployment the main mechanism of mass redundancies in the context of social plans (on this and the following, see Casey 1992: 431–3). Table 8.1 lists the proportion of unemployed social plan recipients by age and industry. It shows the importance of early retirement as a means of reducing labor supply in the 1970s and 1980s. The majority of social plan beneficiaries were over 55 and about half of them came from three industries: energy and mining, iron and steel, and automobiles. These data also show that in the 1980s the importance of energy and mining, where the social plans had been invented in the 1950s, had diminished, while iron and steel and automobiles had grown to become the most important early retirement sectors in the mid-1980s (see also Esser and Fach 1989).

Unification

While early exit had spread widely across West Germany throughout the 1980s, German unification exported early retirement to East Germany as well. Not prepared for the consequences of unification and the loss of east European export

Table 8.1 Proportion of unemployed social plan recipients to all social plan beneficiaries by age and industry, 1974–84

	1974 (%)	1980 (%)	1984 (%)
Age			
55–64	73.4	74.1	85.4
59–64	57.7	54.4	40.1
Industry			
Energy, water, and mining	30.9	8.1	5.0
Iron and steel	14.2	25.8	35.8
Vehicles	5.0	22.5	9.7

Source: Casey (1992: 432, table 2).

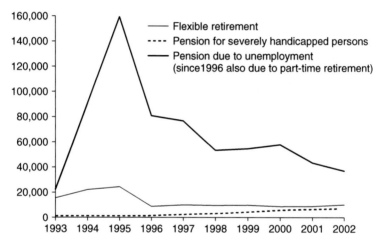

Figure 8.2 Early retirement in East Germany: inflow of male employees between 1993 and 2002
Source: VDR (2004).

markets, employers and employees turned to the well-known tools in order to restructure enterprises. Early exit financed by social insurance became the most important instrument of dealing with the East German labor market crisis (see Figure 8.2). Between 1993 and 2002, about 675,944 East German men retired due to unemployment (VDR 2004, own calculation). In 1995 alone, in the former GDR almost 160,000 employees retired due to unemployment, compared to 111,000 people in the old *Länder* (VDR 2004). Using panel data Ernst (1993: 211) estimates that, in 1992, 30 percent of all departures from gainful employment in East Germany took place through pre-retirement, age-bridging benefits, and pension due to unemployment.

Summarizing the main data on the practice of early retirement in the 1980s and post-German unification, one can see that public programs dominated. Early retirement was mainly financed and regulated as a part of state social policy, in particular by pension and unemployment insurance. However, the use of pension and unemployment insurance for early retirement diverged from the initial goals of the policy's designers. The expansion of the social practice of early retirement was an unintended consequence and an undesired outcome. At the same time, however, the 1980s had also seen the emergence in the chemical sector of an alternative arrangement for financing and regulating early retirement, through collectively negotiated funds. The importance of this alternative would grow in the subsequent period when policymakers began casting about for solutions to the fiscal crisis created by early retirement's overextension.

Reforms and the social practice of early retirement in the 1990s

Already in the 1980s dissatisfaction with early retirement financed as state social policy had increased. Not only did early retirement take up a growing part of the revenues of the social security systems, but the government also directly bore significant and growing expenses as a result of the subsidies it provided to the pension and unemployment insurance schemes.

Resistance of employers against reforms

Federal Government accused German business of abusing the law and sought to change regulations to make firms share the costs (Mares 2001: 310–12). The Christian Democratic Labor Minister and chairman of the party's labor wing, Norbert Blüm, called early retirement 'a conspiracy between management and works councils and a social policy with built-in privileges [for employers and trade unions]' (cited in Mares 2001: 311). In 1982 the government amended the Employment Promotion Act (*Arbeitsförderungsgesetz*) to make firms reimburse the unemployment insurance fund for benefits paid to workers dismissed at the age 59. In 1985 and 1986, the government tried to extend the reimbursement duty to include both the unemployment insurance fund and the pension fund (Rosenow and Naschold 1994: 65).

Employers, however, refused to pay and looked for ways to circumvent the law. Large firms, in particular, 'systematically undermined' the reimbursement duty and were supported in this by works councils, and in some cases were abetted through 'their close contacts to the local employment offices' (Naschold et al. 1994: 168). Other firms found loopholes and exploited exemptions in the law. For example, as companies were not obliged to pay for employees who were under age 56 at the time of dismissal, managers sometimes offered employees the option to leave at age 55 in return for voluntary redundancy payments (George 2000: 181). Such practices brought about the opposite of what had been intended, as the age limit for early retirement fell even further.

Heated conflicts between employers and the government ensued. Employers raised legal objections against the reimbursement duty and took their case to the Federal Constitutional Court. In October 1990, they scored a victory over the government when the Court deemed the reimbursement duty unconstitutional on grounds that it imposed an undue burden (*unzumutbar*) on firms and violated a worker's right to choose his occupation (Art. 12 GG; BVerfG 1990). In 1993, the government responded to the legal setback with a less controversial law that lowered the payments employers were expected to make to the funds (Rosenow and Naschold 1994: 66).

Conflicts among employers

Alongside the strife between government and large firms, a further rift was opening within Germany's employer associations as small firms listed under the weight of rising nonwage labor costs. Figure 8.3 shows the steady and significant increase in contribution rates, especially for pension insurance, in Germany. Large firms contributed massively to this through the widespread use of early retirement to trim their workforces, making up for its effects through productivity gains as a result of working time arrangements and rationalization (Streeck 2003: 6). As they slimmed down their workforces, large firms were also increasingly willing to agree to higher wage increases in collective bargaining as an alternative to disruptive labor strife, as long as they could in turn cut labor costs by sending workers into early retirement.

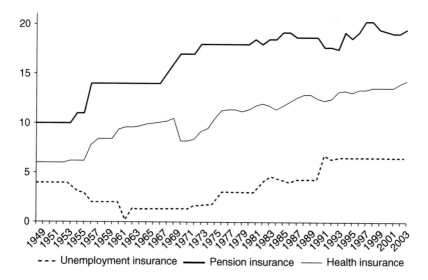

Figure 8.3 Contribution rates to pension, health, and unemployment insurance between 1949 and 2002

Sources: Trampusch (2003: table 6); BDA (2004).

A gap opened between big firms and small firms. Smaller firms could not capitalize on the advantages of early retirement because they could not afford the voluntary redundancy payments (Mares 2003: 238). These firms, with their often more labor-intensive production, were hit harder by the increase in nonwage labor costs. While they could not afford higher wage settlements, they were bound to the same industrial agreement as large firms. These tensions polarized Germany's employers associations as small- and medium-sized firms rebelled and challenged the traditional dominance of large companies. One after another, the top three business associations came under the control of managers of medium-sized firms in the mid- to late 1980s.[20]

Government attempts to correct early retirement practices

As the financial burden on the pension system increased, the Kohl administration made its first attempt at pension reform at the end of the decade (Streeck 2003: 7). The second measure against the misuse of pension insurance for early retirement, after the reimbursement duty, was the gradual increase initiated in 1989 in the age of eligibility for almost all pensions to sixty-five years, to take effect in 2001. The legislation passed with the support of employer associations and against only half-hearted union resistance (Nullmeier and Rüb 1993: 268).

On the employer side, the change in the leaderships of the top associations, along with continuing pressure by small- and medium-sized firms struggling under rising nonwage labor costs, helped bring around employers to a pro-reform position. On the union side, resistance was muted because the measure was not to come into effect until more than ten years later. Among the political parties, the increase in the retirement age was uncontroversial because both CDU/CSU (Christian Social Union) and SPD agreed that reform was necessary and indeed inevitable, given the financial strains associated with financing the pension system (Schludi 2002: 140–4). The parties disagreed only on when the measure should take effect (Faupel 1989: 9).

Reform attempts were halted, however, by German unification, which not only stopped the process but in fact set it back. As noted above (Figure 8.2), early exit financed by the state became a preferred and indeed almost irresistible solution to the massive employment problems generated by the collapse of the East German economy, even if use of social insurance to finance downsizing only exacerbated the fiscal crisis. Moreover, and as indicated in Figure 8.4, practices in the East were mirrored by trends in the West as well, where unemployment pensions rose again dramatically between 1993 and 1995.

By 1995–6, the system had become clearly untenable. Due to the increasing nonwage labor costs, the German labor market was confronted with a growing number of unemployed workers, which drove the social insurance contribution rates further up. Rising nonwage labor costs and unemployment strained the loyalties of employers' and trade union constituencies.

Facing increased pressure from small- and medium-sized firms and his own liberal coalition partner, the FDP (Federal Demonstration Partnership), Chancellor

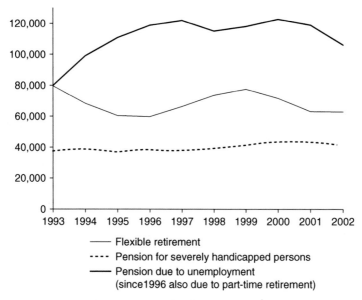

Figure 8.4 Early retirement in West Germany: inflow of male employees between 1993 and 2002
Source: VDR (2004).

Kohl made curbing early exit a governmental priority.[21] In 1996, an 'action program' worked out by FDP Economics Minister Günter Rexrodt laid the ground for more comprehensive legislation later that year, with the most far-reaching reforms of early retirement yet. Most importantly, the 1996 law abolished pensions due to unemployment for individuals born after January 1, 1952. In addition, it raised the age limit for pensions due to unemployment and flexible pensions to sixty-five years of age, to become effective by 2012. Employees wishing to retire early would have to accept a lower pension. Leaving work at age 60 would result in a loss of pension of 18 percent. After 2012, only workers with a long insurance record and severely handicapped persons would be able to retire early.

The increase in the retirement age was explicitly designed to 'correct the present early retirement practice' (BT-Drks. 13/4610: 19; my translation) and, above all, to lower the financial burden of early retirement on the social insurance system. In the lead-up to the legislation Labor Minister Norbert Blüm (1995: 12) condemned the financing of early retirement through unemployment and pension insurance as alien to the purpose of those insurance funds. He argued: 'Part of the nonwage labor costs results from business strategies. I am talking of early retirement that large firms in particular are defining as "social plans," to shift costs onto unemployment and pension insurance funds. The trend toward early retirement must be countered with all possible means' (Blüm 1995: 12).

Liberalization of early retirement

Important for the present argument, government efforts to abolish the early retirement regime and relieve the insurance system of its costs took place parallel to tripartite negotiations over employment policy in the so-called Alliance for Jobs (*Bündnis für Arbeit*). Faced with the changes described above, and loath to give up early retirement entirely, the social partners in effect agreed to absorb some of its costs. In the *Bündnis* negotiations, trade unions and employers successfully lobbied the government to compensate for the reduction in publicly subsidized early retirement by promoting an alternative part-time retirement option through collective bargaining. In doing so, unions and employers suggested shifting welfare from state social policy to collective bargaining. In Germany, collective bargaining can function as an institutional alternative to state social policy. This is because collective bargaining is encompassing and the state has the power to declare collective agreements generally binding (*allgemeinverbindlich*) by extending benefits negotiated at the sectoral bargaining table to nonunion members.

The model on which these proposals were based originated in the chemical industry, where, since 1995, unions and employers had been negotiating over a possible collective agreement on part-time retirement (*Altersteilzeit*). The aim of the chemical industry was to implement early retirement through collective bargaining, thereby organizing part-time retirement as a so-called 'block' model: part-time retirement should be divided into a working phase, during which the employee works full time at a lower wage, and the retirement phase, with full pension. The initiative of the chemical industry reflected the ageing process in the membership of the chemical workers' union. A report of the union in 1997 stated: 'The tendency ... of shifting the age pyramid upward has intensified in the year under review ... the number of pre-retirees [under the membership] increased in the years 1995/1996' (Industriegewerkschaft Chemie-Papier-Keramik 1997: 93, my translation).

The metalworking industry, which had opposed the IG Chemie approach in the past, had in the meantime redefined its strategies and interests. By 1995, IG Metall had reached its 1984 goal of a 35-h working week, and in 1994 the median age of union members had increased to 44 years (Streeck and Hassel 2003: 123, fn. 13). For both reasons, a transition to a reduction of working time over the life course was favorably received by the members. Encouraged by these events, the leaders of the IG Metall changed the unions' strategy from the demand for further reduction of the weekly working hours to the demand for a reduction of working time over the life course. The leadership gained the impression that metalworkers were no longer willing to strike for a further reduction in weekly working hours (IG Metall-Vorstand 2001: 47). Thus in 1996, Walter Riester, then vice chairman of IG Metall, called on employers to create a fund administered jointly and financed from deductions from wage increases (*Tariffonds*), to supplement the benefits of older workers willing to retire.

Although the Riester proposal foundered on opposition from the Metal Employers' Association (Gesamtmetall), the government accommodated an overall shift in the direction of collectively negotiated pension benefits. It passed a new law, the Part-Time Retirement Act (*Altersteilzeitgesetz*) in the same year, 1996. The law encouraged part-time retirement for employees over 55, contingent, however, on a collective agreement between unions and employers. Collective agreements were negotiated in both the metalworking and chemical industries in 1997 on the basis of this new legislation. These agreements complemented the statutory part-time retirement benefits (which amount to 70 percent of previous full-time wages) up to 85 percent (in chemicals, up to 82 percent in metalworking) and sometimes provide compensation for reduced pensions. In sum, these agreements practically offset the pension reduction that had just been enacted by the government to stop early retirement.[22]

After the change of government in 1998, the Red–Green coalition under Gerhard Schröder passed two additional laws on part-time retirement (1999, 2000), which developed this early exit model further. The government also promoted a new pension reform aimed at encouraging new employer-based pension schemes through collective agreements (*Tarifverträge zur Altersvorsorge*). In 1998, the leader of IG Metall, Klaus Zwickel, transformed Riester's idea of a *Tariffonds* into the call for a general retirement age of 60 (*Rente mit 60*). This was to be financed by a wage fund into which employers and employees would each pay 0.5 percent of gross wages (Hassel 2001: 319). Chancellor Schröder in the end rejected the idea of lowering the regular retirement age, creating a deadlock in relations with the union. However, the leader of the chemical workers' union, IG BCE, Hubertus Schmoldt, was able to broker a compromise. His suggestion to conclude collective agreements on early retirement became the leitmotif of the 2000 bargaining round and, for the first time in history, the chemical workers' union signed a collective bargaining agreement before the pattern-setting union IG Metall did. The agreement improved provisions for early retirement and set the pattern for the agreement in the metalworking industry.

In return for the chemical workers union's intervention in the stalemate over the issue of retirement at 60 (*Rente mit 60*), the government improved the legal conditions for collective bargaining on part-time retirement. In June 2000, it extended the 1996 Part-Time Retirement Act, due to expire in 2009, to allow the Bundesanstalt für Arbeit to continue to support part-time retirement until December 31, 2015. In addition, it extended the maximum period of public subsidies for part-time retirement from five to six years. As before, however, the change meant that part-time retirement can now only be used by employees from the age of 55 and only where a collective agreement on this exists.

These measures extend and complete a process of institutional resettlement that over the 1990s has effectively shifted the financing and regulation of early retirement from the public domain (and the public coffers) to the collective bargaining arena. Industrial agreements on part-time retirement and on pensions (*Tarifverträge zur Altersteilzeit und zur Altersvorsorge*) regulate the conditions of entitlement (e.g. the minimum age). They also regulate the so-called transformation of payments (converting pay into contributions for employer-based pension schemes), the financing (for instance, the transformable payment components), and the employer's contribution.[23] In order to manage the occupational pension scheme, a joint pension fund was established in the metal industry in October 2001 under the name of *Altersversorgung Metall und Elektro* (pension in the metal industry), which provides various ways to implement occupational pension schemes.

The government continues to support these measures (as in the case of supplementary pensions, through direct public payments, and tax deductions), but in the case of both pensions (*Altersvorsorge*) and part-time retirement (*Altersteilzeit*) a collective bargaining agreement is a precondition for securing governmental support for such plans (*Tarifvorrang*). The provisions of collective agreements for old-age pensions and for part-time retirement respond to government pension reforms, especially to the increase of the age limit. They almost balance the pension reductions enacted by government to stop early retirement, in fact, since they 'top up' the statutory part-time retirement benefits and compensate for the reduction in pensions. The logic, however, has shifted: from direct government sponsorship and financing of early retirement, to government support for an alternative means of financing and the regulation of early retirement through collective bargaining. Since government subsidizes these collectively negotiated IG Metall benefits, government has to pay a price for the offloading of early exit costs onto collective bargaining. Thus, whether the liberalization of early exit will really ease public funds remains uncertain.

According to surveys of the Federal Labor Office, part-time retirement has been popular. Between 1996 and 2002, the Federal Labor Office approved 168,121 claims for reimbursement where new recruitment replaced retirees (see Table 8.2). The actual number of part-time pensioners is considerably higher since they tend to work full time and then retire earlier (Klammer 2003). Applications for support are made only after the end of the working phase, which means that the official statistics understate the extent of part-time retirement. The Federal Labor Office assumes that the number of partially retired persons is about 3.5–4 times higher than shown by official statistics (BA 2000; Klammer and Weber 2001: 109).

Not only part-time retirement but also the upgrading of state pensions through employer-based pensions has experienced a considerable upswing since 2002. As of December 2003, more than 400 firms with about 200,000 employees in the chemical sector have agreed to payment transformation (IG BCE 2004). In the metal sector 5,500 employers participated in December 2003, accounting for 1,700,000 employees or a full 47 percent of all employees in the metal sector (MetallRente 2004). By the end of 2003, 854 collective agreements on part-time retirement were concluded, covering 16.3 million employees; up to now, collective agreements on pensions cover 19.7 million employees (BMWA 2004: 46, 48).

In sum, reforms in the 1990s changed government social policy, collective bargaining, and the early retirement practice fundamentally. The shift of early retirement from state social policy to collective bargaining was encouraged by governmental reforms in pension policy and taxation. Government social

Table 8.2 Development of part-time retirement: claims for reimbursement to the Federal Labor Office between 1996 and 2002

	1996 (since August 1)	1997	1998	1999	2000	2001	2002	Since August 1, 1996
Number of proposed claims for reimbursement	1,213	7,226	13,202	22,450	38,879	49,953	54,080	187,003
Alte Bundesländer	883	5,475	10,163	18,214	33,234	42,751	46,454	157,174
Neue Bundesländer	330	1,751	3,039	4,236	5,645	7,202	7,626	29,829
Number of granted claims for reimbursement	544	6,062	11,443	19,781	34,623	46,188	49,480	168,121
Alte Bundesländer	367	4,449	8,890	15,899	29,818	39,424	42,191	141,038
Neue Bundesländer	177	1,613	2,553	3,882	4,805	6,764	7,289	27,083
Number of proposed claims for pre-decision (Vorausentscheidung)	761	6,637	14,778	28,674	33,022	37,795	31,745	153,412
Alte Bundesländer	728	6,415	13,244	22,727	25,214	27,860	23,452	119,640
Neue Bundesländer	33	222	1,534	5,947	7,808	9,935	8,293	33,772
Number of granted claims for pre-decision (Vorausentscheidung)				26,766	30,694	36,446	30,900	124,806
Alte Bundesländer				21,115	23,394	26,806	22,712	94,027
Neue Bundesländer				5,651	7,300	9,640	8,188	30,779

Source: Bundesanstalt für Arbeit, Mrs Schmidt, Referat IIa2: Table 'Anträge—Altersteilzeitgesetz (seit 1.8.1996 kumuliert)'; my translation.

policy was reorganized: instead of regulating and financing early retirement as part of social insurance, costs were shifted to collective bargaining by subsidizing collectively funded pensions which in turn could be used to pay for early retirement. The government has since sought to counterbalance cuts in public benefits by promoting collectively negotiated old-age provisions and part-time retirement. Part-time retirement is only possible for those workers who are covered by a collective agreement on early exit. Early exit is no longer designed and introduced by government social policy but by collective bargaining. The relationship between these two institutional structures has been reversed as decisions over the terms and conditions of early retirement have shifted from government social policy to collective bargaining. In this way, the resettlement of early retirement has changed the relationship between government social policy and collective bargaining, in the process changing the practice of early retirement itself.

Conclusion: institutional change as institutional resettlement

The case of early retirement offers valuable lessons with respect to prevailing theories of institutional change. Both in its growth phase and its subsequent retrenchment, we find patterns that do not conform to the models of change that dominate the literature. The growth of early retirement practice shares some similarities with the dynamics identified by Hacker in Chapter 2. As in the case of individual retirement accounts in the United States, so too in the case of early retirement policy in Germany, we see a situation in which relatively minor policy innovations undertaken at one point in time can have quite major downstream consequences as the policy expands through its increasing adoption. However, whereas IRA (individual retirement account) growth was the intended consequence of conservative political actors who faced obstacles to overt retrenchment (therefore, institutional layering to effect policy change as a second best alternative), it is clear that, in the case of the growth of early retirement, policy expansion was a consequence unintended by the policy's authors, who designed the measure under completely different political and economic conditions and mostly envisioned its rather limited application in practice.

The development of early retirement was characterized by a growing gap between the original design of the policy and its subsequent application. Early retirement policies designed in and for a period of prosperity were redeployed under conditions of economic stagnation, as a way of managing structural adjustment while preserving social peace. The situation shares similarities with Margaret Weir's analysis of the temporal 'collision' of Lyndon Johnson's Great Society program with the civil rights movement and urban unrest of the 1960s. Weir shows how programs to alleviate poverty in the United States acquired a racial focus only when they were redirected to deal with urban unrest in the 1960s, a redirection that was highly consequential for the way it alienated poor whites in ways that shaped the political fate of the War on Poverty itself (Weir 1992). In the case of early retirement in Germany, one observes an analogous collision and redirection.

The availability of generous public support for early retirement was eagerly seized on by large firms in a period of economic turmoil. It helped them to cement an alliance with their works councils in favor of industrial restructuring and rationalization, by offering them the opportunity to offload the costs onto the federal budget and the social insurance funds.

The overextension of early retirement led to its exhaustion, setting the stage for its subsequent retrenchment. But in this case, as in many others examined in this volume, retrenchment did not involve the dismantling of the policy, and the process was incremental rather than abrupt. In fact, retrenchment in this instance took the form of what we have called institutional resettlement, such early retirement based on social insurance funds and federal unemployment benefits had to give way in the 1990s to financing and regulation through collective bargaining.

Such resettlement was possible because in Germany collective bargaining institutions offer a functional alternative, to some extent, to state social policy. Levy (Chapter 4) describes how in France the state made attempts to delegate social policy but failed for lack of strong intermediary associations. By contrast, such delegation was achieved in Germany because here intermediary associations are comparatively strong. Unions, business associations, and collective bargaining institutions are more encompassing than in France, and therefore provide the coordination and organization necessary to set standards. Collectively negotiated benefits resemble public benefits to the extent that they are encompassing and in a context in which the state has the power to declare them generally binding for workers not covered by collective contracts.

That said, however, it should be clear that the relocation of early retirement policy subjects its practice to entirely new political dynamics. As emphasized above, in the present case resettlement involves liberalization because it subjects the practice of early retirement more directly to the discipline of the market. This is doubly true. First, collective bargaining—while quite encompassing in Germany—is not all-encompassing, and indeed coverage has been on the decline since the 1980s as a significant number of firms (especially in key sectors like metalworking) have opted out of the system. As most state support for early retirement is now explicitly linked to the existence of an industrial bargain and industrial funds, workers outside the bargain also fall outside the early retirement regime. Second, the resettlement of early retirement to the collective bargaining arena forces the social partners to absorb its costs, and this shift from government and political parties to the bargaining partners themselves exposes the use and application of early retirement to market pressures.

Moreover, and as especially emphasized by Hacker, 'alternative ways of providing social welfare goods and services differ tremendously in their characteristics and social effects, and hence, in who supports them and how political debates over them unfold' (2002: xiii). In previous work, Hacker had demonstrated that what distinguishes the United States is not so much the overall level of social spending and support but the source of social benefits, which are overwhelmingly private (including, above all, employer provision negotiated with unions). The politics surrounding private benefits are different from public programs: '[b]ecause private benefits are distributed quite differently than are public benefits, they activate interests and coalitions that are distinct from those that we usually associate with social policy' (2002: 8). For example, once union-ized workers and unions in strong firms were invested in private, company-based social policies, they were no longer available as political lobbies for more univer-salistic programs, which inevitably would be inferior to what they already had.

While the line between public and private social benefits in Germany has always been more blurred than in the United States, the shift in emphasis from public to private does expose social policy to different political dynamics.[24] In the United States, where unions are weak and many private benefits are granted at the will of the employer, retrenchment has taken the form of unilateral employer retreat. In Germany, the collective bargaining regime involves a more complex public–private mix. Here the more likely dynamics is one in which coalitions of works councils and managers in the country's strongest 'core' firms are able to defend privileged policies, but only at the expense of shrinking coverage. In that sense, the liberalization of early retirement is driven forward by the same political dynamics that have driven its growth as well.

Notes

1. On unintended consequences, see also Ebbinghaus (2002: 179), who compares early retirement policies in Europe, Japan, and the United States.
2. In sheer numbers, age-free disability pensions (*Berufs- und Erwerbsunfähigkeitsrente*) account for more early exits than the early retirement policies that are the subject of this chapter. However, the logic of their use is quite different: they do not respond, for example, to economic fluctuations and therefore are not subject to the same political dynamics that are of interest here.
3. On this issue, see the speech of Labor Minister Anton Storch delivered to the parliament in 1956 (Deutscher Bundesrat, Wortprotokoll, 160. Sitzung am 15. Juni 1956: 203).
4. See the speech of Storch delivered to the parliament in 1956, in which he argues against unemployment pensions for blue-collar workers (Deutscher Bundesrat, Wortprotokoll, 160. Sitzung am 15. Juni 1956: 203).
5. So-called 'social plans' (negotiated between works councils and management to establish the terms under which layoffs would occur) emerged for the first time in the coal industry in the 1950s. The first agreement in the iron and steel industry dates back to 1962, for Rasselstein AG. During the 1960s, social plans became a dominant instrument in the steel industry and hard coal mining (Wenzel 1979).
6. In the parliamentary debates, the sole voice of concern was Adolf Müller (CDU; Deutscher Bundestag, Wortprotokoll, 160. Sitzung am 16. Dezember 1971: 9244(B)).
7. In the memorandum accompanying the 1972 legislative proposal, the Federal Government explained the purpose of the flexible age limit as follows: 'It is necessary to replace the past rigid age limit by a more flexible regulation which grants more freedom and self-determination to the individual at the end of his working life' (BT-Drks. VI/2916: 67; my translation).

8. The 1972 reform introduced pensions for severely handicapped persons at age 60 (*Schwerbehindertenrente*), though this measure never gained as much importance as the other early retirement options discussed here.

9. Such agreements were necessary because of employment protection.

10. In fact, the state subsidized these as well, through tax exemptions.

11. Only few studies exist that analyze early exits by sector. For qualitative case studies, see Rosenow and Naschold (1994) and George (2000).

12. Their subsequent success in establishing a collectively negotiated pension model, as we will see, was facilitated by government support for the measure in the 1984 bargaining round.

13. The different approaches in the chemical and metal industry sector reflected the different age structure of the two unions—IG Metall's members being on an average younger. An additional factor is the inability of the IG Chemie to strike (Schudlich 1982), a consequence of both sector-specific production techniques (process character of production engineering and high capital intensity) and a tradition of company-based social policy that has operated since the early years of the twentieth century and was certainly solidified by a failed strike in 1971 (Schudlich 1982: 128, 160–1). Since that defeat, the union has offered itself as coadministrators of company social policy, taking those costs into account in its wage demands.

14. During the collective bargaining round of 1984/5 collective bargaining contracts on early retirement (*Vorruhestandstarifverträge*) were concluded for a total of 7 million employees. By 1986, 145 collective agreements and 210 company agreements on early retirement were recorded (Prognos 1986: 6). In 1985 *IG Chemie* concluded an industrial agreement on early retirement under the provision of the *Vorruhestandsgesetz*. Under the agreement, workers at age 58 or older had the option of retiring early on 75% of their previous full-time gross wage (the 10% above the statutory 65% being made up by employers; Naegele 1987: 146). In exchange, the union agreed to a regular 40-h week until the end of 1988.

15. The agreement provided for a range of 37–40h, to achieve an average of 38.5 over a maximum of eight weeks. It also contained the possibility to bundle worktime reduction in nonworking shifts. New working time schemes were developed by firms in the wake of the 1984 agreement, allowing for an internal adaptation of working time volume to short-term variations in production. Above all, the large automobile producers worked out new working time systems through which they achieved significant productivity gains by economizing on labor (Vogler-Ludwig 1990: 6; Zwiener 1993: 94–5).

16. As Norbert Blüm (CDU), the Federal Minister of Labor at that time, pointed out in his speech in the German Parliament: 'It fits my idea of solidarity that those who have paid their solidarity tax for a longer period also have a claim for longer support by solidarity funds' (Deutscher Bundestag, Wortprotokoll, 108. Sitzung am 6.12.1984: 8111(C)–8111(D); my translation).

17. In Germany, unemployment assistance consists of 'unemployment benefit' (*Arbeitslosengeld*), administered by the Federal Labor Office and financed by workers' and employers' contributions, and 'unemployment assistance' (*Arbeitslosenhilfe*), financed through the Federal budget. Unemployed workers generally draw unemployment benefit first and only move onto unemployment assistance if they continue to be unemployed after their eligibility runs out (long-term unemployed).

18. After the rapid increase between 1982 and 1985, from DM 5 billion to DM 9.2 billion, the costs for unemployment assistance were reduced to DM 8.2 billion in 1989 (Trampusch 2002: 52).
19. This possibility was neither discussed nor, apparently, even entertained in the parliamentary debates on the subject (Wortprotokoll, Deutscher Bundestag, 10. Wahlperiode, 108. Sitzung am 6.12.1984, 8103 (B)–8116 (C); Wortprotokoll, Deutscher Bundestag, 10. Wahlperiode, 182. Sitzung am 6.12.1985, 13870(D)–13888(A); Wortprotokoll, Deutscher Bundestag, 11. Wahlperiode, 17. Sitzung am 5.06.1987, 1067(D)–1078(C); Wortprotokoll, Deutscher Bundestag, 11. Wahlperiode, 175. Sitzung am 15.11.1989, 13259(C)–13270(A)).
20. In the mid-1980s the interests of big and small firms in the metal industry had already drifted apart. Smaller firms withdrew their support to collective bargaining by leaving employer associations and collective agreements (Silvia 1997; Hassel and Rehder 2001: 7). The business organizations that experienced leadership changes included the DIHT (Deutscher Industrie- und Handelstag or Association of German Chambers of Industry and Commerce), the BDI (Bundesverband der Deutschen Industrie or Federation of German Industries), and the BDA (Bundesvereinigung der Deutschen Arbeitgeberverbände or Confederation of German Employers' Federations), all of which came under the leadership of managers of medium-sized firms (DIHT: Hans-Peter Stihl, 1988–2001; BDI: Tyll Necker 1987–90 and 1992–4; BDA: Klaus Murmann, 1986–97).
21. The BDI and the economic wing of the government coalition (a group of CDU/CSU members of the Bundestag based around Wolfgang Schäuble, together with the FDP) exerted strong pressure on the Chancellor to lower nonwage labor costs through social policy reforms.
22. Under the law, the employer has to top-up the wage during the working phase by around 20% and at least up to 70% of the last net wage. In addition, he has to pay the contributions to the pension insurance on the basis of 90% of the gross salary. The part-time retirement is subsidized by the Bundesanstalt für Arbeit with the reimbursement for employers' expenditure if the part-time retiree is replaced with an unemployed person or a freshly trained apprentice (so called *Wiederbesetzung*).
23. Collective agreements on part-time retirement were concluded in 1997 and 2000 (in 2000 they were renewed), whereby the chemical agreement provides for substantially better conditions for the employees, thus higher payments by the employers (about which, see BDA 2001; IG BCE 2001; WSI 2001). Collective agreements on pensions were concluded in 2001 (see Handelsblatt; Frankfurter Allgemeine Zeitung).
24. And the difference to the United States may not be as great as initial appearances suggest. As Hacker (2002: 8) points out with regard to private (including collectively negotiated) social policy in the United States:

> Widespread collective benefits do not spontaneously arise through decentralized market processes. To become a significant source of social protection, they have almost always required government intervention and support, whether through tax breaks, regulation, or other means. Equally important, as political leaders have sought to bolster private benefits, they have also attempted to make them serve ends different from those that private actor would otherwise have pursued . . . The political forces at work, however, are not identical to those that animate the development of public social programs.

References

BA (Bundesanstalt für Arbeit) (2000). Presseinformation Nr. 5 vom 28. Januar, Nürnberg.

BDA (Bundesvereinigung der Deutschen Arbeitgeberverbände) (2001). Tarifverträge zur Altersteilzeit, Zusammenstellung der BDA, Berlin.

—— (2004). Beitragssätze zur Sozialversicherung, available at www.bdaonline. de/www/bdaonline.nsf/id/GraphikBeitragssaetzezurSozial/$file/Beitragssätze.pdf.

Bergmann, J., Jacobi, O., and Müller-Jentsch, W. (1975). *Gewerkschaften in der Bundesrepublik. Gewerkschaftliche Lohnpolitik zwischen Mitgliederinteressen und ökonomischen Sachzwängen,* Studienreihe des Instituts für Sozialforschung, Band 1. Frankfurt am Main: Europäische Verlagsanstalt.

Blüm, N. (1995). Konkurrenzfähig bleiben. *Bundesarbeitsblatt,* 1996(9): 5–12.

—— (1996). Vertrauen in die Rentenversicherung. *Bundesarbeitsblatt,* 1996(3): 5–10.

BMWA (Bundesministerium für Wirtschaft und Arbeit) (2004). *Tarifvertragliche Arbeitsbedingungen im Jahr 2003,* Stand 31. Dezember 2003. Bonn: BMWA.

BT-Drks. (Drucksache des Deutschen Bundestages) VI/2916.

—— (Drucksache des Deutschen Bundestages) 13/4610.

BVerfG (Bundesverfassungsgericht) (1990). Urteil des Ersten Senats vom 23. Januar 1990 in den Verfahren 1 BvL 44/86 und 48/87, Karlsruhe.

Casey, B. (1992). Redundancy and Early Retirement. The Interaction of Public and Private Policy in Britain, Germany, and the USA. *British Journal of Industrial Relations* 30(3): 425–43.

Deutscher Bundesrat, Wortprotokoll, 160. Sitzung am 15. Juni 1956.

Deutscher Bundestag, Wortprotokoll, 160. Sitzung am 16. Dezember 1971.

——, Wortprotokoll, 108. Sitzung am 6. Dezember 1984.

——, Wortprotokoll, 182. Sitzung am 6. Dezember 1985.

——, Wortprotokoll, 17. Sitzung am 5. Juni 1987.

——, Wortprotokoll, 175. Sitzung am 15. November 1989.

Ebbinghaus, B. (2002). Exit from Labor. Reforming Early Retirement and Social Partnership in Europe, Japan, and the USA. Habilitationsschrift, Wirtschafts- und Sozialwissenschaftliche Fakultät der Universität zu Köln. Köln.

Ernst, J. (1993). Der vorzeitige Ruhestand in Ostdeutschland und einige Aspekte der sozialen Lage der Frührentner in den neuen Ländern. *Sozialer Fortschritt* 42(9): 211–16.

Esser, J. and Fach, W. (1989). Crisis Management 'Made in Germany': The Steel Industry. In: P. Katzenstein (ed.), *Industry and Politics in West Germany. Toward the Third Republic.* Ithaca and London: Cornell University Press, pp. 221–48.

Faupel, G. (1989). Rentenreform: Großer Konsens für sozialen Rückschritt. *Soziale Sicherheit,* 38(1): 4–8.

Frankfurter Allgemeine Zeitung (2001). Die Finanzdienstleister kamen von ganz alleine, 29 October. Frankfurter Allgemeine Zeitung GmbH.

George, R. (2000). *Beschäftigung älterer Arbeitnehmer aus betrieblicher Sicht: Frühverrentung als Personalanpassungsstrategie in internen Arbeitsmärkten.* München: Hampp Verlag.

Hacker, J. (2002). *The Divided Welfare State: The Battle over Public and Private Social Benefits in the United States.* Cambridge: Cambridge University Press.

Handelsblatt (2001). Tarifverträge zur staatlich geförderten Altersvorsorge im Betrieb, 19 September.

HASSEL, A. (2001). The Problem of Political Exchange in Complex Governance Systems: The Case of Germany's Alliance for Jobs. *European Journal of Industrial Relations* 7(3): 305–32.

—— and REHDER, B. (2001). Institutional Change in the German Wage Bargaining System—The Role of Big Companies. MPIfG Working Paper, 01/9, Köln: Max-Planck-Institut für Gesellschaftsforschung.

HEMMER, E. (1997). *Sozialpläne und Personalanpassungsmaßnahmen. Eine empirische Untersuchung.* Köln: Deutscher Institutsverlag.

HERMANN, C. (1988). Die Rentenreform 1972 – Bilanz und Perspektive nach 15 Jahren. *Deutsche Rentenversicherung* 43(1–2): 1–21.

—— (1990). Entwicklungslinien der 100jährigen Geschichte der gesetzlichen Rentenversicherung: Die Zeit von 1957–1991. In: F. Ruland and VDR (Verband der Deutschen Rentenversicherungsträger) (eds.), *Handbuch der gesetzlichen Rentenversicherung. Festschrift aus Anlaß des 100jährigen Bestehens der gesetzlichen Rentenversicherung.* Neuwied/ Frankfurt am Main: Luchterhand, pp. 105–39.

HOCKERTS, H. G. (1980). *Sozialpolitische Entscheidungen im Nachkriegsdeutschland. Alliierte und deutsche Sozialversicherungspolitik: 1945 bis 1957.* Stuttgart: Klett-Cotta.

—— (1990). Entwicklungslinien der 100jährigen Geschichte der gesetzlichen Rentenversicherung: Die Rentenreform 1957. In: F. Ruland and VDR (Verband der Deutschen Rentenversicherungsträger) (eds.), *Handbuch der gesetzlichen Rentenversicherung. Festschrift aus Anlaß des 100jährigen Bestehens der gesetzlichen Rentenversicherung.* Neuwied/Frankfurt am Main: Luchterhand, pp. 93–104.

—— (1992). Vom Nutzen und Nachteil parlamentarischer Konkurrenz: Die Rentenreform 1972—Ein Lehrstück. In: K. D. Bracher (ed.), *Staat und Parteien: Festschrift für Rudolf Morsey zum 65. Geburtstag.* Berlin: Duncker & Humblot, pp. 903–34.

HOFFMANN, E. (1996). Frühverrentung und Beschäftigung – Teil 2: Ältere Arbeitnehmer zwischen Beschäftigung, Arbeitslosigkeit und Ruhestand 1980–1995. *IAB Kurzbericht*, 1996/9, Nürnberg: Institut für Arbeitsmarkt und Berufsforschung.

HUBER, E. and STEPHENS, J. D. (2001). *Development and Crisis of the Welfare State: Parties and Policies in Global Markets.* Chicago: University of Chicago Press.

IG BCE (Industriegewerkschaft Bergbau, Chemie, Energie) (2001). Tarifverträge zur Altersteilzeit, Zusammenstellung der IGBCE, Hannover.

—— (2004). Medieninformation VIII/4 vom 5. Februar 2004, Hannover, available at www.igbce.de.

IG Metall-Vorstand (Vorstand der Industriegewerkschaft Metall) (2001). *IG Metall—Zukunftsreport. Ergebnisse im Überblick—Zuspitzungen und Diskussionsanreize.* Frankfurt: IG Metall.

Industriegewerkschaft Chemie-Papier-Keramik (1997). *Geschäftsbericht 1995–1997 zum 4. Außerordentlichen Gewerkschaftstag in Hannover, 9.Oktober 1997.* Hannover: Industriegewerkschaft Chemie-Papier-Keramik.

JACOBS, K., KOHLI, M., and REIN, M. (1991). Germany: The Diversity of Pathways. In: M. Kohli, A.-M. Guillemard, and H. van Gunsteren (eds.), *Time for Retirement. Comparative Studies of Early Exit from the Labor Force.* New York: Cambridge University Press, pp. 181–221.

KLAMMER, U. (2003). Altersteilzeit zwischen betrieblicher und staatlicher Sozialpolitik. *Sozialer Fortschritt* 52(2): 39–47.

—— and WEBER, H. (2001). Flexibel in den Ruhestand?—Ergebnisse und Überlegungen zur Altersteilzeit. *WSI Mitteilungen* 54(2): 102–12.

LÖWISCH, M. and HETZEL, M. (1983). *Früherer Ruhestand durch Vorverlegung der Altersgrenze.* Berlin: Duncker & Humblot.

MARES, I. (2001). Enterprise Reorganization and Social Insurance Reform: The Development of Early Retirement in France and Germany. *Governance* 14(3): 295–318.

—— (2003). *The Politics of Social Risk. Business and Welfare State Development.* Cambridge: Cambridge University Press.

METALLRENTE (2004). MetallRente News 1/2004, Berlin. Available at www.metallrente.de.

MYLES, J. and PIERSON, P. (2001). The Comparative Political Economy of Pension Reform. In: P. Pierson (ed.), *The New Politics of the Welfare State.* Oxford: Oxford University Press, pp. 305–33.

NAEGELE, G. (1987). *Theorie und Praxis des Vorruhestandsgesetzes. Ergebnisse einer empirischen Ergebnisstudie.* Augsburg: Maro Verlag.

NASCHOLD, F., OPPEN, M., PEINEMANN, H., and ROSENOW, J. (1994). Germany: The Concerted Transition from Work to Welfare. In: F. Naschold and B. de Vroom (eds.), *Regulating Employment and Welfare.* Berlin: de Gruyter, pp. 117–82.

NULLMEIER, F. and RÜB, F. W. (1993). *Die Transformation des Sozialstaats: Vom Sozialstaat zum Sicherungsstaat.* Frankfurt: Campus.

PETZINA, D. (1986). The Extent and Causes of Unemployment in the Weimar Republic. In: P. D. Stachura (ed.), *Unemployment and the Great Depression in Weimar Germany.* Houndmills, UK: Macmillan Press, pp. 29–48.

PIERSON, P. (1996). The New Politics of the Welfare State. *World Politics* 48(2): 143–79.

PROGNOS (1986). *Bestandsaufnahme und Bewertung praktizierter Modelle zur vorgezogenen Ruhestandsregelung.* Bonn: Bundesministerium für Arbeit und Sozialordnung.

ROSENOW, J. and NASCHOLD, F. (1994). *Die Regulierung der Altersgrenzen: Strategien von Unternehmen und die Politik des Staates.* Berlin: Edition Sigma.

SCHARPF, F. W. (2000). Economic Changes, Vulnerabilities, and Institutional Capabilities. In: F. W. Scharpf and V. A. Schmidt (eds.), *Welfare and Work in the Open Economy. Volume I. From Vulnerability to Competitiveness.* Oxford: Oxford University Press, pp. 21–124.

SCHLUDI, M. (2002). The Reform of Bismarckian Pension Systems. A Comparison of Pension Politics in Austria, France, Germany, Italy, and Sweden. Dissertation, Humboldt-Universität zu Berlin. Berlin.

SCHUDLICH, E. (1982). Kooperation statt Korporatismus. In: U. Billerbeck (ed.), *Korporatismus und gewerkschaftliche Interessenvertretung.* Frankfurt am Main: Campus, pp. 127–75.

SILVIA, S. J. (1997). German Unification and Emerging Divisions within German Employers' Associations: Cause of Catalyst? *Comparative Politics* 29(2): 187–208.

STOLLEIS, M. (2003). *Geschichte des Sozialrechts in Deutschland.* Stuttgart: Lucius & Lucius.

STREECK, W. (2003). From State Weakness as Strength to State Weakness as Weakness, Welfare Corporatism and the Private Use of the Public Interest. MPIfG Working Paper, 03/2. Köln: Max-Planck-Institut für Gesellschaftsforschung.

—— and HASSEL, A. (2003). The Crumbling Pillars of Social Partnership. In: H. Kitschelt and W. Streeck (eds.), *Germany Beyond the Stable State.* Special Issue of West European Politics 26(4): 100–24.

TRAMPUSCH, C. (2002). Die Bundesanstalt für Arbeit und das Zusammenwirken von Staat und Verbänden in der Arbeitsmarktpolitik von 1952 bis 2001. MPIfG Working Paper, 02/5. Köln: Max-Planck-Institut für Gesellschaftsforschung.

—— (2003). Ein Bündnis für die nachhaltige Finanzierung der Sozialversicherungssysteme: Interessenvermittlung in der deutschen Arbeitsmarkt- und Rentenpolitik. MPIfG Discussion Paper, 03/1. Köln: Max-Planck-Institut für Gesellschaftsforschung.

VDR (Verband der Deutschen Rentenversicherungsträger) (2004). Versicherungsrenten nach Rentenarten—RV Männer, Frankfurt am Main. Available at www.vdr.de/ internet/vdr/statzr.nsf/($URLRef)/DB3A6D55E0AE07CCC1256AEE003DB4BD/$FILE /rvz31pub.xls.

VOGLER-LUDWIG, K. (1990). Betriebszeit der Produktionsanlagen. *Ifo-Schnelldienst* 43(1–2): 3–8.

WEIR, M. (1992). Ideas and the Politics of Bounded Innovation. In: S. Steinmo, K. Thelen, and F. Longstreth (eds.), *Structuring Politics. Historical Institutionalism in Comparative Analysis.* Cambridge: Cambridge University Press, pp. 188–216.

WENZEL, W. (1979). Zur Geschichte und Entwicklung von Sozialplänen in der Bundesrepublik Deutschland. In Autorengemeinschaft (ed.), *Sozialplanpolitik in der Eisen- und Stahlindustrie—Mit ausgewählten Sozialplänen.* Köln: Bund-Verlag, pp. 11–26.

WIESENTHAL, H. (1987). *Strategie und Illusion. Rationalitätsgrenzen kollektiver Akteure am Beispiel der Arbeitszeitpolitik 1980–1985.* Frankfurt am Main: Campus Verlag.

WSI (Wirtschafts- und Sozialwissenschaftliches Institut der Hans-Böckler-Stiftung) (2001). Tarifarchiv, Düsseldorf. Available at www.tarifarchiv.de.

ZWIENER, R. (1993). Zu den Effekten der Arbeitszeitverkürzung in den achtziger Jahren. In: P. Hampe (ed.), *Zwischenbilanz der Arbeitszeitverkürzung.* München: Verlag Hase & Koehler, pp. 91–103.

9

Contested Boundaries: Ambiguity and Creativity in the Evolution of German Codetermination

Gregory Jackson

> to say that it is ambiguous is to assert that its meaning is never fixed, that it must be constantly won.
>
> (The Ethics of Ambiguity, Simone de Beauvoir)
>
> It was all different; that, at least, seemed sure. We still agreed—but only that she'd changed.
>
> (Mutability, W. D. Snodgrass)

Institutions are commonly seen as formal and informal 'rules of the game' that provide economic agents with incentives and constraints, and thereby induce stable patterns of behavior.[1] Institutional constraints from political, legal, and social environments often lead to institutional isomorphism whereby organizations adopt similar structures and routines (Meyer and Rowan 1977). Institutional theory has thus offered powerful explanations of why organizations have diverse responses to similar economic pressures.[2] Conversely, institutions may present comparative advantages for different types of activities (Streeck 1992; Whitley 1999; Hall and Soskice 2001). These insights have laid a valuable foundation for international comparisons of business, corporate governance, or industrial relations.

Institutional change has nonetheless remained a theoretical puzzle. Institutional theory itself falls into several distinct paradigms that characterize the creation, stability, and change of institutions differently (Powell and DiMaggio 1991; Hall and Taylor 1996; Thelen 1999). Institutions may be seen in regulative, normative, or cognitive terms. But institutional analysis generally shares an emphasis on the constraining character of institutions. To the extent that behavior is consistent with institutional rules (choice-within-constraints), institutional change seems almost inevitably exogenous.[3] Meanwhile, institutions remain resistant to change because of increasing returns, sunk costs, complementarities between different institutions, or power differentials that make change largely path dependent (Mahoney 2000).

In this chapter, I argue that understanding institutional change requires taking seriously the ambiguity of social life. Institutions may reduce uncertainty,[4] but the meaning of an institution is never completely clear. Actors face institutions in ever changing situations. Institutionalized rules and expectations represent these contingencies in only general terms, and can often be interpreted in more than one way.

The social boundaries and interpretations of what an institution demands or allows may remain ambiguous. Ambiguity leads actors to continually reinterpret institutional opportunities and constraints, as well as adapt and modify institutional rules. Since institutions remain an imperfect guide for action, actors may 'discover' new faces of an institution over time through learning, experimentation, and historical accidents. Likewise, ambiguity gives scope for contention and conflict over the meaning of an institution. Many institutions are based on political compromises whose contents are only loosely defined. Such ambiguity may help appeal to (or limited objections from) a wide range of actors *ex ante*, but requires continuous working out and renegotiation in particular local situations *ex post*.

This chapter explores the role of ambiguity and creativity in processes of institutional change both theoretically and empirically. The chapter first provides a theoretical discussion about ambiguity drawing upon recent sociological conceptions of action, and then relates ambiguity to the concept of institutions as 'summary representation' of a strategic game (Aoki 2001). This concept is closely related to 'typifications' where under certain conditions X, a particular type of actor Y is expected to do Z (Berger and Luckmann 1966), or generalized values that make diverse contingencies comparable across different situations and networks of actors (White 1992). While institutions coordinate expectations, ambiguity may remain that poses an interpretive gap to be filled. Actors may thus gain scope for strategic responses to institutions (Oliver 1991) that involve creative reinterpretation and redeployment for new purposes.

Next, the chapter examines the role of ambiguity in the empirical case of German codetermination. Codetermination refers to a complex set of legal and social institutions that shape employee participation in company decisionmaking through works councils and representation in the Supervisory Boards of large firms. Since its origin in the nineteenth century, codetermination survived major economic shocks, as well as social and political upheavals. But the continuity in formal legal rules contrasts with remarkable diversity as an organizational practice—over time, across industrial sectors and between individual firms.

Initially, codetermination developed through state intervention into the private social order of the firm in an effort to integrate employees, but also circumvent independent unions. This political compromise resulted in a dual orientation of works councils to represent the interests of employees, but promote cooperation with management in the interests of the company. This ambiguous role left many latent alternatives that could develop in different directions. Unions first saw codetermination as a paternalistic firm-based rival to industrial unionism, but later came to embrace and utilize codetermination to project union power onto the shop floor. Likewise, management opposed codetermination, but later learned to use codetermination as a means to reduce postwar labor conflicts and improve employee commitment in support of Germany's high-skill, high-quality manufacturing sector. Recently the postwar compromise is being renegotiated again in light of new capital market pressures and corporate governance reforms.

Codetermination illustrates how ambiguity originated in political compromise, and also how ambiguous agreement allows scope for institutional innovation.

Actors continue to contest the various boundaries of codetermination—between public intervention and private ordering; the scope of sectors and firms and issues subject to codetermination; or the balance between cooperation and interest representation within the firm. Since ambiguity remains what codetermination is or should do, actors may pull institutions in different directions as new situations emerge. This stretching of horizons involves new sorts of strategic behavior, including conflict over how rules are to be interpreted and renegotiation over how to apply them. But rather than undergoing wholesale breakdown and replacement, codetermination has evolved in a very incremental fashion through what Streeck and Thelen (see Introduction) call institutional 'conversion'. Ambiguity is thus central for understanding how codetermination was partially reproduced and partially changed over time.

Grounding institutional change in pragmatic social action

Institutional change presents a puzzle, in no small part, due to a rather 'oversocialized' view of how institutions shape action. If institutions are coercive, normative, or cognitively taken-for-granted rules that constrain action, how may actors change their relationships to those constraints in ways that transform institutions?[5] Institutions coordinate individual behavior as 'summary representations' (Aoki 2001) or 'typifications' (Berger and Luckmann 1966) or 'values' generalized across situations (White 1992). While institutions thus constrain action, substantial indeterminacy and situational ambiguity remain. However, the gap between institutional constraint and intentional action has not been sufficiently explored within institutional theory.[6]

Indeterminacy and ambiguity are often neglected because most social science implicitly relies on a teleological conception of action. In *The Creativity of Action*, German sociologist Hans Joas (1992) reviewed existing theories of action and demonstrates the predominance of means-ends schema for understanding of human intentionality. Here action is conceived as the pursuit of preestablished ends or preferences that remain stable from context to context. The perception of the world is given, and is separate from our actions. Actions are then 'chosen' by their anticipated consequences—in what might be termed 'portfolio models' of the actor (Whitford 2002). The rational choice variant postulates maximizing on a fixed order of preferences, but normative models also tend to only 'tinker' with this view by widening the portfolio to include social norms. Both views take ends as given preferences, norms, or worldviews exogenous to the framework. The cognitive or practical model of action used recently in institutional theorizing (DiMaggio and Powell 1991) is potentially different, since action involves enacting preconceived and taken-for-granted worldviews. Routines and taken-for-granted concepts may constitute a 'toolkit' for creative action. Yet even this view brackets how individuals interpret and evaluate their choices in dialogue with situations. Action is focused on the choice of appropriate means, and creative dimensions of human behavior remain unexplained.

Alternatives to a teleological view of action are not yet well developed. But pragmatist thinkers such as John Dewey and George Herbert Mead suggest important elements. Drawing upon their works, Joas (1992) suggests the concept of 'situation' as a basic category. Our actions do not follow predefined ends, but particular 'ends-in-view' emerge concretely out of situations. Ends-in-view are based on judgments and assumptions about the type of situation and the possible actions that flow from it. Conversely, the situation itself is not a fixed, objective given. Situations are interpreted and defined in relation to our capacities for action. Starting from the situation, action follows a series of various ends-in-view that remain relatively undefined at first, but are specified through ongoing reinterpretation and decisions about means. Actors test out and revise their courses of action as each end-in-view itself becomes a means for a further end-in-view. Means and ends flow in a continuous stream—the distinction between them is only an analytical and temporal one.

Pragmatism matters for institutional theory because it reminds us of the potential ambiguity of institutions. Pragmatism suggests an ongoing 'reorganization and reconstitution of habits and institutions' occurs in dialogue with new and changing situations (Joas 1992: 24). Institutions are just one element of a situation, and actors pull institutions in different directions within this horizon through acts of problem solving. Institutional rules do not anticipate every contingency, and actors initially imagine only a limited set of the potential ends to which an institution can be used. No one-to-one relationship exists between an institution and its meaning in a specific situation (Friedland and Alford 1991: 255). Exploring and achieving these meanings through interpretation also opens institutions to active political contestation (Zilber 2002).

Ambiguity thus involves perceived discrepancies between a problem situation and institutionalized rules or routines. But unlike uncertainty or vagueness, ambiguity suggests institutions can take on two or more specific meanings. Such multiplicity of meanings is commonplace as institutions become part of changed situational horizons and ends-in-view. Ambiguous contexts allow scope for creative action through processes of iteration, projection and evaluation (Emirbayer and Mische 1998).[7] Just as well-crafted ambiguity is central for literary metaphor, it is also a powerful catalyst for creativity in social contexts. Creativity is not a mysterious leap as often implied. Rather, creativity is a bounded process that arises from practical situations, but transcends them through contingency, reflexive intentionality, and experimentation (Beckert 2002: 269–81). Actors may thereby reinterpret and adapt institutions to suit new purposes—what Streeck and Thelen call institutional conversion (see Introduction).

Ambiguity and institutional change

To elaborate on the above point, I first introduce a framework for institutional analysis proposed by Masahiko Aoki (2001). This framework incorporates elements of the rational/economic approaches and cognitive/sociological approaches to institutions. It also highlights institutionalization as a dynamic process of reproduction, disruption, and responses to disruption (Clemens and Cook 1999).

	Exogenous	Endogenous
Micro (individual) dimension	(A) Capacities as active repertoires	(S) Strategies as best-response choice
Macro (collective) dimension	(CO) Consequences through inference rules	(E) Expectations as private beliefs
	(I) Institutions as shared beliefs	

Figure 9.1 A subjective game model of institutionalization
Source: Adapted from Aoki (2001).

In his game-theoretic framework, Aoki (2001: 202) defines institutions as a 'compressed, commonly perceived representation of ways in which a game is played'. His definition builds from feedback mechanisms represented by the COASE box whose four elements are reconstructed in Figure 9.1 (Aoki 2001: 203–6). Subjective expectations (E) about the behavior of other actors coordinate the strategic choices of individual agents (S). This allows individuals to economize on information, while their choices are thereby constrained. As expectations are shared and serve as stable guides for strategy, collective behavior comes to confirm and reinforce such expectations about others' strategic choices. Institutions also have consequences (CO) within a given technological and institutional environment that constrain the sets of feasible actions (A) and shape the capacities for action accumulated by actors.

For Aoki (2001: 231), institutional change 'may be identified with a situation where agents' beliefs on the ways a game is played are altered in critical mass . . . In effect, understanding the process of institutional change may be tantamount to understanding the ways in which the agents revise their beliefs in a coordinated manner'. A 'cognitive disequilibrium' emerges between expectations and actual outcomes. Actors question their expectations, perceive existing capacities as inadequate, and seek new strategies. Disequilibrium may be triggered by consequences (CO) of environmental change such as war, financial market collapse, rising costs of the welfare state, etc. Or changed capacities for action (A) may alter strategic options. New capacities may result from learning or accumulation of power. Capacities may also be lost due to exposure to competition or generational change, thereby exhausting preconditions for past strategies. Institutional change begins as actors begin to experiment with, learn, or emulate new strategies (S). New strategies may remain marginal. But beyond a certain scale, shared beliefs (E) undergo a crisis and face competition with other beliefs.

A narrow reading of the COASE box might equate a given objective set of consequences and capacities with a given institutional equilibrium. The term 'equilibrium' seems to denote a discrete and stable state, whereas change occurs through the breakdown of one equilibrium and replacement with another. However, Aoki (2001: 243) cautions against drawing too stark a contrast between periods of stability and transition. Aoki stresses a subjective notion of games wherein institutions are a focal point around which a range of behavior emerges. Here expectations (E) involve both shared cognition and private beliefs. Consequences (CO) are not objectively known, but only inferred by actors and may therefore be unintended. Capacities for action (A) are only a subset of all technologically feasible actions based on active repertoires. And strategies (S) are based on incomplete information that may be revised through information gathering. While these features appear as exogenous and fixed in the short-term, they must be considered variable in the long run because they can be incrementally altered through the operation of the institution itself (Greif 2004). Unintended consequences accumulate, repertoires for action evolve, and new information leads to strategic experiments that challenge institutionalized expectations.

When seen in action-theoretic terms, institutions represent situations in a summary form that must remain loose enough to be transposable across situations, but specific enough to allow actors to mobilize efforts of control in enforcing an institution (White 1992). Institutions often remain ambiguous. More than one set of behaviors may be consistent with an institution. One strong implication is that institutionalization is not a discrete state, but a matter of degree (Jepperson 1991). In the extreme, Erving Goffman (1961) used the metaphor of a 'total institution' where all situations are governed by an institution and action is only possible 'backstage' through deviations in the performance of fixed roles. But while some institutions may be rigidly prescriptive (actors 'must' follow a certain rule), others may establish more limited boundaries of what is not possible (actors 'must not' do something), and others may provide only loose models around which actors engage in substantial improvisation (Crawford and Ostrom 1995). Allowing for the ambiguous nature of 'summary representations' within the COASE framework helps us understand how institutional change may occur through incremental modification, rather than breakdown and replacement of equilibrium outcomes.

Reinterpretation and conversion (E & S)

Within the COASE framework, expectations or values (E) coordinate strategic choices (S). Institutions rest on expectations and values about how actors behave in a range of situations. Yet different degrees of ambiguity confront actors as they attempt to enact institutionalized behaviors or pursue new ends-in-view at the boundaries of institutions. Ambiguity arises as situational contexts shift and create questions about how expectations apply to a particular situation or whether a strategy is actually consistent with expected norms or values. Such ambiguity may remain local and without any impact on the institution.

However, ambiguity may also become more global to an institution as a result of repeated collisions or tensions among different 'faces' of an institution. While institutions are defined as 'shared beliefs' or 'common understandings', Aoki (2001: 202) also mentions how 'the variety of meanings attached to an established institution by agents in different roles may be identified as ideologies'. Conflict is often built into institutions. Interpretation is not merely a technical issue, but involves a micro-politics where underlying conflicts of interest may lead to contention across different groups. If institutions are capable of being understood in more than one way, gaps between institutionalized expectation (e.g. rule or value) and strategic action must be filled by creative interpretation, application, and enactment. Actors must test out different courses of action, and these may lead to the mutability or reinterpretation of an institution (Clemens and Cook 1999: 448) or the conversion of institutions to new ends and purposes (Thelen 2003). The implications of ambiguity will be briefly discussed in relation to the consequences of institutional interdependence (CO) and the capacities of actors (A).

Reconfiguration (CO)

A non-teleological perspective implies that action has multiple effects that are hard to estimate *ex ante*. Institutions gain autonomy to the degree that contingencies and consequences can be externalized from the action context across a boundary of two institutional domains. But any institution exists within a complex environment of where the consequences (CO) of one institution constitute the environment for another institution to different degrees.[8] Recent work uses the concept of *institutional complementarities* to describe reenforcing properties, where one institution becomes more viable given the presence of a corresponding institution elsewhere (Milgrom and Roberts 1995; Aoki 2001; Hall and Soskice 2001). But what may be functional in one domain may lead to dysfunction in another. *Institutional tensions* may arise that destabilize or disrupt the reproduction of another institution. Institutions often embody conflicting principles of rationality, as stressed within Weberian sociology (Lepsius 1990; Sewell 1992: 16–19). Of course, contradictory principles may sometimes serve to balance inherent weaknesses, such as institutionalized power sharing between property rights and employee codetermination (Dahrendorf's 'institutionalized class conflict'), majority rule and constitutional rule of law, or free markets and product regulation.

We can refer to changing relationships between different institutions generally as institutional *reconfiguration*.[9] The concepts of 'unintended fit' between institutions (Aoki 1997) or 'unintended consequences' reflect the mutual adjustment of institutions as an ongoing process needed to reduce ambiguities, debug frictions, and establish satisfactory performance. Institutional tensions may provoke modification, adaptation, and repair of an institution. But often tensions exert strong contradictory pressures that lead political actors or organizations to deal with institutional dilemmas by dealing with one 'face' of the problem at a time, while exacerbating another 'face' whose consequences will have to be dealt with later in time—sometimes beyond the lifetime of those actors. These all represent potential endogenous dynamics for institutional change.

Changing capacities for action (A)

This may produce institutional change even under broadly stable institutional rules. Stark (2001) uses the term 'ambiguous assets' to describe how existing resources may be used to new ends. Likewise, cognitive schemas may be transposed to new situations. Institutions also vest power that becomes a means to new ends. The incorporation of new groups into an institution may thus introduce new capacities for action unforeseen when the institution was created (Thelen 2003). Finally, emergent processes such as experimentation, learning, and emulation may all lead to new organizational or individual capacities (Levitt and March 1988). While capacities are often seen as skills and resources, a broader discussion might also include *values* as a capacity for institutionalizing behavior. Values arise in experiences of self-formation and self-transcendence that lead to enduring modifications of the self—both through positive and negative experiences (Joas 1997). While noneconomic value commitments may become important elements of economic institutions, their instrumentalization in service of utilitarian aims may erode those very values. Here the experiential basis of those value commitments fails to be reproduced, and cannot be reproduced on the basis of rational utilitarian calculation alone.

In sum, ambiguity plays an important role in understanding how institutions may be reproduced in varied ways. Ambiguity implies an interpretative gap between situations and institutions. But unlike the breakdown implied by 'cognitive disequilibrium', ambiguity stresses the potential scope for creative reinterpretation and innovative deployment of institutions for new ends-in-view. The COASE framework points to different sources of ambiguity. Ambiguity may be local and situational, but may also result from reinterpretation through diverse ideological lenses or contention over institutionalized compromises. Ambiguity may also result from efforts to adjust institutions to changed consequences of its institutional environment, resulting in a reconfiguration across different institutional domains. And changing capacities may lead to reinterpretation of institutions in light of changed values or new resources for action. Whether such variation leads to 'institutional change' depends on a critical mass.[10]

Institutional change: the case of codetermination in Germany

This section turns to an empirical examination of ambiguity in the case of German codetermination. German codetermination displays remarkable continuities since the nineteenth century. Yet the stability of legal rules contrasts with its diversity as a social institution that has coevolved with shifts in ideas, power relationships, and coalition building among company stakeholders (Jackson 2001). This section presents only a brief historical sketch to highlight some theoretical themes.

Codetermination rests on a contradictory imperative. Works councils should represent the interests of employees, while pursuing peaceful cooperation with management in the interests of the firm. This duality has made codetermination a highly ambiguous, but remarkably adaptable institution. The balance between representation and cooperation has undergone shifts in response to new economic demands and sociopolitical circumstances. New constellations of actors emerged, and led to contention and reinterpretation of codetermination. As shall be discussed below, the history of codetermination can thus be divided into several distinct phases as a repressive paternalistic institution, a platform of revolutionary socialism, an element of political democratization and social partnership, and a style of comanagement shaping how German firms adapt to international capital market pressures (see Table 9.1).

Political origins of ambiguity (Imperial and Weimar Germany)

The idea of 'codetermination' (*Mitbestimmung*) arose in the mid-nineteenth century having complex roots in Christian, socialist, and romantic philosophies, as well as the notion of parity (*Parität*) and economic democracy (Teuteberg 1961, 1981). Codetermination represented a socially integrative alternative to revolution or socialism, but had different meanings to different people. Employees framed codetermination as a demand for 'industrial citizenship' often analogous to constitutional rights in politics. Employers saw it as a paternalistic practice that used employee representation in company welfare schemes as a way to foster employee loyalty.

Table 9.1 Codetermination as an institution: a schematic overview

	Imperial Germany	Weimar	Postwar	1990s
Codetermination	Coercive paternalism	Contested authority	Social partnership	Comanagement
State	Repression, co-optation	Democratization	Further democratization	Regime competition
Management	Herr-im-Haus, paternalism	Resistance	Increasing recognition of labor	Challenge of shareholder-value paradigm
Unions	Weak	Fear of syndicalism	Political demand, enabling codetermination as a long arm of unions	Framework agreements, decentralization
Employees	Struggle for political citizenship	Political revolution, individual interests	Experience of reconstruction, quality of life issues	Individualization

An increasingly nonliberal German state (Lehmbruch 2001) used codetermination as a strategy of intervention to co-opt labor with the goal of circumventing unions and dampening political support for socialism. Following the 1889 coal mining strike and the rise of the Social Democrats in the 1890 *Reichstag* elections, commercial code reforms gave workers' committees limited consultation rights in 1891. Following another strike in 1905, the state required the work rules of the mines to have consent from a workers committee (Weisbrod 1989).[11] These committees restricted employer prerogatives, but also circumvented independent labor unions. Councils gained little acceptance among management, who clung to autocratic and paternalist models of authority captured by the phrase *Herr im Haus* (Braun, Eberwein, and Tholen 1992: 193–8). Unions likewise retained an ambivalent stance.

During the First World War, wartime 'industrial truce' integrated the Social Democrats and labor unions into national politics (Feldman 1966). Employee mobility was restricted within war-related industries, and the state scrambled to maintain order in industrial production. The Patrial Auxiliary Service Law of 1916 mandated elected workers' committees that held rights for consultation regarding the 'demands, wishes and complaints of the work force with regard to the factory, wage and other employment conditions and the social welfare policy of the firm' (Teuteberg 1961: 511). The controversial law gave councils more power than anticipated because the War Ministry was directly involved with the mediation of disputes. To avoid binding decisions by the state, employers sought cooperation with councils.

Following the war, conflicting views of codetermination existed. Employers saw councils as a temporary wartime institution, whereas union demanded for their extension. Here the changing political circumstances help put works councils on a new footing—specifically, the revolutionary council movement and political democracy of the Weimar state. The new state sought to limit the revolutionary council movement by institutionalizing a less radical version. Codetermination was a right anchored in the Weimar constitution and the Works Councils Law (Betriebsrätegesetz) passed in 1920. The law mandated the formation of works councils with parity representation of blue- and white-collar employees in all establishments with over twenty employees. The supplementary law passed in 1922 allowed the works council to also send two employee representatives to the Supervisory Board.

The law contained many features of contemporary codetermination: the obligation toward peaceful cooperation of the works council in the interests of the firm, the separation of collective bargaining from the activities of works councils, and codecision rights in personnel affairs of the firm. The works council had a 'dual' role in representing the independent interests of workers while supporting the business interests of the employer (Fuerstenberg 1958). Unions made sure that works councils did not engage in collective bargaining, while employers sought the obligation to cooperation. From the mid-1920s, works councils spread to around half of all plants with over fifty employees (Plumpe 1992). Yet despite their new footing, works councils remained a somewhat weak institution. A seminal article by Kurt Brigl-Matthiass (1926) documents the highly ambiguous social context of Weimar works councils which faced contradictory pressures from three conflicting 'faces' of codetermination—as representatives of rank-and-file employees, as part of the broader labor movement alongside political parties and industry-wide unions, and in their legal relationship of cooperation with management.

First, works councils faced strong pressures to respond to the material interests of rank and file workers due to election rules, short terms in office, and close social contact. To maintain legitimacy, works councilors were pressured to take even 'irrational' demands of employees to the management. Conflictual tactics were often employed to demonstrate independence from management, even when cooperation with management was clearly needed. These shop floor pressures also created tension with unions. The 'opportunistic' rules negotiated with shop floor management to gain small benefits within the system often contradicted the broader political and solidaristic goals of unions. The position of works councils is much more dependent on the economic situation of the firm than industrial unions, and made councils more likely to cooperate with the management. Unions consequently remained ambivalent toward works councils, which they saw as a possible source of 'syndicalism' that would undermine union discipline and capacity for multiemployer collective bargaining.

Second, works councils remained part of the political labor movement aimed at transforming the political and economic order. Many councilors were members of socialist political parties, and often the large works councils were factionalized along party lines. Councils spread socialist political propaganda within the company, and sometimes attempted to restrict management authority in the name of socialist workers' democracy. Where works councils became more politicized, their focus moved away from the pragmatic goals of shaping working conditions and created a wide gap with the business concerns of management.

Trade union agendas also played an important role in coordinating works council demands across firms—for example, opposition to overtime in order to realize the 8-h work day. Unions also provided auxiliary support through economic and legal advice. Such linkages with trade unions were crucial in giving works councils a greater capacity for independence from the management. Despite increasing educational opportunities for the working classes through *Volkshochschulen* and popular publications, lack of education greatly limited the capacity of works councils given their insufficient knowledge to make informed judgments about business and legal matters.

Third, the internal and external relations of works councils influenced the capacity of works councils to make credible commitments in cooperating with company management. Employers had politically opposed the Works Council Law, but their experiences with the councils were mixed (Plumpe 1992: 43–55). Political turmoil and the rise of social democracy made labor the single reliable bargaining power. Some employers learned to use the works council as an instrument of constructive communication within the firm. Works councils served as a vent for employee unrest and helped renew the legitimacy of management following the breakdown of authority following the war. Lesser industrial conflict came at the price of increased negotiations and smaller conflicts on a daily basis. Elsewhere, steel firms and employers' associations continued strong opposition, particularly to board representation, and sought to discourage cooperative relations between firms and works councils.

Codetermination thus developed through a state strategy to co-opt labor in the absence of political democracy. But codetermination was built on a wide array of cultural frames and was interpreted by key actors through the lens of very divergent values: company loyalty, the firm as family or community, or codetermination as negotiation among independent parties. The emerging institution remained ideologically charged and its role highly ambiguous. During Weimar, the growing independence of the labor movement did not lead to the end of codetermination, but its reinterpretation. Works councils were liberated from their paternalist origins, but many of their internal and external contradictions were sharpened. Shop floor constituents, unions, and management all pulled works councils in different directions. Works councils remained based on very uneasy compromises, rather than consensus about their legitimate role. Codetermination resulted in a wide diversity of practices spanning from pragmatic cooperation to extreme distrust. This social experiment was then interrupted as the Nazi regime eliminated organized labor and reorganized councils as new 'councils of trust' based on the notion of organic relations between firm and employees as part of a coerced national community.

Democratization and social partnership (1945–60s)

After the Nazi period, codetermination reemerged during postwar democratization. Codetermination found new political legitimacy by being reinterpreted in light of Nazism and postwar reconstruction. While key actors continued to have different visions of codetermination, codetermination stood in a somewhat less ambiguous relationship to the existing social and economic order. The door was opened to substantial institutional innovation beyond the legacies of prewar codetermination.

The first councils arose spontaneously during the immediate aftermath of the war. Their activities concerned the immediate reconstruction and reopening of production plants, as well as housing and rationing of food. Employers did not oppose council efforts to assist in the immediate aftermath of the war. Labor was sometimes able to gain representation in the Supervisory Board and elect a labor director to the management board. Many council members were anti-fascist or communist party members who created personal continuities with the Weimar works councils, influencing their early capabilities and ideological bents.

Meanwhile, employers contemplated how to deal with the councils in the absence of legal norms. The 1920 Works Council Law was an important reference point and signified the maximum scope of rights (Mueller 1987: 76–85). A variety of models emerged in practice, particularly concerning board representation. Unions were cautious in taking a stance. After twelve years of illegality, German unions scrambled to rebuild themselves. They could not easily return to their political program of the Weimar era, although concepts such as 'democratization of the economy' or 'codetermination' reappeared. Socialism continued to play a role, but was supplemented by a broader aim to prevent the political abuse of economic power in war-related industries. Union thus had an ambiguous set of positions, aiming to both transform the existing economic order and participate in the existing order through codetermination. This ambiguity itself helped the left achieve consensus by speaking in general terms to its various factions, while allowing a wide range of policies to be legitimated *ex post*.

The Allies intervened to encourage works councils in the coal and steel industry through the Control Council Law (KRG) in 1946. Due to differing positions among the Allied authorities, the law only vaguely defined rights and duties. Ambiguities were later worked out by negotiated agreements. Rights were substantially expanded in firms with strong union presence, while weaker firms fell behind the standard of the 1920 law. A key question was how to interpret the KRG Paragraph 22 (Mueller 1987: 94–101). Unions sought a legal guarantee for boardroom representation and participation in economic affairs. However, employers saw this interpretation as too broad, since the law did not specify limits. Many employers opposed council demands for representation within the supervisory and management boards. Employers associations feared that generous agreements at particular firms might set precedents that would place unwanted pressure to expand codetermination rights. While the unions also supported uniform legal rights in principle, strategically they hoped firm-level agreements would create facts that positively affected legal developments.

Meanwhile, a separate solution developed in the iron and steel industry. In August 1946, the Allies took direct control of the sector through the North German Iron and Steel Control (NGISC). The Allies planned to break-up the industry into some thirty new firms to avoid the concentration of economic power among industrialists (who had supported the Nazis) in this militarily important industry. NGISC faced the issue of membership in the Supervisory Boards in these newly created companies. Here the British authorities sought employee representation into the boards as a balance of power in the absence of a functioning German state and given the mistrust of industrialists. Some employers supported these practices by entering into pragmatic alliances with the works councils in an effort to stall plans for further dismantling or socialization of industry.

These practices later influenced national legislation. In 1950 the West German state was established and firms again fell under German corporate law, which provided no codetermination rights. The metalworkers' union called for a strike in 1951, leading to the involvement of Chancellor Adenauer in brokering Law on Codetermination in the Mining and Iron and Steel Industries (*Montanmitbestimmung*). The law mandated the parity model of Supervisory

Board within the coal and steel industries. Even here, however, the boundaries of the *Montan* model remained sharply contested (Teuteberg 1981: 58–60). In 1953, legal conflicts about the application to holding companies erupted. The 1958 'Luedenscheid Agreement' used private works agreements to contractually preserve codetermination rights where independent companies were reintegrated into parent companies. And in 1967 and 1971, laws were passed that aimed to prevent the defection of particular firms from the *Montan* model. Meanwhile, other sectors followed a weaker model as unions proved unable to realize their demands due to opposition by the liberal coalition partner (Freie Demokratische Partei, FDP) and employers. The 1952 Works Constitution Act mandated only one-third of Supervisory Board seats for labor, more limited rights for works councils, and no provisions for a labor director in the management board.

Despite the success of the *Montan* model, employees interpreted this institution in diverse ways (Popitz et al. 1957: 156–63). Interviews of steel workers from the 1950s show a high degree of indifference and resignation toward codetermination—few practical effects were perceived and workers remained skeptical about the development of durable codetermination as the postwar crisis receded. Furthermore, socialist workers rejected codetermination as a detrimental compromise. Only about one-third of workers reported a positive evaluation of codetermination. These workers perceived codetermination in pragmatic terms, but did relate participation in the workplace to greater societal and political democracy. Their values were closely related to their experiences in the postwar reconstruction of factories (p. 177). More than political ideologies or agendas, this collective memory was decisive for establishing the legitimacy of codetermination for this generation.

The *Montan* sectors also proved to be highly innovative in applying the rules in ways that influenced the development of codetermination. The formal legal rights stronger, the management and labor were also able to develop new capacities through dense social networks. These social networks outside the firm were important in promoting learning effects, stabilizing expectations, and generating new organizational capacities. On the management side, a working group developed among the personnel department staff from various establishments and enterprises. This group had twenty-five to thirty members meeting twice a month, plus convening with the union for two days a year. The union also became progressively less hostile to works councils and promoted them as an 'extended arm' of unionism within the factory. Specifically, unions provided extensive legal and educational services to works council members, helping to upgrade their competence on economic issues. The regional office of the IG Metall also played an important role as the sources of nominations for labor directors. As the industry faced crisis and decline in the 1970s, this strong local culture of cooperation proved to be the source of extremely innovative employment adjustment policies that relied on a strong comanagement role of works councils in negotiating new practices. Many negotiated rights were incorporated in later national legislation.

Diffusion and consolidation in the 1970s and 1980s

As the postwar generation began to retire, a new younger generation began to emerge as shop stewards and union activists in the late 1960s. These stewards challenged the practices of the works councils in attempting to 'risk more democracy' within the economic sphere. Unlike works councils, local union branches and shop stewards had no obligation to uphold cooperation with the management. Old conflicts reemerged as to whether the labor movement was limited to industrial relations or a society-wide political movement. These challenges from below coincided with peak employment in the German steel industry during 1974 and subsequent period of declining employment.

Meanwhile, sharply contested reforms in 1972 under the Social Democratic Party formalized new rights for works councils (Thelen 1991), and a 1976 revision widened Supervisory Board representation, although it remained weaker than the coal and steel model. Substantial gaps remained between legal principles and organizational practices, leaving substantial ambiguity and heterogeneity across firms. Unions had to struggle at the shop floor level to implement the Works Council Law. A landmark study by Kotthoff (1994) compared the same group of fifty-five firms in 1974/5 and 1989/90, and examined the continuity and change in the role of works councils. Striking evidence was that 53 percent of the firms having deficient interest representation in 1975 had moved toward a more effective and cooperative pattern by 1990. Consequently, the proportion of firms with effective interest representation increased from one-third to two-thirds.

Even more revealing are the patterns of change. The largest change was among firms having works councils under control of a paternalistic management. Here, twelve of the sixteen firms developed more autonomous and effective works councils. By contrast, 'isolated' works councils were reproduced in six of the nine firms. Here, authoritarian styles of management remained unchanged. In only two cases were works councils able to develop greater influence, but through aggressive opposition rather than cooperative negotiation. Kotthoff also points out interesting dynamics at firms with effective works councils in 1975. One typical pattern was a period of stagnation and growing irrelevance of works councils, followed by a revitalization that crystallized around economic crisis and changes of management or works council personnel. But the most common pattern among larger firms was the consolidation of codetermination based on close informal cooperation. Cooperation depends strongly on the personal relationships between the labor director and the head of the works council. Whereas the dual role of the works councils as employee representative and as comanager is ambiguous, it is continuously renegotiated in a very thick local context of interpersonal trust.

The patterns of change show that codetermination, as a formal legal institution, depends closely on how it is socially embedded within patterns of social exchange (e.g. paternalism). This social context is where the ambiguities of the legal doctrine are interpreted and worked out in practice terms. As Kottoff notes:

the patriarchic and paternalistic forms of social order within the factory, which are so common in Germany, were a key prerequisite for transforming conflicts over industrial citizenship into a form of cooperation oriented by the notion of 'codetermination' . . . In factories with more instrumental forms of social order, conflict did not lead to such cooperation, but to spirals of distrust and continuous confrontation.

(Kotthoff 1994: 180, own translation GJ)

Once established, the stability of codetermination also shows how the ambiguity of an institution may support the stability of that institution in the face of external change. Works councils were not only able to shield themselves from internal challenges and factionalism among the employees, but also avoid co-optation by the management that would render it ineffective. Strong personal authority and reputation of the works councilors can help legitimate tough management decisions among employees, but management must honor this too making real concessions. The ambiguous 'dual' mandate gives important flexibility for compromise, but social capital must first be built up to give actors capacities for informal social exchange.

The same importance of social embeddedness applies to the labor director (*Arbeitsdirektor*), particularly union-appointed directors in *Montan* industries. The labor director also has a dual task in representing management, while maintaining the trust of the union and works council. However, if the director favors labor and thereby becomes weak within the board, works councils will not perceive the director as a credible and trustworthy bargaining partner. The complexity of this social milieu places great demands on social skill. Works councilors often point out big differences in the individual qualities of labor directors. Thus, strong labor directors and strong works councils reinforce each other in a positive-sum manner, but each side paradoxically depends on the other side not giving into all their demands. These checks and balances represent a greater social capacity for problem solving.

The diverse patterns of codetermination exist in apparent contention with the fact that codetermination is nearly universally considered to be a stable institution in Germany. Works councils remain unrivaled as the means of interest representation within the firm, and enjoy a high rate of diffusion. But their institutionalization is fraught with challenges. As works councils were recognized by employers and accumulated competence in economic affairs, codetermination took on many new functions and underwent substantial professionalization. Works councils became less deeply embedded within the lifeworld of employees (e.g. lesser input legitimacy), but gained importance in economic governance and the management of employment adjustment (e.g. higher output legitimacy)—particularly in industries such as mining and steel, which were strongholds of labor but underwent massive technical rationalization.

The ambiguity of codetermination and institutional change

In sum, codetermination was fraught with substantial ambiguity from its early days. During different periods, codetermination was deployed to legitimate or enable a very wide range of actions. Codetermination subsequently developed many different 'faces' as it was pulled in different directions—both in political and economic terms. Politically, codetermination was a compromise, resulting from particular state strategies to repress organized labor, employer strategies to maintain a paternalistic authority, and employee strategies to democratize the workplace and establish rights of industrial citizenship. Works councils emerged having a 'dual' mandate to represent the interests of employees and cooperate in the interests of the firm.

Over time, works councils became increasingly cooperative as codetermination took on a growing scope of economic and regulatory functions. However, this required reducing a tension that existed between the broader agenda of German industrial unions and the firm-specific interests of core employees. These tensions were held in check during the 1970s and 1980s, as unions developed capacities to support works councils as a useful extension of their collective aims. Independent unions also strengthened the internal bargaining power of works councils and employee representatives to the Supervisory Board. However, as we shall see, corporate governance reforms since the mid-1990s have swung the pendulum back toward greater tensions given the greater risks and rewards for firms facing capital market pressures.

Ironically, the very ambiguity of codetermination *ex ante* seems to have allowed flexibility in adaptation to new circumstances *ex post*. Codetermination cannot be equated with a specific set of strategic ends or outcomes, but rather a long series of ends-in-view interpreted through a particular shared (albeit ambiguous and contested) set of values. Over time codetermination was put to new purposes— 'institutional conversion'. And only by transforming itself in this way was codetermination sustained as an institution. Change often involved reconfiguration in the light of new institutional and economic environments—such as the emergence of political democracy, industrial unionism, or the internationalization of capital markets. Learning new capacities for action among local networks of actors were important in filling the large gap between codetermination as legal doctrine and an economically beneficial institution of workplace and corporate governance that could be imitated more broadly. For example, innovative norms and practices diffused from coal and steel firms to the rest of the German corporate economy.

The evolution of codetermination suggests institutional change that falls short of crisis or collapse. Codetermination has never given rise to a uniform set of organizational practices. Many local variations or 'styles' of codetermination developed as broad ambiguous institutionalized values were worked out in different local contexts. But this variation in local practices influenced the path of institutional change as synchronic variations unfolded diachronically.

Codetermination under shareholder value: change since the 1990s

The discussion of the postwar era showed that codetermination was no longer seen as an instrument for transforming the economic system into a mixture of capitalist and socialist elements (*Wirtschaftsdemokratie*). Unions accepted that codetermination operates in firms whose goal is to generate cash flows and earnings. Codetermination came to be interpreted as legitimate itself, not only in terms of values of democracy and social inclusion, but increasingly as an efficient model for organizing employment relationships. In terms of its dual mandate, an evolution took place from cooperation to representation, and back to a qualitatively new form of cooperation where both sides see themselves more as partners than as opponents in class confrontation. The scope of codetermination thus moved beyond its legal foundations in social and personal issues to include a wider scope of economic issues that blur boundaries between management functions and codetermination. The 1998 report of the Codetermination Commission (Mitbestimmung 1998) documents the high degree of legitimacy and positive effects of codetermination on social integration and economic cooperation.[12]

While the story of codetermination often ends here, recent trends show that codetermination has continued to change. Since the late 1980s, German capital markets have undergone substantial liberalization and these prompted substantial reforms in corporate governance since the mid-1990s (see Chapter 7 by Deeg). These trends include the weakening of traditional bank monitoring, growth in new institutional investors, expansion of equity-based finance, and the opening of the market for corporate control (Jackson 2003). Changes in corporate governance institutions have strong implications for codetermination, and have led to growing tensions and institutional reconfiguration.

Historically, codetermination evolved as an element of 'organized capitalism' alongside a dense network between banks and large industrial firms. German banks, family owners, or interfirm holdings all represented patient capital that could live with codetermination as long as it delivered cooperation and quality production in the long run, even if decisionmaking and employment adjustment were slower and more costly. But new types of investors face more short-term pressures. Institutional investors focus more exclusively on financial returns, rather than underwriting interfirm cooperation. In addition, regulatory changes have strengthened shareholder rights and promoted greater transparency and disclosure in decisionmaking. Reforms have also enabled greater capital market-orientation by removing past restrictions on managerial stock options, share buy-backs, share swaps, and other uses of equity. This pattern of reform fits well with the concept of institutional layering (see Introduction, Chapter 1 by Streeck and Thelen), since legislation has not sought to directly reform Supervisory Board codetermination but enable boards to engage in new behaviors or follow new social norms embodied in voluntary codes of conduct rather than law.

As a result, many large corporations have adopted new strategies to promote shareholder value. As a criterion of business rationality, shareholder value runs contrary to the normative legitimacy of participation rights and sharing of organ-izational rents that characterize codetermined firms. That is, their logics appear incompatible, at least in principle. The symbolic claims for shareholder primacy have rarely been used as a direct challenge to codetermination given the legal anchoring of codetermination rights. However, the implications of shareholder value for business strategy confront codetermination with new economic problems that typically provoke conflicts:

- Focus on *core competencies* creates conflicts with employees over the defini-tion of core business units and strategies of growth by diversification used to stabilize employment. Divestment from noncore units raises issues of finding good buyers who honor existing employment agreements.

- Ending cross-subsidization of business units and establishing *equity-oriented performance* targets create conflicts over performance criteria, profitability hurdles, time horizons, and disciplining poorly performing units. Greater independence of business units may weaken solidarity among employees being more directly exposed to market risks and rewards.

- *Performance-oriented pay* raises issues of balancing individual and group incentives, defining performance criteria, and the risks of contingent pay. Managerial stock options provoked controversy over income inequality and short-termism.

- Increased *disclosure* and market-oriented accounting may conflict with buffering risks through internal reserves and favor higher distribution of profits to shareholders. However, improving investor information may also increase transparency for employee representatives.

Several recent studies document the role of codetermination under share-holder-value (Hoepner 2001, 2003; Hoepner and Jackson 2001; Jackson, Hoepner, and Kurdelbasch 2004). In many ways strong ambiguities exist between codeter-mination and shareholder value that have left much leeway for mutual adjustment in practice. Works councils may retain their basis of power through continued cooperation with management, while minimizing the negative impact on core employees (Kotthoff 1998). Cooperative works councils may promote a relatively enlightened or incremental and long-term approach to corporate restructuring that helps curtail excessive short-term pressures. But these continu-ities also bring change. Managers are using this cooperation to new ends and thereby modifying the functions of codetermination in light of capital market pressures and changing boundaries of firms.

For example, corporate restructuring during the 1990s resulted in a modest redistribution of corporate wealth from employees to shareholders (Beyer and Hassel 2002). Shareholder value strategies favor lower rates of internal growth and declining employment, while raising targeted return on investment. Management negotiated adjustment by maintaining but modifying commitments to core employees, while allowing the core of stable employment to shrink. This com-promise resulted in the increased use of negotiated employment adjustment and benevolent methods such as natural fluctuation, early retirement, part-time work, etc.[13] Works councils have become active in negotiating site pacts to preserve high value-added production (Rehder 2001). But in order to assure investment in core plants, works councils grant cost-cutting concessions: lower social standards, the elimination of premium wages above collective bargaining rates, or cuts in bonuses for overtime and shift work. Employment alliances are also made through concessions on wages or working hours in exchange for employment guarantees. Work may also be redistributed through reduced or flexible working time, or made cheaper by reducing company premiums above collective rates. Thus, while works councils retain a strong role, the boundaries of codetermination itself are shrinking.

The restructuring of business portfolios also plays into otherwise latent rank-and-file pressures on works councils. While employees may prefer a solidaristic policy of diversification to maintain employment, they often 'discover' new interests as business units face very different fortunes. Core employees may prefer a stronger core business, rather than continued support for ailing businesses that are less central economically. For example, at *Mannesmann* before the hostile takeover, both employee representatives and shareholders pressed the management into planning hive-offs of several major divisions. Traditional machine tools employees wanted to secure more investment, rather than cross-subsidizing expansion into new areas. Meanwhile, telecommunications employees preferred separation to avoid the conglomerate discount of their share price that made acquisitions expensive and increased the danger of a hostile takeover. Here capital market orientation and codetermination are hardly irreconcilable opposites.

Likewise, the introduction of variable performance-related pay also has an ambiguous relation to existing institutions. Works councils have become increasingly used to negotiate variable pay programs. These schemes have been implemented in conformity with sectoral collective agreements—either being paid 'on top' of the collective agreement or under special firm-level collective agreements. But this issue has raised substantial debate. Collective agreements function increasingly as framework regulations, while the formation of the remuneration scheme is left to the company level in consultation with works councils. Such variable components threaten the notion of industry-wide collectively agreed wages or at least lowers the portion of income regulated by collective bargaining. Moreover, greater scope is given to works councils to negotiate over wages—thereby blurring the traditional division of labor between unions and works councils.

Consequently, the relationship between works councils and unions is again becoming more tenuous. Codetermination increasingly supports the micro goals of employees, and their firm-specific interests rather than wider goals of working class solidarity, for example, principles such as equal pay for equal work. Because the interests of employees as producers in a particular firm are more heterogeneous than class interests (Streeck 1992), the heterogeneity of interests inside unions increases and has also led to changing forms of collective agreements—the use of corridors and opting-out clauses, etc. Likewise, codetermination as a politically guaranteed legal right is becoming more private and contractual. For example, the rights of works councils are becoming increasingly contractualized (Jackson 2003) as corporations have set up 'working groups of works councils' to adapt to new organizational structures through negotiated rules, rather than using legally based options such as the *Konzernbetriebsräte*.

The current success of codetermination belies a potential danger. While code-termination continues to provide a number of beneficial economic functions, the legitimacy of an institution cannot rest on functionality alone. Codetermination originated in deep-seated political values, as well as formative experiences of the postwar generation in rebuilding German industry. These value commit-ments were refreshed during the political climate of the late 1960s and early 1970s where the meaning and boundaries of democracy were again tested by collective action. As codetermination becomes an increasingly professionalized domain of comanagement, it is less clearly grounded in broader societal value commitments. In short, by successfully 'managing' workplace conflicts, codetermination may itself erode the preconditions necessary for its own reproduction in the longer term. For example, works councils were often created in new economy firms only after they announced their closure as the IT Bubble collapsed in 2000 or 2001. After winding up these firms, the councils then disappeared. Likewise, the internationalization of corporations themselves poses serious challenges. German unions are unlikely to have the capacities to broaden codetermination and represent corporate workforces overseas. The developments in the European legal context reflect these difficulties of exporting German codetermination. Again the boundaries and interpretations of the institution continue to be challenged.

Conclusion

This chapter has argued that understanding institutional change requires us to rethink the action–theoretic foundations of institutional theory. Institutions are a product of human actions, but are also collective phenomena that confront particular individuals as an external and objective 'social fact' that form part of their situational context. Rather than debate the merits of rational/utilitarian, normative, or cognitive approaches to institutions, I have argued that the debate should be more focused on the creative aspects of action related to a non-teleological understanding of human intentionality (Joas 1992).

Specifically, I have stressed the importance of situational ambiguity in allowing scope for creativity within institutionalized contexts. Ambiguity is not a compet-ing explanation of institutional change on the same level as interests, norms, or ideas. Rather, ambiguity is an element that can be applied to all these models to develop more realistic theoretical applications. To show its implications, the con-cept of ambiguity was applied to the COASE framework developed by Aoki (2001) in order to better interpret processes of variable reproduction or incremental bounded innovation of institutions.

These concepts were then applied to the case of German codetermination. Codetermination exemplifies how ambiguity may lead to variation in organizational practices in ways that engender change over time. The mutability of codetermination, in fact, rests on its ambiguous dual mandate or what we might see as two 'faces' of codetermination—limiting managerial authority and upholding cooperation in the interests of the firm. Throughout its history, codetermination has been pulled in different directions within this horizon without ever leaving it entirely. Codetermination survived a number of macro-social crises, but was reinterpreted in the light of these new experiences and by a changing constellation of key actors. Rather than undergoing collapse and replacement by a new institution, the 'working out' of ambiguous relationships led codetermination to gradually evolve into an institution very different from its nineteenth-century origins.

Empirically, I have highlighted the contentious nature of how institutions are interpreted over time. Even once basic values and principles of codetermination were institutionalized, contention persisted about the social boundaries of these very same institutional norms—the economic sectors, firms, and range of managerial issues to which codetermination might be applied. This synchronic variation also led to diachronic changes over time. Capacities generated and accumulated on small local scales were slowly institutionalized more widely. Whereas cooperation was initially rare, the capacities for cooperation were gradually learned and diffused, while also undergoing substantial modification during this process. Had it not done so, the importance of codetermination for the German economy would have never been so large. Now the social partners again face the challenge of adapting codetermination to new capital market pressures or face its erosion.

Whether or not we see such historical episodes as discontinuity or continuity depends on the analytical problem at hand. But dramatic ruptures may look less dramatic over time, while small modifications may accumulate in ways that we see only later. The overriding lesson is to recall the dialectical manner in which institutional reproduction and change condition one another (Seo and Creed 2002) in a continuously changing world where actors are creative and situations often ambiguous.

Notes

1. The author thanks Peter Hall, Wolfgang Streeck, Kathy Thelen, Josh Whitford, and two anonymous reviewers for their insightful comments. All errors are my own.
2. In practice, institutional factors are often 'added on' to baseline models of an institution-less economy to explain why reality deviates from the pure model.
3. For example, Douglas North (1990) outlines two mechanisms of institutional change: changes in relative prices and changes in preferences. Yet North treats both change in (objective) prices or (subjective) preferences as exogenous parameters.

4. In economics, the concept of uncertainty refers to situations where the magnitude or value of an outcome is unknowable. Ambiguity refers more specifically to situations where more than one interpretation is possible. Philosophers also distinguish ambiguity from vagueness where the meaning is not clear in context.

5. Conceptualizing institutional change faces similar issues as the 'duality' of structure and agency examined by Bourdieu (1990) and Giddens (1984), who focus on how actors and social structures exist in a dialectical relation of mutual influence (Sewell Jr. 1992).

6. I am not arguing here that all institutional theory is deterministic, rather only that the indeterminate aspects of institutional contexts have not been adequately examined and integrated within institutional theory.

7. Iteration involves actors' variable relation to past events through selective attention, recognition of types, categorization, shifting repertoires of action, and 'repair' of violated expectations. Projection involves actors' variable relation to projected future scenarios—anticipation of events, construction of narrative, hypothetical resolution to dilemmas, or experimental enactment. The practical–evaluative dimension involves actors' variable relation to the present through the characterizing experience, deliberation, decision, and execution.

8. As Sewell (1992: 16) argues, 'a theory of change cannot be built into a theory of structure unless we adopt a far more multiple, contingent, and fractured conception of society—and of structure. What is needed is . . . to show how the ordinary operations of structures can generate transformations'.

9. Aoki discusses reconfiguration through geographic integration or segmentation of domains (e.g. protectionism, internationalization, etc.), or where organizations strategically integrate or decouple different domains (e.g. outsourcing, vertical integration, etc.).

10. The question of defining thresholds to conceptualize institutional emergence or deinstitutionalization remains beyond the scope of this chapter.

11. Coal mining was important in developing a model for codetermination, because the legacy of direct state control over the mines made employment relations a concern of the public interest (Fischer 1974: 142; Berg 1984).

12. This section does not discuss the issue of institutional transfer of codetermination to East Germany following German unification. Nor do I discuss legal reforms in areas such as environmental regulation and discrimination confronted works councils with new tasks and led to a further expansion of their activities.

13. Here tools developed to manage industrial decline in the *Montan* sectors are being redeployed to new ends of greater shareholder orientation.

References

AOKI, M. (1997). Unintended Fit: Organizational Evolution and Government Design of Institutions in Japan. In: M. Aoki, H.-K. Kim, and M. Okuno-Fujiwara (eds.), *The Role of Government in East Asian Economic Development: Comparative Institutional Analysis.* Oxford, UK: Clarendon Press, pp. 233–53.

—— (2001). *Toward a Comparative Institutional Analysis.* Cambridge, MA: MIT Press.

BECKERT, J. (2002). *Beyond the Market. The Social Foundations of Economic Efficiency.* Princeton, NJ: Princeton University Press.

BERG, W. (1984). *Wirtschaft und Gesellschaft in Deutschland un Grossbritannien imübergang zum organisierten Kapitalismus.* Berlin: Duncker & Humboldt.

BERGER, P. L. and LUCKMANN, T. (1966). *The Social Construction of Reality: A Treatise in the Sociology of Knowledge.* Garden City, NY: Doubleday.

BEYER, J. and HASSEL, A. (2002). The Effects of Convergence: Internationalisation and the Changing Distribution of Net Value Added in Large German Firms. *Economy and Society* 31(3): 309–32.

BOURDIEU, P. (1990). *The Logic of Practice.* Stanford, NY: Stanford University Press.

BRAUN, S., EBERWEIN, W., and THOLEN, J. (1992). *Belegschaft und Unternehmen. Zur Geschichte und Soziologie der deutschen Betriebsverfassung und Belegschaftsmitbestimmung.* Frankfurt am Main: Campus Verlag.

BRIGL-MATTHIASS, K. (1926). *Das Betriebsraeteproblem.* Berlin: Gupnter.

CLEMENS, E. S. and COOK, J. M. (1999). Politics and Institutionalism: Explaining Durability and Change. *Annual Review of Sociology* 25: 441–66.

CRAWFORD, S. and OSTROM, E. (1995). Grammar of Institutions. *American Political Science Review* 89: 582–99.

EMIRBAYER, M. and MISCHE, A. (1998). What is Agency? *American Journal of Sociology* 103: 962–1023.

FELDMAN, G. D. (1966). *Army, Industry, and Labor in Germany: 1914–1918.* Princeton, NJ: Princeton University Press.

FISCHER, W. (1974). *Wirtschaft und Gesellschaft im Zeitalter des Industrialisierung.* Goettingen: Vandenhoeck & Ruprucht.

FRIEDLAND, R. and ALFORD, R. R. (1991). Bringing Society Back In: Symbols, Practices, and Institutional Contradictions. In: W. Powell and P. DiMaggio (eds.), *The New Institutionalism in Organizational Analysis.* Chicago, IL: University of Chicago Press, pp. 232–66.

FUERSTENBERG, F. (1958). Der Betriebsrat-Strukturanalyse einer Grenzinstitution. *Koelner Zeitschrift fuer Soziologie und Sozialpsychologie* 10: 418–29.

GIDDENS, A. (1984). *The Constitution of Society.* Berkeley, CA: University of California Press.

GOFFMAN, E. (1961). *Asylums. Essays on the Social Situation of Mental Patients and Other Inmates.* Garden City, NY: Doubleday Anchor.

GREIF, A. (2004). On Recent Developments in Institutional Analysis. Stanford University, mimeo.

HALL, P. A. and SOSKICE, D. (2001). *Varieties of Capitalism: The Institutional Foundations of Comparative Advantage.* Oxford: Oxford University Press.

—— and TAYLOR, R. C. R. (1996). Political Science and the Three New Institutionalisms. MPIfG Discussion Paper, Koeln: Max-Planck-Institut fuer Gesellschaftsforschung.

HOEPNER, M. (2001). Corporate Governance in Transition: Ten Empirical Findings on Shareholder Value and Industrial Relations in Germany. MPIfG Discussion Paper 01/5, Koeln: Max-Planck-Institut fuer Gesellschaftsforschung.

—— (2003). *Wer beherrscht die Unternehmen? Shareholder Value, Managerherrschaft und Mitbestimmung in grossen deutschen Unternehmen.* Frankfurt am Main: Campus.

—— and JACKSON, G. (2001). An Emerging Market of Corporate Control? The Case of Mannesmann and German Corporate Governance. MPIfG Discussion Paper 01/4, Koeln: Max-Planck-Institut fuer Gesellschaftsforschung.

JACKSON, G. (2001). The Origins of Nonliberal Corporate Governance in Germany and Japan. In: W. Streeck and K. Yamamura (eds.), *The Origins of Nonliberal*

Capitalism: Germany and Japan in Comparison. Ithaca, NY: Cornell University Press, pp. 121–70.

—— (2003). Corporate Governance in Germany and Japan: Liberalization Pressures and Responses. In: K. Yamamura and W. Streeck (eds.), *The End of Diversity? Prospects for German and Japanese Capitalism.* Ithaca, NY: Cornell University Press, pp. 261–305.

—— HOEPNER, M., and KURDELBUSCH, A. (2004). Corporate Governance and Employees in Germany: Changing Linkages, Complementarities, and Tensions. In: H. Gospel and A. Pendleton (eds.), *Corporate Governance and Labour Management in Comparison.* Oxford: Oxford University Press, pp. 84–121.

JEPPERSON, R. L. (1991). Institutions, Institutional Effects, and Institutionalism. In: W. W. Powell and P. J. DiMaggio (eds.), *The New Institutionalism in Organizational Analysis.* Chicago, IL: University of Chicago Press, pp. 143–63.

JOAS, H. (1992). *Die Kreativitaet des Handelns.* Frankfurt am Main: Suhrkamp.

—— (1997). *Die Entstehung der Werte.* Frankfurt: Suhrkamp Verlag.

KOTTHOFF, H. (1994). *Betriebsraete und Buergerstatus. Wandel und Kontinuitaet betrieblicher Mitbestimmung.* Muenchen: Rainer Hampp Verlag.

—— (1998). Mitbestimmung in Zeiten interessenpolitischer Rueckschritte. Betriebsraete zwischen Beteiligungsofferten und gnadenlosem Kostensenkungsdiktat. *Industrielle Beziehungen* 5: 76–100.

LEHMBRUCH, G. (2001). The Institutional Embedding of Market Economics: The German 'Model' and its Impact on Japan. In: W. Streeck and K. Yamamura (eds.), *The Origins of Nonliberal Capitalism: Germany and Japan in Comparison.* Ithaca, NY: Cornell University Press, pp. 39–93.

LEPSIUS, M. R. (1990). *Interessen. Ideen und Institutionen.* Opladen: Westdeutsche Verlag.

LEVITT, B. and MARCH, J. G. (1988). Organizational Learning. *Annual Review of Sociology* 14: 319–40.

MAHONEY, J. (2000). Path Dependence in Historical Sociology. *Theory and Society* 29: 507–48.

MEYER, J. M. and ROWAN, B. (1977). Institutionalized Organizations: Formal Structure as Myth and Ceremony. *American Journal of Sociology* 83: 340–63.

MILGROM, P. R. and ROBERTS, J. (1995). Complementarities, Industrial Strategy, Structure, and Change in Manufacturing. *Journal of Accounting and Economics* 19: 179–208.

MITBESTIMMUNG, K. (1998). *Mitbestimmung und neue Unternehmenskulturen Bilanz und Perspektiven.* Guetersloh: Verlag Bertelsmann Stiftung.

MUELLER, G. (1987). *Mitbestimmung in der Nachkriegszeit. Britische Besatzungsmacht—Unternehmer—Gewerkschaften.* Duesseldorf: Schwann.

NORTH, D. C. (1990). *Institutions, Institutional Change and Economic Performance.* Cambridge: Cambridge University Press.

OLIVER, C. (1991). Strategic Responses to Institutional Processes. *Academy of Management Review* 16: 145–79.

POWELL, W. W. and DIMAGGIO, P. (1991). *The New Institutionalism in Organizational Analysis.* Chicago, IL: University of Chicago Press.

PLUMPE, W. (1992). Die Betriebsraete in der Weimarer Republik: Eine Skizze zu ihrer Verbreitung, Zusammensetzung und Akzeptanz. In: W. Plumpe and C. Kleinschmidt (eds.), *Unternehmen zwischen Markt und Macht: Aspekte deutscher Unternehmens- und Industriegeschichte im 20.Jahrhundert.* Essen: Klartext Verlag, pp. 42–60.

POPITZ, H., BAHRDT, H. P., JUERES, E. A., and KESTING, H. (1957). *Das Gesellschaftsbild des Arbeiters. Soziologische Untersuchungen in der Huettenindustrie.* Tuebingen: J. C. B. Mohr.

Rehder, B. (2001). The Impact of Plant-Level Pacts for Employment and Competitiveness on the Institutional Change of the German System of Industrial Relations. Paper presented at the 13th Annual Meeting of the Society for the Advancement of Socio-Economics. Amsterdam, June 28–July 1.

Seo, M. G. and Creed, W. E. D. (2002). Institutional Contradictions, Praxis, and Institutional Change: A Dialectical Perspective. *Academy of Management Review* 27: 222–47.

Sewell W. H., Jr. (1992). A Theory of Structure: Duality, Agency, and Transformation. *American Journal of Sociology* 98: 1–29.

Stark, D. (2001). Ambiguous Assets for Uncertain Environments: Heterarchy in Postsocialist Firms. In: P DiMaggio (ed.), *The Twenty-First Century Firm. Changing Economic Organization in International Perspective.* Princeton, NJ: Princeton University Press, pp. 69–104.

Streeck, W. (1992). *Social Institutions and Economic Performance: Studies of Industrial Relations in Advanced Capitalist Economies.* London: Sage Publications.

Teuteberg, H. J. (1961). *Geschichte der industriellen Mitbestimmung in Deutschland.* Tuebingen: J. C. B. Mohr.

—— (1981). Urspruenge und Entwicklung der Mitbestimmung in Deutschland. In: H. Pohl (ed.), *Mitbestimmung: Urspruenge und Entwicklung.* Wiesbaden: Franz Steiner Verlag, pp. 7–73.

Thelen, K. (1991). *Union of Parts.* Ithaca, NY: Cornell University Press.

—— (1999). Historical Institutionalism in Comparative Politics. *American Review of Political Science* 2: 369–404.

—— (2003). How Institutions Evolve: Insights from Comparative-Historical Analysis. In: J. Mahoney and D. Rueschemeyer (eds.), *Comparative Historical Analysis in the Social Sciences.* New York: Cambridge University Press, pp. 208–40.

Weisbrod, B. (1989). Arbeitgeberpolitik und Arbeitsbeziehungen im Ruhrbergbau. Vom 'Herr-im-Haus' zur Mitbestimmung. In: G. D. Feldman and K. Tenfelde (eds.), *Arbeiter, Unternehmer und Staat im Bergbau.* Muenchen: Verlag C. H. Beck, pp. 107–62.

White, H. C. (1992). *Identity and Control: A Structural Theory of Social Action.* Princeton, NJ: Princeton University Press.

Whitford, J. (2002). Pragmatism and the Untenable Dualism of Means and Ends: Why Rational Choice Theory does not Deserve Paradigmatic Privilege. *Theory and Society* 31(3): 325–63.

Whitley, R. (1999). *Divergent Capitalisms: The Social Structuring and Change of Business Systems.* Oxford: Oxford University Press.

Zilber, T. B. (2002). Institutionalization as an Interplay Between Actions, Meanings, and Actors: The Case of a Rape Crisis Center in Israel. *Academy of Management Journal* 45: 234–54.

10

Adaptation, Recombination, and Reinforcement: The Story of Antitrust and Competition Law in Germany and Europe

Sigrid Quack and Marie-Laure Djelic

We consider, in this chapter, national business system change in relation to transnational institution building. Our field of exploration is antitrust regulation and competition law, its emergence and development both in Germany and at the European level. It is increasingly acknowledged that legal frameworks structure market economies and constrain economic behavior (Laporta et al. 1998; De Soto 2000; Fligstein 2001; Berglöf, Rosenthal, and von Thadden 2001). We see the legal treatment of competition issues as important in that respect (Dobbin and Dowd 2000; Djelic 2002).

Until 1945, antitrust regulation was an American legal tradition with no impact beyond American borders. Sixty years later, this has changed to a remarkable extent and antitrust is 'going global' (Evenett, Lehmann, and Steil 2000). Today, close to a hundred countries have adopted a competition law and a transnational space such as the European Union (EU) is also structured by antitrust principles (Djelic 2002).

We use the terms antitrust and competition law interchangeably to refer to legal regimes that have as their objective the protection of competition. Modern competition law encompasses two broad categories of provisions. The first category aims at preventing restraints of competition through agreements or concerted practices such as trusts or cartels. The second category deals with undue

Earlier versions of this chapter were presented at a workshop on National Business Systems in the New Global Context, held in Oslo in May 2003 and sponsored by the University of Oslo and the Norwegian Research Council, and at the Standing Working Group on Comparative Studies of Economic Organization at the EGOS Colloquium in Copenhagen in July 2003. We are grateful to the participants in these workshops for their comments and criticism. Our thanks go also to Kathleen Thelen and Wolfgang Streeck for their helpful discussions around issues related to this chapter. Ariane and Rachel Berthoin Antal read earlier versions and made helpful suggestions. We also thank three anonymous reviewers at Oxford University Press who gave us food for thought. Last but not least, we thank Emily Richards for his thorough language editing and Sylvia Pichorner for her careful word processing.

acquisition of economic power through monopolization, abuse of dominant position, or mergers (Goyder 1998; Pittman 1998). Antitrust and competition laws, however, are not just a matter of substantive provisions but also of legal interpretation, implementation, and enforcement (Rheinstein 1974; Haley 2001). In this chapter, we focus on formal legal changes and how they have been interpreted, implemented, and enforced by legal and administrative actors. Changes in formal rules do not necessarily lead to immediate behavioral change. There may be considerable resistance and actors may find ways to circumvent certain legal prescriptions. In a longer-term perspective, however, the introduction of new legal standards—with an impact, for example, on what is allowed and not allowed in terms of competitive behavior—opens a window on new cognitive and normative frames that actors may gradually start to use to approach reality. This progressive habitualization is likely to be reinforced when a professional community gets structured around those new legal rules—in charge of reading, implementing, and enforcing them (Heintz, Müller, and Roggenthin 2001; Stryker 2003).

Antitrust first came to Germany in 1947, while the building of an antitrust framework was constitutive of forming of the European Coal and Steel Community (ECSC) in 1951—the first step toward the creation of a European Community. However, during the first ten years, these two developments remained only loosely coupled. After 1957, a year marked both by the passing of the first German antitrust act and the signing of the Treaty of Rome, the German and European antitrust stories became much more closely interconnected. We look at the interplay between rule change in Germany and rule building in Europe and at the evolving logics of that interplay up until today. We argue that, over time, the two processes reinforced and stabilized each other.

From our analysis of the development of the German competition regime, we draw some conclusions about the conditions for national institutional change and its mechanisms. This case provides an interesting illustration of how new templates or institutional logics diffuse and call in question old ones—institutional change by 'displacement' (see Introduction to this volume). In particular, this chapter highlights the salience of coalitions between 'foreign invaders' and 'local outsiders' in this process of displacement and institutional change.

Building upon earlier work (Djelic and Quack 2003a,b) we point to the need to think about national system change as resulting from a succession and combination of phases with different logics of change. The process may start with radical reorientations that come at moments when national systems face some degree of crisis. Initially, radical reorientations may be more formal than real, with a significant degree of resistance and decoupling. They will not stabilize nor be long-lasting if this early period is not followed by others where radical changes are appropriated, institutionalized, reinforced, or even partially reoriented through a succession of slow, incremental but significant and consequential steps (see also the introduction to this volume).

Crossing the Atlantic—antitrust comes to Europe

In 1890, the United States passed the Sherman Antitrust Act. Initially, the intent had been to curb the multiplication of cartels and informal agreements and to reestablish conditions for free and fair competition. The unique context in which the Sherman Act was enacted, however, limited its domain of applicability and had unintended consequences of significance (Peritz 1996). Early court cases showed that cartels and other restraints of trade across the States of the Union would be prohibited per se. As a piece of Federal legislation, however, the Sherman Act did not apply within individual States, and tight combinations and mergers within the legal frame of one particular State hence seemed to lie outside its reach (Djelic 1998). Soon, corporate lawyers were identifying mergers as an alternative to cartelization, that was legal under the Sherman Act (Thorelli 1954; Sklar 1988; Fligstein 1990).

The passing of the Sherman Act was thus indirectly a triggering force for the first wave of mergers in the United States (1895–1904). In an irony of history, the fight for competition in the United States led to the emergence of large, integrated firms and contributed to the oligopolistic reorganization of American industries. The Sherman Act was read as generally and in principle outlawing cartels and loose forms of agreements. With respect to size, however, and hence to mergers, the interpretation that ultimately came to dominate in the Supreme Court was that illegality stemmed not from size in and of itself but from unreasonableness as revealed by a proven intent and purpose to exclude others and stifle competition. In 1914, the Clayton Act confirmed and institutionalized this so-called rule of reason argument for size and mergers, prohibiting mergers and acquisitions only when their effect was to 'unreasonably' lessen competition or to create a monopoly (Peritz 1996). By the 1920s, both the per se prohibition of cartels and the use, for mergers, of the rule of reason had become trademarks and defining features of the American antitrust tradition.[1]

Germany discovers antitrust

Until the First World War, the perception prevailed in Germany that organized markets, cartels, and agreements were natural and progressive developments, leading economies, and societies away from the chaos and disruption associated with competition and price wars. In the German intellectual tradition of historicism then dominant among economists, lawyers, and politicians, policymaking and legislation should not attempt to mould business conditions or restrict freedom of economic activity. This meant that cartels and agreements were essentially left to multiply and extend their reach.

After the First World War, however, public concern about cartel abuses increased significantly in Germany. It reached a high point in 1923, during the dark period of hyperinflation, when interfirm agreements were used by member firms to pass on the costs of inflation to retailers and customers (Michels 1928). Yielding to public pressure, the Weimar government issued in November 1923 a regulation against abuses of economic power (Gerber 1998). The impact of this regulation proved limited, leading mostly to a systematic notification of cartel agreements to public authorities (Michels 1928; Liefmann 1938). In 1933, it was replaced by National Socialist legislation that rendered cartels mandatory and gave the Ministry of Economic Affairs a free hand in organizing and monitoring them (Levy 1966: 159).

The Freiburg school—a minority and dissonant voice   That same year, 1933, one economist (Walter Eucken) and two lawyers (Franz Böhm and Hanns Grossmann-Doerth) met at the University of Freiburg. They shared a common conviction: that the inability of the German legal and political system to prevent the creation and misuse of private economic power had contributed to the disintegration of the Weimar Republic. Their academic collaboration gave birth to the Freiburg or ordo-liberal school (Gerber 1994a). In stark contrast to the German *zeitgeist*, members of the ordo-liberal school were in favor of competition, both on economic and political grounds. Competition was a necessary condition, they believed, for political democracy. The competitive economy they envisaged—a multitude of productive units, each one more or less corresponding to a private household—had neoclassical features.

At the same time, they did not believe in competition as self-maintaining equilibrium. A *laissez-faire* policy in Germany, after all, had only brought about collusion and a curtailment of competition. Markets and competitive conditions had to be created by enlightened political authorities and protected by legal frameworks (Peacock and Willgerodt 1989: Ch. 2). They argued for a legislation prohibiting cartels and agreements. They believed that monopoly power should also be prevented, for example, by requiring firms to divest certain operations. However, situations in which this would be necessary were then quite rare. The cartel issue appeared much more problematic (Gerber 1994a: 51).

When the Second World War came to an end, the Freiburg school was neither well known in Germany nor well connected (Wallich 1955; Nicholls 1984). Its programs and the convictions of its members, however, happened to fit in reasonably well with the emerging American project for Germany. American occupation authorities in Germany were therefore instrumental in propelling the ordo-liberal school to the forefront of the political and economic scene (Nicholls 1984; Djelic 1998). In January 1948, the Americans appointed Ludwig Erhard as chairman of the newly constituted German Economic Council (*Deutscher Wirtschaftsrat*). Erhard had been in contact with the ordo-liberal school for a number of years and many members of his close advisory council were connected to that school.

The direct impact of American occupation   A widely shared conviction that cartels had played an important role in the build up of Nazi power led Western allied forces to introduce decartelization laws in 1947. These laws grew out of the long-standing American antitrust tradition and prohibited cartels, combines, syndicates, or trusts (Damm 1958). In the treaty allowing Germany to return progressively to sovereignty, the American government demanded that German agencies prepare their own competition law. Once accepted by German and Allied authorities, this law, it was agreed, would replace the 1947 legislation.

While targeting cartels, American occupation authorities had also aimed at 'deconcentration' (Berghahn 1986: 84) of German industry by splitting up large undertakings. However, well into 1947 there was considerable controversy within the American administration as to how far deconcentration should go (Martin 1950). The onset of the Cold War settled the issue. After that, West Germany became a key bulwark in the fight against communism and was turned into the 'cockpit' of American policy (McCloy, quoted in Schwartz 1991: 29). In consequence, the deconcentration program lost its significance and American occupation authorities came to advocate an oligopolistic structure for the German economy. The model was American and the idea was that 'oligopolies, when policed by the vigorous enforcement of antitrust laws as in the United States, yield pretty good results' (OMGUS 1947: Vol. 18). American policymakers were aware that radical transformations of the sort they were fostering would survive only if Germans actively appropriated them. They had identified the ordo-liberal school as a local relay, but appropriation of the American antitrust tradition was not easy. To smooth the process, the United States sponsored training and 'indoctrination' missions (OMGUS 1950: Vol. 42). In June 1950, a German delegation led by Franz Böhm visited the United States for several weeks, meeting representatives of the Federal Trade Council (FTC), the Antitrust Division, and the Securities and Exchange Commission (SEC), antitrust experts and lawyers, industrialists and trade union members. Upon its return, the delegation published a detailed report (Bundesanzeiger 1950) that became an important source of knowledge on American antitrust in Germany, and some of its members became closely involved in the drafting of the German anticartel act. Back in Germany, they could also use other American resources. Robert Bowie, an antitrust lawyer who was General Counsel to the US High Commissioner in Germany, helped throughout the drafting. The US Department of Justice prepared an enforcement manual, using American antitrust cases. Finally, Americans did not hesitate to adopt a tougher strategy—threatening to impose their own version of anticartel legislation when the drafting process stalled or slowed down (Damm 1958: 212 *ff.*).

Running into obstacles   In 1949, a team of ordo-liberal experts proposed a first draft. The Josten draft, as it was known, called for a total ban on cartels and for legal and political intervention to prevent concentrations of economic power. This draft was quickly filed away, though, for at least three reasons (Berghahn 1986: 160). First, the resistance of business communities was strong, both to the ban on cartels and to the tough deconcentration clause. Then, Erhard's close advisors—including Eberhardt Günther—would rather endorse a philosophy of abuse control than one of strict prohibition. Erhard himself, finally, was not fully convinced, and his opposition to the draft paralleled the opposition of American authorities (Robert 1976). Erhard's own position combined a strict opposition to cartels with a more lenient approach to concentrations of economic power, which placed him close to the position at the time of American occupation authorities. The vision of a social market economy (*soziale Marktwirtschaft*) relied on a combination of large-scale enterprises and efficient competition that together would drive the German economy towards US type consumer capitalism (Erhard 1958: 169–71; Berghahn 1986: 185).

In March 1949, the Allied High Commission prepared a directive asking German authorities to build upon Chapter 5 of the Havana Charter for the drafting of a German anticartel legislation. This Charter, drawn up in the context of the United Nations Conferences on Trade and Employment in 1947, was part of the American attempt to establish a multilateral trading system. It recommended the liberalization of world trade and urged the signatories to introduce national anticartel legislation, but said nothing about the curbing of concentration (Berghahn 1986: 157). Erhard used this directive to reject the Josten draft and to initiate a new drafting process. By October, Günther had prepared a new draft, but since it upheld the principle of abuse control rather than prohibition it was rejected by American authorities.

By 1952, a new version was ready that provided for a prohibition of cartels, with a number of exceptions. It also included provisions on mergers and combinations; a Federal Cartel Office would be entitled to prohibit mergers that led to market dominance. The draft included a definition of market dominance that brought it closer to the Josten draft (Robert 1976: 165). However, by the time of legislative elections in 1953, discussions of the bill in Parliament were still pending.

Industry pressure was a key factor behind the deadlock. Traditional German heavy industries that dominated the Federal Association of German Industries (*Bundesverband Deutscher Industrien*, BDI) were vehemently against any ban on cartels or serious deconcentration. As their capacity to organize was gradually reestablished in the early 1950s, they lobbied strongly (Damm 1958; Braunthal 1965; Djelic 1998). For example, they threatened to reduce their campaign contributions for the 1953 elections and launched a virulent media campaign against Erhard, whom they accused of acting on American orders (Erhard 1963: Ch. 16).

Overcoming the deadlock   In October 1953, following elections, a new attempt was made to reach an agreement. Erhard created an ad hoc commission that brought together officials from the Ministry of Economic Affairs and a few members of the BDI. At the same time, he put pressure on the BDI by deploying a Trojan Horse strategy, attempting to work through minority groups within the business community with more to lose than to gain from cartels. The Community of Entrepreneurs (*Arbeitsgemeinschaft Selbständiger Unternehmer*, AsU), an association of small independent businessmen, joined somewhat later by representatives of the consumer goods industries at the BDI, became his main institutional relays within the business community. These groups became increasingly vocal from 1954, challenging the dominant position of the BDI and its leader Fritz Berg (Braunthal 1965; Berghahn 1986).

The ad hoc commission finally agreed on a revised draft in 1955. Erhard had insisted on the prohibition principle—the bill included a prohibition of cartels largely similar to the provisions of the Sherman Act—but had accepted a number of exceptions. The bill was put to the Bundestag in 1955. Hostilities were immediately reopened and the confrontation lasted until 1957 when the Law against Restraints on Competition (*Gesetz gegen Wettbewerbsbeschränkungen*, GWB) was finally passed. In the meantime, some last-minute changes had been made. The 1955 draft, for example, contained provisions on merger control that had received agreement from the Bundestag at first reading but were then changed at the end of the legislative process (Schmidt and Binder 1996). The same happened to a provision that prohibited oligopolies, the scope of which was reduced (Robert 1976: 312 *ff*.). These last-minute changes revealed once again the strength of opposition coming from parts of German industry, which was represented mostly, but not only, by the conservative party (the *Christdemokratische Union* or CDU). The *zeitgeist* among German political decisionmakers was that concentration was a necessary precondition for German reconstruction (Müller-Henneberg and Schwartz 1963: 615).

The Law Against Restraints on Competition took effect on January 1, 1958. Section 1 declared agreements with restrictive effects on competition as null and void (§1). Section 2 extended the prohibition to vertical agreements that had a negative effect on competition. In their basic principles, German provisions on cartels and agreements thus became congruent with American antitrust tradition. The prohibition principle, however, was qualified in German law by two types of exemptions. First, certain types of agreements were altogether excluded from the general ban. Among these were term-fixing, rebate, and specialization agreements that merely had to be reported to the Federal Cartel Office. The continued toleration of specialization cartels, in particular, allowed small- and medium-sized firms in postwar Germany to establish collaborative networks that enabled them to compete successfully with large industrial firms (Herrigel 1996: 172). Second, certain sectors such as agriculture, sea and air transport, banking and credit institutions, insurance or public utilities were entirely exempted. It would take more than twenty years before these sector exemptions came under serious attack, from national and European actors. Section 3 dealt with market power and prescribed control of its abusive exploitation (§22). The newly created Federal Cartel Office (*Bundeskartellamt*, BKA) was entitled to impose measures and fines against undertakings and groups of undertakings with a view to terminating abusive conduct. From a certain size onwards, mergers had to be reported to the BKA (§23). If the BKA found that the behavior of merged firms represented an abuse of dominant position, it could require the termination of this behavior. The BKA, however, had no authority to prevent the merger itself. The German control of abuse approach with regard to dominant market position paralleled the American rule of reason doctrine and arguably went further in its leniency toward concentration.

The enforcement framework of the German law differed in important ways from its American counterpart. First of all, the legislative traditions in which both laws were embedded differed. The German act was drafted in the tradition of statutory law and its provisions were therefore more detailed, specific, and comprehensive than those of the American Acts. The German law created a relatively autonomous Federal Cartel Office in charge of enforcing the law. This office became the motor of the competition law system because it was virtually the only actor that could initiate, investigate, and decide upon cases in which firms were suspected to violate provisions of the Law Against Restraints on Competition. In stark contrast to American practice, the German law did not allow private antitrust suits except in very specific conditions. In practice, the procedure was developed very much along judicial principles under the influence of Eberhardt Günther, who became the first president of the BKA. Decisions have been subject to judicial review by ordinary courts in the first instance and by the Federal Court of Justice (*Bundesgerichtshof*, BGH) in the second instance.

Planting the seeds transnationally—the ECSC

In May 1950, France proposed a plan for pooling French and German coal and steel industries, with the possible participation of other European countries. The idea was to create the conditions for peace between a core of European countries by institutionalizing mutual economic dependence. Jean Monnet and the French Planning Council were behind the proposal and by the end of June negotiations had begun between six countries—France, West Germany, Italy, Belgium, the Netherlands, and Luxemburg.

A European cartel or the United States of Europe? In an immediate reaction to the French proposal, the American Secretary of State Dean Acheson praised the initiative but held back from giving it full support. This initial American hesitation was mostly due to wariness that the project could turn into a European cartel. Two days later, the French team sent a memorandum to the American State Department, documenting differences between the French proposal and an international cartel. The memorandum emphasized that the main objective was to create a competitive space to stimulate production and productivity and not to 'maintain stable profits and acquired positions' (FRUS 1950).

What really made a difference, however, and got the better of American hesitation, was the fact that Monnet was behind the project. Members of the American administration knew that Monnet believed in the model of expanded production and competitive markets and entertained the vision of a peaceful and united, mass-producing and mass-consuming Europe, with the United States as a model. They were also aware of the close collaboration between the French planning council and American experts, lawyers, and consultants

(Djelic 1998: 151). A key figure again was Robert Bowie, who traveled from Germany to Paris in June 1950 and wrote the competition provisions of the ECSC Treaty (Monnet 1976).

Antitrust legislation as a key bone of contention   Monnet had anticipated difficulties and the probable opposition of business communities. To preempt conflicts, industry representatives were excluded from negotiation proceedings. The French team had insisted that official country delegates should not be members of national industries but 'independent personalities who [had], besides technical capacity, a concern for general interest' (FRUS 1950). As expected, French, Belgian, and German business communities vehemently denounced the project from the start, in particular its anticartel orientations. The impact of these lobbies on country delegates was real, albeit indirect; as a consequence, early drafts of the ECSC Treaty reflected and to some extent incorporated those pressures.

This soon aroused concern within the American administration and prompted intervention. In the autumn, the Americans imposed a redrafting to bring the future treaty into line with initial objectives. As Walter Hallstein, head of the German delegation, described it: 'Monnet's ideas are probably also influenced by the American desire that all cartel-like institutions be rejected . . . The French side will examine the cartel question once more from this perspective. The [German] Ministry of Economic Affairs is likewise asked to submit an appropriate proposal . . ' (quoted in Berghahn 1986: 140).

At the end of October, the French came back with a draft that essentially rekindled the spirit of the early proposal. Two articles, 60 and 61, written in large part by Robert Bowie, dealt explicitly with the cartel issue. Article 60 prohibited cartels and agreements although it made partial exception for crisis cartels. Article 61 dealt with abuse of market power due to excessive concentration, without prohibiting concentration as such. Mergers were allowed if they created conditions for increased efficiency and productivity without threatening competition. The German draft was much less restrictive on the cartel issue, only preventing abuse. All national delegations except the French backed this second draft, which was also more acceptable to industry representatives. The French draft, however, received full American support.

Reaching a compromise   Negotiations stalled for three months, although Monnet continued to hold intensive behind-the-scene talks with both Ludwig Erhard and Konrad Adenauer, the West German Chancellor. Eventually the American High Commissioner, John McCloy—a personal friend of Monnet's—was instrumental in bringing parties back to the negotiating table. In the end, the version of the ECSC Treaty finally adopted was a compromise.

Article 60 had become Article 65 and declared 'all agreements, decisions and concerted practices as void which tend to prevent, restrict or distort "normal competition" within the Common Market for coal and steel'— a per se prohibition of cartels congruent with American antitrust tradition. As part of the compromise, subsection 2 of the same paragraph gave the High Authority the right to authorize specialization agreements, joint buying, or joint selling agreements of particular products if they would 'make for substantial improvements in the production or distribution of those products', were 'not more restrictive than necessary for this purpose' and 'not liable to give the undertakings concerned the power to determine the prices, or to control or restrict production or marketing of a substantial part of the products in question within the Common Market, or to shield them against effective competition from other undertakings within the Common Market'.[2]

Article 61 had become Article 66 but was essentially unchanged. It subjected mergers to the prior approval of a 'High Authority' (§1). The latter would agree upon a merger if the transaction did not create an entity with the power to fix prices, to control or restrict production or distribution to the detriment of competition (§2). Under §3, the High Authority could 'exempt from the requirement of prior authorization' concentrations between smaller undertakings. Thus, in line with American antitrust tradition, Article 66 was designed to prevent the emergence of monopolies but not to combat concentration as such. As a complement to merger control, §7 dealt with firms that already had achieved market dominance when the Treaty came into effect or that could get there afterwards through internal growth. This paragraph and the 'abuse of dominant market position' concept would be reused five years later in the Rome Treaty in a somewhat different form (Joliet 1970: 218 *ff.*).

Whereas Articles 65 and 66 ECSC by and large reflected the influence of American antitrust tradition, a new Article (67) was added that included provisions more in line with European practices. The High Authority in charge of applying the Treaty could allow national states to accept certain agreements under particular conditions, such as during economic or social crises. The introduction of Article 67 left open the possibility for coal and steel producers and their national governments to reestablish certain prewar practices of collaborative market control when economic downswings and increasing global competition brought the European coal and steel industry under increasing pressure in the following decades. In fact, it was Article 67 that rendered ECSC competition law provisions so ineffective in later periods (Schmidt and Binder 1996).

European antitrust becomes a force of its own

As it turned out, the Coal and Steel Community was relayed in 1958 by the European Economic Community (EEC). In the following years, competition policy became an important dimension of European integration, particularly once the EEC became EU in 1992. Today, the European competition authority has grown into a global player—forty years ago this would have seemed unthinkable. Throughout those forty years, American antitrust legislation and practice have exerted influence on the European competition framework, but that impact has varied in character and intensity. At the same time, influences coming from member states or Community institutions gradually contributed to building up European antitrust as a force with dynamics of its own.

Laying the groundwork

The Rome Treaty laid the groundwork for the operation of a European competition law system. Formal provisions were subsequently turned into a living law through regulations issued by the Commission as well as through European Court of Justice (ECJ) case law. Many characteristics of the contemporary competition regime and of recent attempts at reform can be seen as going back to decisions made during the early foundation period.

From the ECSC to the EEC   In May 1955, Foreign Ministers of the ECSC met at Messina, Sicily, to discuss the possibility of an extended Common Market. The context was different then to that four years before. Germany was reimposing itself in Europe, economically and politically, and this worried France. At the same time, attempts at setting up a European defense system had failed in 1952, dealing a blow to political integration projects. These changes in the European balance of power impacted upon the Messina discussions. The French were wary and championing as a consequence a free trade area with limited supranational power. The German government was more ready to envision a European confederation of national states (El-Agraa 1980).

All delegations agreed that the creation of a Common Market required a joint competition policy. Opinions differed considerably, however, as to the nature and scope of such a policy. Germans were in favor of a strict prohibition of restrictive agreements and of a preventive control system run by a strong competition authority. From the start this position was influential, not least because Germany was the only country about to pass and implement a national competition law. Following the Messina meeting, a group of experts worked under the leadership of the Belgian Foreign Minister Paul Henri Spaak to consider the necessary preconditions for a Common Market. A German, Hans von der Groeben, and a Frenchman Pierre Uri drafted the final report, outlining in particular a common competition policy.

Published in April 1956, the Spaak Report prepared the ground for further negotiations. The preamble called for the creation of a Common Market as a way to raise European productivity and efficiency and bring them closer to American levels. The section on competition policy suggested a prohibition of cartels and restrictive agreements with a merger control system similar to that of the ECSC Treaty (Schwarz 1956, 1980: 277–335). The French delegation strongly opposed those propositions, favoring instead a weak system of abuse control. The Dutch perspective combined compulsory notification of cartels with provisional validity (Goyder 1998; Forrester 2000). During negotiations, participants explored concepts unfamiliar to most of them or at least (as in the German case) untried. Paragraphs were changed until the last minute. Ultimately, the German delegation got its way, with a rigorous ban on restrictive agreements as *quid pro quo* to French demands on Euratom and the association of overseas territories (Bayliss 1980: 118). Initial reluctance left some trace, however, in the form of exemptions that were integrated in the final text of Article 85 of the Rome Treaty.[3]

The treatment of concentrations and market power was less controversial. With American firms as benchmark, European politicians believed that further concentration in the integrated market would be both inevitable and desirable—a view also influential among officials of the European Commission (Joliet 1970: 3). Therefore, the proposition of the Spaak Report to establish a merger control system similar to that of the ECSC Treaty did not find its way into the Rome Treaty.

Competition provisions in the Rome Treaty   Article 85 (1) prohibits 'agreements between undertakings, decisions by associations of undertakings and concerted practices which may effect trade between Member States and which have as their object or effect the prevention, restriction or distortion of competition within the Common Market'.[4] This formulation is similar to that of Article 65 in the ECSC Treaty, and in all likelihood derives from the latter (Goyder 1998: 98). The American legacy of a per se prohibition of cartels had entered, via the ECSC path and under German pressure, the competition law of the European Community. However, Article 85 (3) stated that cartels and concerted practices may be accepted when they 'contribute to improving the production or distribution of goods or to promoting technical or economic progress, while allowing consumers a fair share of the resulting benefit'. Here, we see parallels to the exemptions under Article 65 (2) of the ECSC Treaty or those in the German Act of 1958. Given the complex and lengthy negotiations described above, the wording of Article 85 is surprisingly close to that of Article 65 ECSC except for somewhat broader exemption provisions in the Rome Treaty (Joliet 1970: 225).

Article 86 stated, on the other hand, that 'any abuse by one or more undertakings of a dominant position within the common market or in a substantial part of it shall be prohibited as incompatible with the common market insofar as it may affect trade between Member States'. The focus of Article 86 on abuse of dominant position was inspired by §7 of Article 66 ECSC. But unlike competition law provisions of the ECSC, the Rome Treaty did not deal with mergers (Joliet 1970: 225). Article 86 is directed only at the misuse of dominant power; it cannot deal with the attempt to monopolize, in contrast to Article 66 ECSC. The 'abuse of dominant position'—a concept that originally had constituted a supplementary provision in the ECSC Treaty—became of key importance in the Rome Treaty. This approach comes very close in fact to the concept of 'abuse of dominant power' that the German Act of 1958 introduced to deal with concentrations.

Altogether, the influence of American antitrust tradition on European competition law is unmistakable, at least in its fundamental principles. However, the introduction of exemptions and the granting of considerable discretion to the

Commission created a situation where in practice, and through procedural judgment, the European antitrust act could develop a dynamism of its own.

Regulation 17/62: German midwifery for a strong Directorate General IV   In contrast to its ECSC predecessor, the Rome Treaty did not define enforcement mechanisms. The Council of Ministers had four years to adopt an implementation legislation. Hence, debates started again, showing that there were different national interpretations of the law. Germans argued that restraints of trade should be generally forbidden until exempted by the Commission. The French proposed that Article 85 (3) should be interpreted as directly applicable exemption—which would give national authorities greater leeway.

Under the leadership of two Germans—Walter Hallstein, first president of the Commission, and Hans von der Groeben, first commissioner for competition policy—the European Commission resisted the French position. Member states, national courts, and business communities should be prevented from watering down competition provisions (Forrester and Norall 1984). In parallel, members of the Commission balked at the scope of jurisdictions involved; this was bound to exceed the limited resources of the Commission. Directorate General (DG) IV, the newly founded Directorate-General for competition policy, then had about twenty officials, far fewer than its new German counterpart (Goyder 1998).

Initially, DG IV focused on preparing a procedural regulation and hence consulted broadly with member states and experts. German lawyers, academics, and competition officials played an influential role there since they could refer to the German experience (Gerber 1998; Goyder 1998). A first version of Regulation 17/62 confirmed the direct applicability of Articles 85 and 86, imposed notification, reasserted the principle of prohibition, gave the Commission sole jurisdiction for approval of exemptions and imposition of penalties and provided that decisions of the Commission could be appealed in the ECJ. Tense discussions followed, in the European Parliament and in the European Council. The French delegation disagreed strongly with the obligation to notify agreements and proposed that decisions under Articles 85 and 86 should be taken jointly by the Commission and member states concerned. The French finally relented on their opposition to Regulation 17/62 when offered an agreement on agricultural policy (Bayliss 1980: 118; Von der Groeben 1987).

Regulation 17/62 came into force in March 1962 and has shaped since then, without major amendments, the European approach to competition policy.[5] The Regulation gave the Commission exclusive powers in defining exemptions under Article 85 (3). Altogether, it strongly empowered the Commission relative to national competition authorities and laid the foundation for a far-reaching delegation of decisionmaking powers from the Commission to DG IV (Gerber 1998). Few other DGs had such widely delegated powers. This enabled DG IV to continue enforcement including when political deadlocks made it difficult for the Council to decide on other matters (Goyder 1998).

Implementing antitrust   The 'German' approach that prevailed in Regulation 17/62 reflected the belief that a literal reading of the Treaty and strong enforcement authority were necessary to overcome the resistance of national business and political communities. There was, however, an obvious risk in this approach. Critics had pointed out that the 'mesh of the net for catching notifications was so fine that the anticipated number of agreements likely to be registered [...] would be extremely high' (Goyder 1998: 47). And this was the case. By 1963, the Commission had received 920 notifications for multilateral agreements and 34,500 for bilateral ones. DG IV was confronted with a mass problem. The European Parliament and the Council understood that quickly and adopted regulations allowing the Commission to grant block exemptions (Regulations 19/65 and 67/67).[6]

As a consequence of this mass problem, DG IV concentrated its efforts during the 1960s on vertical agreements, often of a bilateral nature. It focused particularly on agreements dealing with distribution, the licensing of industrial property rights, or cooperation for example in research and development (R&D). Preoccupation with these kinds of agreements, some have argued, absorbed resources which DG IV might have better employed investigating multilateral agreements. Most multilateral agreements were horizontal with a dimension of market sharing at least at the national level. They were generally threatening competition more than bilateral agreements on distribution or patent licensing (Goyder 1998: 70). The tendency for DG IV (and the Commission as a whole) to avoid cases likely to generate political resistance among national members explains in part that strategy (Gerber 1998).

The Commission also gave scant attention to abuse of dominant position during this period. In 1963, thinking about implementation of Article 86, the Commission created a working group, again with strong German representation. This group concluded that mergers should be seen more positively than cartels; the former were efficiency-enhancing while the latter were perceived as preserving inefficient structures. These conclusions shaped the Commission's Memorandum on Concentration, where effective competition between oligopolistic enterprises was claimed to be in conformity with Treaty objectives (Joliet 1970: 261).

Altogether, the first years of DG IV were characterized by a steady development of the legislative base for competition policy in the European Community. This development went faster than many European industrialists (and governments) had expected. By the mid-1960s, however, it faced two major challenges: the limited resources of DG IV and the political deadlock created by De Gaulle's 'empty chair' politics.

The ECJ: stimulating supranational dynamics   In this context, the ECJ took over leadership on competition issues. Timing was a critical factor. The first competition cases reached the Court in the mid-1960s, just as De Gaulle's request for unanimous decisionmaking threatened to destroy the European Community (Gerber 1994*b*). In a situation where the Council was all but paralyzed, the Court had increasing importance for maintaining the momentum of integration

(Mattli and Slaughter 1998; Stone Sweet and Caporaso 1998). Rather than limiting itself to particulars of individual cases, the Court enunciated broad principles. It looked to the future, guiding the Commission in its development of competition policy. As Goyder (1998: 578) suggested, the Court provided the Commission with 'windows of opportunity', indicating willingness to support certain developments in competition doctrine.

In its 1964 *Grundig Case* decision [Cases 56 and 58/64 ECJ], the Court gave, for example, a wide interpretation to the 'trade' clause of Article 85 ['which may affect trade between Member States'], thereby increasing the reach of competition policy (Goyder 1998: 52 *ff.*). Similarly, after the mid-1970s, the ECJ developed an interpretation of 'concerted practices'—signaling that it would support a more rigorous enforcement of Article 85. Decision on *Continental Can* in 1972 is another example [6/72 ECJ]. For the first time, the Commission had sought to use Article 86 to prevent an acquisition that would lead to an abuse of dominant position. The Court agreed, thus opening up the possibility to deal with anticompetitive mergers using Article 86 (Gerber 1994*b*: 117). Finally, the Court's decision in the *United Brands Case* [27/76 ECJ] set the stage for enhanced enforcement activities on the part of the Commission against abuse of dominant position (Goyder 1998: 320 *ff.*).

As in constitutional law (cf. Alter 1998), the Court interpreted competition provisions in light of its conception of what was needed to foster integration. Believing that a strong Commission was necessary, it developed a competition law doctrine that empowered the latter relative to national authorities. Hence, the Court confirmed the partial autonomy that Regulation 17/62 had granted the Commission. It also fostered the development of legal doctrines and practices that were (relatively) beyond the reach of intergovernmental negotiations or direct national pressure.

New challenges for the enforcement activities of DG IV The economic crisis of the early 1970s confronted the Commission with a dilemma. On one side, the Commission was intent on securing compliance with established norms and the European Parliament insisted on competition law enforcement, with a view to maintaining the faltering process of integration. On the other, economic difficulties increased incentives for firms to engage in anticompetitive conduct and enforcement became more complex. The integration, in 1973, of the United Kingdom, Ireland, and Denmark, only compounded difficulties. Educational and advocacy efforts were necessary to disseminate European competition norms in these countries. And still, DG IV's resources remained extremely limited (Gerber 1994*b*).

DG IV reacted to the challenge of bridging multiple tasks and limited resources by adopting a 'low economic cost, minimum political risk' strategy (Gerber 1994*b*: 121). From the 1970s onwards, it imposed significant fines in a limited number of cases, focusing increasingly on multilateral horizontal agreements—cartels using concerted practices (Lilja and Moen 2003) or on cases where firms abused a dominant market position (Gerber 1994*b*).

Moving further

Until the mid-1980s, the European competition law system was organized around a clearly delineated division of labor between the Commission and the ECJ. The Commission aimed at improving compliance with competition rules while the Court was developing a European competition law doctrine and expanding its reach. The interplay between national courts and competition officials and the European competition law system remained limited.

Beyond apparent stability, however, considerable change was under way. Basic legal doctrines and institutions remained the same, but from the mid-1980s onwards the respective roles of the Commission, the Court, and member states would change (Gerber 1994*b*). In the following, we briefly outline the context of this transformation.

The Single European Act and merger control   The Single European Act (SEA) of 1986 changed the scene in two ways. First, it increased the range of issues for which qualified majority voting applied. In the process, it gave the Commission back some of the room for maneuver that the latter had lost in the 1960s. Second, it engendered confidence that economic integration was progressing, hence fostering a wave of mergers and acquisitions. Together, those two developments led to the passing of a Merger Regulation in 1989.[7] The Commission had been asking for such legislation since the 1970s but member states had resisted it (Bulmer 1994).

The Merger Regulation provided that 'concentrations' (mergers and certain joint ventures) with a 'community dimension' were subject to Community regulation and removed from the jurisdiction of national competition authorities. The Commission should get advanced notification and it could prohibit the merger where it would 'create or strengthen a dominant position as a result of which effective competition would be significantly impeded in the Common market or in a substantial part of it'.

The introduction of the Merger Regulation fundamentally altered the European competition regime. It enhanced the influence of the Commission, putting it back—rather than the Court—at the center of the system. The Merger Regulation has itself become a key focus of DG IV, shifting attention away from other activities. The establishment of a merger control system has also brought political issues back, while they had been pushed aside in the 1960s in favor of a judicial approach. Even more importantly, the building of a merger control system on the foundations of the existing system strengthened elements of American case law in European competition law. From this perspective, the introduction of the Merger Control system is a case of 'institutional layering' (Thelen 2003: 226; introduction to this volume). New coalitions designed new institutional arrangements that were built on top of existing ones, circumventing a basic reform of the old system. The parallel operation of the different layers, however, changed the direction in which the overall system evolved, arguably bringing it back closer to the American competition law system, which in the meantime, of course, had itself been evolving.

Toward decentralization of enforcement Paralleling these developments, members of the ECJ suggested from the mid-1980s that the Court did not need to play as aggressive a role as in the past, now that other institutions were in a position to carry more of the integration burden.

The Commission has since become more proactive in legislation, issuing both formal and binding regulations (e.g. block exemptions) as well as informal, nonbinding general notices, letters of comfort, and other forms of soft law. During the 1990s, DG IV has increasingly turned its attention to public sectors and government intervention in the economy. The Commission report in 1990 stated, for example, that 'at the present stage of economic integration in the Community the barriers are greatest in markets currently subject to state regulation' (Gerber 1994b: 138). This public turn found expression in the activation of Article 90 of the Rome Treaty,[8] which applies competition law provisions to public enterprises. It also translated into increased enforcement of provisions relating to state aid (for sectoral analyses of these trends see Plehwe with Vescovi 2003; Midttun, Micola, and Omland 2003). Sections of the Rome Treaty that had not been invoked for thirty years now were activated by the Commission and other actors aiming at a liberalization of public sectors. This shows how societal and political actors can invoke 'dormant' institutional fragments not only at the national but also at the supranational level to mobilize for institutional change (see also introduction to this volume).

Finally, the introduction of the concept of *subsidiarity* during the Maastricht Treaty negotiations has also had a significant impact. Recent Commission proposals envisage a far-reaching re-delegation of enforcement activity to national competition authorities, in order to free DG IV resources in particular for merger control. This only makes sense, however, in the context of an evolution—over the last twenty years—where European competition law has had a significant impact at the level of member states, shaping, structuring, or transforming national competition systems (Djelic 2002; ENA 2002).

Discussion—toward national system change

When the Rome Treaty was signed, Germany was the only member state with a competition law—and even there it was only emerging. Today, all member states have competition regimes, shaped and inspired, in one way or another, by the European Community competition regime. When entering the EEC in 1981, Greece adopted a legislative framework fully modeled on the Community blueprint. France significantly reformed its set of loose competition-related norms and institutions in 1986, with European standards in mind. Spain and Italy introduced competition law systems in 1989 and 1990, respectively (Gerber 1994b: 142; ENA 2002).

The Commission has never attempted to put direct pressure on member states (i.e. through regulations and directives) to align national competition laws to European law. Neither have case decisions by the Commission or the ECJ attempted to influence national competition law directly (Van Waarden and Drahos 2002). In fact, the ECJ ruled in 1969 that national competition law could be applied in parallel to EU law, but that EU law had precedence in those areas where it applied. Nevertheless, all member countries have created national competition law regimes, and those regimes, furthermore, have gained in congruence through time if not fully converged (ENA 2002). This increasing congruence provides an interesting case of harmonization occurring without significant direct coercion. Indirect pressures, however, played an important role.

Indirect pressures for harmonization

Growing congruence between European and national competition regimes does not mean full convergence. Differences in substance and procedure persist, and, for reasons identified below, some of these differences will probably not disappear. Nevertheless, we observe a progressive alignment, on general principles, enforcement mechanisms, and administrative practice (ENA 2002). This growing congruence has emerged from the combination of at least three mechanisms.

The first mechanism consisted of subtle 'top-down' pressures exerted by the Commission and ECJ. Decisions of the Commission and ECJ created pressure on member states by banning practices at the European level (e.g. cartels) hitherto accepted at the national level (Drahos 2001; Van Waarden and Drahos 2002: 925). This placed national authorities in the difficult position of having to develop arguments justifying differences between national and European norms and practices. It also provided previously marginal groups of actors, nationally, with windows of opportunity to question the dominant approach. In many instances, such subtle top-down pressures set in motion a process of gradual deinstitutionalization (Djelic and Quack 2003a). The reaction of national authorities to a succession of indirect European attacks potentially relayed nationally was in general to adapt national to European law.

A second mechanism, operating in close interaction with the first, was the emergence of an 'epistemic community' of legally trained officials (Van Waarden and Drahos 2002: 914). This community channeled information, ideas, and solutions between the European and national systems of competition law. EU case law provided an important model and source of norms for this community. Part of this development was the gradual delegation of European competition cases from ECJ to national courts. Already in 1973, the ECJ had ruled that Treaty provisions on competition were directly applicable in national courts. It took more than a decade for national courts to become really involved. Once they did, though, it meant that justices and lawyers became increasingly familiar with European competition law standards and drew comparisons between those standards and national practice. Progressively, those national members of a budding European 'epistemic community' would put pressure on their national systems, fostering change (Quack 2003).

Finally, the 'public turn' in the enforcement activities of DG IV in the 1990s put quite direct pressures on national governments to bring their policies on public sectors in line with the European competition regime. These pressures often led in practice to a general overhaul of existing national competition rules.

Taken together, these three mechanisms suggest a process of 'hollowing out'. The creation, gradual expansion, and subsequently successful operation of a European competition regime gradually undermined the operation of differently patterned national competition regimes and pushed actors within these systems to contemplate, and finally accept, at least partial adaptation to the European model.

The German case: reluctant adaptation

This process can be illustrated with the German case. As described above, German lawyers and competition officials significantly influenced European competition law during the foundation period of the EEC. German ordo-liberal thinking left its mark on the Rome Treaty and on procedural regulations implementing the Treaty during the early years. At the same time, the parallel existence of a European competition regime, structured along similar principles, probably contributed more to the stabilization of the German competition regime than it was realized then. In fact, by the late 1960s, German competition officials referred explicitly to the European competition regime in order to mobilize support against reemerging pro-cartel attitudes at the national level.[9] Interactions between the two systems continued over time, although they changed in nature. While at the beginning of the period influence went predominantly from Germany to Europe, this changed progressively and since the late 1980s the direction of influence has overall been reversed.

As in other member states, German courts have eventually come to borrow concepts and definitions from European case law. German competition authorities have also come to apply EU law in areas that benefited from exemption under national law. German competition officials meet Commission inspectors regularly in the context of investigations or in advisory Committees. Given the close starting base of German and European systems, and reinforcing interactions between the two systems over time, it is surprising that the 'former best pupil' has turned today into a rather reluctant adapter (Van Waarden and Drahos 2002: 915). In fact, German competition officials continue to oppose full adaptation to European competition norms.

Interestingly, and somewhat ironically considering the history recounted above, it was the Federation of German Industry (BDI) that suggested, in 1995, harmonization of national and European competition law in order to enhance the competitiveness of German business. The Federal government responded with a proposal aiming at full harmonization. The advisory Academic Council of the German Minister for Economic Affairs, however, mirroring the views of the Federal Cartel Office and Monopoly Commission (both bastions of ordo-liberal thought) rejected the initiative and the idea of 'Europeanization'. Criticism was mostly directed at the inclusion of a general exemption clause along the lines of Article 85 (3). This was condemned, together with the introduction of the notion of 'decisive influence' in merger provisions, for importing industrial policy goals into competition law (Lodge 2000: 95). In 1999, after four years of controversy, the German law was finally reformed—meaning a far-reaching but not full adaptation to European legislation. There were less sector exemptions, for example, but there were still some. The German merger regime continues to differ from the European, particularly on the concept of dominance (Stadler 1998).

This shows that cross-border model transfer, even when a model has, in earlier periods, been influenced by one's own heritage, always amounts to more than mere copying. The European system, starting as a recombinant of national elements, has evolved over the years its own characteristics and dynamics, as have competition regimes in member states. Despite subtle top-down pressures and an emerging community of episteme and practice, beyond borrowing, modeling, and recombination, there are still some differences between the European and German competition regimes.

Conclusions

The above narratives document two interwoven processes. On the one hand, we have a case of transnational institution building, where rules for the competitive game are progressively structured and stabilized at the European level. On the other hand, in partial interconnection, we document a case of progressive, incremental but consequential institutional change in one country, Germany.

Transnational institution building—recombination and layering

The story of European antitrust recounted above is an illustration of transnational institution building. New rules were progressively institutionalized in a space that was itself being structured. The process of institutional emergence did not start from scratch. It was closer to *bricolage*—recombining institutional fragments—than to ex-nihilo creation (Djelic and Quack 2003a: 30).

At the beginning, the impact of American antitrust tradition and experience was undeniable. The German postwar antitrust experience also had some impact on the construction of a European competition regime. This German development itself reflected an encounter between strong American influence, national ordo-liberal thinking, national institutional legacies, and local resistance.

Altogether, this early period of recombination was characterized by a dominant mode or logic (Djelic and Quack 2003a: 324 *ff*.). One particular set of institutional fragments—here associated with American antitrust tradition —became the dominant element in the recombination process. In the ECSC story, this influence combined a direct and an indirect effect. The direct effect was the impact of American tradition and experience on the ECSC competition regime. The indirect effect was the impact of American antitrust on the German competition regime that in turn played a role in the recombination process at the European level.

Yet, once it started to be interpreted and implemented, European antitrust legislation became a force of its own. By the early 1960s the mode of recombination had ceased to be of a clear dominant kind. The interplay between European texts, new European institutions, national interlocutors, and an emergent epistemic community made institution building a complex process. Evidence points to a combination of what we call negotiated and emergent modes. A negotiated mode expresses the friction between multiple national fragments with approximately equal weight. An emergent mode implies presence, in the friction, of actors and institutional fragments not directly associated with a national identity (Djelic and Quack 2003*b*: 325 *ff.*). During the 1990s, institution building around antitrust involved actors and institutions (e.g. the epistemic community, ECJ, or DG IV) with an identity that went beyond a combination of national identities and was, in a sense, transnational. Multiple actors with no clear identity, functioning themselves at the interface of multiple rule systems, collide with each other. What takes place then, we label an emergent process. The resulting construction is decoupled somewhat from national roots and develops a dynamic of its own as a truly transnational space (Barnett and Finnemore 1999).

While modes and logics of recombination changed during the period, we also document institutional layering and sedimentation (see introduction to this volume). Until the mid-1980s, the European competition regime dealt mostly with cartels and/or abuse of dominant position. With the Merger Regulation, a new layer of institution building was superimposed in 1989, this time with a focus on merger issues. European institution building around the merger issue was strongly influenced by the American experience. On that layer, a dominant mode was again at work, albeit with quite different characteristics from the dominant mode of the 1950s.

The United States could not attempt to impose their model as they had done then. The impact was more subtle and indirect. As the Chairman of the American Federal Trade Commission said in 2002, 'no treaty forced foreign nations to borrow ideas from the US Merger guidelines' (Muris 2002). Nevertheless, they did, seizing upon, in the words of Muris, 'best practices'. An institutionalist perspective would point to a successful process of socialization, to cultural diffusion, and to legitimacy-seeking mechanisms (Strang and Meyer 1993). By the 1990s, Europe and other countries had been 'converted to the value of antitrust' that Americans had early on 'been preaching' (Melamed 2000). Even though Europe was itself a missionary by then (Rouam, Thinam, and Suni 1994), with respect to antitrust the United States remained the referent well into the 1990s.

National institutional change—trickle-down and trickle-up trajectories

In parallel to a story of transnational institution building, we have also documented in this chapter a case of incremental but nevertheless consequential institutional change (see introduction to this volume). In 1945, Germany was closely associated with cartels and cartelization. Then, a political window of opportunity opened in that country, allowing a radical and consequential reformulation of economic policy. The institutional entrepreneurs who seized this opportunity were a coalition of outsiders—Americans with an experience of antitrust—and a small group of (then marginal) insiders with a compatible project. In the long run, the reformulation indeed proved consequential. It was not, however, radical in the sense of rapid rupture and clean break with the past—Germany the cartel country one day turned bastion of antitrust the next. Instead, we observe a succession and combination, over a long period of time, of partial steps and incremental transformations that ultimately amounted to consequential and significant change.

In previous work we have used the metaphor of stalactite change to characterize a process where a succession of incremental steps is nevertheless consequential, in order to overcome the classic dichotomy between rare and radical change on the one hand, incremental and inconsequential change on the other (Djelic and Quack 2003*b*: 308, see also introduction to this volume). The image is that of a minuscule drop of water falling from the vault of a cave. In itself, it seems insignificant, with no impact on the cave as a whole. However, under given conditions of temperature, the succession and combination of large numbers of droplets may lead to an aggregation of the calcite contained in those drops. After a long while, the result is a thick landscape of innovatively shaped stalactites and stalagmites and a consequential transformation, one could say, of the cave as a whole.

In the German antitrust story told here, each single step was fragile, particularly at the beginning. The multiplication of steps, their accretion, and aggregation, reinforced each individual step and in time stabilized the process. As is the case with stalactite formation, the overall direction was set by the first steps (drops). Thereafter, however, the process became, as in our imaginary cave, quite open-ended. The result was a German antitrust tradition with features that could not have been fully anticipated. At the same time, we argue that the concomitant and partly interconnected development of European antitrust was a further stabilizing factor, in the long run, for the German transformation. A comparison with the Japanese antitrust story would tend to confirm this (Haley 2001). The Japanese story shared many features with the German (Yamamura and Streeck 2003) but lacked the interconnection with a reinforcing transnational process of institution building such as that took place in Europe. This comparison suggests the importance of including the effect of transnational institutions—through both trickle-down and trickle-up pressures—in future analysis of national institutional change.

The nature and extent of interconnection between European institution building and German institutional change have varied across time. We identify three main periods. From the mid-1950s to the mid-1970s, influence went predominantly from Germany toward Europe—the German antitrust experience having an impact on the budding European attempt at institution building. For the following ten years, we essentially have a lull, where interplays were weaker than at any other moment. Since the mid-1980s, interconnections have increased again in density and influence is going mostly from Europe toward Germany.

These interconnections are mostly in the form of indirect pressures for harmonization, of essentially two types (Djelic and Quack 2003*b*: 315–20). On the one hand, we identify trickle-down pressures. Those are exerted by European institutions—the Commission, DG IV, ECJ—on the German competition regime. As we have shown, those pressures tend to be subtle, discreet, implicit, and of a normative kind, with little legal or institutional coercion. This trajectory of indirect, subtle, but top-down pressures was to some extent institutionalized from 2000, when the European Commission launched a reform to transfer progressively some of its responsibilities and prerogatives to national authorities, in line with the subsidiarity principle. This delegation of powers comes with a systematic effort at structuring and stabilizing cooperation between national competition authorities. A European network of competition authorities was thus created with a view to building the foundations of more solid cooperation. The Commission hopes that these developments will deepen the common antitrust culture and further in time homogenization (ENA 2002).

On the other hand we also find trickle-up pressures. The structuring of a European epistemic community, around antitrust lawyers and competition officials, has created a situation where national members of that epistemic community are putting pressure nationally for competition regimes to adapt to European blueprints. This has been operative in Germany, increasingly so since the late 1980s. The German story points to another example of trickle-up pressure; this time stemming from German business communities. We have noted the irony, there, given the early history of German antitrust. The BDI in particular has since 1995 been urging a reform to bring the German competition regime closer to the European one. This, they claim, is necessary to increase the competitiveness of German business.

Although resistance has not been insignificant, the combination of trickle-down and trickle-up pressures was enough to bring about, in 1999, a reform of the German competition regime. Further research, by comparing the German to other cases could make it possible to specify the conditions under which the interplay of trickle-down and trickle-up pressures brings about gradual but consequential institutional change and the conditions under which it does not.

Notes

1. Needless to say that American antitrust has been throughout its history a 'moving target' and that our summary here is schematic (see Thorelli 1954 and Peritz 1996 for detailed analyses of its historical evolution). For our purposes—and for reasons of space—we only point here to the broad characteristics of that tradition as crystallized by the 1920s.

2. All citations from the ECSC Treaty are taken from http://www.europa.eu.int/abc/obj/treaties/en/entoc29.htm (Download from 18.09.2003).
3. Following the Treaty on the EU of 1992 (TEU hereafter) Articles 85 and 86 were renumbered respectively to 81 and 82 (cf. Official Journal C 191 29/07/1992). We use the pre-1992 numbering throughout unless otherwise stated.
4. Citations from the Rome Treaty are taken from http://europa.eu.int/abc/obj/treaties/en/entoc05.htm (Download from 29.09.2003).
5. EEC Council: Regulation No. 17: First Regulation implementing Articles 85 and 86 of the Treaty. Official Journal P 013, 21/02/1962: 0204–0211.
6. Regulation No. 19/65/EEC on application of Article 85 (3) of the Treaty to certain categories of agreements and concerted practices. Official Journal P 036, 06/03/1965: 0533–0535. Regulation No. 67/67/EEC on the application of Article 85 (3) of the Treaty to certain categories of exclusive dealing agreements. Official Journal 057, 25/03/1967: 0849.
7. Council Regulation (EEC) No. 4064/89 on the control of concentrations between undertakings (Corrigenda—whole text republished in OJ L 257/90: 13). Official Journal L 395, 30/12/1989: 0001–0012.
8. Article 86 in TEU of 1992.
9. In 1967, for example, the German Federal Cartel Office charged major German and European chemical producers of aniline dyes with price-fixing, imposing high fines on these companies. German courts rejected this decision, arguing that no written agreement had been found, and created in the process considerable public debate. The president of the Federal Cartel Office, Eberhard Günther, argued in that context that German regulation should be adapted to the more comprehensive rules of the EC competition regime. It took several years before this proposal would be finally endorsed politically, leading to the reform in 1973 of the GWB. In the meantime, the European Commission had initiated investigations and imposed high fines on the same chemical companies, the ECJ confirming this decision (Nawrocki 1973: 87).

References

ALTER, K. (1998). Who are the 'Masters of the Treaty'?: European Governments and the European Court of Justice. *International Organization* 52(1): 121–47.

BARNETT, M. N. and FINNEMORE, M. (1999). The Politics, Power and Pathologies of International Organizations. *International Organization* 53(4): 699–732.

BAYLISS, B. T. (1980). Competition and Industrial Policy. In: A. El-Agraa (ed.), *The Economics of the European Community*. Oxford, UK: Philip Allan Publishers Ltd., pp. 113–33.

BERGHAHN, V. (1986). *The Americanization of West German Industry*. Cambridge: Cambridge University Press.

BERGLÖF, E., ROSENTHAL, H., and VON THADDEN, E.-L. (2001). The Formation of Legal Institutions for Bankruptcy: A Comparative Study of the Legislative History. Background Paper for the *World Development Report*, The World Bank.

BRAUNTHAL, G. (1965). *The Federation of German Industry in Politics*. Ithaca, NY: Cornell University Press.

BULMER, S. (1994). Institutions and Policy Change in the European Communities: The Case of Merger Control. *Public Administration* 72: 423–44.

BUNDESANZEIGER (1950). Vorläufiger Bericht der deutschen Kommission zum Studium von Kartell- und Monopolfragen in den Vereinigten Staaten. *Beilage zum Bundesanzeiger*, 250 (Dezember 29).

DAMM, W. (1958). *National and International Factors Influencing Cartel Legislation in Germany*. Ph.D. Dissertation, Chicago, ILL: University of Chicago.

DE SOTO, H. (2000). *The Mystery of Capital*. New York: Basic Books.

DJELIC, M.-L. (1998). *Exporting the American Model*. Oxford: Oxford University Press.

—— (2002). Does Europe mean Americanization? The Case of Competition. *Competition and Change* 6(3): 223–50.

—— and QUACK, S. (2003a). Theoretical Building Blocks for a Research Agenda. In: M.-L. Djelic and S. Quack (eds.), *Globalization and Institutions*. Cheltenham, UK: Edward Elgar, pp. 15–34.

—— —— (2003b). Conclusion: Globalization as a Double Process of Institutional Change and Institution Building. In: M.-L. Djelic and S. Quack (eds.), *Globalization and Institutions*. Cheltenham, UK: Edward Elgar, pp. 302–33.

DOBBIN, F. and DOWD, T. (2000). The Market that Antitrust Built: Public Policy, Private Coercion and Railroad Acquisitions, 1825–1922. *American Sociological Review* 65(5): 631–57.

DRAHOS, M. (2001). *Convergence of Competition Laws and Policies in the European Community*. The Hague: Kluwer Law International.

EL-AGRAA, A. (ed.) (1980). *The Economics of the European Community*. Oxford, UK: Philip Allan Publishers Ltd.

ENA (2002). *Dossier Spécial—La Concurrence*, 318 (February).

ERHARD, L. (1958). *Prosperity through Competition*. New York: Frederick Praeger.

—— (1963). *The Economics of Success*. Princeton, NJ: Van Nostrand.

EVENETT, S., LEHMANN, A., and STEIL, B. (eds.) (2000). *Antitrust Goes Global*. Washington DC: Brookins Institution Press.

FLIGSTEIN, N. (1990). *The Transformation of Corporate Control*. Cambridge, MA: Harvard University Press.

—— (2001). *The Architecture of Markets*. Princeton, NJ: Princeton University Press.

FRUS (Foreign Relations of the United States) (1950). Memorandum of the French Planning Council reprinted in Telegram from Acheson to Dulles, London, May 12. *Collected Original Diplomatic Documents for the Year 1950*, Vol. iii, Washington.

FORRESTER, I. S. (2000). The Modernization of EC Antitrust Policy. Compatibility, Efficiency, Legal Security. European University Institute, Robert Schuman Center, EU Competition Workshop, June 2/3, Florence.

—— and NORALL, C. (1984). The Laicization of Community Law: Self-Help and the Rule of Reason: How Competition Law is and could be Applied. *Common Market Law Review* 11(22): 11–51.

GERBER, D. (1994a). Constitutionalizing the Economy: German Neo-Liberalism, Competition Law and the 'New Europe'. *American Journal of Comparative Law* 42: 25–84.

—— (1994b). The Transformation of European Community Competition Law. *Harvard International Law Journal* 35(1): 97–147.

—— (1998). *Law and Competition in Twentieth Century Europe*. New York: Clarendon Press.

GOYDER, D. (1998). *EC Competition Law*. Oxford: Oxford University Press.

HALEY, J. (2001). *Antitrust in Germany and Japan*. Seattle, WA: University of Washington Press.

HEINTZ, B., MÜLLER, D., and ROGGENTHIN, H. (2001). Gleichberechtigung zwischen globalen Normen und lokalen Kontexten: Deutschland, Schweiz, Marokko und Syrien im Vergleich. *Kölner Zeitschrift für Soziologie und Sozialpsychologie* 41 (Special issue): 399–430.

HERRIGEL, G. (1996). *Industrial Constructions*. Cambridge: Cambridge University Press.

JOLIET, R. (1970). *Monopolization and Abuse of Dominant Position*. Faculté de Droit, Liège, La Haye: Martinus Nijhoff.

KUDO, A. and HARA, T. (1992). *International Cartels in Business History*. Tokyo: University of Tokyo Press.

LAPORTA, R., LOPEZ-DE-SILANES, F., SCHLEIFER, A., and VISHNY, R. W. (1998). Law and Finance. *Journal of Political Economy*, 106(December): 1133–55.

LEVY, H. (1966). *Industrial Germany*. London: Franck Cass.

LIEFMANN, R. (1938). *Cartels, Concerns and Trusts*. New York: Dutton.

LILJA, K. and MOEN, E. (2003). Coordinating transnational competition: changing patterns in the European pulp and paper industry. In: M.-L. Djelic and S. Quack (eds.), *Globalization and Institutions*. Cheltenham, UK: Edward Elgar, pp. 137–60.

LODGE, M. (2000). Isomorphism of National Policies? The Europeanisation of German Competition and Public Procurement Law. *West European Politics* 23(1): 89–107.

MARTIN, J. (1950). *All Honorable Men*. Boston, MA: Little Brown.

MATTLI, W. and SLAUGHTER, A.-M. (1998). Revisiting the European Court of Justice. *International Organization* 52(1): 177–209.

MELAMED, D. (2000). Promoting Sound Antitrust Enforcement in the Global Economy. *Speech of the Acting Assistant Attorney General, Antitrust Division, US DoJ, before the Fordham Corporate Law Institute 27th Annual Conference on International Antitrust Law and Policy*, New York, October.

MICHELS, R. (1928). *Cartels, Combines and Trusts in Postwar Germany*. New York: Columbia University Press.

MIDTTUN, A., MICOLA, A. R., and OMLAND, T. (2003). Path-dependent national systems or European convergence? The case of European electricity markets. In: M.-L. Djelic and S. Quack (eds.), *Globalization and Institutions*. Cheltenham, UK: Edward Elgar, pp.161–92.

MONNET, J. (1976). *Mémoires*. Paris: Fayard.

MURIS, T. (2002). Competition Agencies in a Market Based Global Economy. *Speech of the Chairman of the FTC at the Annual Lecture of the European Foreign Affairs Review*, Brussels, July 23. Available at www.ftc.gov/speeches/muris /020723brussels.htm.

MÜLLER-HENNEBERG, H. and SCHWARTZ, G. (eds.) (1963). *Gesetz gegen Wettbewerbsbeschränkungen und europäisches Kartellrecht*. Köln: Carl Heymanns.

NAWROCKI, J. (1973). *Komplott der ehrbaren Konzerne*. Hamburg: Hoffmann und Campe.

NICHOLLS, A. (1984). The Other Germany, the Neo-Liberals. In: R. J. Bullen, H. P. Von Strandmann, and A.B. Polonsky (eds.), *Ideas into Politics*. London: Rowman & Littlefield, pp. 167–70.

OMGUS (Office of Military Government for Germany US) (1947). Explaining Decartelization to the Germans, Vol. 18, September 10, #11/11–3/7.

—— (1950). Internal Memo, Antitrust Project L501, Vol. 42, September 20, #17/246–1/6.

PEACOCK, A. and WILLGERODT, H. (eds.) (1989). *Germany's Social Market Economy*. New York: Saint Martin Press.

PERITZ, R. (1996). *Competition Policy in America*. New York: Oxford University Press.

PLEHWE, D. (with Vescovi, Stefano) (2003). Europe's Special Case: The Five Corners of Business-State Interactions. In: M.-L. Djelic and S. Quack (eds.), *Globalization and Institutions*. Cheltenham, UK: Edward Elgar, pp. 193–219.

PITTMAN, R. (1998). Competition Law and Policy in the United States. Working Paper US Department of Justice. Washington DC.

QUACK, S. (2003). Internationale Wirtschaftskanzleien im Spannungsfeld von Wandel und Kontinuität des Rechts. In: C. Dörrenbächer (ed.), *Modelltransfer in multinationalen Unternehmen*. Berlin: Edition sigma, pp. 173–98.

RHEINSTEIN, M. (1974). *Einführung in die Rechtsvergleichung*. München: C.H. Beck'sche Verlagsbuchhandlung.

ROBERT, R. (1976). *Konzentrationspolitik in der Bundesrepublik*. Berlin: Duncker & Humblot.

ROUAM, C., THINAM, J., and SUNI, L. (1994). La Politique de concurrence de la communauté à l'échelle mondiale: l'exportation des règles de concurrence communautaires. *EC Competition Policy Newsletter* 1(1): 7–11.

SCHMIDT, I. and BINDER, S. (1996). *Wettbewerbspolitik im internationalen Vergleich*. Heidelberg: Verlag Recht und Wirtschaft.

SCHWARTZ, T. A. (1991). *America's Germany*. Cambridge, MA: Harvard University Press.

SCHWARZ, J. (ed.) (1956, 1980). Spaak-Bericht: Bericht der Delegationsleiter des von der Konferenz von Messina eingesetzten Regierungsausschusses an die Außenminister. In: *Der Aufbau Europas*. Bonn: Osang Verlag GmbH, pp. 277–336.

SKLAR, M. (1988). *Corporate Reconstruction of American Capitalism, 1890–1916*. New York: Cambridge University Press.

STADLER, S. (1998). The German Competition Law Reform of 1999. *European Competition Law Review* 8: 542–6.

STONE SWEET, A. and CAPORASO, J. (1998). From Free Trade to Supranational Polity: The European Court and Integration. In: W. Sandholtz and A. Stone Sweet (eds.), *European Integration and Supranational Governance*. Oxford: Oxford University Press, pp. 92–133.

STRANG, D. and MEYER, J. (1993). Institutional Conditions for Diffusion. *Theory and Society* 22: 487–511.

STRYKER, R. (2003). Mind the Gap: Law, Institutional Analysis and Socioeconomics. *Socio-Economic Review* 1: 335–67.

THELEN, K. (2003). How Institutions Evolve. Insights from Comparative Historical Analysis. In: J. Mahoney and D. Rueschemeyer (eds.), *Comparative Historical Analysis in the Social Sciences*. Cambridge: Cambridge University Press, pp. 208–40.

THORELLI, H. (1954). *The Federal Antitrust Policy*. Baltimore, MD: Johns Hopkins University Press.

VAN WAARDEN, F. and DRAHOS, M. (2002). Courts and (Epistemic) Communities in the Convergence of Competition Policies. *Journal of European Public Policy* 9(6) (December): 1–22.

VON DER GROEBEN, H. (1987). *The European Community—The Formative Years*. The European Perspectives Series. Brussels, Luxembourg: Office for Official Publications of the European Communities.

WALLICH, H. (1955). *Mainsprings of German Revival*. New Haven, CT: Yale University Press.

YAMAMURA, K. and STREECK, W. (eds.) (2003). *The End of Diversity?* Ithaca, NY: Cornell University Press.

Index

Acheson, Dean 262
action, institutional change and pragmatic social
    action 231–2
adaptive expectations
    and the German and Italian financial systems
        193–4
    and path dependence 171
Adenauer, Konrad 205, 241, 263
African Americans, and health insurance 58
ageing population, and pay-as-you go pension
    systems 134
agency
    and actor-centred institutionalism 84
    and structure 7, 19
agenda formation, and American welfare state
    retrenchment 41
Ahmadjian, C. 157
ambiguity
    and codetermination in Germany 230, 230–1,
        237–40, 241, 243–4, 245, 250
    and conversion 26–7
    and institutional change 229–30, 232–6, 249
    and pragmatic social action 232
antitrust and competition law in Europe 22,
        255–77
    and American antitrust 255, 257, 258–9,
        266–7, 275
    and the EEC 264–6, 271, 273
    and the European Commission 266, 269–70,
        272
    and the European Court of Justice 265, 266,
        268–9, 272–3
    Germany 256, 257–62, 271, 273–4, 276–7
    and harmonization 272–3, 277
    and Japan 276
    and layering 270–1, 274–5
    and the Merger Regulation 270–1, 275
    and national institutional change 276–7
    and the Single European Act 270
    and the Spaak Report (1956) 265–6
    and transnational institution building 274–5
Aoki, Masahiko 162, 232, 233–4, 235, 249
Aso, Taro 160

Balladur, Edouard 108, 114, 139
Bank of England 89
bank-based financial systems 173
bankruptcies

in France 52
in the United States 52
banks
    Germany 175, 177, 178–80, 182–3
        coordination effects 192–3
        'Frankfurt Coalition' 180
        loans to firms and manufacturing industry
            178
    Italy 184–5, 186–8, 189–91
        coordination effects 193
        Mediobanca 184, 186, 187, 190–1
    Japan 149, 154–5, 156, 159, 162–3, 164
BDI (Federation of German Industry) 273–4,
    277
Bendix, Reinhard 14
Berger, S. 16
Blüm, Norbert 215
Böhm, Franz 258, 259
bounded change, and path dependence 172
bounded innovation, in Japan 163–5
Bowie, Robert 259, 263
Brigl-Matthiass, Kurt 239
Britain see United Kingdom
Bush, President George H.W. 56
Bush, President George W. 63, 65, 68

capital mobility, and Japan 149
capitalism, liberalization within 30, 33
Castaldi, C. 21
Chirac, Jacques 107, 111, 114, 121, 122
Clayton Act (United States) 257
Clemens, Elizabeth 27
Clinton, President Bill 55
    defeat of health care plan 61–2
CMEs (coordinated market economies) 5, 83
    and Japan 17, 148
COASE framework, and institutional change
        233–6, 249
codetermination
    in Germany 18, 27, 32, 230, 236–49, 250
    and institutional reconfiguration 235
collective bargaining
    in Germany
        and codetermination 238–9
        and early retirement policies 204, 217–18,
            220, 221
competition law see antitrust and competition
        law

conversion 19, 26–9, 30, 31, 33
  and American welfare state retrenchment 42,
    45, 46–8, 49, 70
  and the COASE framework of institutional
    change 234–5
  and creativity 232
  institutional conversion in France 104–5
  in Japan 163
coordinated market economies *see* CMEs
    (coordinated market economies)
coordination effects
  in German and Italian financial systems
    192–3
  and path dependence 171
coordination gains, in the German financial
    system 176
core competencies, and codetermination in
    Germany 247
corporate governance, in the German financial
    system 175–7
creativity, and ambiguity 232
Crouch, Colin 20–1, 28
Cuccia, Enrico 184, 186
cultivation of increasing returns, and path
    dependence 174

Deeg, R. 18, 19, 21, 33
defection, displacement through 20
democratization, and codetermination in
    Germany 240–2
Dewey, John 231–2
disclosure, and codetermination in Germany
    247
displacement 19–22, 30, 31
  and antitrust and competition law 256
  through defection 20–1
  through invasion 21–2
Djelic, Marie-Laure 22, 27
Dosi, G. 21
downsizing, in Japan 157
drift 19, 24–6, 30, 31
  and American welfare state retrenchment 42,
    45–6, 48, 49, 56, 69, 70, 71, 75
  pensions 64–5
  and exhaustion 29
Durkheim, E. 16

early retirement policies
  France 107–8, 109, 114–15, 119, 121, 122
  Germany 29–30, 32, 115, 203–22
    and conflicts among employers 213–14
    exhaustion of 29–30, 203–4, 221
    flexible retirement option 206, 207

    and German unification 210–12, 214
    government attempts to correct 214–15
    and government social policy 205–12
    and institutional resettlement 220–2
    liberalization of 216–20
    and the Metalworkers' and Chemical
      Workers' Unions 217
    resistance of employers to 212–13
    and trade unions 208–9, 216
  Japan 154
East Germany, and early retirement policies
    210–12, 214
ECJ (European Court of Justice), and antitrust
    and competition law 265, 266, 268–9,
    272–3
economic dualism 16
ECSC (European Coal and Steel Community)
    256, 262–4, 265, 275
EEC (European Economic Community), and
    antitrust and competition law 264–6,
    271, 273
elderly people in France, welfare benefits for 111
Elster, J. 26
employees, and codetermination in Germany
    237, 248–9
employer-provided health plans, and American
    welfare state retrenchment 41
employers
  in Germany
    and codetermination 237, 239–40, 240–1
    and early retirement policies 212–14,
      217–18
employment
  changing patterns of, and American welfare
    state retrenchment 50, 51
  illegal 15–16
  in Japan
    and institutional change 150–1, 154
    'lifetime' employment patterns 148, 150,
      165
    policy reforms 158–9
  and Keynesian economic policies 3
  see also labor market policies
EMS (European Monetary System), and France
    103
endogenous change
  in German and Italian financial systems 174,
    194–5
  and neo-institutionalism 83, 86
  and path dependence 173
ends-in-view, and pragmatic actions 232
epistemic community, and European antitrust
    and competition law 272–3, 277

equity-oriented performance targets, and
      codetermination in Germany 247
Erhard, Ludwig 258, 259–60, 261, 263
Esping-Andersen, G. 40, 46, 70
Eucken, Walter 258
European Commission, and antitrust and
      competition law 266, 269–70, 272
European Council, and antitrust and
      competition law 267
European Court of Justice *see* ECJ (European
      Court of Justice)
European integration, and France
      123, 124
European Parliament, and antitrust and
      competition law 267, 269, 270
European Single Market
   and the German financial system 177
   and the Italian financial system 186
European Union (EU)
   and antitrust regulation 255
   interest group behaviour 27
exhaustion 19, 29–30, 31
exogenous shocks 1
   and American welfare state retrenchment
      41, 70
   and German and Italian financial systems
      170, 195
   and transformational change 18

family allowances, France 116
family benefits, in France 141
family structure
   changes in
      France 116
      United States 25, 50–1, 51–2, 75
FDI (foreign direct investment), in Hungary 91,
      92, 94–7, 97–8
Federal Reserve Bank 12
feedback mechanisms
   and Aoki's game-theoretic framework 233
   and the German financial system 174, 194
   and the Italian financial system 194
   and path dependence 171, 172, 173
financial systems
   bank-based 173
   City of London 88–90
   Germany 169–70
   Italy 170, 174, 184–91
   Japan 146, 148, 149, 154–5
   market-based 172–3
   and path dependence 172–4
First World War 238, 257
flexible working in France 108–9

France 103–42
   antitrust and competition law 271
   banque-industrie 117
   'cohabitation' in government 114
   and deconcentration 118
   dirigisme 17, 103–4, 112, 113, 117, 119, 122
      dismantling of 105–7, 116
   health care 110, 117, 118–19
   institutional redeployment in 103–4
   labor market programs 107–9
   liberalization in 32
   Movement of French Enterprises (MEDEF)
      122
   national champions 103, 118
   National Front 121
   post-*dirigiste* state intervention 107–13, 119,
      122–3
      and economic liberalization 114–16, 119,
         122
      and non-state capacity 116–19, 122–3
      and party competition 113–14
      and the social anaesthesia state 104,
         119–22
   SMEs in 107, 111, 112–13, 117, 118, 123
   social insurance in 115–16, 127, 132–8, 139,
      141, 142
   social policy 127–42, 221
      APA (aide personnalisée à l'autonomie)
         111
      CMU (universal health insurance) 111,
         116, 128, 130, 139, 140
      CSG (general social contribution) 128,
         130, 133, 137, 139–40
      decisions based on ambiguous agreement
         131, 137–8, 141–2
      diagnosis of failure 130, 131–5, 141
      and historical institutionalism 129
      as incremental but cumulatively
         transformative 131, 138–41, 142
      LFSS (Social Security Budget Act) 128,
         130, 133, 140
      opposing the past 131, 135–7, 141, 142
      paradigm 142
      path-shifting reforms in 131, 135,
         141–2
      reinsertion policies 135–6
      retrenchment policies 132
      RMI (guaranteed income) 110–11, 116,
         119, 121, 127, 128, 130, 133, 137, 138,
         139, 140
      and the social security deficit 134–5
      third-order changes in 128–9, 130, 142
   state-led political economy in 17, 28, 103

unemployment in 107–8, 109, 115–16, 118,
122, 131, 132–3, 139, 141, 142
welfare state reform 23–4, 27
Freiburg school, and antitrust and competition
law in Germany 258

Gaulle, General Charles de 106, 113, 114, 268
Genoa, governing institutions 29
Germany
antitrust and competition law 256, 257–62,
271, 273–4, 276–7
and American occupation 258–9
and the BDI 260–1, 273–4, 277
and the Freiburg school 258
Law Against Restraints on Competition
261–2
banks 175, 177, 178–80, 182–3
coordination effects 192–3
'Frankfurt Coalition' 180
loans to firms and manufacturing industry
178
CDU (Christian Democratic Union) 205, 214
codetermination in 18, 27, 32, 229–50, 230,
236–49, 250
the 1970s and 1980s (diffusion and
consolidation) 243–4
change since the 1990s 237, 246–9
Codetermination Commission report
(1998) 246
Imperial and Weimar Germany 237–40
postwar period 237, 240–2
corporate governance codex 181–2
early retirement policies 29–30, 32, 115,
203–22
financial system 21, 169–70, 174–84, 192–7
adaptive expectations 193–4
and bifurcation 175
change to a new path 177–84
existing path 175–7
set-up investments 192
and Japan 148
Law on Control and Transparency in
Enterprises 181
and liberalization 32
and ordo-liberalism 22, 259–60, 273–4
shareholder capitalism in 182, 183–4
SPD (Social Democratic Party) 181, 206,
214
stock exchange 180–1
vocational training system 28
Weimar Republic 205, 238–40, 257–8
Ghosn, Carlos 156
Gingrich, Newt 60

globalization
and economic liberalization 3
and France 122, 123–4, 129
and Japan 149
Goffman, Erving 234
Gottschalk, P. 52
Gourevitch, Peter 158
Goyder, D. 269
gradual transformation 2, 9, 19
liberalization as 30–3
Greif, Avner 29
Grossmann-Doerth, Hanns 258
group competition, in the German financial
system 176
Günther, Eberhardt 259–60

Hacker, J.S. 6, 17, 23, 24–5, 204, 220, 221–2
Hall, P.A. 5, 83, 88, 90, 130, 142, 172
Hallstein, Walter 263, 267
Hashimoto, R. 160
Havana Charter (1947) 260
health care spending/system, France 110, 117,
118–19, 140, 141
health insurance
in France 111, 116, 119, 120,
128, 130, 139
in Germany 213
in the United States 53–4, 56, 57–62,
73, 75
defeat of the Clinton health plan 61–2
employment-based 57–9, 62
Medicaid 56, 57, 60–1, 62
Medicare 55, 56, 57, 59–60, 62, 75
Hirschman, A.O. 196
Hispanics in the US, and health insurance 58
holding companies, Japan 165
Hungary 91–9, 100
compared with the United Kingdom 84
Győr region 20, 92–9, 99
comparisons with Szabolcs-Sszatmár-Bereg
97–8
Industrial Park 93, 95
local development 98–9
state socialism in 91, 92–7, 98
uprising (1956) 91
and 'Western style capitalism' 91–2
hybridization, and the German and Italian
financial systems 195

illegal employment, and institutions as regimes
15–16
income distribution, and American welfare state
retrenchment 41, 50, 51

income inequality
  and American welfare state retrenchment 50,
    51, 52–3, 54–5
    and health insurance 58
incomes
  incomes policy in the United Kingdom 87
  RMI (guaranteed income) in France 110–11
incremental change 2, 8–9
  and transformative change 18–19
  with transformative results 9
industrial relations
  in France 106–7, 118
  see also trade unions
inflation
  and economic liberalization 3
  in France 103, 105–6
  in the United Kingdom 87, 91
institutional change
  and ambiguity 229–30, 232–6, 249
  and antitrust and competition law 256
  and codetermination in Germany 229–30
  dynamics of 16–33
  and early retirement policies in Germany 220–2
  five modes of 19–30, 31, 33
  and the German and Italian financial systems
    195–7
  grounding in pragmatic social action 231–2
  and institutions as regimes 9–16, 17–18
  as liberalization 2–4
  and path dependence 6–8, 170–4
  and pragmatism 232
  punctuated equilibrium model of 1, 7, 8–9,
    16, 19, 233–4
  see also incremental change; transformative
    change
institutional complementarities 235
institutional reconfiguration 235–6
institutional tensions 235–6
invasion, displacement through 21–2
Italy
  adaptive expectations 193–4
  Amato Law 187
  antitrust and competition law 271
  Banking Law 187–8
  banks 184–5, 186–8, 189–91
    coordination effects 193
    Mediobanca 184, 186, 187, 190–1
  CONSOB 188, 189
  Consolidated Law 194
  financial system 170, 174, 184–91
  state-dominated capitalism in 184–5
  stock market 185, 186, 188–9
  Telecom Italia 189, 191

Jackson, Gregory 18, 27, 32
Japan 17, 28–9, 103, 145–66
  antitrust regulation 276
  banks 149, 154–5, 156, 159, 162–3, 164
  bounded innovation 163–5
  Commercial Code 161
  conversion 163
  coordinated market economy 17, 148
  economic liberalization 29, 32–3
  financial crisis 119–20, 149–50
  financial system and policies 146, 148, 149,
    154–5
    future prospects 163–4
    reform 159–61, 164
  firms
    economic restructuring 155–7
    future prospects 162–3, 164–5
    holding companies 165
  forces for change 147–50
  future prospects 162–5
  and Germany 148
  government ministries 163
  IRC (Industrial Revitalization Corporation)
    164
  labor market policies 145–6, 148–9, 151,
    153–4
    future prospects 162, 164, 165
    reform 158–9, 161
  layering 163
  LDP (Liberal Democratic Party) 150, 158, 160
  and the liberal market model 146, 156
  LTCB (Long-Term Credit Bank) 156
  Mitsukoshi 157
  model of institutional change 147, 150–7
    macro level (specifics) 152
    micro level (logic) 151–2
    micro-macro interaction 152–3
    and patterns of corporate adjustment
      153–7
  Nissan 153, 156, 157
  policy reform patterns 158–62
  political reforms 161
  Seiya supermarket chain 157
  state spending 120
  statist system 119–20
  tax and welfare reforms 162
  Toyota 156
  and the United States 148
  variations across policy issue-areas 161–2
Joas, Hans, *The Creativity of Action* 231
Johnson, Lyndon 220
Jones, C.O., classical approach to public policy
  130

Jospin, Lionel 108, 111, 121, 122, 139
Juppé, Alain 108, 111, 118–19, 128, 139

Katznelson, Ira 7, 8, 19
Keune, Maarten 20, 28
Keynesian economic policies 2–3, 20
  in France 105, 123
  in Germany 115
  in the United Kingdom 87–90, 91, 99, 100
Kohl, Helmut 214–15
Koizumi, Junichiro 160
Korea, statist crisis in 120
Kotthoff, H. 243, 244
Kristol, William 61

labor market policies
  and early retirement policies in Germany
    205–6
  France 107–9, 115, 118, 122, 128
  Japan 145–6, 148–9, 151, 153–4, 158–9, 161,
    162, 164, 165
Laitin, David 29
layering 19, 22–4, 30, 31, 33
  and American welfare state retrenchment 42,
    45, 48, 49, 56, 70
    pensions policy 63, 75
  and antitrust and competition law 270–1,
    274–5
  in France
    institutional layering 104–5
    and the social welfare system 127, 131,
      138–41
  in Japan 163
Le Pen, Jean-Marie 121
learning curve, and neo-institutionalism 85, 86,
  99
learning effects
  in German and Italian financial systems 192
  and path dependence 171
legitimacy
  in the German financial system 177
  and path dependence 172
Levy, Jonah 17, 18, 24, 27, 28, 30
liberal market economies 5, 83
liberalization
  economic liberalization in France 114–16
  as gradual transformation 30–3
  institutional change as 2–4
  of UK financial markets 90
LIS (Luxembourg Income Study), and American
  welfare state retrenchment 54–5
LMEs (liberal market economies), and Japan
  148

logic of action 18
logic of exit
  in financial systems 173
  in the German financial system 192
logic of hierarchy, and the Italian financial
  system 185
logic of voice
  in financial systems 173
  in the German financial system 175–6, 192
London, City of 88–90
lone-parent families, and American welfare state
  retrenchment 50, 51, 52

Maastricht Treaty 186, 271
McCloy, John 263
macroeconomic policy in France 105–6
Mahoney, J. 7, 171–2
male workers, and early retirement policies in
  Germany 207, 208, 215
manufacturing industry in Germany
  and antitrust and competition law 260
  banks and loans to 178
  and early retirement policies 206–7, 211, 210.
  and postwar codetermination 241–2
Mares, I. 207
market economies
  coordinated and liberal 5
  transitions to 6
market-based financial systems 172–3
Marx, K. 29
Mead, George Herbert 231–2
Mediobanca 184, 186, 187, 190–1
Merger Regulation 270–1, 275
Mettler, S. 54
Milstein, A. 54
minimum wage in France 108
Mitterand, François 103, 107, 113, 117
Miura, Mari 120
Moffit, R. 52
monetarist economic policies, in the United
  Kingdom 90–1
monetary policy, in France 105–6
Monnet, Jean 262, 273
Moore, Barrington 20

Nargis, N. 52
nationalisations in France 106
Nazi Germany, and codetermination 240, 241
neoliberalism, in the United Kingdom 20, 30,
  86–91
NIE (New Institutional Economics), and Japan
  150
Nissan 153, 156, 157

ordo-liberalism, in Germany 22, 259–60, 273–4

Palier, Bruno 23–4, 26, 32, 116
part-time retirement, in Germany 216–17, 218, 219, 220
part-time workers, in Japan 154
path dependence
    and American welfare state retrenchment 41, 44, 68–9, 72–4
    and endogenous change 173
    and French welfare programs 127, 128–9, 131–2, 134
    and the German financial system 169, 170, 177–8
    and institutional change 6–8, 170–4
    and the Italian financial system 169, 170
    and the learning curve 85
    and neo-institutionalism 8, 101
    Pierson's theory of 6, 8, 170–1, 177
pay systems, Japan 163
pay-as-you go pension systems 22
    France 110, 128, 134
    United States 68
Pempel, T.J. 7
pension insurance, and early retirement policies in Germany 204, 209–10, 212, 213, 215
pensions
    France 110, 128, 132
    Japan 148–9
    see also pay-as-you go pension systems
performance-oriented pay, and codetermination in Germany 247
Pierson, P. 22, 27
    and American welfare state retrenchment 42, 43–5, 72
    and early retirement policies in Germany 203
    theory of path dependence 6, 8, 170–1, 177
Piore, M. 16, 20
Polanyi, Karl 4, 30
policies, and institutions as regimes 12
policy changes, and American welfare state retrenchment 44
political mobilization, and liberalization 33
political parties, and party competition in France 113–14
postwar capitalism
    'Golden Age' of 2–3
    transformation of 5
postwar corporatism, in the United Kingdom 87
poverty relief
    in France 116, 122, 128, 139, 141
    in the United States 52, 53, 60

power relations
    in the German financial system 176–7
    and neo-institutionalism 85, 86, 99
pragmatic social action, and institutional change 231–2
private social benefits, and American welfare state retrenchment 45
privatization
    and economic liberalization 4
    in France 106
process of change 8–9
PSID (Panel Study of Income Dynamics), and US income inequality 52–3
punctuated equilibrium model of institutional change 1, 7, 8–9, 16, 19, 233–4

Quack, Sigrid 22, 27

rational choice theory
    and conversion 26
    and institutional change 7
    and institutions as regimes 11
Reagan, Ronald 49, 67
reciprocity, and institutional change in Japan 150–1
recombination, and antitrust and competition law 274–5
reconfiguration
    and the COASE framework of institutional change 235–6
    and codetermination in Germany 245
redundancies, and early retirement policies in Germany 206–7
regimes, institutions as 9–16, 17–18
results of change 8–9
retirement pensions, and American welfare state retrenchment 41, 56, 62–8
Rexrodt, Günter 215
Riester, Walter 216, 217
risk protection
    and American welfare state retrenchment 41, 42, 44–5, 49–50, 57, 69, 71
    and health insurance 62
risk-privatization
    and American welfare state retrenchment 50, 70–1
    pensions policy 63
risk-socialization, and American welfare state retrenchment 50, 71
Robinson, P. 157
Rocard, Michel 110, 115
Rome Treaty (1957), and antitrust and competition law 256, 264, 265, 266–8, 271
Roth, Guenther 13

Roth, William 65
Rothstein, Bo 23
RPR (French Gaullist Rally for the Republic)
    113–14
rule makers/rule takers
    and German codetermination 27
    and institutions as regimes 13–15
rules, and institutions as regimes 10–11

Sabel, Charles 20
Scandinavian welfare states 54
Schickler, Eric 22, 23, 24, 26
Schmoldt, Hubertus 217
Schröder, Gerhard 217
Schumpeter, J. 124
Second World War 258
shared decision making, in the German financial
    system 175–6
shareholder capitalism, Germany 183–4
shareholder value, and codetermination in
    Germany 247–9
Sherman Act (United States) 257, 261
Single European Act, and antitrust and
    competition law 270
Skocpol, T. 25–6
SMEs (small and medium-size enterprises)
    in France 107, 111, 112–13, 117, 118,
        123
    in Hungary 94, 95, 96, 97
social democratic countries, and France
    121
social exclusion, and French social policy 128,
    131, 132, 133, 134, 139, 141
social insurance, in France 115–16, 127, 132–8,
    139, 141, 142
social partnership, and codetermination in
    Germany 240–2
social protection, France 109–11
Soskice, D. 5, 83
Spaak Report (1956), and antitrust and
    competition law 265–6
Spain, antitrust and competition law 271
stock market
    Germany 180–1
    Italy 185, 186
Storch, Anton 205
Streeck, Wolfgang 130, 131
structure, and agency 7, 19
subsidiarity, and antitrust and competition law
    271
Sweden, and France 121
Swidler, Ann 7
Szabolcs-Sszatmár-Bereg, Hungary 97–8

taxation
    and American welfare state retrenchment 45,
        49, 53, 55–6
    and health insurance 57, 73
    and pensions 62, 63, 67
    and French social policy 104, 122, 128, 136,
        139, 140, 141
Teles, S. 56, 68
Thelen, K. 46, 73, 129, 130, 131
third party enforcement, and institutions as
    regimes 10–11, 12
time, and institutional change 27–8
Tocqueville, Alexis de 116–17
Toyota 156
trade unions
    and American welfare state retrenchment 71
    in France 107, 115, 132, 133, 135, 137, 140
    in Germany
        and codetermination 32, 237, 238, 239,
            241–2, 246, 248–9
        and early retirement 115, 208–9, 216
    and institutions as regimes 10, 12
    and Keynesian economic policies 3, 87, 88
    see also industrial relations
Trampusch, Christine 29–30
transformative change 2
    and French social policy 127, 142
    gradual 2, 9, 19, 30–3
    and incremental change 18–19
    transformation without disruption 4–9
transnational institution building, and antitrust
    and competition law in Europe 274–5
Tsebelis, G. 47

unemployment
    and American welfare state retrenchment 50,
        51
    and early retirement policies in Germany
        29–30, 205–6, 208, 209
    and economic liberalization 3
    in France 107–8, 109, 115–16, 118, 122, 131,
        132–3, 142
        benefits 132, 139
        insurance 141
        unemployment traps 139
    in the United Kingdom 87
unemployment benefits, and early retirement
    policies in Germany 210
unemployment insurance
    and American welfare state retrenchment
        45
    and early retirement policies in Germany
        204, 209–10, 212, 213, 214, 215

United Kingdom
  City of London 88–90
  Keynesian economic policies 87–90, 91, 99,
    100
  and neo-institutionalism 84
  transition to neoliberalism 20, 30, 86–91, 99
United States
  and antitrust regulation 255, 257, 258–9, 275
  civil war benefits 25–6
  institutional reform of Congress 23
  and Japan 148
  retirement accounts 23
US welfare state retrenchment 17, 40–76, 204
  and Aid to Families with Dependent Children
    54
  analysis of 43–5
  and changes in employment structure 50, 51,
    75
  and changes in family structure 25, 50–1,
    51–2, 75
  conservative influences on 71–2
  and early retirement policies in Germany
    220, 221–2
  and EITC (Earned Income Tax Credit) 54,
    122
  and ERISA (Employee Retirement Income
    Security Act) 58–9, 62–3, 63
  and family support 53–4
  and health care policy 24–5
  and health insurance 53–4, 56, 57–62, 73, 75
    defeat of the Clinton health plan 61–2
    employment-based 57–9, 62
    Medicaid 56, 57, 60–1, 62
    Medicare 55, 56, 57, 59–60, 62, 75
  and path dependence 41, 44, 68–9
  and pensions 41, 56, 62–8, 75
    401(k)plans 65–6
    and employer contributions 62–4
    Individual Retirement Accounts (IRAs) 64,
      65–6, 67, 220
  and policy feedbacks 46–7
  and policy strategies 74–5
  and private benefits 73–4, 75

  and pro-welfare state coalitions 72
  and public social programs 73
  and risks 17, 25, 41, 42, 44–5
    new social risks 49–57
  and social protection 75–6
  and Social Security 46, 55, 63, 67–8, 75

Venice, governing institutions 29
VOC (Varieties of Capitalism) literature, and
  Japan 150, 151
Vogel, Steven 17, 18, 28–9, 32–3

Walmart 157
Warren, Elizabeth 52
Weber, M. 13
Weir, Margaret 220
welfare spending in France 110
welfare state retrenchment
  and continuity 6
  and early retirement policies in Germany 203
  see also US welfare state retrenchment
welfare states
  France 23–4
  and Keynesian economic policies 3
  and layering 23
  mismatch between risks and social
    protections 40–1
women, and American welfare state
  retrenchment 50, 51, 52, 54
'work line' approach, and social democracy 121
working class, and early retirement policies in
  France 115
working hours in France 108–9, 115
works councils, and codetermination in
  Germany 238–40, 240–1, 243, 244, 245,
  247–9
WTO (World Trade Organization), and Japan
  149

youth employment, training programs in France
  108, 115

Zwickel, Klaus 217